E-Commerce:
Real Issues and Cases

Michael C. Knapp
University of Oklahoma

THOMSON

SOUTH-WESTERN

Australia · Canada · Mexico · Singapore · Spain · United Kingdom · United States

THOMSON

SOUTH-WESTERN

E-Commerce: Real Issues and Cases 1e
Michael C. Knapp

Editor-in-Chief:
Jack Calhoun

Team Leader
Melissa Acuña

Acquisitions Editor:
Jennifer Codner

Developmental Editor:
Rebecca von Gillern

Marketing Manager:
Julie Lindsay

Production Editor:
Dan Undem

Manufacturing Coordinator:
Doug Wilke

Compositor:
Cover to Cover Publishing, Inc.

Printer:
Globus
Minster Ohio

Design Project Manager:
Rik Moore

Internal Designer:
Jennifer Lambert, jen2 Design

Cover Designer:
Jennifer Lambert, jen2 Design

Library of Congress Cataloging-in-
Publication Data

Knapp, Michael Chris
    E-commerce : real issues and
cases / Michael C. Knapp.
    p. cm.
    Includes index.
    ISBN 0-324-07469-7
    1. Electronic commerce. 2.
Electronic commerce--Case studies.
I. Title.

HF5548.32 .K595 2002
658.8'4--dc21
                    2002017686

Dedication

To Mom, Paula, Suzie, and Becky

Preface

A few semesters ago, several senior faculty members of the Price College of Business at the University of Oklahoma called an ad hoc meeting one Friday morning. The purpose of that meeting? To discuss electronic commerce; more specifically, how we planned to respond to the dramatic growth in e-commerce over the previous few years. We all recognized that our curriculum was quickly becoming outdated. More important, we admitted publicly for the first time that we were graduating students who lacked an important knowledge base and skill set they needed to compete effectively in the job market. Several of us passed on complaints voiced to us by students, bright young men and women puzzled by the absence of e-business issues and topics in their accounting, finance, management, marketing, and other business courses. As you might expect, the first decision we made was to create a committee to study the problem. So, there you have it. I have just explained how I became a member of the e-commerce curriculum committee of the Price College of Business.

After talking to colleagues at other universities, I discovered the reaction of the OU faculty was being repeated across the nation. The rapid growth of e-commerce had caught many, if not most, business faculties off guard. Granted, a few forward-looking schools had already been discussing this "problem" and developing a response strategy. Those schools threatened to leave the rest of us looking foolish and leaving our graduates ineligible for many coveted, fast-track positions. But, even the latter schools faced a shortage of appropriate instructional materials for their new e-commerce programs and courses. To help fill the void in e-commerce instructional materials and hopefully to trigger the integration of more e-commerce topics and issues into the curricula of business schools, I decided to write this casebook.

This text can be used in several ways. My casebook can be used as the primary text for a non-technical, broad-based and cross-functional "Introduction to E-Commerce" course offered at the undergraduate level. The instructor's manual for this text includes a syllabus for such a course. That same syllabus, supplemented with selected readings, could also be used for an MBA-level course intended to provide students with a thorough introduction to e-commerce. My casebook can be used as a supplemental text by instructors who want to expose their students to e-commerce issues and topics relevant to specific functional areas of business such as accounting or marketing. This casebook is particularly well-suited as a supplemental text for courses in the areas of business strategy or policy, entrepreneurship, business ethics, and management information systems. Finally, this casebook could be used as an ancillary for the Introduction to Business course where it would serve to introduce novice business students to the emerging New Economy. Instructors who choose to use this casebook as a supplemental text may want to take advantage of the customization option offered by South-Western.

A series of case questions and assignments accompanies each of the 25 cases included in this text. The instructor's manual contains suggested solutions to those items as well as a synopsis, list of key facts, instructional objectives, and suggestions for use for each case. Listed next are brief descriptions of the five modules of cases in this text. Refer to the Contents for a description of each case.

THE BIG ISSUES

These cases examine the handful of major issues and concerns that will likely shape, if not determine, the future of electronic commerce. Among these issues is the matter of privacy. For example, to what extent do e-businesses have a responsibility to protect their customers' privacy? Another controversial issue posed by the New Economy is whether online retail sales should be subject to sales taxes. Brick-and-mortar retailers insist that they will be burdened by a huge competitive disadvantage if their online counterparts are not required to collect sales taxes. Challenges presented by the increasingly global nature of e-commerce are highlighted in one of these cases, while another examines important regulatory issues posed by the growth of online commerce.

FORTUNES MADE

In earlier generations, accumulating an enormous fortune in the business world required decades, if not an entire lifetime, for even the most industrious and imaginative entrepreneurs. Not so in the world of e-commerce. The cases in this module examine five of e-commerce's biggest success stories and the individuals who nurtured path-breaking concepts into multibillion-dollar businesses. Individual cases introduce students to the business models developed by Jerry Yang and David Filo (Yahoo!), Steve Case (AOL), Pierre Omidyar (eBay), Jeff Bezos (Amazon.com), and Mark Cuban (Broadcast.com). These cases also highlight several strategic successes—and blunders—made by these captains of e-commerce.

E-BUSTS

For every success story in electronic commerce, one can identify a host of revenue streams that failed to materialize for virtual businesses—businesses that began and ended as electronic blueprints. Likewise, many professional services that seemed ideally suited for the world of e-commerce never found a market. The two-part "Internet Bubble" case introduces students to five dot-com companies. Part I provides an overview of these companies, including the grandiose expectations that accompanied each of them. Part II examines the factors that eventually led to the downfall of each of those companies. This section also contains a discussion of the Y2K phenomenon and the accompanying gloom and doom predictions that vaporized on 01/01/00. Although Y2K proved to be less than menacing for most businesses, the huge expenditures incurred to prepare for the event had far-reaching implications for most major corporations—implications that are still lingering today.

THE DARK SIDE OF E-COMMERCE

Dishonesty, skullduggery, and the darker side of the human spirit plague businesses of all types. The openness of the Internet and the ease of access to the information superhighway have allowed skilled and determine pranksters to rifle through the accounting records of online companies, steal credit card numbers of their customers and, in some cases, completely shut down their websites. Kevin Mitnick, the Master Hacker, easily qualifies as the most infamous of these ne'er-do-wells. Two other cases in this module examine accounting gimmicks used by many dot-com executives to window dress their financial statements and the disruptive role that "cybersquatters" have played in the early days of the commercial Internet. The final case in this module highlights several new and problematic ethical dilemmas faced by the executives and employees of e-commerce firms.

STATUS REPORTS

This final module includes reports on several of the key developments and trends in e-commerce over the past decade. One of the most important but also most under-appreciated contributors to the Internet Revolution has been e-mail. Internet experts recognize that this rudimentary technology has quietly fueled much of the dramatic growth in online commerce over the past decade. The B2B phenomenon and the rise of the Wireless Internet are also examined in this section. The remaining three cases in this section provide status reports on three new types of businesses spawned by the Internet, namely, Internet incubators, online stock brokers, and e-consulting firms.

I faced many challenges in developing this casebook. The most problematic of those challenges stemmed from the rapid, chaotic, and largely unmanaged growth and change that has characterized e-commerce over its first decade. In fact, while I was developing this book, the New Economy suffered a wide range of growing pains. Who hasn't read of the hundreds of dot-coms or e-tailers that have failed? Surprisingly, many students, and even some professors, see those failures as evidence that e-commerce is slowly receding. Not true; nothing could be further from the truth. Although scores of hastily organized and poorly financed e-tailers have disappeared, the Internet business sector is bigger and healthier than ever. The Internet has arrived in the business world and that world will be forever changed as a result. Our responsibility as business instructors is to make certain that our students recognize the impact the Internet is having and will have in the future on the national economy, international commerce, and individual companies and industries. Likewise, we need to ensure that students understand and are prepared to cope with the impact that the Internet will have on the specific job responsibilities they will assume as they enter the business world in coming years.

ACKNOWLEDGEMENTS

Thanks to the many instructors whose comments and suggestions have helped me significantly in the preparation of this first edition of *ECommerce: Real Issues and Cases*. In particular I'd like to thank:

Bradley J. Alge
Purdue University

France Belanger
Virginia Polytechnic Institute and State University

Eric T. Bradlow
The Wharton School of the University of Pennsylvania

Ramanarao Chamarty
Fox School of Business, Temple University

Edward J. Cherian
George Washington University

Karen B. Clay
Heinz School of Public Policy and Management, Carnegie Mellon University

Stephen H. Craft
Towson University

Mark L. Gillenson
University of Memphis

Greg Gogolin
Ferris State University

Phillip Gordon
Hass School of Business, UC-Berkeley

Ping Lan
University of New Brunswick Saint John

Cindy Joy Marselis
Fox School of Business, Temple University

Jamshed Mistry
Worcester Polytechnic Institute

Shelley M. Rinehart
University of New Brunswick Saint John

Nick Voigt
DuPree College of Management, Georgia Institute of Technology

An electronic commerce textbook faces the risk of having a short shelf-life given the rapid changes in the technology underlying e-commerce processes. You will find that my text largely sidesteps this potential problem. My casebook is not a technical "how to develop and maintain an electronic storefront" text. Instead, it serves to introduce students to the broad issues shaping the nature and future of e-commerce, examines e-commerce strategies that have succeeded—or failed, and explores a wide range of challenges and opportunities pertinent to the e-commerce domain. Unlike the technology issues, which many students will address in other courses, these macro topics do not become quickly outdated. Nevertheless, these topics do certainly evolve and the issues relevant to them often morph into other issues fairly rapidly. To help instructors "stay on top" of recent developments affecting the cases in this text, I will establish an online ancillary for this casebook. At this website, I will periodically post discussions and descriptions of new events and circumstances relevant to the cases in my text.

Thank you for your time. I hope that you share my enthusiasm and interest in the fascinating New Economy. If you have thoughts or comments to share with me, please don't hesitate to contact me (mknapp@ou.edu).

Michael C. Knapp, PhD, CPA, CMA
John Mertes, Jr., Professor of Accounting
University of Oklahoma

Brief Contents

Contents

To date, the federal government has largely adopted a "hands-off" attitude toward regulating the Internet. Despite that attitude, Lawrence Lessig, a Stanford law professor and the "dean" of cyberlaw, insists that cyberspace is being heavily regulated. Lessig argues that major online companies are imposing a subtle but pervasive form of regulation on this new business frontier. This regulation occurs in the form of "code," that is, software code that those companies use to mold the architecture of cyberspace to benefit their own economic interests. Lessig maintains that in the absence of government intervention, these companies will soon jeopardize the freedom and openness that has characterized the Internet over its first several decades.

Like most segments of online commerce, the rise of international e-commerce has been met by great expectations, enthusiastic and optimistic projections, and a huge amount of pure, unadulterated hype. Before the grand potential of global e-commerce can be realized, numerous challenges and problems must be overcome. This case examines the key obstacles to global e-commerce, provides an overview of several companies' efforts to become involved in international commerce via the Internet, and concludes with a discussion of the global market most coveted by online companies—the rapidly developing economy of the People's Republic of China.

Lou Montulli dropped out of the University of Kansas in the early 1990s and migrated to California's Silicon Valley where he accepted a job with a small Internet company that was soon to be renamed Netscape Communications. In 1994, Montulli developed what he initially referred to as "magic cookies." Online companies soon discovered that they could use Montulli's creation to identify visitors to their websites and to develop a file of biographical information for each of those visitors. Within a few years, thousands of online companies made extensive use of Lou Montulli's cookies. As cookies became pervasive on the World Wide Web, civil rights advocates began insisting that these miniscule pieces of electronic matter violated one of the most basic rights of Internet users—their right to privacy.

Does "Big Brother" have the right to monitor and intercept private e-mail messages exchanged by Internet users? The answer to that question is "yes," at least in certain countries. These countries include Russia, the People's Republic of China, Great Britain, and . . . the United States. The revelation in July 2000, that the FBI had developed a "packet-sniffing" software program known as Carnivore to intercept private e-mail messages spawned a nationwide controversy. Many elected officials, civil rights advocates, and journalists charged that the FBI was imposing a nightmare of Orwellian proportions on millions of unsuspecting Internet users.

A crucial question that hangs ominously over e-commerce is whether, or to what extent, legislative authorities will subject online retail transactions to sales taxes. This case outlines the arguments of those parties who advocate taxing those transactions similar to offline or conventional retail sales. Equal time is given to those individuals who believe that imposing sales taxes on e-tail transactions would likely stall the development of an important new sector of the national economy.

Jerry Yang and David Filo majored in engineering at Stanford during the early 1990s. The two close friends whiled away their spare time by developing a Yellow Pages-like directory to catalog websites that they and their friends frequently visited. As the World Wide Web grew exponentially in size, so too did the two friends' online catalog and search engine, which they referred to as "Jerry and David's Guide to the World Wide Web" before deciding on the shorter and more enigmatic name, "Yahoo!." Yang and Filo's creation became so popular among Internet surfers that they decided to drop out of Stanford and convert their hobby into a business venture. Their plan worked. By the age of 30, their net worth exceeded $5 billion—each! This case tracks the evolution of Yahoo! from an online hobby of two college students to one of the premier e-commerce companies worldwide.

CASE 2.2
CITIZEN CASE

In the early 1980s, Stephen Case worked in the marketing department of PepsiCo. Fascinated by personal computers, Case spent countless hours tinkering with the development of online computer networks—networks that would allow him to interact with other personal computer buffs. In 1989, Case created the online service provider, America Online (AOL). During the company's early years, AOL operated in the shadows of its two larger competitors, CompuServe and Prodigy. But, thanks to the persistence and hard work of Steve Case, AOL's subscriber base steadily grew. By early 2000, AOL claimed tens of millions of subscribers, easily making it the largest provider of online services. Case would stun Wall Street later that year when his company effectively acquired Time Warner to create the world's largest media company, AOL Time Warner.

CASE 2.3
THE ACCIDENTAL BILLIONAIRE:
PIERRE OMIDYAR, FOUNDER OF EBAY

Want to sell something on the Internet? Check out eBay, the largest online auction house. Pierre Omidyar, a French citizen living in the Silicon Valley, founded eBay so that his girl friend and eventual wife could exchange information with individuals in the San Francisco Bay area who shared her hobby of collecting Pez candy dispensers. Omidyar nurtured his company though its early years of existence, helping it survive a series of technical glitches and shutdowns, many of which were triggered by hacker attacks. Eventually, Omidyar recognized that his swiftly growing company needed a professional manager to oversee its operations. So, in 1998, he resigned as eBay's chief executive officer, replacing himself with Margaret Whitman, who had served as a corporate executive with Disney and Procter & Gamble. Under Whitman's leadership, eBay has continued to grow and consistently produce profits.

CASE 2.4
ABRACADABRA, INC.

Jeff Bezos gave up a lucrative career as an executive of a Wall Street hedge fund to pursue his dream of being a business owner. Bezos intended to create an Internet-based company but had no idea what product or service his company would market. After extensive research, he decided that his firm would sell books. Bezos dreamed of organizing an online bookstore that would offer more than one million titles to Internet users. Within 12 months of leaving his former job, Bezos had chosen Seattle as the headquarters of his new business, had handpicked a small group of high-tech associates, and settled on Amazon.com as the new firm's name—his original choice was Abracadabra. In July 1995, Bezos launched his online bookstore's website. Throughout the late 1990s, Amazon grew rapidly, thanks to the relentless energy and efforts of its founder and master strategist. In fact, "Getting big fast" served as Bezos's mantra for his new firm. That goal proved to be much easier to accomplish than producing profits. This case documents Amazon's tumultuous climb to the top of the e-tailing world and the challenges that must be faced and overcome for it to remain a leading e-commerce firm.

Mark Cuban founded Broadcast.com on a simple premise: individuals should be able to listen to any of the thousands of radio stations scattered across the globe on their personal computers. More to the point, the Dallas-based Cuban wanted to listen to the radio broadcasts of his beloved Indiana Hoosiers basketball team. Cuban and his close friend, Todd Wagner, invested a few thousand dollars in computer equipment that they set up in a spare bedroom in Cuban's apartment. Within a matter of weeks, the tech-savvy Cuban had converted a personal computer into a radio and, in doing so, created a new Internet industry. Over the coming years, Cuban and Wagner's company would deliver streaming audio and video services to millions of Internet users. After making a name for himself in the e-commerce field, Cuban sold his company to Yahoo!, receiving nearly $3 billion for his ownership interest in the firm. Next, the young entrepreneur used a small chunk of those funds, $280 million to be exact, to purchase the NBA's Dallas Mavericks.

PointCast pioneered push technology in 1996 when it created a web broadcasting service. PointCast users automatically received customized, real-time information they had requested in a screen-saver format. At the height of its popularity, five million Internet users subscribed to PointCast. In late 1996, Microsoft announced that it had agreed to bundle PointCast with its Internet Explorer browser. A few months later, media mogul Rupert Murdoch launched an effort to buy PointCast. But, an in-depth investigation by Murdoch's subordinates revealed major glitches in PointCast's revolutionary technology. Those revelations spelled the end to Murdoch's interest in PointCast and contributed to the company's swift demise.

The second coming of the bubonic plague awaited civilization as January 1, 2000, approached. Or, so claimed hordes of twentieth century Chicken Littles, most notably Peter de Jager, a Canadian citizen who became the principal spokesperson for millions of Y2K doomsayers. When 1/1/00 came and went with little more than a ripple of electronic bugaboos, de Jager and other Y2K prophets of doom emerged from their underground bunkers red-faced and scorned. Were the hundreds of billions of dollars spent on the Y2K fix necessary? This case examines that question plus the pervasive implications that the Y2K debacle has had for the information technology functions of major corporations.

Similar to his idol, Jeff Bezos, Disney executive Toby Lenk walked away from a prestigious and high-paying job in corporate America because he had a burning desire to start his own company. Although he had no experience in the toy industry or with e-commerce, Lenk decided that he would create an online toy company that would mimic the business model Bezos had developed for Amazon.com. Lenk believed his firm, eToys, could eventually become the dominant toy retailer, replacing the industry leader, Toys 'R' Us. Following an initial public offering (IPO), eToys' market capitalization of $8 billion made Lenk's venture the most valuable toy company on Wall Street. To many skeptics, that valuation seemed ludicrous since the company's sales accounted for only 0.1 percent of the toy industry's annual sales. Economic reality soon caught up with Toby Lenk and his company. Less than two years after eToys' wildly successful IPO, the company was floundering in bankruptcy court.

Internet mania gripped Wall Street during the mid- and late 1990s prompting the cyberspace equivalent of the Oklahoma Land Rush. Entrepreneurs and opportunists tripped over each other to create thousands of Internet-based companies across a wide range of industries. Ownership interests in hundreds of these companies, most of which had little or no history of producing profits or even revenues, were sold to millions of individual investors in initial public offerings. The prices of many dot-com stocks skyrocketed in the first few hours they were publicly traded. By late 1999, the dramatic run-up in the prices of such stocks had created a huge "Internet Bubble" in the stock market. This case examines some of the excesses associated with the Internet Bubble and tracks the early history of five well known and widely hyped dot-com companies.

The Internet Bubble in the stock market popped during 2000, resulting in trillions of dollars of losses for mutual funds, other institutional investors, and throngs of individual investors who had been captivated by the unrealistic expectations created for most dot-com companies. As the year progressed and the carnage in the stock market worsened, "burn rate" became a widely used phrase on Wall Street. That phrase referred to the speed with which an Internet-based company was consuming its remaining cash resources. This case examines the downward spiral in Internet stock prices that began in early 2000 and the resulting implications for the U.S. economy. Also discussed in this case are the financial problems eventually encountered by the five high-profile dot-coms introduced in the previous case.

Hackers have plagued the Internet since its inception. When the Internet went commercial in the early 1990s, hackers proved to be among the most troublesome problems faced by companies linked to the Internet. Invisible hoodlums prowled the Internet, searching for entry points into those companies' computer systems, hoping to peer into their accounting records and steal their customers' credit card numbers. In the shady world of computer hackers, the exploits of Kevin Mitnick, the Master Hacker, are legendary. Because of the persistence of a cyberspace detective, Mitnick spent five years in prison and was banned from the Internet for life. This case examines the hacking phenomenon, profiles the life and times of Kevin Mitnick, and discusses security measures that online companies can use to deter and detect hacking incidents.

Many businesses that arrived late on the new frontier of e-commerce found they were victims of "cybersquatting." During the early 1990s, thousands of cyberspace carpetbaggers began snapping up website addresses that replicated the names of well-known companies, products, or services. These individuals paid nominal registration fees to claim copycat Web domain names and then attempted to sell them to the companies that held the exclusive legal rights to the "offline" versions of those names. Cybersquatters often commanded prices well into seven digits for website addresses they claimed in the Internet's infancy. When an increasing number of companies refused to pay ransoms for what they perceived to be their rightful website names, the courts became clogged with lawsuits filed against cybersquatters. This case explores several of the more contentious cybersquatting battles and the measures taken to resolve this controversy.

CASE 4.3
DEBITS, CREDITS, AND DOT-COMS

Corporate executives have always wrestled with the temptation to misrepresent their firms' reported operating results and financial condition. Recent history suggests that the management teams of e-commerce companies may be particularly predisposed to engage in accounting and financial reporting shenanigans. This case describes various gimmicks used by executives of e-commerce companies to window dress financial statement data and reviews several recent measures intended to improve the accounting and financial reporting practices of cyberspace firms.

CASE 4.4
CYBERETHICS: MEANS, ENDS, AND MEAN ENDS

Many business journalists claim that the phrase "business ethics" qualifies as an oxymoron comparable to "jumbo shrimp" or "cruel kindness." The rapid development of e-commerce over the past decade has produced many unique and troubling ethical dilemmas for online companies, their executives, and their employees. This case highlights several of these dilemmas and identifies obstacles that must be overcome to ensure that ethical challenges posed by the New Economy are properly addressed and resolved.

MODULE FIVE STATUS REPORTS

CASE 5.1
E-MAIL: *THE* KILLER APP

The most sought-after commodity in the Internet era is the "killer application." Online entrepreneurs, computer scientists, college students, and hosts of other Internet devotees have spent years searching for the next killer app that would revolutionize the business world—and, at the same time, fatten their bank accounts. Internet experts typically agree that the two most successful killer apps to date in cyberspace have been the World Wide Web and that elegantly simple but incredibly useful communications medium known as e-mail. This case documents the history of e-mail, reviews how it has been used within the marketing function of online companies, and examines its impact on the work roles and responsibilities of millions of individuals employed in the business world.

CASE 5.2
TO B OR NOT 2B

In the early days of e-commerce, business-to-consumer or B2C companies grabbed most of the headlines in the business press. But, inept business models doomed large numbers of these firms to failure. As the B2C craze died down in the late 1990s, the business world turned its attention to the next generation of online companies, business-to-business or B2B firms. Among these firms were hundreds of new companies that promised to streamline the purchasing function of businesses by bringing corporate buyers and sellers together in virtual marketplaces. Although the B2B domain has also suffered from excessive hype and unrealistic expectations, most prominent business periodicals and business leaders still expect that electronic marketplaces will eventually allow companies across a wide range of industries to become more efficient while slashing their operating costs.

CASE 5.3
WAPATHY AND WAPLASH:
WELCOME TO THE WIRELESS INTERNET

By the late 1990s, the era of the information appliance had dawned on the business world. Mobile phones, pagers, Palm Pilots, and various other PDAs—personal digital assistants—became indispensable tools of harried, on-the-move business executives and their subordinates. Not surprisingly, many high-tech companies recognized an opportunity to merge this new trend with the ongoing Internet revolution. Cellular phone manufacturers, giant firms in the telecommunications industry, and first-generation Internet companies, such as AOL and Amazon, were soon touting the huge business potential of the Wireless Internet. Executives of these companies believed that by linking the growing number of information appliances to the Internet, they could create a new and lucrative sector of the Internet economy, namely, "m-commerce" (mobile commerce).

CASE 5.4
ONLINE BROKERS: GOING FOR BROKE ON THE INTERNET

Count among the earliest success stories of e-commerce the online brokers. In a span of a few years, Charles Schwab & Co., E*Trade, and a slew of other e-brokers pried millions of investors from the clienteles of Merrill Lynch and other traditional, full-service brokers. This new breed of brokerage also created millions of new investors—individuals who previously had never ventured onto Wall Street. This case focuses on the two leading online brokers, Charles Schwab & Co. and E*Trade, highlighting key differences in the operating strategies of the two firms. Also featured in this case are the challenges and opportunities faced by online investors.

CASE 5.5
ELECTRONIC HATCHERIES

Among the many revolutionary business models developed during the 1990s was the Internet incubator. The best known of these firms is idealab!, a company founded by Bill Gross, the individual generally credited with originating the concept of an Internet incubator. Gross intended his firm to serve as an electronic hatchery, of sorts, for Internet business ventures. Prospective entrepreneurs would bring ideas for new online companies to Gross. Then, Gross and his small army of Internet specialists would rely on their technological and administrative skills to create sustainable Internet-based businesses from those ideas. Like most e-commerce business models, Gross's concept was soon replicated by hundreds of other would-be Internet moguls. Many of these second-generation Internet incubators quickly fell by the wayside.

The dramatic growth of e-commerce during the 1990s prompted an enormous need for experts in online business operations. Many companies that linked to the Internet did not have the in-house expertise needed to cope with the idiosyncrasies of cyberspace business, so they relied on consulting firms to supply that expertise. By the late 1990s, a new breed of consulting firm had arisen—firms specializing in website design and related services for online businesses. This new genre of consulting firms was led by Razorfish and four other "e-consultancies" that came to be known as the "Fast Five" or the "New Guard." This group of upstarts stole large numbers of clients from old-line consulting firms, such as McKinsey & Co. and Deloitte & Touche. But, the Old Guard firms soon responded to this challenge by revamping their product line of consulting services to compete more effectively with the pure-play e-consulting firms.

MODULE ONE

THE BIG ISSUES

Regulating Cyberspace:
Paul Revere vs. the Corporate Raiders

We can build, or code cyberspace to protect values that we
believe are fundamental, or we can build, or architect, or
code cyberspace to allow those values to disappear.

Lawrence Lessig

In early April 2001, California-based Pacific Gas & Electric (PG&E), one of the nation's largest public utilities with nearly $5 billion in assets, filed for protection from its creditors in federal bankruptcy court. Just two years earlier, PG&E had posted an impressive profit of nearly three-quarters of a billion dollars. What caused PG&E's sudden financial problems? One word: deregulation. During the mid-1990s, California began deregulating its in-state electric utility industry. State officials believed that relaxing many of the restrictive conditions under which electric utilities had historically operated would allow those companies to become much more efficient. The bulk of the projected cost savings would be passed on to the Golden State's residents and businesses in the form of lower electricity bills. Although PG&E and Southern California Edison, California's two major utilities, initially cut their operating costs, the deregulation plan soon backfired, leaving those companies in financial turmoil and many Californians in the dark, literally.

California's deregulation plan allowed its electric utilities to invest in businesses outside of the state. Funds that previously would have been used to build new power generation plants were funneled into business ventures in Texas, New England, and even Great Britain. Most California residents were more than happy to have PG&E and Southern California Edison invest in out-of-state businesses. Why? Because they did not want huge and unattractive power generation plants built in their backyard or, at least, within eyesight of their backyard.

California's booming population, rapidly expanding economy, and shortage of new power generation plants began producing power shortfalls throughout the state within a few years after the deregulation plan took effect. To remedy these shortfalls, PG&E and Southern California Edison were forced to purchase significant amounts of electricity from out-of-state suppliers. Alleged price gouging by those suppliers and simple supply and demand forces caused the two utilities to pay previously unheard of prices per kilowatt-hour for electricity. Since the state's deregulatory program effectively prevented the two companies from passing these higher operating costs on to consumers, executives of the once proud firms had to resort to pleading for financial relief from state agencies and the state legislature. Frustration stemming from the inability of state officials to solve the crisis and growing pressure from increasingly anxious creditors persuaded PG&E's management to file a bankruptcy petition in hopes that a federal judge could develop a plan to rescue the company.

During the latter decades of the twentieth century, many politicians and economists argued that allowing economic markets to operate with as few regulatory restraints as possible was the "American way." Those arguments apparently convinced Congress to begin deregulating several important industries, including the banking, savings and loan, brokerage, and airline industries. These efforts to reintroduce open market forces into long-regulated industries often resulted in enormous costs and inconveniences being imposed on the parties that deregulation was intended to benefit, namely, everyday citizens. Consider the federal government's deregulation of the banking and savings and loan industries during the 1980s. Within a few years, financial institutions that had been financially sound for decades began crumbling into insolvency due to high-risk investment and lending decisions made by their executives—decisions those executives would have been prohibited from making just a few years earlier. Federal taxpayers eventually absorbed the massive cost of a bailout plan passed by Congress in the late 1980s to rescue hundreds of financially troubled banks and savings and loans.

Regulation is a fact of life for the executives and owners of businesses that operate in industries central to the U.S. economy. Many of these industries experience regulation cycles: initial regulation, followed by some degree of deregulation, followed by re-regulation. The ebb and flow of public opinion regarding the proper role of government agencies in overseeing the private business sector, the rise and fall of different political ideologies, the health of the national economy, and numerous other factors mold the regulatory philosophy embraced by each generation of elected officials and government bureaucrats.

When e-commerce appeared on the scene of the U.S. economy in the early 1990s, business journalists soon began mentioning the "r" word. During the late 1990s, a passionate debate arose regarding whether, or to what extent, online commerce should be regulated. Most e-commerce pioneers maintained that regulatory authorities should "let the Net be," while other parties openly questioned why the revolutionary new businesses sprouting online should escape the regulatory restraints that had burdened most Old Economy companies for decades. That debate still continues and its eventual outcome will have profound consequences for the future of e-commerce. The outcome of this debate will also impact the owners, executives, and employees of both New Economy and Old Economy companies as well as the millions of everyday citizens who simply enjoy spending idle hours surfing the Net.

OPEN 24/7

The team of scientists and engineers that created the Internet during the early 1970s were charged with developing a communications network capable of surviving a massive catastrophe, including a nuclear holocaust. Surging interest in the Internet during the 1990s prompted major advertising agencies to produce a series of trendy television commercials portraying that team of Internet founders. Those commercials typically depicted the creators of the Internet as a group of hard-working but cheerful computer geeks who had an obsessive desire to complete a complex but intriguing assignment given to them by their superiors, much like a group of enthusiastic high school students working on a tough but fascinating physics lab assignment.

Commercials occasionally capture reality. Verbal accounts by founders of the Internet tend to support Madison Avenue's portrayal of them and the work environment that led to the creation of the information superhighway. These individuals had little, if any, interest in political or bureaucratic matters related to their project. They simply wanted to build a nationwide computer network capable of serving as an effective and, hopefully, indestructible communications medium.

The two individuals principally responsible for designing the Internet's architecture, Vint Cerf and Robert Kahn, intended this new network to be as open or "dumb" as possible. Cerf, Kahn, and their colleagues wanted communications and other information to travel unhindered through all branches of the large computer network that they assembled, the so-called "end-to-end" or openness principle. Two decades after the forerunner of the Internet came into being, a British computer scientist, Tim Berners-Lee, developed the sister technology of the Internet, the World Wide Web. Berners-Lee also predicated his creation on the end-to-end principle. "There's a freedom about the Internet. As long as we accept the rules of sending packets around, we can send packets containing anything to anywhere."[1]

One of the biggest concerns of early cyberspace enthusiasts was that the Internet would eventually be broken down into compartments. Rather than being a libertarian paradise available to every individual with the means to access and operate a computer, the Internet might become a series of cyberspace cubicles, access to which was controlled by a few powerful and self-interested parties.

During the first two decades of the Internet's existence and during the early years of the tandem technology formed by the merger of the Internet and the World Wide Web, cyberspace operated as a "functional anarchy." The government agencies responsible for funding the development of the Internet allowed the scientific and academic communities to assume primary responsibility for overseeing or "regulating" the new cyberspace frontier. Members of both of those communities firmly believed that information should flow freely on the Internet, largely unimpeded by political, governmental, or bureaucratic restraints. As a result, the Internet and World Wide Web were burdened by few formal rules and regulations until the early 1990s.

The federal government's decision to open the Internet to commerce in the early 1990s changed cyberspace forever. First, that decision triggered enormous growth in the number of Internet users. Second, the decision created a large population of Internet users, principally profit-oriented businesses and companies, that wanted to impose their will on the structure and nature of cyberspace. Unlike the scientists and academics who had ruled the Internet for two decades, these captains of commerce were not wedded to the openness creed of the Internet.

---

1. *The Economist* (online), "Upgrading the Internet," 24 March 2001.

Instead, they saw cyberspace as a new and potentially vast market for their goods and services, a market that had to be subdued and controlled if it was to be commercially exploited. The commercialization of the Internet brought to the forefront once more the worst fears of its founders and early users.

> The demise of the end-to-end principles that have served the Internet so well would be a tragedy: users might find themselves fenced off within 'walled gardens' of content, and the emergence of unimagined new applications might be stifled. Were that to happen, the last decade of the 20th century might come to be seen as an all-too-brief golden age of openness and innovation that was fatally undermined by short-termism and greed.[2]

REGULATION: THE HOT POTATO OF CYBERSPACE

Most early efforts by elected officials, government agencies, or the courts to impose some degree or type of regulation on the Internet were reactionary or firefighting measures. Occasionally, a crisis arose in cyberspace that demanded some authoritative party to take action. For example, in the mid-1980s, "hacking" became the subject of numerous front-page articles in metropolitan newspapers. Public concern and outrage over several successful efforts by hackers to gain access to the computer systems of key military installations and the computer networks of other important government agencies finally forced Congress to act. In 1984, Congress passed the Computer Fraud and Abuse Act, a federal statute that provided law enforcement authorities with the means to vigorously prosecute individuals charged with breaking into a computer network.

In an excellent article that appeared in *Legal Times*, James Johnson, a prominent Washington, D.C., attorney, traced the sketchy regulatory history of the Internet.[3] Johnson pointed out that despite the critical and growing importance of the Internet and the World Wide Web to the U.S. economy and culture, there is still no Department of Cyberspace or even a national cyberczar. During the 1990s, President Clinton's administration created a series of policy-making committees and organizations to oversee the Internet and e-commerce. These organizations included the Working Group on Electronic Commerce, the Information Infrastructure Task Force, and the Advisory Council on the National Information Infrastructure.

The individuals on the Internet policy bodies formed by the executive branch are typically members of one or more Cabinet departments or key federal agencies. Not surprisingly, these individuals tend to focus on the mission of their governmental unit when addressing important policy matters concerning the Internet. "The Commerce Department . . . looks at the Internet as a way of promoting U.S. businesses . . . [while] the Justice Department worries about it as a crime scene."[4] These differing points-of-view complicate efforts to develop an integrated and comprehensive national policy agenda for the Internet and account for the minimal number of formal rules and regulations issued for the Internet by the executive branch of the federal government.

---

2. *Ibid.*

3. J. H. Johnson, "The Working Group Behind Cyberlaw Policy," *Legal Times*, 17 July 2000, 21.

4. *Ibid.*

According to James Johnson, the Federal Communications Commission (FCC) is the only agency of the executive branch with a "statutory mandate broad enough"[5] to oversee the Internet. The FCC has become involved in several important debates and controversies arising from the Internet's impact on the nation's communications infrastructure. For example, during the late 1990s, the FCC investigated the dramatic growth of instant messaging (IM) on the Internet. AOL had developed this new communications technology and controlled the two largest IM systems. Many parties complained to the FCC that AOL was not operating in the public interest since only subscribers to its two IM systems were allowed access to those systems. Subscribers to other, smaller IM services were prevented from engaging in online, real-time chitchat with AOL's IM subscribers. After studying this controversy and issuing several policy statements, the FCC chose not to force AOL to open its IM systems to users of other IM services. That decision was consistent with the "hands-off" approach the FCC has invoked toward the Internet.

Despite the relatively lax efforts of the executive branch to oversee the Internet, the other two branches of the federal government have done even less to regulate cyberspace. Congress has sporadically passed legislation that affects the Internet or Internet users, including the Computer Fraud and Abuse Act. However, Congress generally has been reluctant to tackle the highly technical and often politically sensitive regulatory issues involving cyberspace, meaning that there "isn't a consistent or coherent body of law regulating conduct on the Internet."[6] In fact, there is not a congressional committee devoted exclusively to the Internet, although there is an informal and bi-partisan Congressional Internet Caucus that meets periodically to discuss important issues relevant to the Internet.

State and federal courts have also been prone to sidestep important legal questions that arise regarding the Internet. A problem that judges face is their relative unfamiliarity with the critically important technology issues that underlie Internet-related legal cases that come before them. Additionally, the state and federal statutes that are most relevant to such cases were typically drafted well before the Internet emerged. "Existing law can fit poorly with technological developments, mostly because the legislators who drafted the laws did not anticipate them."[7] When judges have asserted their authority in litigation involving the Internet, they have often relied heavily on the testimony of expert witnesses or "special masters" who are well versed in the Internet and related high-tech issues.

LAWRENCE LESSIG: FROM COMPUTER WHIZ TO CYBERLAW WIZARD

The complex legal and regulatory issues posed by the Internet spawned a new body of law during the 1990s called cyberlaw. Lawrence Lessig, a Harvard Law School professor, quickly established himself as the most recognized expert in this

5. *Ibid*.

6. *Ibid*.

7. A. Liptak, "Is Litigation the Best Way to Tame New Technology?" *The New York Times* on the Web, 2 September 2000.

new legal field. In 1999, Lessig published a best-selling book on the subject entitled *Code, And Other Laws of Cyberspace*.[8] In that book, Lessig maintains that despite the hands-off regulatory philosophy the federal government has adopted toward cyberspace, the Internet and the World Wide Web are being subjected to a subtle but pervasive form of regulation. Lessig argues that the regulatory vacuum created by the federal government has invited and encouraged commercial interests to step in and impose their own regulation on cyberspace in the form of "code," meaning the key software applications woven into the infrastructure of the Internet and the World Wide Web. That code includes, but is not limited to, Web browsers, operating systems, encryption modules, Java, and e-mail systems. In the absence of aggressive, proactive measures to reclaim cyberspace from the code-writers of the major e-commerce companies, Lessig warns that much of the benefit of the Internet will be lost to the public forever.

Lawrence Lessig was fascinated by technology, particularly the Internet, from an early age. By the time he enrolled as an undergraduate at the University of Pennsylvania, Lessig easily qualified as a computer whiz. After finding his fraternity's accounting records in disarray, Lessig wrote a software program to manage the fraternity's financial affairs. After graduating from Penn where he majored in economics and philosophy, Lessig traveled to England to study political philosophy at the University of Cambridge before returning to the States and entering Yale Law School. Upon graduation from law school, he accepted a clerkship to work for Justice Antonin Scalia of the U.S. Supreme Court.

Justice Scalia, who is widely recognized as the most conservative member of the Supreme Court, enjoyed debating controversial legal issues and cases with his young clerk. Justice Scalia believes that the courts should stick to the original intent of the United States Constitution instead of attempting to reshape or interpret key constitutional dictates so that they apply more readily to modern society. Lessig, a committed libertarian on most legal and political issues, has just the opposite view. He believes the Constitution was designed to be a blueprint that could and should be modified to address the unique challenges faced by each generation, including new economic developments, technologies, and social issues.

Not surprisingly, Lawrence Lessig failed to change Justice Scalia's outlook on the Constitution, nor did the judge persuade his subordinate to adopt a more rigid or judicially conservative view of that document. In fact, Lessig's debates with Justice Scalia only served to reinforce his libertarian views on important constitutional matters, particularly those involving the Internet. Lessig was successful in changing one attitude held by Justice Scalia, namely, his aversion to high-tech devices. The young law clerk convinced Justice Scalia and his colleagues to use computer-based tools to assimilate, organize, and digest the copious amount of information they had to review for each case placed on the Supreme Court's docket.

After completing his clerkship, Lessig accepted a position as a law professor with the University of Chicago. Lessig devoted his scholarly research and writing to his favorite topic, cyberspace. In the early 1990s, he developed one of the first cyberspace legal courses in the nation at the University of Chicago. A few years later, he taught a similar course at Harvard after joining that university's law faculty. Although well known in legal circles by the mid-1990s, Lessig first came into national prominence in 1998. Judge Thomas Penfield Jackson, the federal judge

---

8. L. Lessig, *Code, And Other Laws of Cyberspace* (New York: Basic Books, 1999).

presiding over the controversial antitrust lawsuit filed against Microsoft by the federal government, appointed Lessig a special master in the Microsoft case. In that role, Lessig would serve as the principal consultant to Judge Jackson on technological and related legal issues that arose in the landmark lawsuit.

Lessig held the special master position on the Microsoft case for all of six weeks. After studying Lessig's extensive writings on the subject of cyberlaw, attorneys for Microsoft recognized that his views on most issues relevant to the antitrust lawsuit differed sharply with their arguments and would almost certainly be detrimental to their client. After weeks of wrangling with Judge Jackson, they succeeded in having Lessig dismissed from the case. Despite Lessig's removal and over the strenuous objections of Microsoft's legal counsel, Judge Jackson continued to consult regularly with Lessig and rely heavily on his arguments in arriving at important decisions during the course of the lawsuit. The print and electronic media also frequently interviewed and quoted Lessig concerning key developments in the Microsoft case.

Attorneys and judges also sought out Lawrence Lessig's opinions on several other major legal cases during the late 1990s. Justice Sandra Day O'Connor, who, like Antonin Scalia, had made extensive use of Lessig's impressive computer skills during his clerkship for the high court, cited his scholarly work when she wrote the Supreme Court decision that overturned key provisions of the 1997 Decency in Communications Act. That federal statute criminalized the transmission over the Internet of certain "indecent" or "patently offensive" materials to minors. Lessig maintained that the law violated the First Amendment or freedom of speech rights of Internet users, an opinion shared by a majority of the Supreme Court.

The FCC also relied on Lessig's arguments when it debated the critical "open access" issue while reviewing the proposed merger of AOL and Time Warner. Apparently because of Lessig's writings on that subject, the FCC ruled that the merged company could not prevent other Internet service providers and telecommunications companies from accessing its nationwide broadband network. Finally, Lessig testified in support of Napster, Inc., the company responsible for developing file-swapping software that resulted in widespread violations of federal copyright laws. Lessig's high profile in such cases resulted in the *National Law Journal* naming him one of the 100 most influential lawyers of 2000 and *Business Week* including him on its list of the top 25 "eBiz" leaders of 2000.

PROFESSOR LESSIG SAYS, "CODE IS LAW"

Throughout the late 1990s and into the new century, Lawrence Lessig carried out a forceful, one-man campaign to convince the general public, Congress, the federal courts, and anyone else who would listen that the world of cyberspace faced a huge crisis. Because of this campaign, *Business Week* declared that the young law professor had become a modern-day Paul Revere.[9] Lessig insisted that the widely held belief that the Internet was essentially an open, unregulated frontier where ideas and information flowed freely was not consistent with the reality of cyberspace. Although the federal government had adopted a hands-off attitude to regulating the Internet, federal authorities had not discouraged or prevented large

---

9. *Business Week*, "The Paul Revere of the Web," 6 March 2000, 74.

companies from imposing their own "subtle but omnipresent" form of regulation on the Internet.[10] Lessig argued that these companies had used computer software code and other high-tech means to quietly but effectively mold cyberspace to benefit their own economic interests.

> [The Internet] has been shaped not by edicts, but by code—the bits and bytes that form the wired world's digitized backbone. . . . A handful of companies are transforming cyberspace into a marketer's paradise, to the detriment of all forms of communication that lack obvious revenue-generating potential. Lessig eloquently summarizes the pessimistic paradigm in a catchy three-word slogan: 'Code is law.'[11]

In his book, *Code, And Other Laws of Cyberspace*, Lessig provides numerous examples of how large companies use code to dictate the "architecture" of cyberspace and, in doing so, create a form of privatized law. According to Lessig, "code writers . . . determine what the defaults of the Internet will be; whether privacy will be protected; the degree to which anonymity will be allowed; the extent to which access will be guaranteed."[12] Consider the extensive rules that AOL imposes on the millions of individuals that use its services. Lessig questions why AOL is allowed to limit the number of individuals who can gather in a chat room to communicate with each other, while the company's executives can contact and communicate with all AOL users; why AOL has the ability to monitor and record the activities of its subscribers during their visits to the company's website; why AOL has the unquestioned right to determine when and how to disguise the identities of its users while they are roaming through its various online cubicles.

In legal briefs submitted to Judge Jackson during the Microsoft antitrust lawsuit, Lessig argued that Microsoft's executives had used code to obtain an unreasonable advantage over their competitors. For example, Lessig testified that Microsoft's combination of certain software modules for its Web browser and Windows 98 operating system made "it impossible for either computer makers or consumers to separate the browsing functions without compromising Windows."[13] By maintaining the confidentiality of the source code for its major software products, Microsoft allegedly deterred many companies from developing competing products. A CEO of a Microsoft competitor, Red Hat Inc., echoed this argument when he remarked that "in the proprietary software world, it's as if someone is passing laws but not telling you what they are."[14]

Lawrence Lessig identifies three principal threats to the public interest posed by the efforts of private companies to code cyberspace to further their own economic interests. The first of those threats is the ability of private companies to gain inordinate control over intellectual property rights and thereby limit the extent to which the public benefits from technological discoveries and other advances in cyberspace. Lessig supports "open source code" software applications, such as those developed by the Finnish company Linux. Making the source code of key software applications freely available would allow the general public,

---

10. B. I. Koerner, "The Accidental Activist," *Business2.com*, 20 March 2001.

11. *Ibid.*

12. Lessig, *Code, And Other Laws of Cyberspace*, 60.

13. D. Bank, "Legal Scholar Could Influence Microsoft Trial," *The Wall Street Journal*, 23 February 2000, B1.

14. *Ibid.*

rather than principally the stockholders of specific companies, to benefit from new advances in software design. Lessig also rails against recent efforts of e-commerce companies to patent online business methods. For example, he believes that Amazon's effort to patent its "one-click" shopping method is, well, patently unreasonable. In his view, every online business should be able to freely use such perfunctory methods even though other companies developed them.

The ability of individuals to maintain their privacy is the second threat to the public interest posed by code writers, according to Lessig. Existing technology allows companies such as Yahoo!, AOL, and DoubleClick to accumulate extensive databases of biographical information on the users of their services, including those individuals' online browsing habits. Lessig contends that Internet users are often coerced, or at least goaded, into sacrificing some degree of personal privacy in exchange for access to online information. Finally, Lessig maintains that the architecture of cyberspace imposes limitations on freedom of speech that could not have been imagined by the drafters of the Constitution. Again, out of expedience or ignorance, Internet users often readily accept limitations on their ability to communicate online and to have access to other points of view. "Because the Internet makes it so easy to seek out others with the same views, and to tailor our news consumption to our personal tastes, many people will voluntarily block out any chance of being exposed to new or unsettling ideas."[15]

Lawrence Lessig spends considerable time and energy spreading his "code is law" message while investing comparatively little effort in developing concrete solutions to the problems posed by the commercial coding of cyberspace. He has repeatedly urged federal authorities to require software companies to develop open source code products. At the very least, Lessig maintains that software companies should make their new products modular so that consumers can readily substitute competing products for each other instead of being forced to purchase bundles of interrelated software applications. Lessig has also called for the courts and legislative bodies to educate themselves regarding the subtle but effective efforts of private companies to build a cyberspace architecture that benefits their own narrow economic interests. He believes that if federal officials come to recognize the threat that commercial interests pose to the Internet, those officials will be more likely to adopt a more proactive strategy to protecting the openness and freedom of the Internet.

Does Lawrence Lessig expect that his warnings will resonate with those parties in power who have the ability to make what he believes are desperately needed policy changes regarding cyberspace? No. In fact, he is very pessimistic. He warns that the government has been captured by the large companies that are imposing their will on cyberspace. "We're in the worst possible time to have to rely on our government to do the right thing. Government has been captured."[16]

DIFFERING POINTS OF VIEW

Lawrence Lessig is admired by throngs of Internet users who want to keep cyberspace an open frontier dominated by the libertarian philosophies that he

---

15. *The Economist*, "The Internet—Founding Myths," 17 June 2000, 4.

16. Koerner, "The Accidental Activist."

embraces. Professor Lessig also has many critics who do not share his views. Understandably, executives of major software and e-commerce companies find his arguments objectionable. Microsoft, in particular, has disparaged many of Lessig's positions, particularly his recommendation that federal authorities encourage software companies to develop open source code products. In May 2001, Microsoft announced a large-scale campaign to blunt the public relations efforts of Lessig and other advocates of open source software products. Microsoft executives claim that those products tend to be less reliable and sophisticated than competing products protected by intellectual property rights. Those executives also claim that allowing new software products to enter the public domain immediately, that is, making the source code for those products freely available, would stunt economic development in cyberspace.

No less an authority than Gary Becker, a professor of economics at the University of Chicago who received the Nobel Prize for economics in 1992, supports Microsoft's position that moving toward open source software would be detrimental to economic development. Becker maintains that Lessig's arguments are naïve and grossly simplify complex economic phenomena.[17] Becker believes that rather than stifling competition, allowing intellectual property rights to be controlled by private companies serves to promote technological advances. Companies realize that because of existing intellectual property laws, they will benefit significantly from successful new products they develop. That realization motivates business executives to assume large risks by investing huge sums in research and development activities. Likewise, protection of intellectual property rights triggers what another well-known economist has referred to as "creative destruction."[18] Companies realize that because federal statutes protect existing products and technologies, they must develop superior products and technologies to overcome that important advantage.

Ironically, Lawrence Lessig's harshest critics include other civil libertarians who have embraced the Internet in recent years. Principal among these critics is Declan McCullagh, who serves as the Washington, D.C., bureau chief of the cyberspace media outlet *Wired News*. Unlike Lessig, McCullagh views the federal government as the principal threat to the Internet. McCullagh preaches a simple "let the Net alone" ideology under which cyberspace would be allowed to evolve essentially free of governmental restraints or intervention. Lessig suggests that, like so many Internet devotees, McCullagh fails to understand that commercial interests, not government agencies, present the most lethal threat to an open Internet. In Lessig's view, it matters little whether the source of cyberspace regulation is the private or public sector, the result is the same: a less open, a less free Internet. Although Lessig opposes most forms of government regulation, he is convinced that at this point only the federal government can protect the public from the overreaching commercial interests that threaten to take over cyberspace.

Declan McCullagh is unimpressed by Lessig's arguments and continues to insist that essentially any government intrusion in cyberspace is uncalled for and counterproductive to society. In a more personal attack, McCullagh told a reporter for the Internet-related publication *Business2.com*, that Lessig is "a very

---

17. G. S. Becker, "Uncle Sam Has No Business Busting Up Microsoft," *Business Week*, 19 June 2000, 36.

18. *Ibid.*

smart fellow who hangs out with other very smart fellows who think that the world would be a better place if they were running things."[19]

Many leading business publications have also discredited Lawrence Lessig's arguments, including *The Economist*, a respected British periodical. According to that publication, Lessig's belief that the Internet should be a "libertarian paradise beyond the constraints of law and the manipulation of big companies" was always unrealistic.[20] Instead of mandating government intervention to break the grip of big business on the Internet, *The Economist* suggests that control mechanisms operating within a free society and free market economy should be given a chance to correct the problems identified by Lessig. In fact, many of the companies that Lessig routinely criticizes have been "punished" by Internet users, government authorities, or the simple economic forces that drive a free market. For example, during 2000, both Microsoft and DoubleClick abruptly changed their online privacy policies following "fierce criticism that they were breaching consumers' privacy."[21]

Only time will tell whether Lawrence Lessig or his critics were right. But, in the meantime, Lessig's "code is law" theory and related arguments will "be the starting point for all discussions of Internet governance."[22] While continuing to campaign for an open Internet, Lessig has gone on to other projects including becoming the director of the Center for Internet and Society at Stanford Law School. In that position, he hopes to refocus his time and energy on teaching and academic research and writing. But, his fondest hope is even more basic. Lawrence Lessig dreams of once again being "someone whose phone never rings."[23]

QUESTIONS

1. Choose an industry other than one discussed in this case. Explain how the industry you chose is regulated. List and briefly describe what you believe are the key advantages and disadvantages of the regulatory scheme used for that industry.
2. Provide additional examples of how online companies use software code to "regulate" cyberspace. For each example you list, indicate whether you believe the given policy or procedure improperly limits the rights of Internet users or is inappropriate in some other way. Defend each of your answers.
3. Identify a federal law passed by Congress over the past decade that is directly relevant to the Internet. List several key features of that law. What do you believe Congress hoped to accomplish by passing this law?
4. Search online or hard copy databases and find a recent criminal or civil lawsuit involving an important issue related to the Internet. Provide a brief summary of the lawsuit you selected, including the parties involved, the nature of the dispute, and other essential information. Would more extensive or effective

---

19. Koerner, "The Accidental Activist."

20. *The Economist*, "The Internet—Founding Myths."

21. *Ibid.*

22. Koerner, "The Accidental Activist."

23. *Ibid.*

regulation of the Internet have prevented the problem that led to the filing of the lawsuit? Defend your answer.

5. Choose one of Lawrence Lessig's key arguments or opinions. Write a brief essay explaining why you agree, disagree, or partially agree/disagree with that given argument or opinion.

6. Do you believe the federal government should become more actively involved in regulating the Internet? If not, which party or parties, if any, do you believe should have the primary responsibility for regulating or overseeing the Internet? Defend your answer.

Global E-Commerce:
Competition, Conflict, . . . Cooperation

The world only exists in your eyes—your conception of it.
You can make it as big or as small as you want it.

F. Scott Fitzgerald

The commercialization of the Internet and the World Wide Web during the 1990s presented a golden opportunity for thousands of companies scattered across the globe. Large multinational companies realized that the Internet provided them with the means to better coordinate their worldwide operations; to slash certain operating costs; to market their goods and services to millions, if not billions, of new customers; and, generally, to become more efficient, more competitive, and more profitable. The owners and managers of throngs of small and mid-sized companies recognized that the Internet gave them, for the first time, a feasible method for expanding their operations into international markets.

Throughout the 1990s and early years of the new century, international e-commerce spread like a proverbial wildfire: rapidly but unevenly. Retail commerce on the Internet, or e-tailing, exploded in the United States. By the late 1990s, tens of thousands of retail websites based in the United States hawked merchandise and services of all types, while comparatively few retail websites had been established in countries of the European Union and even fewer yet in the nations of the Far East. Many factors account for the uneven spread of retail e-commerce across the globe. For example, marketing research has revealed that catalog shopping serves as an important precursor to online shopping. Since catalog shopping has not been as prevalent overseas as it has been for several decades in the United States, citizens of most countries have not been properly "prepped" to become online shoppers.

Certain types of e-commerce have flourished in given countries, while being totally banned in other regions of the world. Take the case of online gaming. Federal laws in Australia have allowed online gambling to become a popular pastime among Aussies. In the United States, law enforcement authorities constantly scramble to shut down gambling sites sprouting on the Web since most of those sites violate restrictive state and federal gaming laws. On the other hand, websites selling access to a wide array of adult-oriented entertainment rank among the most profitable e-tail businesses in the United States, while such businesses are effectively outlawed in many countries.

In the early years of international e-commerce, dozens of Israeli companies helped pioneer the technology to provide for secure online business transactions and communications. Most of those companies were organized and managed by former Israeli military officials who had helped develop fail-proof security systems, high-tech surveillance methods, intricate encryption schemes, and other technologies that allowed Israel to survive despite being surrounded by neighboring countries with hostile intentions. Tuvalu, a tiny Polynesian nation consisting of a string of islands located between Hawaii and Australia, also took advantage of the spread of e-commerce around the world. How? By selling its name—its Internet domain name, that is. With the financial backing of the Internet incubator idealab!, a Toronto-based company obtained the rights to market Tuvalu's two-letter, Internet domain suffix ".tv" to international companies involved in the television industry. By 2001, that arrangement had allowed Tuvalu, which has a population of approximately 10,000, to double its gross domestic product.

In most countries of the world, including the United States, federal authorities have encouraged the development of Internet-based businesses but have provided little financial support specifically earmarked for New Economy firms. Not so in Dubai, one of the seven emirates that make up the United Arab Emirates, a small Middle Eastern country located on the Arabian Peninsula. Sheikh Mohammed bin Rashid Al Maktoum, the crown prince of Dubai, decided to make his country a haven for cyberspace companies by investing billions of dollars to create the "Internet City." That city consists of a large industrial park catering to high-tech companies and an adjoining community containing thousands of new homes comparable to those found in suburban communities throughout the United States. The Sheikh expects that more than 100,000 executives, technicians, and support personnel recruited from nations around the world will eventually work in the Internet City and live in its adjacent residential area. By early 2001, almost 200 high-tech companies had committed to becoming tenants of Internet City, including Oracle, Microsoft, IBM, and Sun Microsystems.

Like most segments of e-commerce, the rise of international e-commerce has been accompanied with great expectations, enthusiastic and optimistic projections, and a huge amount of pure, unadulterated hype. Several challenges and problems must be addressed and overcome before the grand potential of global e-commerce is realized. This case begins by highlighting some of those challenges and problems. Next, the case examines successes and failures experienced by major U.S. firms that have used the Internet to go global and then reviews a key strategy that smaller businesses have relied on to become involved in international e-commerce. The final section focuses on the nation that many Internet experts believe will eventually prove to be among the most lucrative e-commerce markets for multinational companies, namely, the People's Republic of China.

ROADBLOCKS TO SUCCESS IN GLOBAL E-COMMERCE

A slew of cultural, economic, and technological obstacles did not prevent large numbers of U.S. firms from plunging headfirst into international e-commerce during the 1990s. But, those obstacles did prevent most of those companies from producing significant revenues from the foreign markets they targeted. In late 1999, one report indicated that only 5 percent of online retail sales by U.S. companies were to residents of foreign countries and two-thirds of those sales were to Canadians.[1] Although the bulk of e-commerce transactions to date has involved U.S. companies and citizens, that will change in the near future as increasing numbers of businesses and individuals around the globe gain access to the Internet. One market research firm estimates that by 2005 nearly two-thirds of all goods and services sold over the Internet will be purchased by individuals or businesses from countries other than the United States.[2]

Several factors have proven to be major impediments to international e-commerce. These factors include language and other cultural barriers, economic constraints, and the perplexing problem that countries around the world have faced in levying taxes on revenues of multinational companies produced via the Internet.

WEB OF BABBLE

Among the most obvious barriers faced by U.S. companies that want to use the Internet to tap international markets is the large number of languages and dialects spoken across the globe. To date, English has clearly been the language of e-commerce. In late 2000, more than 70 percent of all sites on the World Wide Web were in English, although English-speaking countries account for only 8 percent of the world's population. The English language's dominance of the Web will likely erode in coming years since the percentage of Internet surfers whose first language is English has been falling rapidly. In 1996, English was the primary language of 80 percent of Internet users. That percentage had fallen to less than 50 percent by late 2000 and is projected to fall to 25 percent, or even less, by 2005.[3]

Online companies doing business in Western Europe must wrestle with the difficulties posed by the large number of languages officially recognized by the European Union (EU)—11, to be exact. The European Commission, the EU's executive body, maintains a staff of more than 130 translators just to ensure that all member countries of the EU receive official edicts promptly and in their native language. Although Western Europe presents a major communications problem for online companies marketing goods and services there, the language barrier posed by the Far East is, by comparison, enormous. Approximately 60 percent of the world's population lives in Asia where hundreds of languages and dialects are spoken. One journalist commented that the maze of languages in the Far East threatens to convert the World Wide Web into the Web of Babble in that important and rapidly developing region of the world.[4]

---

1. D. Biederman, "Global E-Headaches," *Traffic World*, 25 October 1999, 21.

2. R. O. Crockett, "Surfing in Tongues," *Business Week e.Biz*, 11 December 2000, EB 18.

3. Following is a breakdown of the native languages of Internet users in December 2000: English—49.9%; Chinese—7.6%; Japanese—7.2%; German—5.9%; and Spanish—5.0%. Source: R. O. Crockett, "Surfing in Tongues," *Business Week e.Biz*, 11 December 2000, EB 18.

4. K. Belson, "Asia's Internet Deficit," *BusinessWeek Online*, 23 October 2000.

The impact of the language barrier on companies involved in global e-commerce varies considerably across industries and across different lines of business within given industries. For example, many websites that sell international airline tickets present information only in English and possibly one or two other widely used languages, an option not feasible for car rental sites targeting international customers. Purchasing airline tickets online calls for a few simple decisions, while renting automobiles online is much more complex since car rental contracts tend to be lengthy, written in legalistic jargon, and require customers to make numerous decisions.

Online companies that present key information on their websites in only one or a few languages run the risk of having some of that information "lost in the translation" by customers who are forced to communicate in something other than their native language. Many potential customers of such companies may simply choose to find a more user-friendly website with which to do business. Several studies confirm the positive effect that presenting online information in the target audience's native language has on a website's traffic and sales. One study found that consumers are four times more likely to make purchases on a website that uses their primary language.[5] A U.S. company that retails Chinese food products over the Internet increased its online sales 700 percent by adding to its website descriptions of those products in Chinese.[6]

CULTURE CLASHES

The language barrier that impedes the progress of international e-commerce is actually a component—the predominant component—of a larger barrier to Internet-based global commerce. In recent history, the United States has often been referred to as the world's cultural melting pot. But now, the Internet can easily lay claim to that title. Every moment of every day, a rich and incredibly varied mix of cultural norms, mores, religious beliefs, and political viewpoints meet, and often clash, in cyberspace.

A prerequisite for success for online companies involved in global e-commerce is a comprehensive awareness, understanding, and respect for the cultural norms of the nations in which they do business. Research by business scholars has documented that the definition of "acceptable" or "ethical" business practices varies dramatically from country to country and often across ethnic or other culture-specific groups within a given nation. For example, one study compared and contrasted the attitudes of U.S. and Russian citizens regarding several controversial business practices.[7] That study found that Russian citizens generally believe price-fixing by large corporations is acceptable, while "whistle-blowing" by corporate employees is inappropriate. U.S. citizens have the opposite point of view in each case, perceiving price-fixing as unethical and whistle-blowing as acceptable behavior. Likewise, Americans believe that bribes or "grease" payments in-

5.   B. Vickers, "E-Tailers Find Global Web Sites Need to Learn Local Languages," *The Wall Street Journal* Interactive Edition, 16 November 2000.

6.   Crockett, "Surfing in Tongues."

7.   S. M. Puffer and D. J. McCarthy, "Finding the Common Ground in Russian and American Business Ethics," *California Management Review*, Winter 1995, 29–46.

tended to facilitate major business deals are unacceptable, while Russians view such payments as a normal and necessary expense of doing business.

Cultural differences manifest themselves in various ways on the Internet. Some cultural clashes in cyberspace arise from deeply held beliefs regarding such important matters as individual freedoms and the proper role of government agencies in overseeing a nation's economy. Other culturally induced problems confronted by Internet users and online companies are triggered by simple routines, customs, or habits unique to given countries or regions of the world. For example, retail websites developed by American firms often use a shopping cart icon to help shoppers "store" items while they are browsing a given site. In many foreign countries, individuals have never seen a shopping cart, meaning that a shopping cart icon is, well, foreign to them.

Arguably, the wide variance in attitudes toward online privacy across the globe qualifies as the most contentious cultural issue facing companies involved in global e-commerce. In countries dominated by strong central governments, Internet users generally have much less online privacy than in the democracies of the world. But, even countries that share common heritages and political beliefs have had sharp disagreements regarding online privacy. Recently, the United States and member countries of the EU disagreed over the extent to which U.S. companies should be required to protect the personal data of individual consumers acquired from sources inside the EU. From the inception of e-commerce, the EU has imposed much stricter privacy protection requirements on companies' use of consumer data than the United States. Under the terms of a compromise reached in mid-2000, U.S. companies that obtain consumer data from sources within the EU must agree to abide by that federation's stricter privacy standards when using such data for marketing or other business-related purposes.[8]

Government authorities across the globe have been anxious to reach reasonable compromises to impasses posed by cultural barriers since such compromises promote cross-border e-commerce that benefits all affected countries. Nevertheless, certain cultural differences can present intractable obstacles to online commerce. For example, many Muslim traditions limit or forbid interaction between men and women, particularly unmarried men and women. These cultural norms apply as well to interaction on the Internet involving business transactions. Such restrictions can prevent Muslim women from participating in e-commerce unless "accompanied" by an online chaperone.[9]

ECONOMIC CONSTRAINTS

Economic conditions present one of the most pervasive and difficult-to-overcome barriers to global e-commerce. In many underdeveloped countries of the world, the majority of individual citizens and business enterprises lack the economic resources necessary to participate in online commerce. For a large segment of the U.S. society, ready access to the Internet, the most obvious precursor to online

---

8. A. C. Raul, "World to America: Zip It!" *eCompany* (online), July 2001.

9. S. McFarland, "Internet Can Open—and Close—Doors for Muslim Women Living in Seclusion," *The Wall Street Journal* Interactive Edition, 6 April 2001.

commerce, is a reasonably priced commodity that goes largely unappreciated, similar to electricity, the interstate highway system, and other benefits yielded by the world's most prolific and productive economic system. In early 2001, 43 percent of U.S. citizens regularly surfed the Internet, compared to only 3 percent of citizens of all other countries.[10] In Russia, where the average monthly salary hovers at approximately $50, Internet access fees that range from $0.60 to $1.20 per hour preclude most citizens from spending hour after hour leisurely browsing the World Wide Web.[11] And, buying a book, toy, or babushka doll online is simply out of the question. In fact, in 1999, retail e-commerce in Russia amounted to a negligible $3 million. That figure is projected to rise to a still paltry $900 million by 2003.[12]

Poverty has also severely limited the development of domestic and international e-commerce in Latin America. "Poverty is so persistent that people still lack access to a telephone, and the possibility of buying a computer, let along logging onto the Internet, is reserved for a relatively small group of city dwellers with sufficient incomes."[13] Even most Latin American businesses do not have online access. A recent study found that only 10 percent of small and mid-sized Latin American businesses were wired to the Internet.[14]

Japan boasts the second-largest economy in the world, trailing only the United States in annual gross domestic product. Despite the size and sophistication of that country's economy, comparatively few Japanese households have access to the Internet. In late 2000, 11 percent of Japanese households were linked to the Internet compared to 37 percent of all U.S. households.[15] The culprit: high online access fees charged by the companies that control Japan's telephone lines and broadband networks. The growing popularity of wireless technology in Japan promises to provide its residents a relatively cheap alternative method of accessing the Internet. Practically every wireless device now sold in Japan is Internet-ready, which will likely fuel an increase in domestic and international e-commerce within that country in coming years.

Another factor likely to spur rapid development in online commerce in Japan is the Internet's ability to break down that country's "middleman" economy. Throughout the twentieth century, Japan's economy was characterized by several layers of intermediaries that bloated the prices of goods and services purchased by consumers. The Internet provides the means for Japanese consumers to bypass those intermediaries and purchase goods and services from online sources at much reduced prices. "The Internet allows merchants to circumvent the many

---

10. S. Baker, "A Net Not Made in America," *Business Week,* 26 March 2001, 124.

11. J. Varoli, "In Bleak Russia, a Young Man's Thoughts Turn to Hacking," *The New York Times* on the Web, 29 June 2000.

12. G. Chazan, "Internet Payment Card Is Made to Scratch Russia's Online Itch," *The Wall Street Journal* Interactive Edition, 18 August 2000.

13. A. DePalma, "Getting There Is Challenge for Latin America E-Tailing," *The New York Times* on the Web, 17 August 2000.

14. J. L. Rich, "Staking a Claim in Latin America," *The New York Times* on the Web, 25 September 2000.

15. Associated Press, "Japan Launches Strategy to Catch West in Information Infrastructure," *The New York Times* on the Web, 2 September 2000.

layers of middlemen who clog this country's distribution system, adding costs every time merchandise changes hands."[16]

The economic obstacles that U.S. companies face in their efforts to exploit the rich Japanese market via the Internet are clearly becoming less imposing with each passing year. Overcoming the economic barriers to global e-commerce present in Russia, Latin America, and other developing countries and regions of the world will be more difficult to accomplish. Until a critical mass of Internet users develops in a given country or area of the world, few online companies will invest the time and resources necessary to sell goods and services to the existing Internet users in those markets. So, the question becomes how to spur economic development and growth in those heavily populated regions of the world that could eventually prove to be important markets for online companies. Most economists believe that the only feasible answer to that question is sizable financial commitments by the major industrial countries to promoting economic development in those regions.

In the summer of 2000, the so-called "Group of Eight" or G8, a consortium of nations that includes the United States, Great Britain, Japan, and five other countries, announced a $15 billion aid package to help develop information technology infrastructures in third world countries. The G8 followed up on that commitment during its July 2001, meeting in Genoa, Italy, by implementing a comprehensive action plan intended to close the "digital divide" that had arisen during the 1990s between the industrialized nations of the world and underdeveloped countries.

THE TAX MAN COMETH

Until the early twentieth century, the volume of international commerce was modest by most standards. Transportation and communication barriers, among other factors, limited the incentive and ability of companies, even the largest public corporations, to market goods and services outside of their home countries. Ironically, the destruction and turmoil of World War I persuaded large companies around the globe to turn their attention to foreign markets. Many U.S. firms, in particular, recognized that the need to rebuild much of Europe's economic infrastructure provided them with an opportunity to expand their operations overseas. Similarly, the introduction that millions of American servicemen and women received to foreign cultures prompted greater interest in a wide range of products exclusively available in other regions of the world.

The growth of international commerce following World War I led to another type of warfare: international trade wars. Each country that became heavily involved in international commerce typically had two objectives. The first goal was to export a significant volume of goods and services to foreign countries; the second objective was to protect domestic industries from being undercut by a flood of lower priced overseas goods and from being disadvantaged in other ways by international competitors or their governmental agencies.

---

16. S. Strom, "Log on and Get Your Kimonos Right Here. And Eggs," *The New York Times* on the Web, 7 June 2000.

Taxation has historically been a major source of international trade conflicts. At the heart of most such disputes is a simple question, namely, which nation should be permitted to tax the revenues produced by international trade: the "residence" country, that is, the home nation of the company conducting the international trade, or the "source" nation where the business revenues are actually produced? Allowing both countries to levy taxes on the revenues produced by international trade would impose an undue burden on multinational companies and dramatically inhibit the growth of global commerce.

Throughout the 1920s, numerous multinational agencies and trade groups studied the thorny taxation issue posed by international commerce. After extensive debate, the major industrial countries of the world decided that the fairest and most reasonable international tax regime was to allow source countries to tax the revenues produced by multinational firms as long as those firms had a "permanent establishment" in the given source country. If a multinational company does not have a physical presence in a foreign country in which it sells goods or services, those revenues are taxed only by the company's home country. During the twentieth century, the permanent establishment concept became the lynchpin of a maze of international tax treaties.

The permanent establishment concept worked well until the early 1990s. But, the growth of online commerce during the latter part of that decade re-ignited the debate concerning the taxation of revenues produced by multinational companies. Since many companies that export goods and services to foreign countries via the Internet or with the assistance of the Internet do not have a physical presence in those countries, the permanent establishment concept prevents source countries from levying taxes on those goods and services. Not surprisingly, countries that are net importers of electronic goods and services have insisted that the permanent establishment concept is outdated and unfair. A tax scholar suggests that as international e-commerce continues to grow, changes in the international tax regime will be necessary. "For electronic commerce importing states to continue to accept the permanent establishment principle as currently constituted, it may be necessary for electronic commerce exporting states to make concessions in other areas that will permit sharing of the electronic commerce tax base with electronic commerce importing states."[17]

Several international trade groups and multinational government agencies have studied the question of how revenues produced by international e-commerce should be taxed. These organizations include the G8, the World Trade Organization (WTO), the Organization for Economic Cooperation and Development (OECD), and the EU, among others. Although numerous proposals have been considered, many of which would make sweeping changes in the theory and method underlying the taxation of international commerce in the Internet era, no one proposal has received widespread support. Despite the lack of agreement on how to resolve the taxation problem presented by international e-commerce, the leading international organizations agree that whatever policy is eventually adopted, it must satisfy three broad principles: the policy must maintain the fiscal sovereignty of individual nations, achieve a fair-sharing of the

17. A. J. Cockfield, "Balancing National Interests in the Taxation of Electronic Commerce Business Profits," *Tulane Law Review*, November 1999, 74 Tul. L. Rev. 133.

tax receipts produced by international e-commerce, and avoid double taxation of international e-commerce revenues.[18]

The ongoing debate over the taxation of international e-commerce poses another stumbling block for multinational companies wanting to use the Internet to enter new foreign markets or to expand the scope of their existing operations in foreign countries. Disputes over tax collection methods and the magnitude of tax payments create major headaches for such firms and divert their attention from the more important, day-to-day challenges of mastering the intricacies of marketing goods and services in a wide range of cultures; coping with the challenge of delivering those goods and services on a timely basis; and coordinating their domestic, international, and cyberspace operations. If the nations of the world fail to reach a viable and timely agreement on how to tax international e-commerce, the development of international e-commerce will likely be stunted. "Unless governments revise tax statutes and regulations to address the unique challenges and problems created by e-commerce, the global tax systems may become hopelessly outdated—resulting in confusion, inconsistency, and even retarded economic growth."[19]

THE BIG DOGS OF INTERNATIONAL E-COMMERCE: SUCCESSES AND FAILURES

The large, public companies that dominate the U.S. economy realize that overseas markets, because of their size, offer greater long-term potential than the domestic market. When the Internet went commercial during the 1990s, aggressive corporate executives of many U.S. companies invested heavily in technology applications to access foreign markets via the Internet. But, as noted earlier, most of those companies have experienced little success in selling their goods and services online to international customers. Forrester Research, the large market research firm, reports that even when companies receive online orders from international customers, they are often unable to fill those orders. "Forrester Research estimates that 46% of Internet-based orders to the U.S. from international clients go unfilled because companies lack the proper procedures."[20] The limited success to date of most companies that have adopted global e-commerce initiatives have discouraged other large companies from making a serious commitment to online international sales efforts.

The companies that have had the most success in global e-commerce are those that do not face the daunting task of moving physical goods across international borders. Among these firms are America Online (AOL), the Internet service provider and Internet portal that merged with Time Warner in 2000, and one of AOL's principal competitors, Yahoo!. Both AOL and Yahoo! began moving

---

18. D. L. Forst, "Old and New Issues in the Taxation of Electronic Commerce," *Berkeley Technology Law Journal*, Spring 1999, 14 Berkeley Tech. L.J. 711.

19. K. Frieden, *Cybertaxation, the Taxation of E-Commerce* (Chicago: Commerce Clearing House, 2000), 79.

20. D. Shook, "Cutting Through a World of Red Tape," *Business Week Online*, 28 June 2000.

aggressively into international markets during the late 1990s. Those efforts have paid large dividends. By early 2001, the websites of these companies ranked among the most visited sites in the major online markets around the world, including Great Britain, Germany, France, Brazil, and Japan.

Unlike Yahoo!, which prefers to establish international websites that it totally controls, AOL tends to enter foreign markets by arranging joint ventures with existing companies in those markets. One of AOL's largest international ventures is with Japan's leading mobile phone operator, NTT DoCoMo, Inc., the only telecommunications company to "create a mobile Internet with mass appeal," according to *Business Week*.[21] AOL's executives intend to use this alliance to learn as much as possible about wireless technology and its impact on the future of the Internet, particularly in the Far East where wireless devices are commonly used to access the Internet. In early 2001, AOL's Japan subsidiary, AOL Japan, changed its name to DoCoMo AOL to take advantage of NTT DoCoMo's name recognition among Japanese Internet users.

Steven Case, AOL's founder, reports that "striking the right balance between globalism and localism"[22] is among the biggest challenges his company has been forced to address in expanding internationally. AOL, Yahoo!, and other prominent e-commerce firms headquartered in the United States face the risk of being viewed as "digital colonialists" if they are too aggressive in their efforts to enter foreign markets.[23] AOL stirred a controversy in Brazil when the company used an in-your-face advertising campaign to attract new subscribers. The tag line in that campaign was "We're the biggest because we're the best." Potential customers and Brazilian firms competing with AOL harshly criticized that statement, forcing AOL to quickly drop the phrase.

Yahoo!'s executives have also been forced to deal with controversy prompted, unintentionally, by operating decisions they have made in foreign countries. In May 2000, Yahoo! drew the attention of the worldwide press when a French judge ruled that the company had violated a French law by allowing Nazi artifacts to be auctioned online. Actually, the offending items were not directly available for purchase on the Yahoo! France website, which is operated by Yahoo!'s French subsidiary. But, French citizens who visited Yahoo! France could use links on that website to access Yahoo!'s home site where the items could be purchased.

Another U.S. company involved in global e-commerce that has run afoul of foreign laws is Hewlett-Packard, the computer manufacturer. In 2000, a federal court in Germany imposed a large judgment on Hewlett-Packard for marketing a CD burner that German citizens used to duplicate copyrighted songs. Under German law, companies marketing devices used to make illicit copies of intellectual properties can be held responsible for the resulting damages suffered by the owners of those properties. The legal problems that Hewlett-Packard and Yahoo! have encountered raise two key questions for companies involved in global e-commerce: "Can foreign courts impose their countries' particular laws on Web

21. J. Ewing, C. Yang, and M. Kunii, "AOL Abroad: Miles to Go," *Business Week*, 15 January 2001, 47.

22. J. G. Auerbach, B. Wysocki, and N. E. Boudette, "For U.S. Internet Portals, the Next Big Battleground Is Overseas," *The Wall Street Journal*, 23 March 2000, B1, B4.

23. *Ibid.*

sites based outside their boundaries, and, if so, how can United States e-commerce companies adapt to an international patchwork of [legal] rules?"[24]

Marketing experts and business journalists point to Dell Computer when asked to identify a company selling physical goods that has realized unquestioned success in international e-commerce. Dell began selling computers in the United States from its website in 1996. In less than four years, Dell sold computers online from nearly 90 international websites. From the very beginning, Dell used a decentralized approach to its worldwide sales effort. "Dell created a common technology platform for each of its global sites, including a template for ordering and product information, which ensures a consistent user experience across the sites."[25] Once the management team for a new foreign site has been trained, that management team assumes responsibility for the site, including its "rollout" or launch. Dell has also established a local customer service group for each market that it serves. According to an executive of Dell's worldwide division, "Every time a customer picks up the phone, they're dealing with someone local."[26]

For every success story in international e-commerce, there are dozens of global e-commerce initiatives that have ended in disaster. Probably the most publicized of these failures was the rapid demise of Boo.com, a Swedish firm that marketed high fashion apparel on the Internet. That company's executives attempted to launch websites simultaneously in 18 countries, a task that the company did not have sufficient in-house expertise or financial resources to accomplish. In the spring of 2000, Boo.com filed for bankruptcy just six months after the company went public by selling millions of shares of stock. Another now-bankrupt firm that tried its hand at international e-commerce was eToys. During 1999, eToys invested millions of dollars to begin selling toys online in Europe. Unfortunately, eToys' management had not mastered the fine art of e-tailing merchandise in the United States. Large losses suffered by eToys' ill-fated and poorly organized European operations contributed to the company's collapse in the spring of 2001.

SMALL COMPANIES: GOING GLOBAL BY GOING LOCAL

In the early days of the New Economy, a series of television commercials encouraged small to medium-sized companies to "go global" with the help of the Internet. These commercials insisted that even small wineries, apparel manufacturers, and consumer electronics distributors could use the Internet to compete head-to-head with the large, multinational companies in their industries—companies that had international trade departments developing worldwide e-commerce strategies. The punch lines of such commercials were sales pitches by e-consulting

---

24. R. Raysman and P. Brown, "Yahoo! Decision in France Fuels E-Commerce Sovereignty Debate," *New York Law Journal*, 12 December 2000, 3.

25. B. Tedeschi, "Internet Businesses Find the Global Village Dauntingly Native," *The New York Times*, 22 May 2000, C15.

26. *Ibid.*

firms that offered to help modestly sized companies "globalize" or "internationalize" their businesses via the Internet.

The clunky buzzwords "globalize" and "internationalize" soon fell out of favor with e-consulting firms and the clients they were attempting to attract. Those terms were replaced with the similarly awkward expression "localize." Because smaller companies do not have the resources to undertake large-scale business development efforts around the globe, e-commerce consultants began encouraging these firms to focus their development efforts, at least initially, on one country or even one region of a given country. In other words, the theory became that small companies should go global by going local.

By 2000, the "localization" industry boasted nearly $50 billion of annual revenues. Besides helping clients find the right overseas markets to target, so-called LSPs (localization service providers) provide their clients with an array of services and products they can use to adapt their websites to the language, cultural idiosyncrasies, tax collection and reporting regulations, and other demands of those markets. Although scores of companies market localization services, *The Wall Street Journal* reports that five firms are recognized as the leaders in the industry, including Berlitz GlobalNET, a division of Berlitz International, and Boston-based Lionbridge Technologies.[27]

Berlitz GlobalNET specializes in language translation services. The company can translate a wide range of information into more than 250 languages, including such highly technical materials as product manuals, engineering specifications, and software documentation. In making such translations, the company assures clients that it takes into consideration the cultural differences and language nuances unique to individual countries and to specific regions of those countries.

Lionbridge Technologies offers a full range of localization services including translation, software development, and website design. According to a Lionbridge executive, a company intending to localize a website must address three key issues: strategy, content, and technology.[28] The key issue is the first. To choose the proper strategy for a foreign website, a company must have a clear understanding of the primary objective it wants to accomplish with that website. That objective will typically be to produce sales, subscriptions, or other forms of revenue. However, in some cases, the intent of a foreign website may be solely to increase awareness of a company's products or services. Once a client has determined the purpose of a foreign website, an LSP can assist the company in developing a plan or strategy to accomplish that goal. An LSP can also choose or analyze the content that a client intends to use at the website to determine, among other issues, whether the narrative information is linguistically correct and whether it is expressed in the proper tone. Finally, an LSP can assist a client in choosing the proper technology for a website. The complexity and nature of the information presented at a website, for example, dictate the type of server that should be selected for the site.

The cost of localization services varies considerably depending upon the nature and extent of the services demanded. Developing a simple website for one foreign market typically costs between $50,000 and $100,000, while larger and

27. B. Vickers, "As E-Commerce Goes Global, Firms Push Localization Services," *The Wall Street Journal* Interactive Edition, 30 November 2000.

28. T. Livingston, "Translation and Localization Services," *Web Techniques*, September 2000, 34.

more elaborate localization projects can run into millions of dollars. As one marketing expert observed, localization services are not cheap but they are not nearly as expensive as simply ignoring the business opportunities available in international markets.[29]

The Special Case of China

Internet experts agree that the big plum in international e-commerce is the People's Republic of China. With more than one billion potential customers, thousands of multinational companies covet the opportunity to establish economic beachheads on mainland China. China's recent history provides important insight on the challenges that foreign companies must overcome to market products and services online to the country's citizens and businesses.

In 1976, Deng Xiaoping assumed leadership of the largest nation in the world following the death of Mao Tse-tung. Under the authoritarian rule of Mao Tse-tung, China's economy had failed to keep pace with the rapid development of other major economies around the globe during the post-World War II era, largely because Mao Tse-tung had discouraged efforts to introduce capitalism into his Communist nation's economic structure. Soon after succeeding Mao Tse-tung, Deng Xiaoping brought radical change to China's economy. China's new leader stunned the world when he declared that "To get rich is glorious!" Under Deng Xiaoping, Chinese citizens were not only allowed to establish privately owned businesses but were encouraged to do so. Deng Xiaoping also encouraged foreign investment in his country by large multinational corporations and initiated efforts for China to join international trade groups, principally the powerful World Trade Organization (WTO).

After succeeding Deng Xiaoping in 1993, Jiang Zemin continued his predecessor's open-door economic policy. But, when the Internet barged onto the economic scene during the mid-1990s, the phrase "open-door economic policy" took on a completely new meaning. In the past, Chinese leaders had been able to exert nearly complete control over the flow of goods, services, and investment capital into and out of their country. The Internet threatened not only to loosen those leaders' firm grip on their nation's economy but also to diminish their ability to limit Chinese citizens' exposure to ideological points-of-view that differ radically from those of the Communist Party.

The top echelon of the Chinese government is clearly torn between its interest in maintaining iron-fisted control over the country and using the Internet to further the economic development agenda begun nearly three decades ago by Deng Xiaoping. "Chinese leaders have been ambivalent about the Internet since its first explosive growth in China in the mid-1990s. They want to harness it for business and education, while preventing it from becoming a tool of political discontent."[30] One senior member of the Chinese government recently observed that, "we missed a lot of the Industrial revolution. And we don't want to miss this

29. *Ibid.*

30. *The Wall Street Journal* Interactive Edition, "China Issues Stiffer Internet Rules on News Reports and Chat Rooms," 8 November 2000.

[Internet] revolution."[31] Nevertheless, other top officials insist that any measures taken to encourage more economic freedom via the Internet will surely add to the increasing tide of political dissent that the country's central government has faced in recent years. These latter officials have successfully demanded that the Chinese government take steps to impose tighter restrictions on the Internet within their country.

Measures taken by Chinese governmental authorities to control the online flow of information into their country include requiring ISPs to install filters that block access of Chinese citizens to most media websites of democratic countries. Likewise, online companies operating within China are required to monitor the information made available to Chinese citizens at their websites. Yahoo! relies on the services of Chinese journalists loyal to the nation's Communist leadership to select the news stories and other information suitable for visitors to Yahoo!'s Chinese website. The Chinese government also relies on an army of online observers to monitor information flowing into their country over the Internet. Political observers doubt that such efforts will be effective over the long run. "Total control of today's vast, borderless, redundant cyber-architecture is not possible."[32] In fact, Chinese dissidents opposed to their country's Communist leadership—dissidents who live outside the country for the most part—are committed to undercutting their government's effort to censor the Internet. "We are destined to destroy the Chinese system of censorship over the Internet,"[33] declares Li Hongkuan who heads up a pro-democracy Chinese group based in the United States.

The strict controls that the Chinese government has imposed on the Internet and the political tension spawned by the Internet within China complicate efforts of multinational companies to sell goods and services online to Chinese citizens and businesses. Despite those challenges, multinational companies are tripping over each other to establish a toehold in that vast market. In June 2001, AOL unveiled a $200 million joint venture with a Chinese computer manufacturer. That venture will develop online interactive services to be marketed to Chinese citizens. The efforts of AOL and other companies to enter the Chinese market will likely be rewarded if those firms are persistent and patient. Currently, China has the third most Internet users in the world and will soon overtake Japan for second place behind the United States. Market researchers project that China will have between 100 and 125 million Internet users by 2004.

A large proportion of China's Internet users in coming years will be members of the so-called Generation Yellow, the young, well-educated Chinese who are filling the better paying professional, technical, and managerial positions being created by China's growing economy.[34] No doubt, the growing purchasing and political power of this new generation bodes well for multinational companies hoping to market goods and services online or offline in the People's Republic of China. A sign of the times in China and a possible clue regarding the country's fu-

---

31. N. Hachigian, "China's Cyber-Strategy," *Foreign Affairs*, March–April 2001, 118.

32. *Ibid.*

33. E. Eckholm and S. Faison, "Can the Internet Free China?" *New York Times Upfront*, 20 September 1999, 16.

34. T. Haisong, "The Ranks of Revolutionaries: Hooked Up, Fired Up and Liberated by the Internet; China's 'Generation Yellow' Is Laying the Groundwork for Change," *Time International*, 23 October 2000, 42.

ture is the huge popularity among Generation Yellow of Jerry Yang, Yahoo!'s co-founder and a committed capitalist.

QUESTIONS

1. Choose a multinational organization that plays an important role in promoting international e-commerce. Research that organization and obtain the following information: the organization's headquarters, the countries or other parties that are members or that participate in some way in the organization, and the organization's principal goals. Also provide a brief summary of the major economic policies or proposals the organization has recently sponsored or endorsed.

2. List several proposals that international trade organizations could recommend to provide a fair and feasible approach to taxing global e-commerce revenues produced by multinational companies.

3. Visit the website of a localization service provider (LSP), other than the firms discussed in this case. Document the firm's name, website address, and the location of its headquarters. In a bullet format, list the primary services provided by the firm.

4. In recent years, many U.S. companies have been criticized for conducting business in countries whose governments have a history of human rights abuses. Is such criticism justified? Defend your answer. Would your answer change if the companies in question were only involved in e-commerce in those countries?

5. Censorship on the Internet is an important but sensitive issue for many online companies that operate in countries controlled by strong central governments. Should online companies, such as Yahoo!, agree to censor the information available from the websites they operate in certain countries? Defend your answer.

6. Research online or hard copy databases and identify one or more recent developments that affect the ability of multinational companies to gain online access to the Chinese market. Explain how each development you identified will result in greater, or reduced, online access to China by such companies.

7. Identify a U.S. company involved in international e-commerce, other than the companies discussed in this case. Research this company and write a brief summary of how it has used the Internet to establish or expand its international operations.

Privacy Matters: Cookies

If there is technological advance without social advance,
there is, almost automatically, an increase in human misery.

Michael Harrington

Among the hundreds of new business terms introduced in the Internet Age, journalists may have had the most fun and produced the most puns from "cookies."[1] Computer scientists and programmers had long used that term to refer to miscellaneous pieces of electronic data. In 1994, a self-professed computer geek and college dropout working for Netscape Communications developed a form of "magic cookies" that would revolutionize the way Internet users and online companies interacted. Lou Montulli's magic cookies were soon referred to simply as "cookies" by Internet users and the business press. What originally had been a generic computer engineering term quickly became an important term of the art in the Internet Age.

Lou Montulli enrolled in the University of Kansas in 1989 to pursue his interest in computer technology. The 18-year-old Montulli found working on computer projects linked to the rapidly evolving Internet much more fascinating than working on homework assignments for his math, history, and English composition courses. So, he dropped out of KU and headed west to California's Silicon Valley "where the action was," at least in a cyberspace sense. Montulli accepted a job with Mosaic Communications, a company later renamed Netscape Communications.

Netscape was one of the first companies that recognized and acted on the commercial opportunities the Internet created. One of the problems businesses faced in using the Internet for commercial purposes was the inability of computers to recognize and distinguish among Internet users while they navigated around a website. In the early days of e-commerce, an Internet user browsing a retail website was required to enter identifying information, such as a home address and social security number, each time he or she decided to purchase an item. To make

---

1. I would like to thank Razi Dakhan, a J.C. Penney Leadership Fellow at the University of Oklahoma, for his extensive research assistance on this case.

online purchasing less cumbersome, Montulli developed his magic cookies to identify individual visitors to a website and to maintain a file of personal information for each of them as they wandered around that website.

Several companies involved in e-commerce soon realized that this new breed of cookies had a variety of applications that Lou Montulli and his Netscape colleagues never imagined. Within a few years, cookies ranked among the most popular and controversial Internet technologies used by online companies. The most functional and controversial feature of cookies is their ability to help online companies, particularly online advertisers, capture information regarding the browsing habits of Internet users. This feature allows online companies to place advertisements on Web pages viewed by individuals who have an interest in the goods and services highlighted in those ads. Privacy advocates maintain that the ability of cookies to gather an enormous amount of information regarding Internet users' surfing habits violates those users' privacy. "The breadth of information that can be gathered from someone's online activity is just enormous, and exceeds anything that governments have been able to achieve for all but their most intensely scrutinized suspects."[2]

Lou Montulli profited handsomely from his role in the Internet revolution. In February 2000, *The Wall Street Journal* reported that Montulli had morphed from a "quintessential unkempt geek" a decade earlier into a buttoned-down Internet millionaire with a "great haircut and stylish clothes."[3] In fact, in 1999, *People* magazine named the former Netscape geek the "Sexiest Internet Mogul." Despite the notoriety and fortune that his invention has brought him, Montulli has often expressed concern that his magic cookies are being misused. Such concern caused Montulli to agree to serve on a task force charged with establishing standards to dictate how cookies should and should not be used. Online companies and other firms that rely heavily on the Internet failed to respond favorably to that task force's recommendations. "The fact is, it's too late to tinker with cookies now. They power practically every online shopping cart and every paid advertisement. In less than six years, they've become part of the fabric of the Web."[4]

Not everyone agreed that it was too late to tinker with cookies. By the late 1990s, several civil rights groups had banded together to form a vocal and vigorous coalition to protect citizens' online privacy rights. Among other proposals, the privacy rights coalition lobbied regulatory authorities and the U.S. Congress to impose severe restrictions on the use of cookies.

COOKIES RUN RAMPANT ON THE WEB

In 1994, Netscape integrated Lou Montulli's cookies into the first version of its Internet browser. At about the same time, Netscape released the following brief description of these curious and often misunderstood cyberspace go-betweens: "a general mechanism which server side connections can use to both store and re-

---

2. R. Tomkins, "Cookies Leave a Nasty Taste," *Financial Times* (London), 3 March 2000, 16.

3. T. E. Weber, "The Man Who Baked the First Web Cookies Chews Over Their Fate," *The Wall Street Journal*, 28 February 2000, B1.

4. *Ibid.*

trieve information on the client side of the connection. The addition of a simple, persistent, client-side state significantly extends the capabilities of Web-based client/server applications."[5]

In more concrete terms, cookies consist of a string of text information saved to an Internet user's hard drive when he or she visits a website that uses cookies. Cookies can contain a variety of different types of information, such as the address of the website that issued them. Most important, cookies contain a unique tracking number that a given website accesses each time a user visits the site. This tracking number allows a website to identify the individual Internet user and to retrieve information obtained and archived during the user's previous visits, including passwords, specific Web pages visited, products purchased or reviewed, and credit card numbers.

Journalists who track the Internet have developed several analogies to better explain the nature and use of cookies. One analogy suggests that cookies are comparable to laundry claim checks. You drop your laundry off at the cleaners and you receive a claim check. When you return two days later, the claim check allows the laundry to quickly retrieve your clothes. Another analogy suggests that cookies are comparable to electronic tags or IDs placed on shoppers when they enter a supermarket. Those tags record every movement of shoppers as they browse the aisles of the supermarket, including the products examined but not purchased and those products that find their way into shopping carts.

Some cookies are referred to as "session cookies." These cookies exist only during one online session of an Internet user. Once an individual disconnects from a website, session cookies simply evaporate into cyberspace. "Persistent cookies" are stored on an Internet user's hard drive. Because of their nature, persistent cookies are much more functional for both Internet surfers and online companies . . . and more controversial. Most references to "cookies" within the press and by computer experts involve persistent cookies.

Making online shopping easier is not the only benefit that cookies provide to individual Internet users. Cookies allow us to "click" our way through logon procedures at websites without being forced to recall those cumbersome user names and easily forgotten passwords that we create for those sites on our initial visits. Cookies also allow Internet surfers to develop personalized websites such as a My Yahoo! or My AOL site.

In the late 1990s, bogus rumors circulated within the press regarding the capabilities of cookies. The most common of these rumors suggested that cookies were software programs that could be secretly executed after being stored on an Internet user's hard drive. Once executed, these little monsters could wreak havoc on a user's computer system. Pure fiction, according to the tech-savvy *Seattle Times*. "Cookies cannot spread viruses, steal your personal information, read your hard drive or empty your bank account."[6]

Within a few years after Netscape integrated cookies into the first edition of its Internet browser, cookies were everywhere on the Web. Other Internet browsers quickly made use of Montulli's creation as did dozens of major Internet companies such as Yahoo!, Amazon.com, and DoubleClick. In a June 2000 survey, 87 percent

---

5. *The Irish Times*, "Cookies: The Paparazzi Cyberspace," 8 September 1997, 20.

6. P. Lewis, "Web Cookies: Trail of Crumbs—Each Bite or Click on the Web Serves as Transfer of Data," *Seattle Times*, 9 August 1998, C1.

of the 91 most popular websites among Internet surfers admitted to using cookies.[7] The other 13 percent of those websites refused to disclose whether or not they used cookies. During the summer of 2000, officials of the Federal Trade Commission (FTC) testified before the U.S. Senate Committee on Commerce, Science, and Transportation regarding online companies' pervasive use of cookies.[8] To confirm how prevalent cookies were on the Web, an FTC staff member spent 15 minutes surfing the Internet during an online demonstration before that committee. In that brief time, the individual accumulated more than 120 cookies on his hard drive.

DOUBLECLICK'S COOKIE FACTORY

Online advertisers easily qualified as the most prolific cookie bakeries during the late 1990s, although cookies were a mainstay of hundreds of other Internet-based companies and many private organizations and federal agencies, as well. By the year 2000, annual online advertising expenditures approached $3.5 billion. From the early days of advertising on the World Wide Web, competition among online advertisers was intense. Virtual and conventional companies that advertised their goods and services on the Web often had unrealistic expectations for their online advertising campaigns. When those expectations went unfulfilled, those companies typically blamed their advertising agencies.

Pressure from their clients and competitors forced online advertising agencies to constantly search for new and more effective advertising methods. Soon after the introduction of cookies in the mid-1990s, advertising companies recognized that those miniscule tidbits of electronic matter might be the solution to a major problem they faced. That problem was how to ensure that online advertisements, such as banner ads, appeared on the computer screens of the parties most interested in purchasing the products and services being advertised. Online advertisers, such as DoubleClick, realized that they could use data that documented the browsing habits of Internet users—data "harvested" by cookies—to develop highly targeted advertising campaigns. Such data also gave Internet advertising agencies the ability to deliver advertisements on a real-time basis, that is, while Internet users browsed the Web.

> Their [online advertisers] intent is to target advertisements such as changing banner ads to users whose profiles match those of likely consumers of the advertised products. For example, DoubleClick was retained by the 3M Corporation to help target Internet banner advertising for an expensive multimedia projector to those users who would be most likely to purchase it. DoubleClick made use of the information cookies provided about user browsing habits to match the banners with users who had a history of selecting high-technology sites.[9]

DoubleClick's heavy reliance on cookies to provide targeted advertising campaigns for its clients allowed the New York-based company to quickly become the

7. G. R. Simpson, "Online Advertisers Are Negotiating Deal on Privacy Rules with U.S. Regulators," *The Wall Street Journal* Interactive Edition, 13 June 2000.

8. J. Clausing, "Washington Unconvinced That Internet Advertisers Can Police Themselves," *The New York Times* on the Web, 14 June 2000.

9. L. Eichelberger, "The Cookie Controversy," *cookiecentral.com*.

largest online advertiser. By the year 2000, DoubleClick boasted nearly 5,000 clients and was posting ads on 1,500 websites. DoubleClick accounted for nearly one-half of the estimated one trillion ads placed on the Internet that year, far outdistancing the second largest online advertiser, Engage Technologies, a subsidiary of the Internet incubator CMGI.

When Netscape introduced cookies in the mid-1990s, Internet users could only acquire a website's cookies by actually visiting that site. Since few individuals had any reason to visit DoubleClick's website, the company's executives recognized that they either had to rely on their clients' cookies to collect information on Internet users or develop a method for "planting" DoubleClick's own cookies on users' hard drives. The company's executives adopted the latter strategy. Individuals who click on a Web page ad placed there by DoubleClick acquire a DoubleClick cookie. Cookies planted in this way have allowed DoubleClick to become the Web's Cookie Master and to collect browsing information on millions of Internet users, most of whom have never considered visiting DoubleClick's own website.

DoubleClick's aggressive use of cookies angered many Internet users and prompted the filing of numerous lawsuits against the online advertiser. These plaintiffs charged that DoubleClick had violated their privacy rights by monitoring their travels across the Web and by maintaining a record of those travels. Additionally, many of these lawsuits alleged that DoubleClick had violated one or more federal statutes, including the Computer Fraud and Abuse Act, the Electronic Communications Privacy Act, and the Wiretap Act. Such lawsuits created a major public relations problem for DoubleClick. In response, DoubleClick's executives waged a "publicity war to defend its practice of placing cookies on Internet users' hard drives."[10] Company officials insisted that they had not concealed the fact that they were collecting information on individuals' browsing habits and rejected repeated assertions that doing so posed a threat to those individuals' economic and psychic well-being.

DoubleClick faced even more criticism in 1999 after company officials announced they had spent $1.7 billion to acquire Abacus, the nation's largest offline consumer database. According to the Internet-linked publication *eCompany*, Abacus contains demographic profiles for approximately 90 percent of U.S. households.[11] Those profiles have been compiled from various sources, including department store and credit card companies' purchasing records. From the standpoint of DoubleClick's chief executive officer (CEO), Kevin O'Connor, the key feature of the Abacus database was names, lots of names. Just as important to O'Connor, an address and other identifying information accompanied each of those names. During the late 1990s, DoubleClick had accumulated a huge database of so-called cookie dossiers that documented the browsing habits of individual Internet users. But, that database did not contain names and addresses linking the cookie dossiers to specific individuals.

O'Connor believed that DoubleClick could use the information in the Abacus database to match the company's cookie dossiers with specific households, if not specific individuals in those households. These new consumer profiles would be invaluable to DoubleClick and its advertising clients. "For an advertiser, if you

---

10. M. Meland, "The Other Online Profiler," *Forbes.com*, 25 February 2000.

11. R. King, "Kevin O'Connor Gives People the Willies," *eCompany* (online), October 2000.

marry Abacus information with behavioral data online, you get nirvana."[12] According to *The Wall Street Journal*, DoubleClick's profiles would be so detailed that they would likely identify the clothing sizes worn by many, if not most, of the individuals included in the merged database.[13] So, if Lands' End, a mail-order and online apparel retailer, found itself with an overstock of corduroy trousers, size 34 long, the company could zap out a batch of e-mails to Internet users who wore that size of trousers and who had purchased corduroys in the past.

Before Kevin O'Connor could begin cross-referencing his company's cookie dossiers with his huge new offline database, he had to solve one problem. DoubleClick had pledged since its inception to keep "completely anonymous" those Internet users who accessed DoubleClick ads. In a 1998 interview with the *Seattle Times*, O'Connor insisted that his company ". . . absolutely protects the privacy of individuals. We don't ask for personal information, and we'd never associate a user's name with a cookie."[14] O'Connor and his company could not keep those pledges if they went forward with the plan to merge the two databases.

In late 1999, O'Connor quietly dropped the anonymity pledge from DoubleClick's privacy policy listed at its website. At that point, O'Connor believed he and his company were free to go forward with their plan to put together extensive consumer profiles that could be used to develop precision-targeted marketing campaigns for DoubleClick's advertising clients. O'Connor also intended to market packages of those profiles to other advertisers and to specific companies selling goods or services likely appealing to the individuals included in the profile packages. An Internet privacy consultant charged that DoubleClick's sudden about-face betrayed large numbers of Internet users who had relied on the company's privacy policy. "This is a blatant bait-and-switch trick. For four years, they have said their services don't identify you personally, and now they're admitting they are going to identify you."[15]

Although O'Connor realized that his plan was controversial, he could not have predicted the avalanche of criticism that swamped DoubleClick when the plan was announced to the public. "All hell broke loose in late January [2000] when the news broke that DoubleClick had actually assembled real profiles of 100,000 specific users from a dozen Web sites, and was planning to peddle them to advertisers. The watchdogs howled."[16] Privacy advocates maintained that the use of DoubleClick's profiles for advertising purposes was not their primary concern. Those advocates argued that the use of DoubleClick's profiles by non-advertisers posed the most far-reaching threats to the privacy of individual Internet users. For example, companies selling automobile insurance could use those profiles to determine which of their policyholders regularly accessed websites for liquor companies. Similarly, law enforcement authorities could use DoubleClick's profiles to identify individuals predisposed to engaging in specific types of illegal conduct, such as illicit gambling activities. In effect, those profiles could be used to "brand," or stereotype, individual Internet users.

---

12. *Ibid.*

13. T. E. Weber, "Tricks of the Snoops' Trade," *The Wall Street Journal*, 23 February 2000, B1.

14. Lewis, "Web Cookies."

15. W. Rodgers, "Activists Charge DoubleClick Double Cross," *USA Today* (online), 7 June 2000.

16. King, "Kevin O'Connor Gives People the Willies."

In February 2000, the FTC notified Kevin O'Connor that it was launching an investigation to determine whether his company had engaged in unfair and deceptive practices. Following that announcement, O'Connor admitted that he had made a mistake "by pressing ahead with his Abacus plan without a clear agreement with consumers and regulators about where to draw the line on privacy."[17] O'Connor then postponed DoubleClick's plan to cross-reference the Abacus and cookie dossier databases. A few months later, during an appearance before the U.S. Senate Commerce Committee, DoubleClick's chief privacy officer testified that DoubleClick had complied with its pledge not to use the consumer profiles developed from its two large databases. However, the officer also noted that DoubleClick would have 40 to 50 million such profiles ready for use in the future, assuming that regulatory authorities allowed the company to proceed with its plan to use those profiles.[18]

COOKIES, PRIVACY, AND SELF-REGULATION

From their inception, cookies generated controversy for one major reason: they collected personal information regarding Internet users without first obtaining the consent of those users. This "subversive collection"[19] of personal information rankled civil rights groups, particularly members of several privacy rights groups that sprang up in the mid-1990s as the Internet surged in popularity with the public. Many online companies attempted to quell cookie-related privacy concerns by frequently reminding Internet users that they could easily eliminate the cookies that had collected on their hard drives. With a few dozen keystrokes, individuals can identify the cookies stored on their computer hard drives and then delete those that they do not want. By the late 1990s, several software vendors marketed "cookie management" software programs. Among other functions, these programs permit Internet users to pick and choose the cookies they will allow to be activated.

Efforts to inform the public that cookies could be eliminated from one's hard drive failed to placate Internet privacy advocates. Privacy activists correctly pointed out that such education efforts had little, if any, impact on the tens of millions of technologically-impaired Internet users who did not understand the nature of cookies and how online companies employ them. A nationwide survey in August 2000 revealed that most Americans were concerned about the issue of online privacy. However, that same survey also revealed that 56 percent of Internet users didn't know what a cookie was. "I think some Internet users are overwhelmed by technology. They don't want to be tracked on the Internet, but how can they stop it when they don't even know what a cookie is?"[20] Privacy advocates argued that the public's demand for privacy on the Internet, when coupled with the widespread lack of understanding of Internet privacy issues, mandated

---

17. *Ibid.*

18. Clausing, "Washington Unconvinced That Internet Advertisers Can Police Themselves."

19. Lewis, "Web Cookies."

20. M. Robuck, "Survey Says Internet Privacy a Concern Among Consumers: But Most Users Don't Know How to Protect Themselves," *Boardwatch Magazine*, October 2000, 86.

that regulatory and legislative authorities assume responsibility for establishing and enforcing standards to promote online privacy.

Throughout the 1990s, governmental officials generally adopted a "hands-off" approach to the Internet. No one wanted to be held responsible for disrupting the dramatic technological revolution taking place in cyberspace—a revolution that economists believed was the driving force behind the longest period of economic expansion the United States had ever experienced. Another factor that contributed to this passive regulatory philosophy was not widely discussed by the press, namely, that many regulatory and legislative bodies simply did not have the technological expertise to impose their will on the Internet. One journalist recalled an incident involving a prominent Congressman who was debating the issue of Internet privacy during a televised program on a major network. During that debate, a media representative noted that Internet users could easily "turn off" their cookies.[21] The Congressman's reaction to that statement revealed he had been unaware of that important fact. Ironically, this Congressman had proposed an online privacy bill to regulate the use of cookies.

Key leaders within the Internet industry maintained that extensive government regulation of e-commerce, including the creation of federally mandated rules and regulations governing online privacy, was unnecessary. Why? Because self-regulatory groups had assumed responsibility for ensuring that the Internet was a haven of free enterprise in which Internet users could expect to be treated fairly by online companies. Dozens of such self-regulatory bodies were organized during the 1990s, with the Online Privacy Alliance (OPA) being among the most prominent of these groups. More than 80 online companies and trade associations have joined the OPA, including DoubleClick. A primary role of the OPA is to develop policies and procedures to protect the privacy rights of Internet users.

The public relations fiasco involving DoubleClick in 2000 severely undermined the credibility of the OPA and similar self-regulatory groups. Privacy advocates used that series of events to hammer home a point they had been voicing for years, namely, that the Internet industry could not be relied upon to regulate itself. "We haven't seen anything from the industry side that says they're serious about protecting consumers' privacy."[22] Privacy advocates maintained that the passive regulatory philosophy of the federal government toward the Internet and the less-than-rigorous oversight efforts of self-regulatory bodies such as the OPA had encouraged several leading online companies to adopt an "anything-goes-until-we're-told-otherwise" attitude toward Internet privacy.

LOOKING TO THE FUTURE

Over the next several years, online privacy promises to be among the most controversial topics involving the Internet and e-commerce. The debate on this subject will include the press, civil rights groups, regulatory authorities, the federal courts, individual Internet users, and many other parties. *The Washington Post*

---

21. J. Freeman, "Washington Tries to Move on Internet Time," *Forbes.com*, 13 March 2000.

22. Robuck, "Survey Says Internet Privacy a Concern."

suggests that the outcome of this debate will have pervasive implications for electronic commerce: "The trade-off between personal privacy and personal commerce is rapidly becoming one of the defining business battles of the Internet."[23]

Several issues will be in the forefront of the debate over the extent to which consumer privacy should be protected and promoted on the Internet. Among the more important of those issues is the impact of this country's Internet privacy standards—or the lack thereof—on the increasing volume of international trade completed over the Internet. By the end of the century, U.S. trade with member countries of the European Union [EU] approached two trillion dollars annually. Since the inception of electronic commerce, the United States has had a much more liberal or relaxed attitude toward Internet privacy than its major trading partners in Europe. "U.S. laws on [Internet] privacy are far more liberal than Europe's, permitting a robust market in the exchange of consumer data between companies. European law prohibits companies from sharing data without permission from the consumer."[24]

Officials within President Clinton's administration worried that the U.S.'s attitude toward Internet privacy would eventually impede the growth of international electronic commerce with member countries of the EU. Near the end of the Clinton administration, the U.S. Department of Commerce announced that it had reached an agreement with the EU concerning online consumer privacy. That accord calls for U.S.-based e-commerce companies to abide by European privacy laws when transacting business with citizens of EU countries. Executives of many U.S. companies are unhappy with that agreement for two reasons. First, they claim that the EU's online privacy rules are far too restrictive. Second, these executives believe the agreement establishes a dangerous precedent, namely, allowing foreign governments or trade alliances to impose their regulatory philosophies on U.S. businesses.

A key factor that promises to complicate the ongoing debate on online privacy is the rapid pace of technological change in cyberspace. For example, while privacy advocates campaigned against the widespread and growing use of cookies, a new, more virulent species of Lou Montulli's magic cookies invaded the Internet. So-called "Web bugs" are similar to cookies and can be used for the same purpose, namely, tracking the browsing habits of individuals who surf the Internet. But, the more sophisticated technology that underlies Web bugs makes them much more difficult to detect than cookies, which explains why online advertisers began using them.

No doubt, online companies, particularly online advertising agencies, will continue to develop more high-tech and insidious methods for tracking and obtaining personal information regarding Internet users. Leading those efforts will likely be the long-time nemesis of online privacy advocates, DoubleClick. In January 2001, the FTC completed its nearly one-year investigation of the company. The FTC's report cleared DoubleClick of any wrongdoing, ruling that the company had not infringed on the privacy rights of Internet users, a conclusion that stunned and infuriated the firm's critics. Two months later, DoubleClick received

---

23. L. Walker, "Time to Let the Cookies Crumble?" *The Washington Post*, 4 November 1999, E1.

24. G. R. Simpson, "U.S., EU Negotiators Reach Agreement on Electronic-Commerce Privacy Rules," *The Wall Street Journal*, 15 March 2000, B6.

another piece of good news. A federal judge dismissed most of the pending law-suits filed against the company in federal courts by Internet users. Similar to the FTC, the federal judge found that DoubleClick had not breached the privacy rights of Internet users. The judge also reported that she could find no evidence that DoubleClick had violated any federal statute, as claimed by many of the plaintiffs in the lawsuits she dismissed.

The double-barrel shot of good news received by DoubleClick in the spring of 2001 allowed the company's executives to barge ahead with their plan to merge the huge Abacus database with the information collected by the company's mas-sive army of cookies. In an effort to reassure Internet users and quiet its critics, DoubleClick insisted that it would take appropriate measures when necessary to "anonymize" certain information in that merged database.[25] Likewise, the com-pany's management developed and then posted to DoubleClick's website a ten-point privacy policy and asked Internet users to comment on that policy and sub-mit recommended modifications.

DoubleClick's sudden interest in promoting online privacy did little to subdue critics of the company. Throughout 2001, these critics rigorously lobbied key members of the new George W. Bush administration and the U.S. Congress to take aggressive measures to limit the online "data harvesting" activities of Dou-bleClick and similar firms. The proposal that troubled DoubleClick and other on-line advertisers the most was a recommendation to simply ban the use of cookies on the Internet. A representative of one online advertiser lamented, "If we didn't use cookies, it would horribly affect the way we collect data. We want to know who is looking at what on the Web."[26]

Dozens of bills addressing the issue of online privacy were introduced in Congress during 2001. Eventually, two of these bills garnered the bulk of Con-gress's attention.[27] One bill, sponsored by Senator John McCain and Senator John Kerry, proposed to allow companies to collect personal data from Internet users who had not specifically informed those companies *not* to collect such in-formation. Unlike the so-called "opt-out" bill of Senators McCain and Kerry, Senator Fritz Hollings authored a bill that included an "opt-in" stipulation. Under this proposed statute, online companies would be permitted to collect personal information only from those Internet users who expressly authorized them to do so.

For years to come, Lou Montulli's magic cookies and their descendants will al-most certainly continue to pose an array of perplexing privacy issues and con-cerns for Internet users, online companies, and regulatory authorities. If Lou had only known that his cookies would become the central focus of a major public policy debate, he might have spent a little more time designing them and, possi-bly, given them a name more worthy of their status as important icons of the In-ternet Age.

25. K. Oser, "An Urge to Merge; Inquiry Over, DoubleClick Seeks to Mingle On/Offline Data," *Direct* (online), 1 March 2001.

26. S. Ellison, "Cookies Are Starting to Crumble, Making Online Advertisers Worry," *The Wall Street Journal* Interactive Edition, 24 July 2000.

27. J. Balz, "A Lot of Talk, No Action Expected in Washington," *St. Petersburg Times* (online), 14 May 2001.

QUESTIONS

1. Recent studies suggest that a large segment of the public is unaware of the threats to personal privacy posed by the Internet. Who do you believe is responsible for making the public fully aware of those threats: Internet users, themselves; online companies; regulatory authorities, such as the FTC; the U.S. Congress; or other parties? Defend your answer.

2. Search hard copy or online databases to identify recent lawsuits filed by individuals who claim that an online company violated their privacy rights. Choose one such lawsuit. For the lawsuit you selected, identify the plaintiff, the defendant, and the plaintiff's principal allegations. In your opinion, is the plaintiff likely to be successful in the lawsuit? Why or why not?

3. Choose two companies that operate websites that retail goods or services to the public. Find and print the privacy policy of each company. Summarize the key features of each policy. How do the two policies differ? What factors may account for those differences?

4. Research and write a brief report describing the nature of "Web bugs" and how they are similar to, and different from, cookies.

5. Much of the recent debate over online privacy in the U.S. Congress has focused on whether online companies should employ an "opt-in" or "opt-out" policy in collecting biographical and other information concerning Internet users. Which of these two general policies or strategies do you believe is most appropriate? Defend your answer.

6. Do you believe that Kevin O'Connor acted ethically when he changed DoubleClick's privacy policy? Explain.

7. Research recent developments involving DoubleClick. Summarize those developments in a bullet format.

Privacy Matters: Carnivore

*The right to be left alone—the most comprehensive
of rights and the right most valued by a free people.*

Justice Louis Brandeis

In 1890, a young Boston attorney, Louis Brandeis, co-authored an article for the *Harvard Law Review* destined to become a classic legal treatise on the issue of individual privacy.[1] That article, entitled "The Right to Privacy," focused on what the two legal scholars considered the greatest threats to one of the most basic rights of individual Americans, namely, the "right to be left alone." One of those threats stemmed from the development of mechanical communications devices, principally the new-fangled invention known as the telephone. According to Brandeis and his co-author, such devices posed the hazard that "what is whispered in the closet shall be proclaimed from the housetops."[2]

For nearly four decades, Brandeis practiced law in Boston, building a nationwide reputation as a legal expert on issues having a direct bearing on the rights and privileges of individuals. In fact, Brandeis became known as the "people's attorney" for his work on several high-profile legal cases that pitted the constitutional rights of individuals against the vested interests of large institutions and business organizations. In 1916, President Woodrow Wilson appointed Brandeis to the United States Supreme Court where he served with distinction for more than three decades. While serving on the high court, Brandeis often had the opportunity to argue on behalf of the privacy rights of individuals. Brandeis became so linked to that issue that several decades later the worldwide organization Privacy International initiated the annual Louis Brandeis Award to recognize individuals taking courageous measures to defend citizens' privacy rights.

During his long tenure on the nation's highest court, Brandeis frequently found himself writing dissents to controversial opinions handed down by the majority of his colleagues. In 1928, the Supreme Court wrestled with the issue of

---

1. S. Warren and L. D. Brandeis, "The Right to Privacy," 4 *Harvard Law Review* 193 (1890).

2. *Ibid.*

whether the wiretapping of telephone conversations by law enforcement authorities violated an individual's constitutional rights. The majority opinion handed down in that landmark case, *Olmstead v. United States*, gave government agencies the right to wiretap telephone conversations without obtaining a court order. Predictably, Brandeis strongly dissented to that opinion, insisting that such wiretaps grossly violated individual citizens' right to privacy. Nearly four decades later, another Supreme Court opinion vindicated the view expressed by Brandeis in the *Olmstead* case. In *Katz v. United States*, the high court ruled that individuals have a reasonable expectation that governmental officials will not eavesdrop on their telephone conversations.[3] The Katz opinion forced law enforcement authorities to obtain a court order showing "probable cause" of a crime before wiretapping telephone conversations.

The latter decades of the twentieth century saw the development of new technologies that posed threats to individuals' privacy rights that Louis Brandeis could never have imagined. Foremost among those new technologies were the Internet and the World Wide Web. In the early 1990s, before the Internet and the Web became woven into the fabric of Americans' everyday lives, two political science professors commented on the growing impact that technology developments and related changes in the business world were having on the privacy rights of individuals. "The right of privacy has . . . become more vulnerable to assault from technological advances and a societal and corporate need to acquire more information about individuals. Simply, the right to privacy has become far more complex, far more complicated, and far more extensive today."[4]

In July 2000, *The Wall Street Journal* revealed one of the most startling threats to the privacy rights of individuals in the new Internet Age.[5] The prominent publication reported that a surveillance system developed by the Federal Bureau of Investigation (FBI) had the ability to monitor the content of the approximately 1.5 billion e-mail messages sent each day in the United States. That revelation triggered a public outcry by civil rights advocates and organizations, principal among them the American Civil Liberties Union (ACLU). Critics of the FBI were unswayed by the agency's adamant statements that the new surveillance system was being used sparingly, principally in counter-terrorism efforts and in drug trafficking investigations and only then when specifically approved by a court order. Those critics pointed to several previous cases in which the federal agency had been accused of using its powers and privileges to spy and eavesdrop on prominent individuals who expressed strong political points of view on key issues of the day. These latter parties included Martin Luther King, Jr., John Lennon, and, ironically, William O. Douglas, the famed Supreme Court justice who replaced Louis Brandeis on the high court in 1939.

---

3. *Katz v. United States*, 389 U.S. 347 (1967).

4 J. F. Kozlowicz and C. E. Cottie, "Conceptions of Privacy: A Q-Method Study of Lay and Professional Viewpoints," presented at the 9th Annual Conference on the Science of Subjectivity, University of Missouri-Columbia, October 1993.

5. N. King and T. Bridis, "FBI's System to Covertly Search E-Mail Raises Legal Issues, Privacy Concerns," *The Wall Street Journal* Interactive Edition, 11 July 2000. In fact, the Carnivore system was first publicly discussed during a congressional hearing in April 2000 that went overlooked by the press.

KEEPING PACE WITH CYBER CROOKS

Throughout the late 1990s, the Internet grew in popularity with the everyday American citizen as well as cyber crooks. Increasingly, the FBI found itself attempting to track down criminals plying their trade in the shadowy world of cyberspace. One study reported that stock market-related frauds perpetrated over the Internet alone, imposed more than $1 million of losses *each hour* on honest investors.[6] Other examples of cyber crimes that haunted the FBI during the 1990s included hacker attacks on the computer systems of large corporations and government organizations, damaging viruses that miscreants released on millions of unsuspecting Internet users, and denial of service attacks that effectively shut down Yahoo!, eBay, and many other popular websites. A lack of technical expertise in Internet technology and investigative tools and techniques well-suited for the Internet hamstrung the efforts of FBI agents to track down and prosecute cyberspace criminals. Frustration finally convinced the FBI to create an internal task force that would focus almost exclusively on the Internet.

Marcus Thomas joined the FBI in the mid-1980s. Thomas initially worked on such "mundane" FBI assignments as tracking down bank robbers and investigating bomb scares. In the early 1990s, Thomas transferred to the FBI's Laboratory Division, which provided technical support for FBI investigations involving computer crimes. By the late 1990s, Thomas found himself heading up the FBI's new cybertechnology operations that investigated criminal activities linked to the Internet. Throughout 1998 and 1999, Thomas and several of his subordinates worked on a secret project within the well-guarded FBI compound in Quantico, Virginia. Thomas wanted to develop a surveillance system that would allow the FBI to monitor e-mail communications among criminal elements using the Internet. In his own words, Thomas' objective was to develop a system that would help him and his fellow agents "catch the bad guy."[7]

An FBI official and one of Thomas' superiors justified the development of the new surveillance system by insisting that his organization had become "overwhelmed" by new and sophisticated criminal schemes launched over the Internet.[8] As the Internet became entrenched in American culture during the 1990s, conventional or "low-tech" criminal scams began to benefit from the information superhighway as well. The FBI found that with each passing year more and more technologically inclined criminals were using the Internet as a tool to organize, control, and direct their asocial affairs. Thomas and his superiors reasoned that the only way the FBI could pose a serious challenge to such New Age criminals was to join them in cyberspace.

Thomas' subordinates used the code name "Carnivore" for their new project because the system was intended to find the "meat" they were searching for among the vast number of e-mail messages sent over the Internet each day. That meat was communications linked to criminal conduct. The icon they used to represent the new system on the FBI's computer screens was "a snarling mouth of

---

6. A. C. Raul, "Should You Fear the Carnivore?" *eCompany* (online), November 2000.

7. D. Q. Wilber, "Web Spinners," *Baltimore Sun*, 1 August 2000, 1F.

8. *Ibid.*

bloody teeth about to snap shut on a stream of ones and zeros, the language of computers."[9] Neither Thomas nor his subordinates intended the "Carnivore" name or icon to be released to the public. "Carnivore" was chosen as a tongue-in-cheek code name to be used strictly for internal purposes. In the weeks and months following the public disclosure of the new surveillance system, journalists sarcastically suggested several less inflammatory names that Thomas and his associates could have used for their pet project. Those suggestions included NERD (network e-mail redirection and detection), SNOOP (simultaneous network observation for ongoing probes), or the more uplifting HERO (high-tech e-mail reconnaissance observer).[10,11]

Before the development of Carnivore, the FBI had been forced to seek court orders to retrieve from the computer systems of ISPs (Internet service providers) e-mail messages allegedly linked to some criminal conduct. By the time such e-mails were obtained and reviewed, the FBI often found that the parties they sought had perpetrated additional crimes on unsuspecting victims and in many cases had slipped away by changing their cyberspace identities or by taking more conventional evasive tactics and simply "skipping town."

Disclosure of the Carnivore system immediately created an enormous headache for the FBI. The unfortunate name selected for the new surveillance system provoked widespread concern that the federal agency routinely trampled on the constitutional rights of the millions of honest Americans and businesses that used e-mail as their primary communication medium. Critics most commonly charged that the new system infringed on the Fourth Amendment rights of U.S. citizens, namely, the right to be protected from illegal search and seizure. Almost immediately, several civil rights advocacy groups demanded that the FBI reveal how the system worked, while others lobbied Congress to pass legislation outlawing the system.

IN DEFENSE OF A PREDATOR

Public disclosure of the FBI's Carnivore system prompted widespread rumors and speculation regarding the nature and use of that system. One critic of the new surveillance system noted during an interview on *CNNfn* that "Carnivore is a program that can be installed on an Internet service provider, and once installed, it allows the FBI to tap into any e-mail from any person. So it's roughly equivalent to the government going to GTE or Pacific Bell and installing a device that lets it listen to any phone call from any person at any time."[12] *The San Diego Union-Tribune* reported a similar assertion. "Carnivore just taps everyone's communications and . . . filters them to look for illegal activity. As a result, your pri-

---

9. *Ibid.*

10. M. Himowitz, "Carnivore's Appetite a Mystery," *Baltimore Sun*, 14 August 2000, 1C.

11. B. Mitchell, "Carnivore, Sniffers, and You," *Computer Networking* (online), 19 July 2000.

12. P. Sabga and C. Molineaux, "The N.E.W. Show," *CNNfn*, 26 July 2000, Transcript #00072607FN-107.

vate e-mails to your friends and family, perhaps discussing very personal family matters, will end up in the hands of the FBI."[13]

FBI officials quickly came to the defense of their new surveillance system. Those officials insisted that constant surveillance of e-mail messages transmitted over a given ISP's network was not equivalent to a permanent wiretap on a major telephone network.

> Unlike conventional telephone conversations, e-mail messages are transmitted digitally. A computer slices and dices the outgoing information [e-mail message] into 'packets,' each with an identifying tag. The packets are then dispersed throughout the Internet, finding the most efficient path to their destination. When the packets arrive at their destination, they are reassembled, and the recipient is then able to read the message. As a result . . . the FBI cannot 'tap a line' because there is no discrete line to tap. Instead, some mechanism is required to digitally scan all packets that pass through a link a suspect is known to use—like his ISP—and pick out the packets that belong to him.[14]

The FBI physically attaches a small black box containing the Carnivore software to an ISP's computer system. Since each identifying tag included in an e-mail packet specifies the sender and intended recipient of the message, the FBI can program Carnivore to flag each packet being sent or received by a party under investigation. Those packets are then copied and saved for subsequent review by an FBI agent. The initial version of Carnivore was a fairly standard "packet sniffer." For several years, many business organizations have used packet-sniffing software to monitor e-mails flowing through their computer networks. Computer hackers, such as the infamous Master Hacker, Kevin Mitnick, have also routinely used packet sniffers to intercept confidential e-mail messages of businesses, government organizations, and private individuals.

To employ Carnivore in a criminal investigation, FBI officials must first obtain a court order specifically approving the use of the surveillance system. Such court orders expire after 30 days but the FBI is obligated to stop using the system immediately when the information being sought has been collected. At ten-day intervals, the judge who issues the court order reviews the status of the investigation. Any evidence collected via the Carnivore system must be immediately inventoried. Eventually, a copy of the inventoried transmissions is given to the parties involved in the intercepted messages. Those parties that are the targets of criminal investigations can use that information to help develop appropriate strategies to defend themselves against any charges they may ultimately face. To calm public concerns that "Big Brother" was reading the private e-mails of everyday citizens, FBI officials repeatedly insisted that all "innocent" e-mail messages flow through the system "unimpeded" and "unobserved" by the agency's cyberspace detectives.

> It is important to note that the identification, segregation, and copying of pertinent e-mail messages are digitally accomplished by the [Carnivore] software. Rather than being scrutinized by FBI agents, the vast amounts of innocent, non-pertinent data flow

---

13. W. D. Gore, "FBI Internet Tap Is a Limited Program," *San Diego Union-Tribune*, 16 August 2000, B11 and B13.

14. *Ibid.*

through Carnivore's electronic screen in their digital form, unimpeded by Carnivore and unobserved by the human eye.[15]

Despite assertions to the contrary by critics of the Carnivore system, FBI officials maintained that the system was not programmed to search e-mail messages for key words or terms that might be suggestive of criminal conduct. Key-word monitoring systems have been available for several years and are reportedly used by many companies to flag the use of terms such as "union" or "boss" that appear in e-mail messages transmitted over a company's computer network by employees.[16] A company's security personnel typically investigates flagged e-mail messages to determine whether given employees are engaging in insubordination or other inappropriate conduct.

Supporters of the FBI's aggressive new surveillance system also attempted to mute criticism of the federal agency's efforts by pointing out that several countries were using or planning to use comparable surveillance systems to monitor e-mail transmissions. Those countries included Russia and Great Britain. Apparently, Carnivore-like systems are routinely attached to all ISPs operating in Russia and have been for several years. In 2000, the British Parliament passed a law that authorized the creation of an e-mail surveillance system similar to Carnivore. The new law appropriated more than $30 million to cover the cost of integrating that monitoring system into the computer network of every British ISP. E-mails flagged for review by the system are diverted to the new "Government Technical Assistance Center," a name that British authorities intended to be less eye-catching than "Carnivore."

A final, and somewhat awkward, strategy that FBI insiders used to counter criticism of Carnivore was suggesting that the surveillance system was not as effective as the federal agency had originally intended. For example, FBI officials readily admitted that encryption systems employed by many sophisticated Internet users, particularly sophisticated criminals, to conceal the content of e-mail messages diminished the effectiveness of Carnivore. Following the public disclosure of Carnivore, several software vendors began marketing such encryption systems for businesses and individuals using the Internet. As noted by one such vendor, "Carnivore has been very beneficial for us. People have been shocked into the realization that their mail is not secret when they send it across the Internet."[17]

THE TEMPEST GROWS

The Wall Street Journal's disclosure of Carnivore in July 2000 sparked a flurry of investigative reports by the print and electronic media. Repeated statements issued by the FBI describing the general nature and purpose of the system and repeated denials by the federal agency that Carnivore violated the privacy rights of Amer-

---

15. *Ibid.*

16. L. Landon, "Big Brother Is Watching You: Governments and Private Sector Are Reading Your E-Mail and Monitoring the Sites You Visit," *The Ottawa Citizen*, 22 July 2000, D1.

17. *Minneapolis Star Tribune*, "E-Mail Fears Fuel Demand for Security Devices," 21 August 2000, 11D.

ican citizens failed to placate civil rights advocates. Less than three weeks after the initial public disclosure of Carnivore, the ACLU filed a request to obtain the source code for the system under the Freedom of Information Act. The FBI refused to comply with that request. FBI officials correctly pointed out that releasing the source code for Carnivore would completely defeat its purpose since criminals could use that information to readily circumvent the surveillance system.

Mounting criticism of the Carnivore system quickly caught the attention of several prominent members of the U.S. Congress and key officials within the Clinton Administration. Liberal Democrats and conservative Republicans banded together to criticize the FBI's new surveillance tool. John Conyers, a Democratic congressman from Michigan, bluntly noted, "Constitutional rights don't end where cyberspace begins."[18] Among Republicans, House Majority Leader Dick Armey of Texas questioned the need for Carnivore and expressed concern that the FBI was being less than candid regarding its actual use of the system. By the fall of 2000, legislators had introduced several bills into the U.S. House of Representatives to ban or significantly limit the use of the Carnivore system.

Within the Clinton Administration, Attorney General Janet Reno became the focal point for much of the criticism directed at the Carnivore system. As head of the U.S. Justice Department, Reno had oversight responsibility for the FBI. One of Reno's first actions was to suggest that the system be renamed, a recommendation quickly seconded by Louis Freeh, the Director of the FBI. In early August, Reno ordered that an independent panel of experts be appointed to review the purpose, nature, and use of the Carnivore system.

The independent panel selected by Attorney General Reno issued its report on Carnivore in late November 2000. That report generally supported earlier statements made by the FBI regarding the key operating features of the surveillance system and the manner in which FBI agents were using the system. The report confirmed that Carnivore was essentially a sophisticated packet sniffer, comparable to those that had been used legitimately and illegitimately for many years. Additionally, the independent panel reported that FBI policy required a court order to be obtained before Carnivore was used in a given investigation. Although generally complimentary of the FBI, the independent panel did express several reservations regarding the Carnivore system.

The most serious concern raised by the independent panel's report involved the adequacy of the "human and organizational controls" that the FBI had implemented for Carnivore. Members of the panel were concerned by the potential failure of FBI personnel to comply with explicit standards developed to govern the use of the system. The panel suggested that extensive auditing functions be integrated into Carnivore to ensure that FBI agents complied with all relevant legal safeguards. Since the FBI periodically updates the technology involved in the Carnivore system, the panel also recommended that the system be subject to regular independent reviews.

At approximately the same time that the Justice Department released the results of the independent panel's review of Carnivore, another development reignited the controversy surrounding the system. A civil rights advocacy group, the Electronic Privacy Information Center (EPIC), released copies of FBI documents that it obtained after filing a lawsuit under the Freedom of Information Act.

---

18. S. Lash, "Feds Defend Use of E-Mail Snooper," *The Houston Chronicle*, 25 July 2000, A2.

Those documents included an internal FBI memorandum that discussed the results of a test of the Carnivore system. That test indicated Carnivore "could reliably capture and archive all traffic through an Internet service provider."[19] Critics charged that this test confirmed that the FBI was clearly considering a more expansive role for Carnivore in the future. Following the release of the FBI memo, the U.S. Senate Judiciary Committee requested additional information from the FBI regarding why such a test had been performed and exactly how the agency planned to use Carnivore in the future.[20]

No major legislation impacting the FBI's use of the Carnivore system passed Congress in 2000. As the controversy surrounding the system continued to swirl in late 2000, Carnivore's critics pinned their hopes for a resolution to that controversy favorable to their position on the newly elected Congress and the administration of President-elect George W. Bush. In February 2001, the FBI announced in a brief and matter-of-fact press release that its online surveillance system had been renamed DCS1000. An FBI spokesperson indicated that the new name was due to an upgrade of the system: "With upgrades come new names."[21] When asked to explain the meaning underlying the new alphanumeric name for the system, the FBI spokesperson curtly replied that the new name "doesn't stand for anything."[22]

The FBI's decision to rename Carnivore failed to appease the agency's detractors. When he learned of that decision, the associate director of the ACLU commented that the new name was a superficial measure that did not change the nature of the FBI's surveillance system or the risks it posed to the public's privacy rights. "If it prowls like a wolf, howls like a wolf and has the voracious appetite of a wolf, it's still a carnivore."[23] At approximately the same time that the FBI announced the name change for its surveillance system, privacy advocates received another piece of bad news. An article in *The Wall Street Journal* revealed that the Central Intelligence Agency (CIA), the shadowy sister organization to the FBI, was also using covert means to track Internet users. A senior CIA official candidly observed, "We want to operate anywhere on the Internet in a way that no one knows the CIA is looking at them."[24]

CARNIVORE, E-COMMERCE, AND BIG BROTHER

The controversy prompted by the public disclosure of Carnivore in July 2000 had implications for a wide range of parties, including thousands of companies that relied heavily or exclusively on the Internet to market their goods and services.

---

19. J. Schwarz, "Review Released on Web Wiretap," *The New York Times* on the Web, 22 November 2000.

20. *Reuters* (online), "Senate Panel Presses FBI for Carnivore Data," 27 November 2000.

21. *Reuters*, "Carnivore E-Mail Wiretap System Gets New Name," *The New York Times* on the Web, 13 February 2001.

22. *Ibid.*

23. *Ibid.*

24. N. King, "Small Start-Up Helps the CIA to Mask Its Moves on the Web," *The Wall Street Journal* Interactive Edition, 12 February 2001.

One of the biggest roadblocks that Internet-linked companies have faced in per-suading potential customers to complete transactions over the Internet has been privacy concerns. One study estimated that such concerns reduced the volume of e-commerce revenues by nearly $3 billion in 1999.[25] The Carnivore controversy served to heighten those fears by inciting an "I told you so" campaign by skep-tics anxious to chastise their friends and neighbors for being too trusting of the apparent privacy afforded by the Internet.

Federal law enforcement authorities do not deny that Internet surveillance ef-forts likely discourage some parties from doing business on the Internet. But, those authorities are also quick to point out that failure to employ surveillance technologies such as Carnivore would almost certainly contribute to a much more significant problem facing e-commerce, namely, the rapid growth of fraud scams perpetrated over the Internet. Likewise, representatives of leading e-commerce companies believe that sacrificing some degree of privacy on the Internet is a small price to pay for promoting consumer confidence in the integrity of transac-tions consummated principally or totally in cyberspace.

The public uproar caused by the disclosure of the FBI's Carnivore system fo-cused considerable attention on, and spurred widespread debate concerning, the ability and right of companies, private organizations, and government agencies to use digital technology to monitor the electronic communications of their em-ployees. One legal scholar noted that "Digital technology provides employers with an arsenal of extraordinarily intrusive methods of workplace surveillance. . . . The Orwellian nightmare of the Thought Police and Big Brother appears to reflect reality and has several disturbing similarities to the current widespread use of surveillance technology in American workplaces."[26] Empirical studies tend to confirm that scholar's concerns. *Fortune* magazine reported in the sum-mer of 2001 that 46 percent of all companies regularly monitor their employees' e-mails.[27] Another study found that 54 percent of major U.S. companies "moni-tor their employees' Internet use, while 38 percent store and review e-mail messages."[28]

One of the most widely reported cases of a large corporation monitoring its employees' e-mails involved *The New York Times*. In November 1999, the presti-gious newspaper fired more than 20 employees who circulated reportedly offen-sive materials via e-mails over the corporation's computer network.[29] Are such surveillance efforts necessary? Are they ethically justifiable? Debate over those questions will likely continue for many years to come as the Internet becomes in-creasingly important to the U.S. economy. In the meantime, many corporate ex-ecutives seem to be heeding the mantra of Andy Grove, Intel Corporation's chief executive and one of the most respected leaders in the e-commerce domain. In

---

25. D. Howell, "Electronic Commerce—An Issue of Privacy," *Investor's Business Daily*, 26 July 2000, A8.

26. R. Dixon, "With Nowhere to Hide: Workers Are Scrambling for Privacy in the Digital Age," 4 *Journal of Technology Law and Policy* 1, Spring 1999.

27. A. Cohen, "Worker Watchers," *Fortune/CNET Technology Review*, Summer 2001, 72.

28. Landon, "Big Brother Is Watching You."

29. A. Carrns, "Bawdy E-Mails Were Funny Till Times' Parent Fired 22," *The Houston Chronicle*, 6 February 2000, 3.

discussing the hyper-competitive economic environment ushered in by the Internet Age, Grove warned that "only the paranoid survive."[30]

No doubt, future advances in technology will pose increasingly grave threats to the privacy rights of individuals. Justice Louis Brandeis foresaw those threats some seven decades ago. In his dissent to the Supreme Court's majority decision in the *Olmstead* case, Justice Brandeis observed that, "The progress of science in furnishing the government with means of espionage is not likely to stop with wiretapping."[31] One of Justice Brandeis's successors on the Supreme Court, Justice Antonin Scalia, expressed a similar concern in 2001 in the opinion he wrote for the *Kyllo vs. The United States* case. That case involved the use of thermal imaging technology by law enforcement authorities to "look" through the walls of homes without obtaining a search warrant. In his opinion, Justice Scalia noted that he and his colleagues and society, in general, needed to determine what limits should be placed "upon this power of technology to shrink the realm of guaranteed privacy."[32]

QUESTIONS

1. Internet users' desire for privacy often conflicts with the efforts of law enforcement authorities to protect those users from fraudulent schemes perpetrated over the Internet. Which is more important, protecting the privacy of Internet users or protecting them from Internet-based scams? Defend your answer.

2. In your opinion, who should decide the extent to which the FBI should be allowed to use new technologies to obtain information pertinent to ongoing criminal investigations: FBI officials, the federal courts, the U.S. Congress, or some other party? Defend your choice.

3. Are software vendors behaving ethically when they develop and aggressively market products designed to help Internet users defeat the purpose of the Carnivore system?

4. Several ISPs in the United States took legal action to prevent the FBI from attaching the Carnivore system to their computer networks. Do you believe that those efforts were ethical or morally justifiable?

5. What limitations, if any, do you believe should be imposed on the rights of employers to monitor their employees' e-mails? Identify one scenario in which such monitoring is clearly appropriate and another scenario in which such monitoring seems unwarranted.

30. T. Bunker, "Many Fear Carnivore, with Reason," *The Boston Herald*, 7 August 2000, 24.

31. Reuters, "Privacy Laws No Match for Modern Technology," *The New York Times* on the Web, 8 May 2001.

32. J. Schwartz, "Organized Crime Case Raises Privacy Issues," *The New York Times* on the Web, 30 July 2001.

To Tax or Not to Tax

*The wisdom of man never yet contrived a system
of taxation that would operate with perfect equality.*

Andrew Jackson

Are you one of those people who can't wait to check their e-mail? No doubt, an e-mail from a close friend can brighten anyone's day. But, for the weary salesperson, accountant, or marketing manager nearing the end of a long day, double-clicking the e-mail icon can be a fearful experience. A batch of new e-mail messages can mean the difference between catching the 5:25 Hometown Express or spending the next two hours hunched over the computer screen, staving off hunger with a Diet Coke and a bag of Fritos.

Besides frazzled corporate soldiers, the United States Postal Service ranks high on the list of "victims" of the e-mail society that has emerged in recent years thanks to the Internet. Why buy a stamp, address an envelope, and write a letter when you can dash off a quick e-mail to Mom and Dad, Aunt Suzie, or a college buddy?

A few years ago, a widely circulated rumor suggested that Congress was considering a bill to slap a five-cent tax on every e-mail message zapped across the country. Congressman Schnell, the principal proponent of the bill, wanted to channel the funds raised by the tax to the U.S. Postal Service. Those funds would compensate the Postal Service for lost revenues due to the mega-number of stamps that go unsold each year thanks to the dramatic growth of e-mail as a communications medium.

The proposed e-mail tax set off a storm of protest. Millions of Internet users received an e-mail message encouraging them to swamp elected officials with e-mails condemning the proposed tax. The e-mail tax was even raised as an issue during several political campaigns. During a televised debate in the fall of 2000 between Hillary Clinton and Representative Rick Lazio, who were involved in a heated contest for an open U.S. Senate seat in New York, both candidates were asked to comment on whether or not they supported the proposed e-mail tax. Neither did. In fact, the proposed tax was simply a rumor, a hoax. No such tax bill was ever introduced in Congress. Congressman Schnell did not exist. Ironically, the e-mail tax hoax created such a furor among Internet users that an *actual* congressman proposed an *actual* bill that would have permanently exempted e-mail from being taxed. That bill soon died from lack of support.

Just because Congress has no apparent intention of levying a tax on e-mails does not mean that the Internet has escaped the long arm of taxing authorities. In fact, the controversy involving the bogus e-mail tax was just one element of a far-ranging debate that erupted in the late 1990s. That debate focused on whether, or to what extent, Internet traffic, particularly electronic commerce, should be subject to taxation. On the international scene, scores of countries, including the United States, began squabbling over how best to tax multinational e-commerce. Before resolving the global tax implications of the Internet, most politicians and interest groups in the United States insisted on addressing an extremely contentious and complex domestic taxation issue. That issue was whether the federal government should force online merchants to collect sales taxes from their customers.

A MAZE OF SALES TAXES

In the early 1930s, the Great Depression was draining the financial resources of state governments nationwide. To generate the funds needed to continue providing a wide range of services to its citizens, Mississippi became the first state to pass a retail sales tax. The decision of the Magnolia State soon prompted other states to begin levying taxes on retail sales. The Supreme Court blessed this trend in the late 1930s when it ruled that retail sales taxes were legal. Eventually, 45 states and the District of Columbia would collect statewide retail sales taxes. The five holdout states include Alaska, Delaware, Montana, New Hampshire, and Oregon.[1]

Sales tax fever spread beyond state governments to local governments and other "sub-national" governmental agencies. Presently, an estimated 7,500 state and local governments and agencies collect retail sales taxes. Because multiple sales taxes are levied in many jurisdictions, the actual number of sales taxes being collected in the United States exceeds 30,000. Retail sales tax collections each year approach $200 billion.

Sales taxes vary significantly from jurisdiction to jurisdiction. There is little consensus in sales tax rates and even less consensus on what goods and services are subject to sales taxes. For example, the number of professional or business services taxed by individual states ranges from more than 150 in Hawaii to fewer than 20 in several states. Many states exempt food items from sales taxes but impose taxes on "snack" items. "In New York, large marshmallows are considered taxable snacks, while little marshmallows are tax-exempt food. Plain doughnuts are tax-exempt in some states, while jelly-filled ones are taxable."[2] In California, sales tax authorities consider Evian water a food item. But, Perrier qualifies as a snack and thus must be taxed. Why? Because it has bubbles. Go figure.

---

1. Unlike most developed countries, the United States does not have a national-level sales tax or value-added tax. The federal government does impose excise taxes, which are comparable to sales taxes, on a few items, most notably gasoline.

2. H. Gleckman, "The Tempest Over Taxes," *Business Week e.biz,* 7 February 2000, EB 32.

The importance of sales taxes as a source of revenue also varies sharply across jurisdictions. For a handful of states, including Mississippi, statewide sales taxes account for 50 percent or more of their annual revenues. In Vermont and Virginia, sales tax collections account for only 20 percent of annual revenues. The national average ranges between 35 and 40 percent.

Among the most common complaints leveled at retail sales taxes is that they are regressive. Income tax rates are progressive: the more income you earn, the higher the percentage of your income you pay in taxes. Sales taxes rates are unaffected by the incomes of taxpayers. Since lower income taxpayers tend to purchase goods and services subject to sales taxes in quantities comparable to higher income taxpayers, sales taxes consume a larger percentage of the earnings of lower income taxpayers. Ironically, when sales taxes were first imposed during the 1930s, the theory was that well-to-do citizens would bear the burden of these taxes. The Depression Era had robbed most other Americans of the economic resources needed to purchase retail goods.

Retailers, particularly those engaged in interstate commerce, routinely complain of the problems they face in complying with the tangled and overlapping maze of sales taxes and sales tax regulations. Retailers must determine the items to which the sales taxes in each taxing jurisdiction apply, identify the appropriate tax rates for individual items, remit sales tax collections on a timely basis to the proper authorities, and continually monitor the jurisdictions in which they do business to identify changes in sales tax laws and regulations. One study indicates that dozens of sales taxes expire each year or are cancelled by legislative bodies, while as many as 200 new sales taxes are added each year.

The frenzied growth of electronic commerce in recent years threatens to undermine the unwieldy sales tax system that has evolved on a helter-skelter basis over the past seven decades. That system emerged in an economic environment in which businesses operated exclusively from physical facilities and consumers purchased goods and services principally from local merchants. Today, many consumers purchase goods and services from virtual businesses across the country and around the globe. Using the nation's archaic sales tax system to capture and tax such transactions poses a proverbial square-peg-in-round-hole problem. A corporate executive commenting on the sales tax issue noted, "We now have a significant lag between old legislation and the reality of today's digital economy."[3]

The public often views the Internet as a "tax-free zone," a perception reinforced by the U.S. Congress in 1998 when it passed the Internet Tax Freedom Act. However, that federal statute did not exempt retail sales made via the Internet from sales taxes. Instead, that law simply imposed a three-year moratorium running through October 21, 2001, on any new Internet-based taxes.

Similar to other retail sales, most goods and services purchased over the Internet are subject to state and local sales taxes. However, the difficulty of collecting those taxes results in the large majority of them going unpaid. This *de facto* exemption from sales taxes on electronic commerce ignited a firestorm of controversy in the late 1990s as the volume of online retail transactions spiraled upward. Eventually, the battle lines drawn in this controversy created two factions. One group, the anti-tax crusaders, emphatically argued that the overriding economic

---

3. M. Geewax, "Will Buying on the Net Remain Tax Free?" *The Atlanta Journal Constitution*, 27 February 2000, 1C.

interests of the nation dictated that the Internet be free of sales taxes. On the other side of the issue, a pro-tax contingent maintained just as adamantly that electronic commerce had to be taxed in the same manner as retail sales at brick and mortar establishments.

CASH COWS AND FIRE TRUCKS

The surge in electronic commerce that began in the late 1990s helped sustain one of the longest periods of economic growth in the nation's history. An annual state of the economy report issued by the Department of Commerce in mid-2000 declared that information technology was the principal driver of the American economy. Economists and governmental officials agree that the Internet is the lynchpin of that technology.

> The report showed the benefits of information technology are quickly spreading across the board, and eventually will touch every business from the smallest Mom-and-Pop to the biggest Fortune 100. . . . We believe that when members of the Congress better understand the growing impact technology is having on consumers, job creation, and our economy, then they will make more informed policy decisions.[4]

Many politicians and economists predicted that any effort to impose new taxes on electronic commerce or to force online merchants to collect existing sales taxes on Internet-based transactions would bring this period of economic prosperity to a premature and abrupt end. John Boehner, a prominent member of the U.S. House of Representatives, warned that "Clogging the Internet with sales taxes is the surest way to bring this remarkable engine of economic growth grinding to a halt."[5] His colleague in the U.S. House, John Kasich, reinforced that viewpoint. "E-commerce presents nothing less than a second Industrial Revolution. The biggest threat to this growth is government treating the Internet like a cash cow."[6]

James Gilmore, the governor of Virginia, chaired the 19-member Advisory Commission on Electronic Commerce (ACEC)—a blue-ribbon panel created by Congress to study the taxation of electronic commerce. Governor Gilmore personally lobbied the public and members of the ACEC to build support for eliminating sales taxes on electronic commerce. "To the extent tax-free treatment is viewed as a preference or subsidy of the Internet, American public policy should embrace it in order to realize the Internet's tremendous social and economic potential."[7] Senator John McCain, a leading candidate for the Republican Party's presidential nomination in 2000, made a pledge not to tax Internet transactions a major plank of his campaign platform. Along with John Boehner and John Kasich, McCain sponsored a joint congressional bill to exempt electronic commerce from sales taxes nationwide.

4. J. Clausing, "Digital Economy Has Arrived, Commerce Department Says," *The New York Times* on the Web, 6 June 2000.

5. T. Diemer, "Battle Brewing Over Internet Sales Tax," *The Plain Dealer*, 16 April 2000, 1H.

6. H. Gleckman, "The Great Internet Tax Debate," *Business Week*, 27 March 2000, 228.

7. D. Rigsby, "Total Tax Ban on E-Commerce Gains Steam," *Nation's Cities Weekly*, 15 November 1999, 1.

To support their claims that sales taxes would hamstring electronic commerce, the anti-tax lobby referred to a study that suggested online sales would fall by as much as 30 percent if sales taxes were rigorously enforced on Internet commerce. Another economic study revealed that e-commerce was growing most rapidly in states and localities that levied the highest sales taxes on conventional retail sales. Strengthening the anti-tax lobby's position even more were economic data indicating that most state and local governments were running surpluses by the late 1990s, thanks largely to the economic boom fueled by the Internet. "Tax the Internet, and you might kill the goose that laid the golden egg" cautioned one observer.[8]

Results of public opinion polls consistently showed that a majority of the public supported a ban on Internet taxes. Nevertheless, leaders of the anti-tax lobby soon found themselves opposed by an impressive coalition of politicians, economists, and representatives of state and local governments.

The most influential members of the pro-tax lobby included 37 governors who represented a majority of the National Governors Association. This group, led by Utah governor Michael Leavitt, another member of the ACEC, feared that the mushrooming growth of Internet sales would eventually shrink their states' tax revenues. A study by economists at the University of Tennessee projected that annual sales tax collections nationwide might drop by as much as $20 billion, or approximately ten percent, due to rising Internet sales.[9] Other forecasts projected even larger declines in sales tax revenues for state and local governments.

Since sales taxes provide the funding for schools, hospitals, roads, and fire and police protection, pro-tax lobbyists maintained that those services would eventually face drastic cuts. A petition signed by members of the National Governors Association placed the public on notice that failure to tax electronic commerce could potentially "devastate education funding."[10] The director of the Oklahoma Municipal League pointed out that not collecting sales taxes on retail Internet sales would be particularly crippling to states such as Oklahoma that have relatively modest tax bases. "It would be pretty bad if someone's house is on fire and all we can do is e-mail a picture of a fire truck to them."[11]

The mayor of New Orleans became a national spokesperson for the U.S. Conference of Mayors, a group solidly in favor of taxing electronic commerce. He noted that retail sales tax collections accounted for nearly one-half of his city's annual budget. Cities such as New Orleans that have a large percentage of their citizens employed in retail sales face a potential "double whammy." Soaring Internet sales not only threaten to reduce these cities' sales tax collections but also to swell their unemployment rolls as brick and mortar retailers slash payrolls in the face of declining revenues.

The pleas of state and local government officials to tax electronic commerce rankled members of the anti-tax brigade. John Kasich and other front-line supporters

---

8. M. Castelluccio, "Taxes on the Internet?" *Strategic Finance*, May 2000, 71.

9. *AccountingWeb.com*, "House Leader Plans to Block Online Sales Tax," 21 June 2001.

10. P. A. Gigot, "GOP Governors Join the E-Tax Lobby," *The Wall Street Journal* Interactive Edition, 14 April 2000.

11. S. Colberg, "Oklahoma Cities in Favor of Getting Internet Sales Tax," *Tulsa World*, 21 March 2000, 1.

of the move to ban taxes on electronic commerce responded to those pleas by alleging that states and municipalities had grossly and intentionally overestimated their projected revenue losses due to Internet sales. A public statement issued by the National Taxpayer Union also railed against the demands of state and local government officials to tax the Internet. Those "governments are not starved for revenues. They're just hungry . . . to fund wasteful and unnecessary projects. Taxing the Internet isn't about helping Main Street or funding essential services. It's about greed."[12]

One of the strongest arguments made by pro-tax forces appealed directly to the public and politicians' sense of fairness. An owner of a small appliance store in Omaha spoke up for Mom and Pop retailers when he asked why online merchants "should get a special break? It puts us at a very big disadvantage."[13] That sentiment was echoed by dozens of corporate executives of nationwide retail chains. A senior vice-president of Radio Shack, which operates a large chain of consumer electronics stores, bluntly pronounced that "our tax laws must treat all retailers the same."[14]

Another interest group adversely affected by the informal tax amnesty granted to most Internet sales included those individuals not having ready access to the Internet. "Digital divide" is the phrase coined to refer to the gap developing between taxpayers in the upper and middle income classes who can afford access to the Internet and citizens with more modest incomes who can not. These latter individuals are generally denied an opportunity to purchase goods and services on a tax-free basis. "At a time when the gap between rich and poor is so wide, many question whether it's good public policy to allow Internet-savvy consumers to avoid sales taxes while poorer people without computers bear a hefty tax burden."[15]

One of the most respected economists to weigh in on the Great Internet Tax Debate was Gary Becker, a Nobel Prize winner and professor of economics at the University of Chicago. Professor Becker sided with those forces opposed to taxing Internet sales but not because of the argument central to their position, namely, that the Internet promotes economic growth and thus should not be burdened with taxes. In fact, Professor Becker observed that allowing Internet sales to go untaxed promotes economic inefficiency. Effectively lowering the cost of the products and services sold by online merchants gives them a competitive advantage over conventional retailers, meaning that they can be less efficient than conventional merchants and still remain in business. Over the long run, allowing such economic inefficiency to be institutionalized would be bad for the overall health of the economy.

Professor Becker used "interesting" logic—what else would you expect from a Nobel Prize winner—to arrive at his decision to support the effort to ban sales taxes on electronic commerce. He argued that the obvious unfairness of taxing one group of retail businesses differently from another would eventually focus the attention of politicians on two related but even more important issues,

---

12. Rigsby, "Total Tax Ban on E-Commerce Gains Steam."

13. Gleckman, "The Great Internet Tax Debate," 230.

14. A. Goldstein, "Brick-and-Mortar Retailers Make Plea for Internet Taxation," *The Dallas Morning News*, 21 March 2000, D1.

15. Geewax, "Will Buying on the Net Remain Tax Free?"

namely, steadily rising sales tax rates and the increasingly complex sales tax system in this nation. The strong lobby against imposing sales taxes on Internet sales might eventually result in the reduction, elimination or, at least, simplification of sales taxes on conventional retail sales, which would benefit all retailers and consumers. The key interest group that flinched at this argument was representatives of state and local governments. Professor Becker's hoped-for outcome to the sales tax debate would likely require a new approach to funding state and local governments.

IN THE MEANTIME . . . BACK AT THE STORE

As the philosophical debate over taxing Internet commerce raged on, back in the real world the taxing authorities in the 7,500 or so, sales tax jurisdictions stretching far and wide across the United States continued to demand that merchants collect and remit taxes on retail sales. With a few exceptions, conventional retailers complied. These brick and mortar retailers collected sales taxes and remitted them to the taxing agencies, no doubt grumbling indignantly all the while.

Most virtual retailers, on the other hand, were generally unburdened by the need to collect sales taxes from their customers. These retailers did not deny that their customers had a statutory responsibility to pay sales taxes on the items they purchased. Instead, e-tailers relied on a 1992 Supreme Court opinion that effectively relieved them of the responsibility to collect sales taxes in all but a few jurisdictions. The legal case that had triggered that Supreme Court opinion involved a mail order company sued by the state of North Dakota. The Peace Garden State charged that the mail order company had a responsibility to collect sales taxes from North Dakota residents who ordered merchandise from the firm's catalog. The mail order company maintained that it had no responsibility to do so. Eventually, the two combatants argued their positions before the Supreme Court.

In 1967, the Supreme Court had decided that retail businesses could not be forced by state and local governments to collect sales taxes if doing so would impose an undue burden on them. The general rule handed down by the Supreme Court was that retail businesses had a responsibility to collect sales taxes in a given state only if they had a substantial "nexus," that is, physical presence, in that state. "States could otherwise tax business activities far beyond their borders and end up restricting interstate commerce."[16] Conventional retailers easily satisfy the substantial nexus rule given the stores, warehouses, and other physical facilities they have in every state in which they operate. However, mail order companies typically have a substantial physical presence in only one or a few states. For instance, a mail order company will have a corporate headquarters in a given state and possibly warehouses or distribution facilities in one or a small number of other states.

Throughout the 1970s and 1980s, state legislatures gradually and deliberately attempted to sidestep the substantial nexus rule included in the Supreme Court's 1967 opinion. These efforts to force out-of-state merchants to collect and remit

---

16. A. Caffrey, "Technology States May Hurt Effort to Simplify E-Commerce Tax Codes," *The Wall Street Journal* Interactive Edition, 7 March 2001.

sales taxes on in-state sales culminated in the lawsuit filed by North Dakota against the mail order company. That lawsuit provided a direct test of the Supreme Court's substantial nexus rule. The Supreme Court concluded that the mail order company did not have a responsibility to collect North Dakota sales taxes since it had no physical presence in that state. Although not an issue in that case, the mail order company did not contest its obligation to collect sales taxes in the handful of states in which it maintained physical facilities.

Virtual retailers realized that the 1992 Supreme Court decision effectively exempted them from collecting sales taxes in all states except those in which they had a physical presence. As a result, these retailers typically located their physical facilities in only one or, at most, a small number of states. By the late 1990s, state and municipal tax authorities had filed numerous lawsuits against e-tailers for failure to collect sales taxes. A common question in these cases was whether an e-tailer that operates a computer server in a given state, even if indirectly through a third-party intermediary, satisfies the nexus requirement. A related issue was whether an out-of-state retailer that maintains a presence on a Web "mall" administered by an in-state party has a substantial physical presence in the given state. Generally, the courts have ruled such arrangements do not meet the nexus standard established by the Supreme Court.

By the late 1990s, a hybrid type of retailer emerged to challenge online merchants and brick and mortar establishments. These "click and mortar" retailers blended together features of virtual and conventional retailers to develop a new approach to retailing goods and services. Most click and mortar retailers were initially conventional retailers. As the digital revolution swept through the business world, these old-line businesses soon recognized the benefits of adding an online dimension to their operations. For example, the success of Amazon.com convinced the two largest bookstore chains, Barnes & Noble and Borders, to create websites at which they could market books and other merchandise.

Collecting sales taxes proved to be an even greater headache for click and mortar retailers than for "Old Economy" merchants. These hybrid retailers typically have sales outlets in a large number, if not all, of the fifty states and the District of Columbia. Since they meet the substantial nexus standard created by the Supreme Court, they are obligated to collect sales taxes on merchandise sold through their physical facilities and via their online operations.

One click and mortar retailer observed that collecting sales taxes on online sales is a "nightmare." The specific destination of merchandise being sold online has to be tracked so that the appropriate sales tax, if any, can be computed. ZIP Codes are not particularly helpful in tracking down sales tax jurisdictions since ZIP Code areas may overlap several sales tax jurisdictions, and vice versa. Likewise, as suggested earlier, the applicability of sales taxes to given goods and services varies significantly across tax jurisdictions. The only practical approach for a click and mortar retailer to use to ensure compliance with sales tax regulations is to obtain expensive software designed specifically for that purpose. Even then, the business or its software vendor must continually update that software for changes in sales tax regulations across the United States, such as changes in sales tax rates in given jurisdictions.

Click and mortar retailers devised different strategies to cope with the sales tax issue for their online operations. Many of these strategies were designed with the express purpose of exploiting loopholes in sales tax regulations and related court rulings.

Barnes & Noble created barnesandnoble.com, a wholly owned subsidiary, to assume responsibility for its online marketing efforts. In states, such as New York, where barnesandnoble.com has a physical presence due to offices or other facilities, the management of the parent company and online affiliate developed a strategy of working closely together to promote each other's operations. In those states in which barnesandnoble.com does not have a physical presence, the parent company and its online affiliate were intended to operate independently. For example, in these latter states, corporate policy dictated that Barnes & Noble bookstores would not promote the barnesandnoble.com website nor accept refunds for merchandise purchased online. By keeping the operations of the parent company and online affiliate independent in these states, Barnes & Noble's executives hoped to avoid any suggestion by taxing authorities that barnesandnoble.com had a substantial nexus in those states.

Borders' executives also set up a separate affiliate, borders.com, to manage their company's online operations. However, Borders did not take the conservative measures adopted by Barnes & Noble to keep its physical and online operations independent in those states in which its online affiliate did not have physical facilities. Instead, Borders chose to promote borders.com in all of its retail outlets, including those stores located in states in which borders.com was strictly a "virtual" operation.

A reporter for *The New York Times* asked a Borders executive whether borders.com was violating sales tax laws in those states in which it did not have a physical presence although it was linked closely to the parent company's bookstores in those states. "We don't believe that's the case. On the Internet, there is no clear standard on this issue. So long as there's no physical presence in borders.com in our stores, such as having Internet terminals in the stores, there's no nexus. Otherwise, it wouldn't be fair."[17] A leading economist disagreed with that opinion. "From an economic point of view, it's slam dunk obvious that this is nexus by affiliation. All this monkey business gives you nexus."[18]

Two of the nation's largest retailers, Wal-Mart and Kmart, also faced the nexus issue when they began selling merchandise online. Similar to Barnes & Noble and Borders, both companies established subsidiaries to oversee their Internet operations. Wal-Mart created walmart.com, while Kmart founded bluelight.com. Initially, WalMart.com had a physical presence or nexus in only three states. As a result, walmart.com collected sales taxes only on merchandise sold to residents of those states—Arkansas, California, and Utah.

A major stumbling block that walmart.com soon faced was sales returns. Wal-Mart customers have become accustomed to the company's liberal return policy. When these customers purchased goods from Wal-Mart's new online subsidiary, they expected to have the same opportunity to return damaged or unwanted merchandise. But, rather than going through the hassle of returning goods via the mail or a common carrier, walmart.com customers wanted to make merchandise returns at the nearest Wal-Mart store. To keep their customers happy and to minimize the likelihood of a nexus "problem," walmart.com contracted with Wal-Mart to process its sales returns.

---

17. B. Tedeschi, "Despite Reprieve, Tax Laws Complicate Internet Retailing," *The New York Times* on the Web, 9 February 1999.

18. *Ibid.*

Wal-Mart executives staunchly defended their efforts to avoid the collection of sales taxes while at the same time closely coordinating the operations of their conventional stores and online subsidiary. "If the system allows that to take place, we're going to compete on that field."[19]

Kmart, Wal-Mart's principal competitor, adopted a very different strategy when it established bluelight.com. When asked whether his company collected sales taxes in all sales tax jurisdictions, bluelight.com's chief executive responded, "Absolutely. Did we buy an expensive software package to do that? Absolutely. Do we with think it's right? Absolutely not."[20] That executive went on to note that Kmart decided to collect sales taxes on online sales because it did not want to "alienate" the communities in which its stores were located. "There are municipalities that are counting on this money. We don't want to be the lightning rod for [criticism]. . . . We also don't want to do anything that's illegal."[21]

As the Internet sales tax debate has evolved in recent years, all three types of retailers—conventional retailers, e-tailers, and click and mortar retailers—have continually re-examined and fine-tuned their online sales strategies and sales tax collection policies. In late 2000, Barnes & Noble fully integrated its physical stores and online sales operations. That decision meant that most customers who purchased books from barnesandnoble.com would be required to pay sales taxes on those purchases since Barnes & Noble would have one or more stores in their home state. In the summer of 2001, Borders announced that due to anemic sales for borders.com it was entering into an alliance with Amazon.com. Under the terms of this arrangement, Amazon would assume responsibility for managing Borders' online sales operations.

So, Who Is Going to Fix This Mess?

Both factions involved in the Internet tax debate realized that something had to be done to remedy the chaotic sales tax system in the United States. The 1992 Supreme Court decision re-affirmed the rule that requires merchants to collect sales taxes only if they have a substantial physical presence in a given state. At the same time, the high court explicitly noted in its 1992 decision that the constitutional authority for regulating interstate commerce, which includes imposing sales taxes on cross-border sales, rests squarely with Congress, not the executive or judicial branches of government. In fact, the Supreme Court pointed out that Congress had every right to overturn or replace the substantial nexus rule by enacting appropriate legislation.

Political infighting and posturing rank among the most difficult obstacles that Congress faces in tackling the problem of sales taxes, in general, and sales taxes on electronic commerce, in particular. Most governors and representatives of local governments have a strong interest in supporting maintenance of the current

---

19. M. McCance, "Wal-Mart Unveils Web Site Operations," *Richmond-Times Dispatch* (online), 21 March 2000.

20. B. Tedeschi, "Going Against the Grain in Integrating Web Operations," *The New York Times* on the Web, 5 June 2000.

21. *Ibid.*

sales tax system and extending that system to include electronic commerce. Any significant reduction in sales tax collections would pose a financial crisis for the large majority of state and local governments and increase their dependence on the federal government for funding.

Members of the U.S. House and Senate have generally adopted a "big picture" view of the Internet sales tax impasse, choosing to focus on what is best for the entire country and the overall economy. Nevertheless, U.S. representatives and senators are subject to pressure from powerful interest groups in their legislative districts and states. Not wanting to offend either the anti-tax or pro-tax factions involved in the Internet sales tax debate, Congress took the "politically correct" measure of appointing the ACEC to study the issue in 1998. Most members of Congress hoped that the ACEC would arrive at a logical and feasible plan to resolve the controversy. Individual members of Congress could support such a plan without taking a significant risk of being held personally responsible for the adverse impact it might have on one or more interest groups.

As the ACEC deliberated, several thick-skinned legislators introduced bills to address the sales tax issue. Senator McCain's bill to exempt Internet sales from sales taxes failed to gain significant support in Congress. The same fate befell a bill introduced by Senator Fritz Hollings of South Carolina. That bill would have imposed a 5 percent national sales tax on all Internet and mail order sales. The resulting funds would have been split among the states by way of a revenue-sharing model.

Similar to Congress and the public, the ACEC eventually split into two ideological factions on the Internet tax debate. Governor Gilmore headed the anti-tax majority on the commission, while Governor Leavitt became the spokesperson for the pro-tax minority. Because it was sharply divided, the ACEC could not muster the two-thirds majority that Congress had mandated it had to reach before making a final recommendation on the Internet sales tax issue. Despite that congressional mandate, members of the ACEC insisted on reporting to Congress. So, the commission filed two reports: a majority report written by the 11 members who wanted to ban sales taxes on Internet commerce and a minority report written by the remaining members who generally supported such sales taxes.

The ACEC's majority report recommended that Congress extend the moratorium on new Internet taxes by five years, through 2006. That recommendation pleased the anti-tax lobby, most of whom believed that delaying a decision on the Internet tax debate would be equivalent to banning Internet taxes. These parties reasoned that by the time Congress revisited the issue in 2006 the importance of the Internet to the nation's economy would preclude any serious effort to impose new Internet taxes or to enforce existing sales tax laws that apply to electronic commerce. The principal recommendation of the minority report called for individual states to simplify their sales tax systems. Those states that complied by December 31, 2003, would be allowed to require remote (nonresident) online and mail order merchants to collect sales taxes from their customers.[22]

---

22. Recently, approximately 40 states banded together to sponsor the "Streamlined Sales Tax Project." This project is intended to simplify and standardize state sales tax codes and collection policies. Supporters of this project believe that it will make the collection of sales taxes on retail Internet transactions more feasible.

For more than one year, Congress mulled over and debated the ACEC's dual reports. All the while, the October 21, 2001, expiration date for the five-year moratorium on new Internet-based taxes crept closer and closer. Finally, Congress made its decision . . . sort of. Congress passed a bill extending the Internet Tax Freedom Act by two years, a bill signed into law by President George W. Bush in late November 2001.

The extension of the Internet Tax Freedom Act in the fall of 2001 failed to quell the widespread controversy involving the taxation of electronic commerce. Congress' indecision seemed to goad several states to adopt more vigorous measures to collect so-called use taxes on Internet and mail order sales. Most states have use tax statutes that require residents who purchase goods from nonresident merchants without paying a sales tax to pay a tax for "using" those goods in their home state. As one tax expert remarked, "At the end of the day, everyone is either supposed to pay sales tax or use tax."[23]

Many states initially adopted use tax statutes to capture, indirectly, sales taxes on mail order purchases. Because of the difficulty of tracking down out-of-state purchases made by their residents, few states have made a serious effort to collect use taxes except on certain "big ticket" items. In some states, the only procedure for collecting these taxes is a line item on the state income tax return that instructs residents to list and pay the use taxes they owe on out-of-state purchases of goods and services.

To date, most states have had little success in collecting a larger percentage of the use taxes owed by their residents. One southern governor joked that his state might realize a significant increase in use tax receipts since he was considering paying the few hundred dollars of those taxes his family owed that year. A less jovial governor threatened to use his state's highway patrol to follow out-of-state delivery trucks to their destinations in his state. On arrival, highway patrol officers would ask the purchasers whether they wanted to charge their use taxes to a credit card or pay cash.

QUESTIONS

1. Many companies have taken deliberate measures to avoid collecting sales taxes on online sales. In your view, are such efforts justified? Are they ethical? Defend your answer.
2. State and local governments are not-for-profit organizations. Identify the key differences in the objectives of governmental organizations and business enterprises. Also, compare and contrast the strategies and specific methods that governmental units and businesses use to finance their operations.
3. Three types of retailers were discussed in this case: conventional "brick and mortar" retailers, virtual retailers, and click and mortar retailers. List the comparative advantages and disadvantages posed by each of these approaches to operating a retail business.
4. Professor Becker noted that the absence of sales taxes on Internet transactions provided online merchants a competitive advantage over conventional retail

---

23. P. Louwagie, "Louisiana Has a Lot to Lose from Tax-Free Shopping on Web," *The Times-Picayune*, 27 March 2000, A01.

merchants. Identify several other companies or groups of companies that benefit from competitive advantages. Briefly describe or explain how each of these competitive advantages arose and indicate whether each is a "fair" advantage to the given company or group of companies.

5. Search the Web to identify two sites at which firms market sales tax software and related products and services. Identify each website and the name of the firm operating that site. Provide a brief description of the goods and services offered by each firm that you identified.

6. Discuss the relative merits of a progressive tax rate structure compared with a regressive tax structure. Indicate which tax structure is more "fair." Research and briefly discuss the tax rate structure that the federal government imposes on corporations.

MODULE TWO

FORTUNES MADE

Yoo-Hoo?

If you break for lunch, you are lunch.

Jerry Yang

Names are important. Many psychologists maintain that the name parents give a child can have a significant impact on the child's life. No wonder, then, that expectant parents spend long and often stressful hours choosing between Lindsay Leigh and Jessica Suzanne or between Chase William and John Michael. In the summer of 1994, two Stanford graduate students faced this dilemma. No, these two students were not expectant parents. Instead, they needed a name for a "baby" they intended to launch into cyberspace.

During the early 1990s, Jerry Yang and his close friend David Filo had become captivated by the Internet and the World Wide Web. Like most Internet surfers, the two graduate engineering students found searching for information on the Web a frustrating experience. The exponential growth rate in the number of Web pages and the absence of a Yellow Pages-like directory for the Web complicated the efforts of early Internet surfers to track down statistics needed for a research paper, recipes for apple strudel, or missing limbs on their family trees.

Frustration eventually drove Yang and Filo to develop their own cataloging system for "cool" websites they frequently visited. They hung the moniker "Jerry's Guide to the World Wide Web" on their creation, a name soon replaced with the more even-handed "Jerry and David's Guide to the World Wide Web." As a growing number of friends and acquaintances began using the system, the two graduate students decided to make it available to all Internet users by posting it on the Web. Before going public with their system, they wanted to give it a snazzier, more "hip" name. Two obvious candidates were Akebono and Konishiki, a pair of prominent Sumo wrestlers after whom Yang and Filo had named their computers. Akebono, Yang's computer, served as the storage unit for the Web cataloging system, while the system's search engine resided on Konishiki, Filo's computer.

After considering and rejecting a slew of names, Yang and Filo began thumbing through a dictionary for additional candidates. The two modest and self-deprecating computer "geeks" eventually stumbled across a five-letter word that both agreed was well suited for their purpose since it seemed to describe each of them. According to *Random House Webster's College Dictionary*, a yahoo is "an un-cultivated and boorish person." As a young boy growing up deep in the heart of Dixie, David Filo had often been referred to by his father as a little "yahoo." For emphasis, Yang and Filo added an exclamation point to their system's name.[1]

Initially, Yahoo! caused some consternation for Internet surfers familiar with the bottled chocolate drink "Yoo-hoo." Within a few months, though, Internet surfers quickly learned that Yahoo! was the most effective means for navigating the somewhat mysterious and often mesmerizing World Wide Web. Within a few years, the hordes of dedicated Yahoo! users would number in the tens of millions.

TRAILER TWILIGHT ZONE

Jerry Yang and David Filo became close friends during a six-month visit to Japan on a student exchange program sponsored by Stanford. Other than an interest in computers and engineering, the two Stanford students did not seem to have much in common. Yang, who was born in Taiwan and fatherless at age two, had immigrated as a small child to the San Francisco Bay area with his mother and brother. In grade school, Yang struggled to learn English but always excelled at math and science. Upon graduating from high school, he decided to enroll in Stanford so that he could be close to his mother. Yang majored in electrical engineering, completing an undergraduate degree and master's degree within his first four years at the prominent school in the heart of the Silicon Valley. David Filo spent his formative years in the small Louisiana town of Moss Bluff, located a few miles from an inland bay of the Gulf of Mexico. After graduating from high school, Filo obtained a degree in computer engineering from Tulane University, a school perched on the banks of the Mississippi River, not far from New Orleans' French Quarter.

After completing the exchange program in Japan and returning to Stanford, Yang and Filo were sharing a pizza during one of their frequent late night study sessions when they came up with the idea for a Web search engine. Both Yang and Filo were sports buffs who spent much of their spare time searching for information online that they could use to gain an advantage over the other members of their fantasy sport league. The unwieldy and unmapped World Wide Web made finding that information very time-consuming and difficult.

The two engineering students realized that by developing a classification system for important sites on the Web—that is, sites important to them—they could more readily access specific information when a need for that information arose. Jerry Yang had become very familiar with the benefits of an efficient classification system as a Stanford undergraduate. To help finance his education, he had worked as a book sorter and shelver in the Stanford library, a job requiring him to learn the "ins and outs" of the Dewey Decimal System.

A problem that Yang and Filo soon encountered while working on their after-hours hobby was identifying websites *not* worthy of being included in their clas-

---

1. Dozens of articles regarding Yahoo! that have appeared in business periodicals, and major newspapers suggest that "Yahoo" is an acronym for "Yet Another Hierarchical Officious Oracle." Not true, according to Yang and Filo who insist that they jointly plucked the name out of a dictionary.

sification system. The more they searched the Web, the more interesting, quirky, and fascinating sites they discovered, sites they found difficult to discard. Soon, the two graduate students were including most of the sites they visited in their online catalog of the Web. As the workload for their project became increasingly burdensome, Yang and Filo invited a third student who had traveled to Japan with them to become involved in the project. Later, other friends and colleagues would volunteer to work on the project.

A cramped trailer on the Stanford campus that housed graduate engineering students served as the first headquarters of what would later become Yahoo! Inc. Yang and Filo spent long hours hunched over their computer screens in the trailer, alternately searching the Web and then compiling information on sites they chose to include in their system. As the World Wide Web continued to grow dramatically in popularity and in size, they became preoccupied with their hobby, shirking other responsibilities, such as preparing for their classes—and attending those classes. Eventually, the project became an around-the-clock obsession for Yang, Filo, and several other fellow engineering students.

As the project grew in size and more and more computers were added to the Yahoo! network, heat produced by the generators that powered those computers spiked the temperature inside the trailer to near-intolerable levels. Yang and Filo kept the trailer's blinds closed to fend off additional solar heating and relied on the ghostly glow produced by a cluster of computer monitors to provide much of the lighting for the trailer's interior. Occasional visitors to the trailer stepped in from the sunlit Stanford campus to a surreal, shadowy, and sauna-like Twilight Zone environment. Stacks of textbooks, piles of dirty laundry, and discarded fast-food wrappers and empty cups added to the "ambiance" of the trailer's interior.

When reminiscing on Yahoo!'s trailer days, Yang recalls that he and his colleagues felt like they were frantically laying track for an approaching runaway train that was gaining momentum as it approached. By early 1995, that runaway train threatened to derail Stanford's computer system. University administrators who learned of the Web-mapping project firmly suggested that Yang and Filo begin searching for a more suitable and appropriate home for that project.

Yang and Filo finally admitted to themselves that to justify the time, effort, and resources they were plowing into Yahoo!, they had to convert their 24/7 hobby into a business or simply walk away from it. The two friends spent hours kicking around different ideas for developing a business plan for Yahoo!. In early 1995, most Internet surfers still scorned any effort to use the Internet for a commercial purpose. No doubt, any attempt to charge user fees to Yahoo!'s "customers" would offend the bulk of them and possibly encourage them to try out similar services being developed on the Web. Besides, collecting such fees would pose a logistical nightmare. Ironically, Yang and Filo briefly considered converting Yahoo! into an online bookstore, a business concept later implemented by Jeff Bezos, founder of Amazon.com.

A lack of business experience posed a major stumbling block for Yang and Filo in their effort to create a viable business from Yahoo!. In early 1995, they asked a Stanford business major to join Yahoo!. That individual developed a crude outline of a business plan that Yang and Filo used to file for a corporate charter. With that charter in hand, they went in search of deep-pocketed investors to provide seed money that they could use to rework Yahoo! into a business.

Michael Moritz, a partner with Sequoia Capital, a leading venture capital firm, was among several potential investors who met with Yahoo!'s two co-founders.

Moritz remembers being shocked when he first stepped into the unkempt Yahoo! trailer. But, after talking with Yang and Filo and becoming familiar with Yahoo!'s operations and its worldwide reputation, he recognized that the two young graduate students had stumbled upon something "big." Most striking to Moritz was the dedication of the Yahoo! staff to its goal of organizing the Web to make it useful to millions of computer users around the globe. The Yahoo! trailer served as a "temple of hard work, sheer enthusiasm, and a near-monastic devotion to the cause."[2]

Within a few weeks, Moritz authorized a $1 million investment in Yahoo! by his firm. With those funds in hand, Yang and Filo were ready for their next assignment: finding a chief executive officer (CEO) for Yahoo!. Neither Yang nor Filo considered themselves viable candidates for that job. In fact, neither wanted the job. After taking a leave from their academic studies at Stanford and moving Yahoo!'s computer system off-campus, the two twentysomething entrepreneurs, with the help of Michael Moritz, began interviewing CEO candidates for Yahoo!.

KOOGLE AND MALLETT HAMMER OUT A BUSINESS PLAN FOR YAHOO!

In the late spring of 1995, Tim Koogle met with Jerry Yang and David Filo. At the time, Koogle, a 43-year-old former Motorola executive and a graduate of Stanford and the University of Virginia, served as the president of a large communications firm. Although largely unfamiliar with Yahoo!, Koogle was immediately impressed by the zealous dedication of Yang and Filo and the potential he saw to develop their Internet search engine into a major business.

> I thought about the business. What they had already put on the Web was being used by a fair number of people without any money being spent on marketing. It was a good sign that there was some raw material there. Then, I did my homework and saw that in many ways it was analogous to the broadcast network business. So, I took the job and I went from running a company with $350 million in revenues and 2,000 employees at three factories worldwide to jumping in with six guys and no business plan.[3]

Koogle saw his primary role as developing an overall strategic mission for Yahoo! and obtaining the resources needed to implement that mission. Hiring an experienced business executive to oversee Yahoo!'s day-to-day operations was Koogle's first priority. Yang and Filo had kept Yahoo! operating by working 100-hour weeks and by depending on a few loyal friends willing to do the same. Koogle wanted to hire an individual who would take advantage of the enthusiasm and commitment of Yahoo!'s small staff, while developing a more structured, efficient, and functional business environment.

In the summer of 1995, Koogle hired Jeff Mallett as Yahoo!'s chief operating officer (COO). The 29-year-old Mallet posed a stark contrast to Koogle. Known as

---

2. A. Gumbel, "The Cyberpunks: Four Years Ago David Filo and Jerry Yang Were a Couple of Unknown Geeks," *The Independent* (London), 24 March 1999, 5.

3. C. Ayres, "Yahoo! Puts Web in a Spin with Dynamic Policy of Expansion," *The Times* (online), 14 November 1997.

"T.K." within Yahoo!, Koogle is soft-spoken and laid-back, while Mallet is glib and energetic. Yahoo! insiders quickly hung the nickname "Sparky" on the hyperactive, former all-American soccer player. "You can say I run things like I played soccer—with a lot of energy and purpose. I like to get involved in everything. I'm a dying breed in a high-risk profession: I'm a generalist."[4] Mallett's perky personality meshed well with the irreverent and mischievous work environment that Jerry Yang and David Filo had created within their small organization. Mallett revels in jokes and double entendres. When outside parties arrived for an appointment with Yahoo!'s new COO, his secretary often had to tell them that he was indecent. In fact, Mallett was waiting for those parties in a meeting room named "Decent."

With Jeff Mallett on board and with the full support of Jerry Yang and David Filo, Tim Koogle set out to transform Yahoo! from a free service used by Internet surfers to a profitable business with a steady and sustainable revenue stream. Koogle intended to build Yahoo! into a media company comparable to one of the large television networks. Millions of couch potatoes view network programming at no cost. Networks generate revenues not from their viewers but rather from the companies and other organizations that advertise on the networks in an effort to sell their products and services to Mr. and Ms. Couch Potato.

Koogle realized that scores of companies wanted to tap the pocketbooks of the Internet surfers who regularly accessed Yahoo!'s website. Demographic studies revealed that those individuals tended to be more technologically savvy and economically blessed than the average citizen, two attributes that many potential advertisers found appealing. Within a short while, Yahoo!'s Web pages were plastered with banner ads that invited surfers to click on them to obtain information regarding scads of products and services ranging from personal computers, to mountain bikes, to investment counseling. Koogle's subordinates helped advertisers target their ads to parties most interested in their products and services by tracking the Internet surfing habits of individuals who regularly visited the Yahoo! website.

While Koogle crisscrossed the country to convince companies to fly banner ads on Yahoo!, Mallet supervised a growing squad of Yahoo! surfers who searched the Web for new sites to add to the Yahoo! catalog. In fact, finding new sites was not the problem. Coping with the explosive growth in the number of new websites posed the most significant logistical problem for Mallett's crew. Organizing those sites into a logical and easy-to-use scheme also presented a major headache for Yahoo!'s staff. That responsibility fell to Srinija Srinivasan, the individual who had accompanied Jerry Yang and David Filo to Japan on the student exchange program and who later became the third member of the Yahoo! family. A longstanding tradition within Yahoo! was awarding an ostentatious title to each new employee, a title that referred to the individual's role within the organization. Yang and Filo quickly tagged Srinivasan with the title of "Ontological Yahoo." Yang and Filo share a title, namely, "Chief Yahoo," the title that appears on their business cards.

Shortly after assuming Yahoo!'s top management position, Tim Koogle declared that he not only wanted to make Yahoo! a successful media firm, he

---

4. J. Swartz, "Yahoo!'s Other Dynamic Duo," *The San Francisco Chronicle*, 6 August 1998, D3.

wanted to make it the world's largest media firm. A key element of his strategy to achieve that goal was "branding" Yahoo!. Koogle intended to imprint the Yahoo! name into the minds of Internet surfers so that they would equate the World Wide Web with his company. Koogle wanted anyone who went online to find a website or other information to automatically call up Yahoo! to find that site or information. "Branding" Yahoo! would serve the dual purpose of building a loyal following of Internet users, while at the same time allowing Koogle to extract increasingly large fees from the companies that placed ads on the Yahoo! site. Koogle relied on an advertising campaign of his own to develop a strong brand name for Yahoo!. That series of television commercials asked the now familiar question, "Do you Yahoo!?"

Yahoo!'s growing prominence on the Internet drew the attention of other major Internet firms, including America Online (AOL) and Microsoft. In the fall of 1995, AOL attempted to purchase Yahoo!. Jerry Yang and David Filo rebuffed that attempt, insisting that their company remain independent of the big Internet and media firms. The two Chief Yahoos realized that if AOL or another large firm purchased Yahoo!, they and the management team they had retained would forfeit their right to direct the company's future. AOL's strategy of establishing a "toll-gate" for using the Internet particularly troubled Yang and Filo. Unlike Yahoo!'s free search service, AOL charged Internet users subscription fees for the right to use its services. Both Yang and Filo believed that forcing users to pay a fee for simply accessing the Internet conflicted with the free service ideal that had reigned as one of the most important features of the information superhighway since its earliest days.

Tim Koogle's announced intention to build the world's largest media company served as a wake-up call for several large media companies. Executives of those companies immediately began developing strategies to respond to the challenge laid down by Koogle. In early 1996, worldwide media giant News Corporation, probably best known for its Fox television network, issued a press release indicating that it intended to "bury" upstart Yahoo!.[5] Several major media companies, including News Corporation and NBC, began developing Internet services to compete directly with Yahoo!. By the spring of 1996, approximately two dozen search engines were available on the Web. Many of those search engines cataloged a larger percentage of the millions of Web pages than did Yahoo!—most search engines capture only a fraction of all Web pages in their classification schemes. Nevertheless, Yahoo!'s more logical and easier to use classification scheme and the goodwill it had accumulated with throngs of Internet users allowed Koogle's company to maintain its status as the leading search engine for the World Wide Web.

Tim Koogle's aggressive growth strategy for Yahoo! when coupled with the need to fend off competitive threats posed by such prominent firms as AOL, News Corporation, and NBC, required money, lots of money—money that Yahoo! did not have. Yahoo!'s advertising revenues were growing rapidly, but the company had yet to turn a profit, meaning that Koogle had to obtain the funds he desperately needed from external sources. Instead of turning to Sequoia Capital or another venture capital firm, Koogle decided to sell a stake in Yahoo! to the general public via an initial public offering (IPO).

---

5. A. Gumbel, "The Cyberpunks."

On April 12, 1996, Yahoo!'s common stock hit the market at an initial selling price of $13 per share. Within hours, the stock leaped to $43 per share before settling back to close the day at $33. The first-day increase in the price of Yahoo!'s stock easily ranks among the largest percentage gains for an IPO in the long history of the stock market. By the end of that first day of trading, Yahoo!'s collective market value approached $1 billion. Yahoo!'s employees shared in that fortune since most of them held a substantial amount of stock in the company. The two Chief Yahoos, who together owned slightly less than 50 percent of the company's stock, suddenly had a net worth exceeding $200 million, each!

Tim Koogle quickly went to work spending the cash raised by Yahoo!'s IPO. Unlike most companies, Yahoo! had not established a research and development (R&D) department. Instead of relying on in-house R&D to improve its search engine technology and to develop new services, Yahoo! acquired other companies that had the expertise or services its executives wanted. Investors responded favorably to Koogle's aggressive expansion campaign, sending Yahoo!'s stock price ever higher. In December 1997, the $1 million investment that Sequoia Capital made two years earlier in Yahoo! Inc.—which at the time was no more than an online hobby of two bright graduate students—had a market value of nearly $600 million.

On the Portal of Success

During 1998, Tim Koogle continued to acquire Internet-related companies either by paying cash or by giving their owners previously unissued Yahoo! stock. Many Internet analysts questioned Koogle's seemingly haphazard acquisition strategy. Unknown to those analysts and Yahoo!'s competitors, Koogle was pioneering the concept of a Web "portal." In late 1998, Koogle finally discussed this new strategy publicly. "We've set out to make Yahoo! the only place anyone needs to go to get connected to anything. There's nothing in the real world to compare to that."[6]

In the early days of Yahoo!, Jerry Yang and David Filo compared their website to an airport hub. Individual Internet users congregated at the Yahoo! site before departing for their final destinations. Koogle wanted to convert Yahoo! into the *final* destination for Internet surfers. Yahoo! would serve as a doorway or portal to the Web. Once Internet users entered that portal, they would effectively be inside a gated community in cyberspace. Inside that community, a surfer could access e-mail, get up-to-the-minute scores for sporting events, enter a chat room, check stock quotes, or go to a My Yahoo! site to read news and other materials customized to his or her special interests.

In commenting on the reengineered Yahoo!, *Business Week* observed that "Yahoo! has morphed from an ordinary search service into the be-all, do-all of the Net, offering a dizzying array of services and information. Need a daily fix of news, stock quotes, weather and e-mail? Head to Yahoo!. Want to house-hunt, figure out a retirement plan, or research the Ebola virus? Yep—Yahoo!."[7] Koogle's

---

6. L. Himelstein, H. Green, R. Siklos, and C. Yang, "Yahoo! The Company, The Strategy, The Stock," *Business Week*, 7 September 1998, 66.

7. *Ibid.*

new strategy caused Yahoo! to leapfrog its competitors to become the most visited site on the Web. By late 1998, more than 40 million surfers logged on to Yahoo! each month, one-third more than the audience garnered by NBC's top-rated show, *ER*. When asked to comment on Yahoo!'s new business model, Chief Yahoo Jerry Yang responded matter-of-factly, "Portals are an extension of what we have always done."[8]

Koogle's portal strategy caught his company's major competitors off guard. But not for long. Those competitors quickly copied his strategy and began constructing their own portals. *Business Week* noted that Koogle effectively retooled not only Yahoo!, but every other major website attempting to flag down surfers on the information superhighway. "What was stunning was how thoroughly Koogle transformed not just Yahoo! but the world of consumer websites. . . . Now everybody's trying to out-Yahoo! Yahoo!"[9] One Internet media firm reported near the end of 1998 that eight of the ten most popular websites were portals styled after Yahoo!. Other than Yahoo!, those portals included AOL, Microsoft MSN, Lycos, Netscape Netcenter, Excite, Infoseek, and Altavista. The sudden and stunning popularity of Koogle's portal concept caused *Time* magazine to declare 1998 "The Year of the Portal."[10]

Increasing Yahoo!'s advertising revenues was the primary motive underlying Tim Koogle's decision to convert Yahoo! from a search engine into a portal. By converting Yahoo! into a portal, Koogle hoped to increase the "stickiness" of his company's website. Advertisers added the term "stickiness" to the lexicon of business in the late 1990s. One business journalist remarked that "stickiness is the Web buzzword *du jour* and refers to the ability of a website to hold on to visitors and keep them from quickly hopping off to someplace else in cyberspace."[11] The longer Internet users remain at a given website, the more valuable that website is to online advertisers and the more they are willing to pay to place advertisements on the site.

Before converting Yahoo! to a portal, Koogle realized that the website of his company's principal competitor, AOL, was much "stickier" than Yahoo!'s site. Media Metrix, the leading Internet ratings firm, reported in the summer of 1998 that each individual who logged on to AOL remained at that site an average of 42 minutes. The comparable statistic for Yahoo! was a measly 9 minutes. Besides his portal strategy, Koogle planned to upgrade Yahoo!'s entertainment programming to help attract and keep surfers at the company's website. In 1998, that programming featured such captivating offerings as online question and answer sessions with the ever-popular Hansons.

By late 1998, Yahoo! operated in 14 countries and broadcast in 9 languages and seemed well on its way to becoming the Web portal for the world, another of Tim Koogle's announced goals for his company. At the time, Internet users from outside North America accounted for almost one-third of Yahoo!'s daily traffic. Because of Jerry Yang and David Filo's affection for Japan, that country was among the first nations outside North America targeted by Yahoo!. By 1998, Yahoo! Japan easily qualified as the most popular website in Japan.

8. J. Swartz, "Doorman of the Net," *The San Francisco Chronicle*, 29 July 1998, B1.

9. *Business Week*, "Timothy A. Koogle," 27 September 1999, EB 26.

10. *Time.com*, "Digital Year in Review (1998): The Rise of the Portal."

11. J. Stacklin, "Dot.com to Help Sites Stick," *Crain's Cleveland Business*, 5 June 2000, 2.

New Century . . . New Challenges

Tim Koogle's portal concept took Wall Street by storm. Institutional investors, Internet analysts, day traders, and other stock market mavens piled praise on Koogle, the newly crowned "King of the Web," and drove his company's stock price higher and higher. For the three-year period ended December 31, 1999, Yahoo!'s common stock claimed the top slot on *The Wall Street Journal's* list of best-performing stocks. A $1,000 investment in Yahoo! stock on December 31, 1996, was worth more than $152,000 three years later. At one point, the two Chief Yahoos had a net worth of $7.5 billion each. In terms of market value, Yahoo! ranked as the 17th largest U.S. company at the end of 1999, surpassing scores of Old Economy stalwarts such as Coca-Cola and Procter & Gamble.

Yahoo!'s aura of invincibility took a direct hit in early 2000 when the stock prices of dot-coms and other Internet-related companies began plunging in the face of a series of poor revenue reports and earnings "surprises." Unlike most Internet companies, Yahoo! had been profitable since 1998, but those profits were very modest compared to most relevant benchmarks. Increasingly, critics pointed to several factors that posed significant challenges for Yahoo!'s management and threatened the young company's future prospects.

Threats Galore

Ranking high on the long list of threats that Yahoo! faced as the new century dawned was an impressive fraternity of corporate executives who coveted Yahoo!'s leadership position in the New Economy. *USA Today* suggested in August 2000 that "Yahoo is in the cross-hairs of a murderers' row of business titans."[12] That "criminal" line-up included, among many others, Bill Gates, the former CEO of Microsoft; Stephen Case, AOL's chairman of the board and CEO; Gerald Levin, Time Warner's top executive; and media mogul Barry Diller, the CEO of USA Networks.

Particularly worrisome to Tim Koogle and his colleagues was the announcement in early 2000 that Yahoo!'s long-time nemesis AOL planned to merge with media giant Time Warner. That merger guaranteed AOL access to one of the most important assets of a Web portal, namely, "content." In Internet lingo, "content" refers to "anything you read or look at or listen to for its own sake—from news to music to video clips—rather than as a means to make a purchase."[13] Following the merger, AOL would have at its disposal an enormous quantity and array of high-quality media products produced by Time Warner. Clearly, that content would provide AOL with an important competitive advantage over Yahoo! in luring Internet users.

Tim Koogle and his colleagues faced competitive challenges not only from several large, well-established firms but also from a slew of upstart, Web-based businesses. In 2000, two new Harvard graduates proved how easy it was to not only launch a new portal but also to quickly grab a major piece of the leading portal's

---

12. J. Swartz, "Yahoo! Stands Alone in Web Wars," *USA Today*, 24 August 2000, 1B.

13. K. Swisher, "Content on Web Is Under Fire for Not Making Any Money," *The Wall Street Journal* Interactive Edition, 9 October 2000.

market share. Bill Daugherty and Jonas Steinman created a portal that awarded lottery prizes to Internet users who logged on to the site. The more Web pages viewed by the portal's visitors, the more chances they had to win randomly awarded prizes. This new portal, fittingly named iWon, awarded one $10,000 prize each day, thirty $1,000 prizes each week, a $1 million prize each month, and a granddaddy jackpot of $10 million each year on April 15th, "tax day." The simplicity of the concept underlying iWon caused the site's creators to wonder why no other Web portal had used it. "If somebody stands on a roof and throws off dollar bills, people are going to show up," Jonas Steinman astutely observed.[14] Within a few months of being launched, iWon began appearing in Internet media rankings as one of the most popular sites on the World Wide Web.

The widespread financial distress evident among dot-com companies in early 2000 presented an obvious problem for Yahoo!. Tight-lipped Yahoo! executives had historically refused to provide information regarding the sources of the company's advertising revenues. Nevertheless, Internet analysts estimated that dot-coms accounted for nearly one-half of the company's advertising clients. As 2000 progressed and large numbers of dot-coms filed for bankruptcy, investors worried that Yahoo!'s advertising revenues would be adversely affected. In late 2000, a Yahoo! spokesperson reluctantly revealed that the company had lost more than 200 advertising clients due to "financial pressures." At the same time, Yahoo! reported that it still had more than 3,000 advertising clients and that the proportion of its advertising revenues generated from Fortune 500 companies was steadily increasing.

Many financial analysts predicted that wireless technology would pose a significant threat to Yahoo! in the new millennium. AOL and Yahoo! easily ranked as the most dominant Web portals among desktop Internet surfers by the end of the 1990s. But, increasing numbers of Web surfers were turning to mobile devices to access the Internet. "Yahoo! may dominate the desktop, along with AOL, but it will need to figure a way to keep its audience as people begin to take the Web with them wherever they go."[15] As one journalist noted, major telecommunications companies developing wireless capabilities, including Sprint PCS and US West, "hope to send Yahoo! and its likes into obsolescence. They want to be your portals, your main entrance to the Internet."[16]

A final challenge that Yahoo!'s management team faced during 2000 and beyond potentially posed the largest threat to the company's long-term viability. In simple terms, many skeptics questioned the underlying soundness of Yahoo!'s business model that Tim Koogle had developed. That model rested on the simple concept that Yahoo! was analogous to a television network that offers free programming to viewers, while generating the bulk of its revenues from advertisers. "Its New Economy aura notwithstanding, Yahoo! has hewed to an idea born in old media—a vision that declares advertisers will pay a big premium to advertise on the Web's biggest and best-known site, just as they pay a premium to advertise on a top-rated television program."[17] Tim Koogle's business model seemed

---

14. M. Gunther, "Eyes on the Prize," *Fortune* (online), 16 October 2000.

15. M. Veverka, "Embraceable You," *Barron's*, 24 April 2000, 20.

16. N. Hutheesing, "Who Owns Your Portal?" *Forbes*, 22 May 2000, 22.

17. S. Hwang and M. Mangalindan, "Yahoo!'s Grand Vision for Advertising on the Web Takes Some Hard Hits," *The Wall Street Journal* Interactive Edition, 1 September 2000.

very reasonable when he developed it in the mid- to late 1990s. But, the model was untested. By 2000, Internet ratings services and large advertising agencies had collected a huge volume of data that provided important insight on the validity of the central plank of Yahoo!'s business plan. Those data suggested that Web-based advertising was not as effective as traditional advertising.

Banner ads flown on Yahoo!'s website by advertisers served as the staple of Koogle's Web-based advertising program in the first several years of the company's operations. One key barometer used to measure the success of such ads is the "click-through" rate, that is, the percentage of Web page viewers who actually click on a banner ad and access information regarding the given product or service. Initially, click-through rates on banner ads averaged as high as 5 percent. By mid-2000, that average had tumbled to as low as 0.3 percent. "Compare this with the economics of the dowdy junk-mail business, which typically sees 2 percent of its targets not only look at mailings but also respond."[18] Data collected by one major Yahoo! advertising client revealed that the company spent $200 on average to obtain a new customer from ads placed on Yahoo! Web pages, while it spent only $20 to acquire a new customer through more conventional advertising efforts. With such statistics in hand, Internet financial analysts doubted that Yahoo! could continue to charge premium rates to its existing advertisers and questioned its ability to acquire additional clients in the future, particularly the Fortune 500 companies that Koogle had been targeting.

Yahoo! Lays a Heavy Bet on E-Commerce

With the help of Jeff Mallett, Jerry Yang, and David Filo, Tim Koogle responded to each of the strategic threats posed by the cutthroat competitive environment that Yahoo! faced as the Internet industry began maturing in the early part of the new century. One response was to pour more resources into developing Yahoo!'s operations in foreign countries, particularly in the Far East. Yahoo!'s competitors had focused most of their energy and efforts on challenging Yahoo!'s dominant position in the lucrative U.S. market, while largely ignoring the much smaller Internet economies developing across the world.

Initially, Yahoo! addressed the challenge posed by the growing popularity of wireless devices among Internet users by attempting to broker deals with several of the leading wireless companies. For example, Jeff Mallett and Jerry Yang attempted to convince Sprint PCS's management to make Yahoo! the default home page for the growing number of Sprint's wireless customers. Sprint refused but did agree to include a link on its home page to Yahoo!, and AOL, as well. Similar efforts by Yahoo! executives produced similar disappointing results. Eventually, a frustrated Tim Koogle decided to spend $80 million to purchase Online Anywhere, a company that markets software that formats websites for mobile devices. Koogle then negotiated deals with companies, such as Palm that manufacture mobile devices to include the Online Anywhere software as standard equipment on those devices.

The most dramatic move Koogle made to respond to his company's rapidly changing competitive environment was to align Yahoo! more closely and directly

---

18. *Ibid.*

with e-commerce. Since its inception, Yahoo! had viewed itself as the "friend of the little guy"—that individual sitting in front of a desktop computer searching for the score of a college football game, a weather report for south Philly, or a movie critic's opinion on the newest Hollywood release. Koogle recognized that to thrive within the harsh competitive conditions of the Internet industry, Yahoo! could not continue to rely heavily on revenue produced by banner ads directed at Internet surfers. In late 2000, one Internet analyst noted that Yahoo!'s executives "are trying very aggressively to move away from their traditional model. They recognize that anyone who banks their future on banner advertising is in pretty bad shape."[19]

In June 2000, Koogle created Corporate Yahoo!, a new fee-based service designed to develop customized Web portals for large corporations and other organizations. A primary purpose of these portals would be to attract potential customers, but they would also provide a full range of online capabilities to companies that established them, including online billing and buying services. Although Yahoo! had offered fee-based services in the past, the Corporate Yahoo! service would be the first such service expected to produce a significant revenue stream for the company. Industry observers saw this move as evidence that Yahoo!'s management intended to reduce its dependence on Web-based advertising revenues. Several companies partnered with Yahoo! in developing this new service. Inktomi would provide the default search engine for the service, Tibco Software would develop the software needed to integrate the computer systems of clients with the Corporate Yahoo! sites, while Hewlett-Packard would take the lead in marketing the service.

Tim Koogle hoped that Corporate Yahoo! would give his company a foothold in the rapidly developing B2B (business-to-business) sector of the Internet economy. "Commerce is expected to become an increasingly important part of Yahoo! as the company plays the role of an 'enabler,' bringing together buyers and sellers in what company leaders hope will become one of the biggest markets on the Internet."[20] Yahoo! had a sizable head start in establishing itself as a B2B enabler since it had approximately 3,500 corporate advertising clients when the Corporate Yahoo! service was established. Yahoo! was well acquainted with the needs and objectives of those companies, which allowed it to match an advertising client needing a particular product or service with another client that marketed that product or service. Koogle also intended to use the large database of customer preferences Yahoo! had collected from the personalized My Yahoo! websites to funnel individual customers to the portals of Corporate Yahoo! clients that sold directly to the public.

KOOGLE'S LAST STAND

As the year 2000 progressed, the economic conditions facing Yahoo! worsened. Most problematic for the company was the steadily deteriorating financial condi-

19. C. O'Brien, "Yahoo! A Bulwark of Internet Consistency in Age of Uncertainty," *San Jose Mercury News* (online), 2 October 2000.

20. K. Swisher, "Behind the Portal," *The Wall Street Journal* Interactive Edition, 17 April 2000.

tion of hundreds of undercapitalized dot-coms with weak business models and minimal revenues. As increasing numbers of dot-coms lurched toward bankruptcy, Yahoo!'s advertising revenues continued to spiral downward. Once immune from negative press, Tim Koogle and other key leaders of the Internet Revolution became favored targets of criticism by business reporters searching for individuals to blame for the sudden and severe economic malaise gripping the New Economy. More troubling to Koogle than the press's criticism was a rising tide of discontent among Yahoo! insiders, many of whom began expressing doubts regarding his leadership and management skills. Some of those colleagues held Koogle responsible for underestimating the toll that the dot-com crisis was taking on the company. Yahoo! insiders also charged that Koogle's laid-back management style prevented him from taking aggressive enough measures when he finally realized that the company's financial health was fading quickly.

By late 2000, a rift had developed between Koogle and the two other principal decision makers within the company, Jeff Mallett and Jerry Yang. According to *Business Week*, Mallett became increasingly frustrated with Koogle's growing isolation and "lack of involvement" with the other members of the company's management team.[21] Jerry Yang reportedly chose to side with Mallett when disagreements arose between Mallett and Koogle regarding key strategic issues facing the company. Yang's decision to align himself with Mallett apparently undercut Koogle's power within the company and doomed T.K. to losing his position as CEO.

The end came abruptly for Tim Koogle. In early 2001, Yahoo!'s stockholders and financial analysts were shocked when the company's reported operating results revealed the unexpectedly large impact that the dot-com debacle was having on the firm's revenues and profits. Financial analysts immediately slashed their revenue and profit forecasts for the company's first quarter of 2001. By early March 2001, Yahoo!'s executives realized that the company's actual first-quarter results would be even worse than the dismal amounts forecast by analysts a few weeks earlier. On March 7, after reportedly being coaxed to do so by Jerry Yang, Koogle announced that he was resigning as the company's CEO, although he would remain as the chairman of the company's board.

Jerry Yang moved quickly to offer the CEO position to a friend of his. That friend, Terry Semel, had served for nearly three decades as an executive of the media company Warner Brothers, which by early 2001 was a major operating unit of AOL Time Warner. Yang managed to essentially choose Semel as the new CEO since he and another Yahoo! board member, who was Yang's friend as well as a partner of a major investment firm, together controlled nearly one-half of Yahoo!'s common stock. But, a problem arose before Yang could close the deal. Before accepting the CEO position, Semel insisted that he also be named chairman of the board. A reticent Koogle eventually agreed to make way for Semel and resigned as chairman of the board. Upon resigning that position, Koogle reported that he intended to pursue other interests, including hanging out with some artist friends in Italy.

In contrast to Koogle's relaxed management style, Semel was expected to introduce his new subordinates to a "brass tacks" approach to doing business. In terms of strategic measures, Semel planned to focus considerable resources on

---

21. B. Elgin, "Inside Yahoo!" *BusinessWeek Online*, 21 May 2001.

continuing and expanding the Corporate Yahoo! initiative developed by his predecessor. Semel also planned to place a heavy emphasis on other fee-based services offered by Yahoo! and to pursue strategic alliances with other media and entertainment companies. He hoped that such alliances would provide Yahoo! access to high-quality content that would allow the company to compete more effectively with AOL in attracting Internet users.

JERRY YANG: CORPORATE SPOKESPERSON

Despite Tim Koogle's position as Yahoo!'s CEO, Jerry Yang served as the most visible, vocal, and effective spokesperson for the company as it emerged in the late 1990s as one of the dominant companies within the new Internet sector of the economy. Yang's colleague and fellow Chief Yahoo, David Filo, stayed active in the company but preferred to maintain a much lower public profile. Besides fielding difficult questions posed by the press regarding Yahoo!'s strategic initiatives, Yang has also long served as the company's moral compass. "Jerry doesn't think of himself as a businessman trying to exploit this new Internet community. He still thinks of himself as being a citizen of the Internet and makes sure the management team runs the company according to the Golden Rule."[22]

Yahoo!'s success has showered Jerry Yang with wealth and fame. Much of his wealth evaporated during 2000 and 2001 as the stock prices of Internet-related companies nosedived. Yang, still a billionaire, accepted those losses philosophically. "Five years ago, I was worth nothing. If you do this for the money, you are doing it for the wrong reasons. . . . My life is with Yahoo!. I can't imagine what I would be doing otherwise."[23] On frequent trips to his native Taiwan, Yang must register in hotels under fake names since he is one of the country's most popular and recognized celebrities. He is even welcome in the People's Republic of China, Taiwan's principal antagonist, where he has met on occasion with President Jiang Zemin.

When asked to identify the key strategy or policy or asset that has allowed Yahoo! to be successful, what is Jerry Yang's typical response? His company's name. The irreverent, self-deprecating moniker that he and David Filo plucked out of the dictionary in the summer of 1994 has become one of the most respected and recognized brand names in the world and, arguably, the most recognized and valuable on the Internet. . . . Do you Yahoo!?

QUESTIONS

1. Search online or hard copy news databases to find recent articles and news reports regarding Yahoo!. Summarize in bullet form recent significant developments affecting or involving Yahoo!.

---

22. B. Schlender, "How a Virtuoso Plays the Web," *Fortune*, 6 March 2000, F-83.

23. N. Taylor, "Yahoo! Dream Lives; Jerry Yang, Billions of Dollars Poorer, Remains Unshaken by the Dot-com Bust," *South China Morning Post* (online), 14 May 2001.

2. Relying on this case and the information you collected in responding to the previous question, list in descending order of importance the most important strategic threats or challenges that Yahoo! presently faces. Briefly defend or explain your list.

3. Tim Koogle emphasized the importance of "branding" Yahoo!. Identify other Internet companies that have been successful in developing a well-known brand name or identity for their products or services. Explain or describe how these companies successfully branded those products or services.

4. Search the Web for recent Internet-related statistics reported by Media Metrix and other Web ratings firms. Examples of such statistics would include tables reporting "Web page views," "click-through rates," and comparable measures used to gauge Internet traffic and Web usage. Explain the significance of the statistics you find in your search and discuss how companies might use those data to make decisions regarding their advertising budgets.

5. Choose a Web portal other than Yahoo!. Visit Yahoo!'s website and the website of the other portal you chose and write a summary of the key features of each. In your summary, point out the key similarities and differences in the two portals.

6. Identify key strategic decisions that Tim Koogle made for Yahoo! that are identified in this case. Explain how these decisions contributed to the eventual success of Yahoo!. Also, identify one or more other strategic decisions that Tim Koogle might have made for his firm but did not. How do you believe these latter decisions would have impacted Yahoo!?

7. Do you believe that Jerry Yang was justified in orchestrating the removal of Tim Koogle as Yahoo!'s CEO and chairman of the board? Why or why not?

Citizen Case

I can buy 20 percent of you or I can buy all of you. Or I can go into this business myself and bury you.

Bill Gates (statement made to Steven Case, CEO of America Online)

As teenagers growing up in Seattle in the early 1970s, Bill Gates and his close friend, Paul Allen, shared an interest in computers, which at the time were bulky, tediously slow, and very expensive. In 1975, Allen showed Gates an article in *Popular Electronics* that discussed a "personal computer" known as the MITS Altair 8800. The small and affordable computer was designed for use by individuals—individuals who had the patience and mechanical ability to put together the mail order computer when it arrived unassembled on their doorstep. Gates and Allen quickly realized that personal computers would require software, lots of software. Within a few months, the two ardent computer enthusiasts formed a partnership to operate a small software company. They named their new venture Micro-Soft, creating that name from a merger of the two words "microcomputer" and "software." A little more than two decades later, Microsoft Corporation would boast the largest market value of any public company in the United States and catapult Gates and Allen into the ranks of the richest individuals in the world.

Gates and Allen are soft-spoken and in the past were often referred to as "nerdy" by business journalists. Nevertheless, each of them can be feisty and aggressive when circumstances warrant. Gates' competitive spirit was evident during a May 1993 meeting with the young chief executive officer (CEO) of an online service provider. In the late 1980s, that young CEO, Steven Case, had helped found America Online (AOL), a company that provided online services on a subscription basis to computer users scattered across the United States. At the time Case met with Gates, AOL ranked a distant third in terms of total subscribers to the two leading online service providers, Prodigy and CompuServe. Case hoped to strike a deal with Microsoft that would allow AOL to add significantly to its subscriber base. Unknown to Case, Bill Gates had something else in mind.

Case and his colleagues agreed to travel to Microsoft's headquarters in Redmond, Washington, to meet with Gates. Shortly after the meeting began, Gates bluntly told Case, "I can buy 20 percent of you or I can buy all of you. Or I can go into this business myself and bury you."[1] A stunned Case sat silently for a few moments before replying, "The company's not for sale."[2] Bill Gates later denied having made the seemingly threatening statement to Steven Case. Case, a fellow AOL officer who attended the meeting, and one of Gates' subordinates who was also in attendance confirmed that the statement was made. However, Gates' subordinate told Kara Swisher, a reporter with *The Wall Street Journal*, that his boss didn't make the statement in an "obnoxious" or "combative" way.[3] No doubt, that was news to Steven Case.

Ironically, at the same time that Bill Gates was making his not-so-subtle pitch to acquire AOL, his friend and fellow Microsoft founder, Paul Allen, was pursuing the same objective but employing a much different strategy. Allen chose to gradually and quietly accumulate a significant ownership interest in AOL by purchasing the company's stock in the open market. In the early 1990s, Paul Allen described himself as a "private investor." A few years earlier, he had cashed in a sizable portion of his Microsoft stock after health problems forced him to retire from the company. By the spring of 1993, Allen had acquired nearly 25 percent of AOL's outstanding stock. When Case and his fellow AOL directors learned of Allen's growing ownership interest in their company, they quickly changed the company's corporate charter in an effort to prevent him from becoming the firm's principal stockholder.

Case and his colleagues rebuffed Paul Allen's effort to take over AOL. Staving off Bill Gates proved to be a more difficult task. Microsoft officials informed AOL's directors that their company intended to extend a buyout offer to AOL's stockholders. Since AOL's directors effectively controlled a majority of the company's stock, they would decide whether AOL remained independent or whether Microsoft swallowed up the small firm. In June 1993, AOL's board met to discuss the matter. According to *The Wall Street Journal*, two factions developed among the directors. One faction believed that Microsoft's lucrative offer should be accepted. Alexander Haig, a retired U.S. Army general and Secretary of State during President Reagan's administration, served as a leading spokesperson for the group of directors who wanted to sell out to Bill Gates. General Haig worried that AOL did not have the resources or business expertise to compete head-to-head with Microsoft if it chose to enter the online service business. In his typically blunt manner, General Haig noted, "We could get vaporized."[4]

Although Case stood to reap a nearly $25 million windfall if Microsoft purchased AOL, he led the other faction steadfastly opposed to selling out to Microsoft. Case worried that if Microsoft acquired AOL, he and his colleagues would lose control of the company and its future. A board member supporting Case's point of view noted eloquently, "Do we want to be a footnote on Bill Gates' resume, or do we want to be the king of the online industry?"[5]

---

1. K. Swisher, "When Bill Met Steve: A Showdown That Shaped AOL," *The Wall Street Journal*, 22 June 1998, B1, B10.

2. *Ibid.*

3. *Ibid.*

4. *Ibid.*

5. *Ibid.*

After considerable debate, AOL's board of directors decided to vote on whether they would sell out to Microsoft. By the slimmest majority possible, namely, one vote, the directors chose to remain an independent company. That decision proved to be a wise one, at least economically speaking, for the directors, in particular Steven Case. In less than five years, Case realized a twenty-fold increase in the value of his ownership interest in AOL. Case also received sizable paychecks for serving as AOL's top executive. In 2000 alone, Case's compensation for serving as AOL's CEO, including the value of stock options he exercised, easily topped $300 million.

HONOLULU PAPERBOY

Steven Case spent his childhood in the tropical climate of Honolulu. His father, a corporate lawyer, and his mother, a teacher, were natives of the Aloha Sate. Case displayed an entrepreneurial spirit at a young age. Similar to many of his friends, Case worked a paper route; unlike his friends, he used his paper route as a "feeder" for another line of business. Case hawked merchandise of all types to his paper route patrons, including stationery, garden supplies, and even wristwatches. The young businessman enjoyed "strategizing," as he routinely spent hours lying awake at night coming up with new ideas to market merchandise. Closing sales was less enjoyable for him since he was extremely shy. In fact, the young businessman often coaxed his older brother, Dan, into doing the "dirty work" of meeting face-to-face with potential customers.

Steven Case majored in political science at Williams College, a small liberal arts school tucked in the far northwestern corner of Massachusetts, a few miles from southwestern Vermont and New York's eastern border. Despite his major, Case continued his business career during his time at Williams. He sold tickets for rock concerts, helped organize a limousine service, and peddled merchandise of various types to fellow students and residents of Williamstown, the home of Williams College. While at Williams, Case made one foray into the high-tech world—enrolling in a computer programming course—that would foreshadow his subsequent career choice. Years later, he admitted that the programming course had been his least favorite college class.

Like many political science majors, Steven Case found landing a job following graduation a challenging and frustrating assignment. Case knew what type of job he wanted: he wanted to work in the marketing department of a major company, preferably a media or telecommunications firm. Case wrote dozens of letters to corporate executives in those industries asking for a job interview. One corporate executive the 22-year-old college graduate wrote was Gerald Levin, the top executive of HBO, a new company that marketed entertainment programming through cable outlets. Levin and most of the other executives that Case contacted did not respond to his request for a job interview. Eventually, Case settled for a job with Cincinnati-based Procter & Gamble.

At Procter & Gamble, Case helped develop advertising and marketing strategies for a variety of consumer products. Among those products was the towelette, a paper product soaked with hair conditioner. To help sell the public on this new product and new method of applying hair conditioner, Case used the advertising byline, "Towelette? You bet!" Despite that catchy line, towelettes proved to be a hard sell. After a couple of years, Case left Procter & Gamble to accept a position in the marketing department of Pizza Hut, a wholly owned subsidiary of PepsiCo. Case found that job uninspiring as well. In 1983, he abruptly left Pizza Hut to take a job with a small and financially troubled company based in Las Vegas.

Control Video Corporation (CVC) marketed video games produced by Atari. Shortly after Case joined CVC, the company's board dismissed most of the company's management team. For the next two years, the company limped along, barely surviving. In 1985, CVC reemerged as Quantum Computer Services. Quantum's principal line of business was providing online services to owners of personal computers. Those services consisted principally of a series of rudimentary bulletin boards.

Despite his unpleasant introduction to computers at Williams College, by the early 1980s Case had become fascinated by personal computers. He had purchased an early-generation personal computer while working with Pizza Hut in Wichita, Kansas. Although primitive by today's standards, that computer convinced Case that the future would be radically changed by the personal computer. He expected that the key benefit of the personal computer would be allowing businesses and individuals to communicate easily and inexpensively. Drawing on his personal experience, Case once noted during an interview with a *Washington Post* reporter that "there was something magical about being able to dial out to the world from Wichita."[6] During his first few years with Quantum, Case dedicated himself to finding a way to exploit the communications opportunities created by personal computers.

Case quickly became Quantum's top marketing strategist. One of his first major accomplishments in that role was brokering a cooperative arrangement with Commodore, at the time a leading maker of personal computers. That arrangement gave Quantum the right to provide online services to purchasers of Commodore computers. Thanks to Case's efforts, Quantum soon made similar arrangements with other computer manufacturers, including Apple and Tandy Corporation.

Case and his colleagues at Quantum eventually recognized that they were limiting the company's growth by marketing its services to owners of only certain types of computers. So, in 1989, they decided to branch out and offer those services nationwide to owners of all personal computers. To come up with a snappy name to better promote those services, Case organized a company-wide contest. The self-confident Case decided that his entry "America Online" was superior to all others and notified his co-workers that he was the winner of the contest. In 1991, Case and his fellow executives renamed their company America Online, Inc. Within the press, the company is most often referred to as AOL.

One of the first major decisions that Steven Case made after launching AOL in 1989 was to create an "instant messaging" service, a form of online chat that unlike e-mail allows individuals to communicate with each other in real-time. Case hoped that this new and easy-to-use method of communicating online would attract a large number of new subscribers to AOL and, in doing so, permit the com-

---

6. D. Southerland, "America Online Prepares for Shifting Opportunities," *The Washington Post*, 8 November 1993, 15. Author's note: Apologies to Wichita residents and other citizens of the Sunflower State who, no doubt, are firmly of the opinion that they are citizens of the world.

pany to reach a key milestone—100,000 total subscribers. A key feature AOL integrated into its instant messaging service was "buddy lists." These lists allow users of the service to log on and immediately determine which of their friends are also online and available for a *tete-a-tete*.

By 1991, Case served as AOL's CEO. In that position, he saw his principal responsibility as "strategizing." Initially, Case's principal marketing strategy was targeting specific groups of computer users. To capture large blocks of new AOL subscribers, Case negotiated strategic alliances with companies and organizations that controlled or influenced clusters of computer users. For example, he arranged a deal with the Tribune Company, the publisher of the *Chicago Tribune*. Relying on information provided by that newspaper, AOL developed an online news and information service designed for individuals living in or near the Chicago metropolitan area. Both companies benefited from this alliance: the Tribune Company because the online service attracted new subscribers to its newspaper; AOL since it collected a fee for each individual who subscribed to the online service.

Steven Case had one goal in mind as he worked relentlessly to build AOL into a viable and profitable business that would pose a competitive challenge to the two leading online service providers, Prodigy and CompuServe. "Mr. Case's plan has always been to capture the biggest online audience any way he can."[7] His plan to accomplish that objective rested on two key beliefs. "Case didn't waver on two central ideas: first, that the most important use of an online service is communicating with people, and second, that it is better to be easy to use than to have the most sophisticated technology."[8]

SPOCK GOES PUBLIC

Despite a positive reception to instant messaging by the Internet community and Case's aggressive efforts to attract large blocks of new subscribers with common interests, AOL continued to lag behind its two principal competitors in the first few years following the online service's nationwide launch in 1989. In fact, during the early 1990s, AOL faced a series of crises that threatened the company's existence and jeopardized Steven Case's leadership position with the company. Case dealt with those crises with his characteristic coolness. In his early years with AOL, Case's subordinates nicknamed him "The Wall" because of his calm demeanor and his lack of any apparent emotional reaction to important developments affecting his company. Industry insiders who have become acquainted with Case often describe him as impersonal, at best. One critic observed that he can be "as cold as Spock on a bad day."[9] But, those who know him best suggest that Case's aloofness and impersonal nature stem from his shyness, a personal trait that has plagued him since his days as a Honolulu paperboy.

---

7. H. W. Jenkins, "Maybe AOL's Bankruptcy Would Be More Ethical," *The Wall Street Journal*, 22 April 1997, B1.

8. S. Hansell, "Now, AOL Everywhere," *The New York Times*, 4 July 1999, Section 3, 1.

9. J. Sandberg, "Case Study," *Newsweek*, 24 January 2000, 15.

In early 1992, Case's low-key personality cost him his job title. At the time, AOL was preparing an initial public offering (IPO) of its common stock. The investment bankers responsible for organizing the IPO hinted that Case was too introverted and mild-mannered to be an effective spokesperson for AOL. Since Case, more than anyone, wanted AOL's IPO to be successful, he stepped down as the company's CEO and was replaced by James Kimsey. The two men had worked together since 1983 when Kimsey was brought in to serve as CVC's CEO shortly after Case accepted a position with that company. Despite his decision to step down, Case remained a primary decision maker within AOL.

AOL went public on March 19, 1992, selling two million shares at an initial offering price of $11.50 per share. On that date, the company, which had established its headquarters in Vienna, Virginia, a suburb of Washington, D.C., had approximately 150,000 subscribers. Under the leadership of Case and Kimsey, the company's subscriber base continued to grow modestly by industry standards. Industry insiders often pointed to two key factors they believed would prevent AOL from ever competing effectively with Prodigy and CompuServe. First, they criticized Case's strategy of concentrating on market niches, of pursuing groups of computer users with common interests and needs rather than making a broad-based marketing appeal to all computer users. Second, critics believed that Case's strategy of downplaying the importance of technological sophistication would prevent AOL from overtaking its competitors. These skeptics argued that most computer users wanted and, in fact, insisted on, cutting-edge technology. Both Prodigy and CompuServe appealed to such users since they upgraded their services more frequently and offered more "bells and whistles" than AOL.

In 1993, Case regained his title as CEO of AOL just in time for the eventful meeting with Bill Gates in May of that year. After overcoming the takeover bids of Bill Gates and Paul Allen for his company, Case began to pursue several new strategic initiatives to increase AOL's market share. First, Case began pouring large sums into mass marketing and advertising efforts to attract new subscribers. Second, he streamlined AOL's pricing structure, making it much simpler and easier to understand than the fee structures used by Prodigy and CompuServe. Third, AOL began offering a Windows-based version of its service. Finally, Case added all-important "content" to AOL by increasing the number of links to the Internet available to subscribers and by providing them with shopping and other online services.

At the same time Case was implementing his new initiatives to increase AOL's market share, he took steps to capitalize on the growing popularity of his company's instant messaging system. Case realized that his most effective marketing representatives were users of the instant messaging service since they encouraged friends and relatives to sign up with AOL. He also continued to insist to his subordinates, to the business press, and to Wall Street that ease of use, not technological sophistication, was the key to success in the online services industry. "We don't really care about technology. We've tried to recognize that it is a means to an end, and the end is to improve the way people get information and communicate."[10]

Case's aggressive strategic initiatives began paying dividends during 1993. By the end of that year, AOL reported more than 500,000 subscribers. The company

---

10. J. C. Ramo, "How AOL Lost the Battles but Won the War," *Time*, 22 September 1997, 44.

tripled that number during 1994 and approached five million total subscribers by the end of 1995. AOL's exponential growth in subscribers allowed the company to leapfrog Prodigy and CompuServe and establish itself as the largest online services company in the nation.

In 1994, Bill Gates, as long expected by Steven Case, finally entered the online services market. Case had always feared that Microsoft's prominence and technological prowess would make any online service offered by the company an immediate market leader. But, once again, Case was successful in fending off Bill Gates. By the time Gates launched MSN (Microsoft Network), AOL had established a reputation for excellent service and ease-of-use. That reputation prevented MSN from prying subscribers away from AOL and allowed Case and his colleagues to continue capturing a majority of new subscribers to online services.

AMERICA ONLINE AND THE INTERNET

On Christmas Day 1990, Tim Berners-Lee, a British computer scientist working for a research organization based in Geneva, Switzerland, introduced what would become the World Wide Web. For the next several years, Internet users grew increasingly familiar and comfortable with the often homespun, amateurish, and cranky Web pages developed by budding webmasters. By 1995, websites had become more sophisticated and functional, making the Web a mainstay of Internet users. Steven Case recognized that the Web posed both a challenge and an opportunity for AOL. On the downside, the Web threatened to funnel Internet users away from AOL's online service. To capture those users at AOL's website and to add to the company's subscriber base, AOL began offering Internet access in 1995. Overnight, AOL went from being an online service provider or OSP to being an Internet service provider or ISP.

The dramatic growth in the World Wide Web and AOL's decision to become an ISP forced Steven Case to once again reevaluate several of the key elements of his company's business plan. Since AOL's inception in 1989, monthly subscriber fees had accounted for the bulk of the company's revenues. Several AOL executives worried that competition among ISPs and the availability of numerous free Internet services, including Yahoo!, the Internet's leading search engine, might eventually force the company to slash the fees charged to subscribers. To respond to that concern, Case searched for ways to reduce his company's reliance on subscriber revenue. He found the answer in advertising.

In the mid-1990s, companies began recognizing that the World Wide Web provided an opportunity to advertise their goods and services to a lucrative market, namely, computer users. Demographic studies revealed that individuals who surfed the Internet and explored the Web tended to be more affluent and more prone to making discretionary expenditures than other consumers. Suddenly, the websites operated by AOL, Yahoo!, and other leading Internet companies were plastered with banner ads for a wide range of merchandise and services.

To make AOL's website more attractive to advertisers, Case knew that he needed to take steps to make the site more "sticky." The longer Internet users "stuck" to the AOL website, the higher the advertising rates Case could charge to companies flying ads on the site. The key to making the AOL site sticky was having high-quality content available at the site. Throughout the late 1990s, Case and his colleagues wrangled deal after deal with content suppliers such as media companies and news organizations, purveyors of health and nutrition information, stock market and financial database services, among many others. Many of the contracts that AOL arranged with content suppliers included revenue-sharing provisions. For example, some of those contracts provided for the payment of "bounties," that is, certain content suppliers received a fixed payment for each new subscriber they attracted to AOL.

Another change in AOL's business plan involved its marketing strategies. During the early 1990s, AOL began a "carpet-bombing" campaign in which it deluged U.S. households with diskettes offering free trial subscriptions to its online service. Although very successful, the campaign was also extremely expensive. By 1996, AOL was spending nearly $400 to acquire each new subscriber. Company executives realized they had to reduce marketing expenses. So, they scaled back the carpet-bombing campaign and began to rely more heavily on conventional advertising methods to acquire new subscribers.

One of the most effective strategies for attracting and retaining new subscribers was the decision in 1996 to charge a flat monthly fee of $19.95 for unlimited access to AOL. That new pricing structure attracted subscribers in record numbers to AOL. By the end of 1998, AOL's subscriber base had grown to more than 15 million and the company's cost to acquire a new subscriber had fallen to approximately $80.

An initiative that Case pursued even more aggressively after converting AOL to an ISP was growth through acquisitions and strategic alliances. Case had taken to heart Bill Gates' statement in 1993 that he would "bury" AOL if Microsoft decided to enter the online services industry. Despite the weak entry that Microsoft's MSN made into the online services market in 1994, Case worried that MSN would eventually prove to be a major threat to AOL. Case adopted a proactive strategy to preempt any eventual bold effort by Bill Gates to make MSN more of a challenge to AOL. In 1998, Case purchased Netscape Communications for approximately $4 billion. That acquisition immediately added the nine million registered users of Netscape's popular Netcenter website to AOL's subscriber base. Even more important, the buyout of Netscape provided a new revenue stream for AOL. Netscape was the market leader in developing software used by corporations to establish, manage, and operate their e-commerce websites. Financial analysts projected that significant growth in business-to-business (B2B) e-commerce would create an increasing demand for such software.

During 1998, Case also negotiated a large deal with the leading manufacturer of Internet servers, Sun Microsystems. AOL agreed to buy $500 million of equipment and services from Sun. In return, Sun agreed to market AOL's newly acquired Netscape software to its large corporate clients. *Business Week* described the Netscape and Sun deals as an "in-your-face" statement made to Bill Gates by Steven Case and reported that the deals clearly established AOL as the "most dangerous rival" to Microsoft's role as the leading firm in the world of the Internet.[11]

---

11. I. Sager, C. Yang, L. Himelstein, and N. Gross, "A New Cyber Order," *Business Week*, 7 December 1998, 27.

STEVEN CASE, FIREFIGHTER EXTRAORDINAIRE

As Case revamped AOL's business plan during the late 1990s, he faced repeated opportunities to hone his crisis management or "firefighting" skills. During that time frame, AOL experienced a series of shutdowns resulting from technical glitches, hacker attacks, and simple overloading of its computer systems due to the huge growth in its subscribers. In August 1996, AOL's subscribers were denied access to the Internet for almost twenty-four hours when technical problems arose following the installation of new software. A surge of new subscribers overwhelmed AOL's computer systems in January 1997 shortly after the company went to the flat $19.95 monthly pricing structure. Ironically, this latter crisis actually wound up saving the company millions of dollars of marketing expenses. Since AOL was obtaining new subscribers at a rate faster than company personnel could process the subscriptions and install the additional equipment needed to accommodate the new subscribers, company management decided to temporarily suspend marketing and advertising efforts.

Throughout the late 1990s, AOL faced an embarrassing situation resulting from a controversial accounting method the company used in 1995 and 1996 for marketing and advertising expenses. To raise additional capital during that two-year period when the company was expanding rapidly, AOL management needed to convince potential investors and lenders that the company was profitable and financially viable. To help accomplish that objective, AOL executives decided to treat certain expenditures incurred to acquire new subscribers during those years as assets and report them on the company's 1995 and 1996 balance sheets. Generally accepted accounting principles mandated that those expenditures be written off as expenses on AOL's 1995 and 1996 income statements. This accounting gimmick allowed AOL to markedly improve its reported financial results in both 1995 and 1996. In 1996, AOL reported a pretax profit of $62 million when the company actually should have reported a loss of $175 million. After a highly publicized, multi-year investigation of AOL's accounting practices by the Securities and Exchange Commission (SEC), the two parties reached an agreement to settle the matter in May 2000. That settlement required AOL to restate its previously reported operating results for 1995 and 1996 and pay a $3.5 million fine.[12]

Steven Case and his AOL colleagues confronted another challenge in the late 1990s, one posed by Yahoo!. During 1998, Yahoo!'s CEO, Timothy Koogle, introduced the concept of a Web portal. Rather than operating Yahoo! like a bus station or airport, that is, attracting Internet users to the search engine's website and then sending them on their way to whatever eventual destination they desired, Koogle decided to convert the Yahoo! website into a gated community within the World Wide Web. Within that community, Internet users could access e-mail, obtain stock market quotes, chat with friends, and shop at online stores. Koogle's ultimate objective was to significantly increase the traffic on Yahoo!'s website, which would allow him to charge advertisers higher rates for flying banners on Yahoo!'s Web pages. In fact, AOL had been evolving into a portal before Koogle

---

12. M. Schroeder and N. Wingfield, "AOL to Pay $3.5 Million to Settle SEC Charges Over Accounting," *The Wall Street Journal* Interactive Edition, 16 May 2000.

formally conceived the notion of a Web portal in 1998. Never reluctant to borrow a good idea, Case and his colleagues adopted some of the finer points of Koogle's concept and converted AOL into a Web portal as well, a Web portal that also offered Internet access.

The instant messaging service developed by AOL in 1989 proved to be a "killer app" for the company. But, this new service also posed a major headache for Steven Case as the 1990s came to a close. AOL dominated the instant messaging "market" in the late 1990s, accounting for an estimated 80 to 90 percent of all instant messages sent over the Internet. More than 150 million individuals used the two separate instant messaging systems that AOL operated. Most of those users were not AOL subscribers. Not surprisingly, the popularity of AOL's instant messaging systems with non-subscribers persuaded many of those individuals to become AOL subscribers, which explained why AOL management allowed and encouraged "outsiders" to use those systems.

Case and his fellow executives designed AOL's instant messaging systems to be closed systems. Individuals registered with other instant messaging services, such as the much less popular Microsoft Messenger service offered by MSN, could not exchange messages with parties registered with AOL's two systems. By the late 1990s, AOL's competitors, principal among them Microsoft, charged that Case and his fellow officers had an unfair chokehold on the instant messaging communications medium in the United States. Those competitors equated that chokehold to the early days of the telephone industry when telephone calls could only be placed between users of the same telephone company, which placed small telephone companies at an enormous disadvantage to the larger firms in the industry. The CEO of one company that operated a competing instant messaging system angrily accused AOL of improperly using its dominance of instant messaging to scuttle comparable services offered by other firms. "There is a fundamental issue here, that no company with this kind of market dominance should be able to erect barriers."[13]

Although most users of AOL's instant messaging systems accessed those systems free of charge, the company still reaped significant economic benefits from non-subscribers who became "hooked" on instant messaging. Most important, non-subscribers who used the instant messaging systems provided AOL with a valuable database of e-mail addresses, thanks to the company's extensive use of "cookies." AOL also benefited significantly from subscribers who used the instant messaging systems. Those subscribers were prone to access other featured services on the AOL website, which increased the stickiness of the site. No small wonder, then, that Steven Case refused to budge when competitors, including his old pal Bill Gates, demanded that AOL open its instant messaging systems to all Internet users. On numerous occasions, computer engineers for other instant messaging services "hacked" into AOL's two systems so that their own users could access those systems. Following each such incident, AOL's computer technicians quickly patched the "holes" in their instant messaging systems opened by the invaders.

The controversy over AOL's instant messaging systems prompted the filing of numerous lawsuits against the company and spawned considerable criticism of

---

13. J. R. Wilke and N. Wingfield, "Antitrust Concerns Spur FTC to Probe AOL's Instant Messaging," *The Wall Street Journal* Interactive Edition, 14 June 2000.

Steven Case. Some industry insiders and business journalists suggested that Case's refusal to open his company's instant messaging systems to all Internet users was selfish and narrow-minded. Eventually, Microsoft and approximately forty other companies banded together and filed a joint protest with the Federal Trade Commission (FTC) and Federal Communications Commission (FCC) charging that AOL unfairly monopolized instant messaging within the United States.

By the end of the 1990s, Steven Case had vanquished his two early rivals within the online services industry, Prodigy and CompuServe. AOL acquired CompuServe's online service operations in 1998, while Prodigy had slipped into near oblivion by 2000 when it had only a small fraction of AOL's total subscribers. Near the end of 1999, the price of AOL's common stock had soared a split-adjusted 70,000 percent beyond its IPO price a little more than seven years earlier, easily making Case a billionaire. Despite the success that AOL had realized, Case's company faced two more crises as the turn of the century approached—crises that posed huge and potentially devastating implications for AOL.

Dozens of companies, the most prominent being NetZero, provided free access to the Internet by the late 1990s. Industry experts began questioning whether AOL could continue to charge for Internet access given the growing number of free ISPs. Another and more serious problem that AOL faced near the turn of the century was the trend for Internet users to log on to the information superhighway by way of speedy broadband cable networks. AOL subscribers used "narrowband" access modes to tap into the Internet. Steven Case recognized that as the price of Internet service on broadband cables declined, more and more Internet users would opt to sign up with broadband ISPs. Among the leading broadband ISPs was the Roadrunner service offered by media giant Time Warner. What to do, what to do? Facing the challenges posed by free ISPs and broadband ISPs, Steven Case resorted to what he does best . . . strategize.

AOL Acquires Time Warner

In 1980, Steven Case wrote Gerald Levin, the chief executive of HBO, asking for a job. Levin never responded. Two decades later, Case contacted Levin again. By this time, Levin served as the CEO of Time Warner, which owned HBO, *Time* magazine, *Sports Illustrated*, Warner Brothers Studios, CNN, the Turner Broadcasting Network, and many other high profile companies and publications in the media and telecommunications industries. Case proposed that his company, AOL, take over Time Warner. This time, Gerald Levin responded to Case. The two men soon reached an agreement that would result in the largest corporate merger in U.S. history. The merged company would be named AOL Time Warner. Case would become chairman of the new company's board of directors, while Levin would hold the title of CEO. Despite the equal billing given the two companies involved in the merger by the business press, AOL's stockholders would effectively acquire Time Warner since they would own 55 percent of the new firm's common stock.

The daring merger Steven Case arranged with Time Warner helped him address the two key strategic challenges that AOL faced as the 1990s came to an end. First, the merger with Time Warner would allow AOL to begin offering Internet access to its subscribers over the broadband network of Time Warner Cable, a

Time Warner subsidiary. At the time, Time Warner Cable operated the second largest broadband network in the nation. Second, Case planned to use Time Warner's impressive portfolio of periodicals, electronic media properties, and other media and entertainment resources to enhance the value of AOL's website. Case knew that adding Time Warner content to AOL's website would help his company repel the challenges posed to AOL's operations by free ISPs. From the standpoint of Time Warner, the merger gave that company access to the rapidly growing Internet market, something that Gerald Levin had coveted for years. In the words of an AOL executive, the merger would allow the two companies to "unlock the value" of their "complimentary assets."[14] *Newsweek* reported that developing new technology was not among the factors that motivated Steven Case to pursue the merger with Time Warner—an assertion that few Internet experts found surprising given Case's longstanding ambivalence toward technology.

> The venture isn't about creating new technology; everybody already expects content and commerce on desktops and in living rooms, on palm devices and mobile phones. The buyout is about exploiting that technology to ensure that an array of AOL devices will beam out *Fortune* magazine articles and trailers for *Lethal Weapon XV* and track your interests so advertisers can target you even more.[15]

When Steven Case and Gerald Levin jointly announced the AOL Time Warner merger, most business journalists expected that the proposed merger would be scrutinized by regulatory authorities. In the United States, major corporate mergers must be approved by relevant regulatory agencies to ensure that the mergers are in the public's interest. Practically every large merger must receive the blessing of the FTC. The FTC's Web page indicates that the federal agency "seeks to ensure that the nation's markets function competitively, and are vigorous, efficient and free of undue restrictions." For example, the FTC ensures that mergers do not result in violations of federal antitrust statutes by creating monopolistic or near-monopolistic conditions within an industry. Such conditions can limit competition and ultimately result in fewer product offerings, reduced services, and higher prices for the goods or services produced by a given industry. FTC officials focused on several potential antitrust issues in reviewing the proposed AOL Time Warner merger. But, most of the federal agency's investigation targeted two major issues: (1) whether the merged company would limit or deny other ISPs access to its broadband cables, and (2) whether the new company would control an excessive proportion of media content and media delivery properties in the United States. The AOL Time Warner merger also required the FCC's approval since it involved an array of communications mediums and properties, including Internet access and telecommunications lines. Ensuring fair and reasonable access to communications mediums by the general public is the FCC's principal regulatory objective. The key issue that the FCC considered in reviewing the AOL Time Warner merger was the instant messaging controversy that had been plaguing AOL.

The first major issue considered by the FTC in reviewing the proposed merger was referred to as the "open access" issue. Critics of the AOL Time Warner merger worried that the new company could effectively damage competing ISPs, such as EarthLink, the second largest ISP at the time, by denying them access to Time

---

14. S. Levy, "The Two Big Bets," *Newsweek*, 24 January 2000, 41.

15. *Ibid.*

Warner's large cable network or by charging them exorbitant rates for such access. The second substantive issue considered by the FTC in reviewing the proposed AOL Time Warner merger was unique to that merger. Never before had the FTC reviewed a proposed business combination that promised to bring together under one corporate ownership group such a large set of media properties, both content providers and content delivery systems. Some journalists speculated that the breadth of media properties to be controlled by Steven Case and his subordinates could potentially result in prejudicial reporting of important events, particularly events having significant implications for AOL Time Warner.

> Citizen Case may now be a news magnate, but it's hard to imagine he'll micromanage stories in *Sports Illustrated*. The real problem isn't a corporate honcho ordering up a synergistic story but self-censorship—reporters and editors who know which side of their bread is buttered on and are therefore less aggressive and critical.[16]

The FTC formally approved the AOL Time Warner merger in December 2000. To gain approval for the merger, executives of the two merger candidates had to agree not to discriminate against other ISPs in providing access to the new firm's broadband cables. In November 2000, as an act of good faith, Time Warner Cable signed an open access agreement with EarthLink. Under the terms of that agreement, Time Warner Cable charged EarthLink $27 per month for each EarthLink subscriber that used its cable network to access the Internet. That figure was $3 less than the monthly amount Time Warner Cable charged Roadrunner, the broadband ISP operated by Time Warner.

The FTC chose not to impose any explicit restrictions on AOL Time Warner stemming from the merged firm's control of a significant portion of the nation's media properties. However, the federal agency did take the extraordinary step of requiring that the new company be monitored by a federally appointed trustee for five years. That trustee will monitor AOL Time Warner to ensure that the firm does not abuse its responsibility to disseminate news and other information fairly and reasonably to the public and to ensure that the company does not violate federal antitrust laws. The monitoring trustee will have the authority to hire a wide range of experts, including accountants, attorneys, and technology specialists, to determine whether the new company is acting in the public interest. AOL Time Warner must pay for the entire cost of the trustee's operations.

In January 2001, the FCC granted approval for the AOL Time Warner merger. Contrary to the expectations of many parties, the FCC did not force AOL to open its two instant messaging systems to users of other such systems. AOL executives had staunchly opposed such a move. Those executives argued before the FCC that opening instant messaging systems to all users would result in advertisers jamming those systems with "spam," similar to what happened when e-mail systems were converted to open systems. That result, AOL's management contended, would be a great disservice to the millions of Internet users who rely on instant messaging as their primary communications medium.

Executives of the proposed new company agreed to two key concessions to obtain the FCC's approval for the merger. First, those executives agreed to make any future generations of their instant messaging technology open systems. Those future generations of instant messaging will likely include video conferencing and

---

16. J. Alter, "Big Media Gets Even Bigger," *Newsweek*, 24 January 2000, 42.

other capabilities. Executives of the proposed company also agreed not to influence the ISP choices of individuals who expressed an interest in using the company's broadband cable network to access the Internet. This agreement meant that external ISPs using that cable network, such as EarthLink, would be able to reasonably compete with the ISPs of AOL Time Warner that would also be using that network.

The January 2000 press release issued jointly by AOL and Time Warner to announce their planned merger noted that "this unique new enterprise will be the premier global company delivering branded information, entertainment, and communications services across rapidly converging media platforms." Even after clearing the hurdles posed by the FTC and FCC, the new company faced challenges that had to be overcome before it could make good on that promise.

The key remaining hurdle the new company faced was the challenge of blending together the "old" and the "new," that is, the Old Economy culture of Time Warner and the New Economy culture of AOL. "There's a huge cultural gap between AOL's twentysomethings and Time Warner's graybeards. When it comes to making deals or launching new ventures, they move at two speeds."[17] Journalists who tracked the merger from the date it was announced in January 2000 predicted that Steven Case and his entourage of "twentysomethings" would likely prevail over the more deliberate Time Warner executives when differences of opinion arose over key strategic initiatives. Making key strategic decisions quickly, in "Internet time," had been one of the hallmarks of Case's successful career as a corporate executive. Few observers expected him to change that feature of his management style once he presided over AOL Time Warner's board of directors.

CASE-ING THE FUTURE

When the AOL Time Warner merger received final clearance from federal regulators in early 2001, AOL had more than 26 million subscribers. By the end of 2001, AOL boasted over 30 million subscribers, more than four times the number reported by MSN. The merger with AOL allowed Case to not only keep MSN at bay, it also allowed him to subdue the competitive challenge posed by smaller ISPs, particularly those ISPs that offered free access to the Internet. In fact, by late 2001, most of the free ISPs had merged with competitors or simply ceased operating. No doubt contributing to the demise of most free ISPs was the increasing attractiveness of AOL's website, thanks to the merger with Time Warner. By mid-2001, subscribers were spending, on average, 70 minutes per day roaming the AOL website, a more than 50 percent increase over the previous three years.[18]

AOL's executives were so encouraged by the improved operating performance of their company following the Time Warner merger that in mid-2001 they decided to raise the ISP's monthly subscription fee for the first time in three years. AOL's new monthly subscription fee of $23.90 was approximately 10 percent

---

17. C. Yang, R. Grover, and A. T. Palmer, "Show Time for AOL Time Warner," *Business Week*, 15 January 2001, 59.

18. J. Angwin, "AOL Raises the Monthly Charge for Its Flagship Internet Service," *The Wall Street Journal* Interactive Edition, 22 May 2001.

higher than the $21.95 fee charged by MSN. Microsoft's management team saw that increase as an ideal opportunity to launch a raid on AOL's massive flock of subscribers. Almost immediately, Microsoft initiated a $50 million advertising campaign to persuade AOL subscribers to sign up with MSN. Microsoft offered three months of free Internet access to AOL subscribers who switched to MSN and promised not to raise their monthly subscription fee for nearly two years. Microsoft management also hoped that the fall 2001 launch of Windows XP, which contains a menu of enhanced Internet-friendly features, and the company's widely hyped .Net initiative that it was pursuing at the time would help MSN eventually narrow AOL's huge lead in subscribers. The new competitive challenges posed by Microsoft had little impact on Steven Case, at least outwardly. Case and his AOL colleagues publicly shrugged off those challenges, choosing instead to focus their time and energy on fine-tuning the business plan of their company.

Steven Case has not been alone in recognizing the business opportunities presented by the personal computer, computer networks, and the Internet. Scores of other forward-looking individuals have had a similar vision. So, why has Case succeeded when most other New Economy visionaries have failed? One clunky word: strategizing. Unlike many of his contemporaries, Case was never committed to any one strategy. In the dynamic business environment of the Internet Age, he recognized that for AOL to survive and thrive the company's strategies had to be continually challenged, to be rethought, and, in some situations, to be junked in favor of new strategic initiatives. In the words of a *Newsweek* reporter, Case "has built AOL into a colossus despite having to change strategies more often than most chief executives change underwear."[19] A more blunt assessment of Case's strategic wizardry was offered by a reporter with *The Wall Street Journal*. "Steve Case is a strategic genius with a capital G."[20]

In a little more than one decade, Steven Case converted a simple belief that individuals would want to use personal computers to communicate with each other into one of the largest companies in the world. Case's success seems to have impressed other people much more than it has himself. In an interview with *Fortune* magazine, a property he acquired in the Time Warner takeover, Case once noted matter-of-factly, "The ability to . . . connect with people all over the world—how could that not, over time, be a huge business?"[21]

QUESTIONS

1. Steven Case has long believed that "ease of use" is a key, if not the most important, element of any online service marketed to the public. On the other hand, Microsoft tends to stress the importance of state-of-the-art technology in developing and fine-tuning the online services that it offers to the public. Which of these two strategies do you believe is likely to be more successful over the long run? Defend your answer.

19. A. Sloan, "Spooking the Street," *Newsweek*, 27 May 1996.

20. A. B. Perkins, "AOL Beats the Odds—Again," *The Wall Street Journal* Interactive Edition, 12 January 2000.

21. M. Gunther, "The Internet Is Mr. Case's Neighborhood," *Fortune*, 30 March 1998.

2. Compare and contrast the role that the following parties typically play in developing and implementing a company's strategic initiatives: chairperson of the board of directors, members of the board of directors, chief executive officer, chief operating officer, and stockholders.

3. Choose a leading e-commerce firm other than those that are a major focus of one of the cases in this text. For the firm you select, identify what you believe are that company's key strategic initiatives.

4. In your opinion, what are the most important traits that a CEO of a major company should possess? Rank order the traits you identify from most to least important and defend that ranking.

5. In your opinion, did Steven Case behave unethically when he refused to convert AOL's instant messaging systems to "open" systems when asked to do so by competitors in the late 1990s? Explain. Does a corporate executive have a responsibility to consider the "public good" when making important decisions affecting his or her company? Why or why not?

6. Define what constitutes a "monopoly" in the business world. Why does the federal government generally disapprove of monopolies? Under what conditions can monopolies be beneficial for the general public?

7. Research online and hard copy sources to identify a recent corporate merger other than AOL Time Warner. Identify the parties to that merger, their principal lines of business, the name of the post-merger company, and the key factors that apparently prompted the merger.

8. Research online and hard copy sources to identify recent developments involving AOL Time Warner. Summarize those developments in a bullet format.

The Accidental Billionaire: Pierre Omidyar, Founder of eBay

Everything is worth what its purchaser will pay for it.

Publilius Syrus

So, you have always had a "thing" for pink flamingos. You collect pink flamingo tapestry, ties, and towels. How about adding a pink flamingo teapot to your collection? No problem. Recently, an eBay seller provided the following description of an item to be auctioned off to the highest bidder:

> This elegant pink flamingo teapot is new and has never been used. In excellent mint condition. Teapot stands 10 inches high and 8 inches wide. Priority shipping is $5.40 insured. Checks, money orders, Visa, MasterCard, Discover and PayPal are accepted.

No doubt, if you are a collector, you have discovered eBay, the online auction house. Within six years after Pierre Omidyar created eBay, the company had nearly 35 million registered users. The most loyal eBay browsers are collectors—collectors of baseball memorabilia, Route 66 signs, Mennonite quilts, snow globes, and even Pez dispensers. Don't laugh. Omidyar set up the *ebay.com* website because his girl friend and eventual wife, Pam Wesley, had difficulty finding other individuals who enjoyed collecting and trading the Pez candy dispensers modeled after characters from Bullwinkle to the Incredible Hulk to Chewbacca.

When the movie version of John Grisham's novel *The Client* hit theaters nationwide, an Elvis Pez dispenser appeared as a prop. That Pez sighting set off a frenzied search by collectors of the candy dispensers. But, not even Pam Omidyar, with a net worth in the billions thanks to her husband's ingenuity, could purchase an authentic Elvis Pez dispenser. Why? Because the Elvis Pez dispenser was a one-time-only edition created for the big screen.

TUFTS AND THE KING OF STUFF

Pierre Omidyar met Pam Wesley at Tufts University, a private college located a few miles northwest of downtown Boston. He majored in computer science, while she studied biology and eventually earned a masters degree in molecular genetics. Born in Paris to Iranian parents, Omidyar immigrated to the United States when he was six years old. After graduating from Tufts, Omidyar landed a job developing consumer-oriented software applications for a subsidiary of Apple Computer.

Several years and jobs later, the concept of creating an online auction service occurred to Omidyar over a casual dinner conversation with Pam. During that conversation, Pam complained of the problem she had connecting with individuals who shared her interest in Pez dispensers. Omidyar reasoned that many other collectors, particularly those with an interest in offbeat items such as pink flamingos or Pez dispensers, experienced the same frustration as Pam. The thought occurred to Omidyar that the Internet provided the means to bring such individuals together in an online marketplace—a market in which they could exchange information as well as buy and sell collectibles. This simple realization prompted Omidyar to establish a website, initially named Auction Web, to create virtual communities of collectors and other hobbyists.

Omidyar launched his small online business in September 1995. He renamed the company eBay, a truncated variation of "electronic Bay," because he believed his website would be used principally by collectors and other Internet surfers living in or near the San Francisco Bay area where he and Pam had settled. Within months, though, the eBay website was attracting Internet users not only from all parts of the United States but worldwide as well. The dramatic growth in the number of items listed on eBay and the corresponding increase in the amount of time that Omidyar had to dedicate to his "hobby" soon forced him to quit his day job. Another key factor in his decision to become a full-time entrepreneur was the steadily growing profits produced by eBay.

A business reporter noted that the items sold on the eBay site were best classified as "stuff"—stuff that most of us have lying around in the corners of our garage and in dust-covered boxes littering the attic. Another reporter used a less elegant term, "everyday crap," to refer to the most common items marketed at the eBay site. Such characterizations resulted in Pierre Omidyar being labeled the "King of Stuff." Omidyar seemed unaffected by that label and other condescending comments made regarding himself and eBay by executives of more conventional companies. Three years after founding eBay, Omidyar took the company public. By then, a professional management team ran the company while he faded into the background. As the price of eBay's stock gyrated wildly during the first several years of the company's existence, the "King of Stuff's" personal fortune vacillated from a few billion dollars to upwards of 10 billion dollars. Certainly, that amount of wealth can purchase a sizable degree of indifference to disparaging comments made by critics and naysayers.

eBay Essentials

Go to the *ebay.com* website and you will find literally millions of individual items offered for sale across several thousand categories. These categories include antiquities, ceramics, promo glasses, toy soldiers, and a classification simply entitled "weird stuff." A potential buyer scans individual items in categories of interest or uses eBay's search function to determine whether a desired item is being offered by an eBay seller.

Before a potential buyer can place a bid on a given item, he or she must register with eBay. The online registration form requires potential buyers and sellers to provide just a few items of information, including their name, e-mail address, and mailing address. The most important feature of the registration process is reading and accepting the user agreement. Among other responsibilities, this agreement alerts the prospective eBay member that every transaction consummated at the eBay site qualifies as legally binding on both parties. An eBay seller who fails to deliver goods sold in an eBay auction, or a buyer who fails to pay for goods he or she has purchased, assumes some risk of being dragged into court by the other party to the transaction.

After completing the registration process, new eBay members typically establish a "My eBay" page. Members use this page to keep track of the items they have listed for sale, the items on which they have bid, and their eBay account balance, among other information. A member can also use his or her personal page to provide billing information to eBay. Most members have eBay fees debited to a major credit card.

Once a new member is registered and provides the necessary billing information, he or she can place bids on a mint condition Mickey Mantle baseball card, a Movado watch, or a Marvin the Martian Pez dispenser. Each item sold on eBay has an auction item page. Among other information, this page includes a brief description of the given item, the quantity being offered for sale, the amount of time left in the auction, the first bid, the current maximum bid, and payment and shipping terms. To place a bid on an item, an eBay member scrolls to the bidding form that follows the auction item page. The member enters his or her user name, password, and the bid being made on the item in the appropriate windows included in the bidding form.

Sellers can generally choose an auction period of three, five, seven, or ten days. Most eBay auctions are ascending-price or English auctions. That is, over the term of an auction the prices bid by potential buyers continually rise. Once an auction is completed, eBay contacts the winning bidder and the seller of the item. eBay requires the two parties to contact each other and finalize the details of the transaction within three days.

Listing an item to be sold over eBay requires the completion of a "Sell Your Item" page. On this page, a potential seller keys in the title of the item being sold, selects the eBay category in which the item should be included, provides a brief description of the item, chooses the minimum opening bid and the number of days the auction is to run, and enters his or her eBay user name and password, among other information. For an additional listing fee, a seller can include a photo of the item being sold. Another option available to a seller is establishing a "reserve price." If this price—which is not revealed to buyers—is not reached, the seller has the right to reject all bids and retain ownership of the item at the completion of the auction.

Among the most important facets of eBay's auction process is the "feedback" feature. eBay encourages both buyers and sellers to complete an online feedback form for each finalized transaction. Feedback records are maintained for each eBay member. A buyer who is tardy in making payment for a given item or a seller who is lax in properly packing an item for shipment to the buyer will likely receive negative feedback from the other party to the transaction. Feedback compliments and complaints are publicly and permanently posted on eBay for all members to review. Experienced eBay members rely heavily on these records to determine whether or not to buy from, or sell to, given individuals.

eBay serves strictly as a facilitator in its online auctions. The company does not maintain an inventory of the items listed at its website, does not take physical possession of merchandise after it is sold, and does not become involved in the transfer of funds between buyers and sellers. Instead, eBay simply serves to bring buyers and sellers together and to track their interaction over the course of each auction.

For its services, eBay charges a variety of fees. eBay collects insertion fees from members who list items for sale. This nominal fee typically ranges from $0.30 to $3.30 but is higher for big-ticket items such as automobiles and real estate. When an item is sold, eBay receives a sales commission. Generally, this commission is 5 percent of the selling price. eBay also charges fees for special services requested by members. For example, sellers can pay an additional insertion fee to have their items boldfaced in eBay's listings or to have an item tagged with a specific eBay icon, such as the "Great Gift" icon. Members must also pay an additional fee to establish a reserve price for an item being sold.

PIERRE'S GRAND EXPERIMENT

Pierre Omidyar readily admits that he never intended to create a large company when he established eBay. Instead, he viewed his auction website as a "grand experiment"—an experiment in electronic commerce. For many years, the stock market and other financial markets had fascinated Omidyar. In particular, the concept of market efficiency appealed to him. "I'd always been interested in financial markets just generally, and I'd been attracted by the theory that in an efficient market, goods trade at their true value. Supply and demand balance to get to that true value. . . . That's just kind of a neat thing."[1]

When the federal government opened the Internet to commercial ventures in the early 1990s, Omidyar had a perfect opportunity to run his own test of the efficient market theory. What Omidyar did not realize was the vast size of the market that he was tapping. Practically everyone has a large store of "everyday stuff" they no longer want or need. Likewise, millions of individuals collect memorabilia of some type. Just how large is the market for "everyday stuff"? Estimates of the annual sales volume for this market range from $50 billion to $100 billion. In September 1995, Pierre Omidyar anointed himself the leader of that market when he opened eBay for business.

Before Omidyar dreamed up the concept of an online auction, individuals who wanted to sell their extra stuff were essentially limited to running classified ads in the local newspaper or having a garage sale. Collectors faced the daunting task of tracking down their personal Holy Grail by searching the classifieds each day, by poking through boxes of stuff at myriad garage sales, or by crisscrossing the country in their SUVs or station wagons to rummage through dimly lit antique shops from Kittery Point, Maine, to Imperial Beach, California, and from Del Rio, Texas, to Duluth, Minnesota. Suddenly, eBay brought all of these individuals together in one place, a virtual marketplace. eBay consolidated literally thousands of fragmented local and regional markets characterized by confusion, chaos, and

---

1. A. Sachs, "The e-Billionaire Nobody Knows," *GQ*, May 2000, 235.

incomplete information into one centralized and easily accessible market. "He [Omidyar] created an ingenious mechanism for mining value out of cluttered, stuff-filled lives, a 'place' where groping buyers and latent sellers could meet and make order (and a few bucks) out of chaos."[2]

In June 1996, Omidyar quit his job so that he could devote more of his time to expanding and perfecting his online auction house. A computer and software technician by training, he soon realized that he needed someone who had a better understanding of the business world to manage eBay's increasingly complex financial affairs, to formulate corporate strategies and policies, and to develop concrete plans and goals for the company. So, Omidyar hired a buddy, a recent graduate of Stanford's prestigious MBA program, and placed him in charge of "strategic analysis and planning" for eBay.

Over the following year, eBay's auction listings and revenues continued to grow as the number of eBay members approached the one million mark. Although eBay produced profits from the very beginning, those profits were not sufficient to finance the company's rapid growth. By mid-1997, Omidyar faced a choice. Either he could sell eBay or he could seek external financing. A large media company offered him $50 million for his company. Because his experiment was not complete, Omidyar spurned the buyout offer and instead approached Benchmark Capital, one of the leading venture capital firms in the nation.

In June 1997, Benchmark agreed to invest $5 million in eBay. That investment sustained eBay's operations over the remainder of 1997 and through the first several months of 1998. At that point, Omidyar decided to take the company public via an initial public offering (IPO). Going public would not only provide a windfall of funds to finance eBay's continuing growth and its chief executive's ambitious expansion program, it would also provide an economic windfall for Omidyar, for friends who had invested in the company, and for Benchmark Capital.

Before taking the company public, Omidyar made another important decision in the spring of 1998. He chose to step down as eBay's chief executive officer (CEO) and replace himself with a professional corporate executive. After an extensive search, Omidyar and his colleagues settled on Margaret Whitman, a marketing executive who had worked previously with Disney, Procter & Gamble, Bain & Co., and Stride Rite. Although Whitman assumed the CEO position vacated by Omidyar, he remained the chairman of eBay's board of directors.

To many observers, Whitman seemed a strange choice to take over eBay. She had a limited knowledge of the Internet and had no technical expertise or background in Internet technologies. But, she did possess several attributes that Omidyar believed eBay needed in a top executive. Whitman brought to eBay strong organizational skills. She developed a more concrete organizational structure—a structure that clearly documented the responsibilities of each of her subordinates. Under Omidyar, eBay had been characterized by a freewheeling corporate culture that emphasized innovation and camaraderie. Whitman placed greater emphasis on imposing personal responsibility on her subordinates. When something went wrong, she expected someone to take responsibility for the problem or misstep, even if that "someone" was her.

Early in Whitman's tenure, Omidyar, who remained the company's principal owner, expressed concern that Whitman's stricter policies might damage the

---

2. *Ibid.*, 233.

closely-knit, family orientation he had attempted to promote within the organization. Despite Omidyar's reservations regarding her management style, Whitman refused to budge. As chief executive, she insisted on "calling the shots," even if some of those shots offended the person who had hired her. Eventually, Omidyar and his former colleagues who remained in management positions with eBay relented and accepted the new boss's management style.

Whitman's many years as a marketing executive had taught her that to be successful, companies have to pay close attention to their customers. The most common complaints directed at eBay under Omidyar's leadership were that the company did not place a sufficient emphasis on customer service. eBay members often criticized the company's sophisticated website for being difficult to use. Whitman recognized that such complaints would eventually translate into lost customers, particularly when other major auction houses went online. After taking over for Omidyar, Whitman spent considerable time navigating eBay's website. She found the customer complaints justified. No doubt, the site was easy to use for the highly skilled computer and software technicians who had developed it, including Omidyar. But, Whitman found the site frustrating and recognized that other Internet novices would as well. To address this problem, she poured significant resources into a program to make eBay's website more user-friendly.

Another important change implemented by Whitman was imposing restrictions on the items that could be sold at the eBay website. Omidyar and his colleagues had refused to make any moral judgments regarding a wide array of questionable items listed for sale by eBay members. Whitman believed such judgments were necessary, appropriate, and in eBay's best interest. For example, she decided that an online auction house was not the appropriate venue to market guns and other weapons. Likewise, she decided that items smacking of racial or ethnic intolerance should not be made available at eBay's website. She also established an adults only section of the website to reduce the risk that children would access listings that contained explicit material not intended for minors.

Finally, Whitman adopted an aggressive, forward-looking strategy for eBay. She did not want eBay to be relegated to the low end of the evolving online auction industry. That is, she did not want her company to be primarily society's dispersal agent for low-priced, everyday stuff. Shortly before Whitman became eBay's CEO, the company had acquired one of the leading old-line and offline auction houses, Butterfield & Butterfield. That acquisition gave Whitman and eBay greater access to high-priced auction items such as rare art and prized antiques. Examples of other big-ticket items for which Whitman wanted to develop online auction markets included real estate, automobiles, furniture, and computer equipment.

Margaret Whitman's no-nonsense management style and rigorous corporate policies did not stymie the impressive financial and operating trends begun by eBay's founder. In fact, the company's new listings, revenues, and profits rose even more rapidly under her leadership. By the late summer of 2001, *Investor's Business Daily* reported that each day 2.1 million Internet surfers visited eBay's website and that 600,000 new items were listed for sale daily by the site's 34 million registered users.[3] During the previous year, 265 million items had been listed for sale at the site. Monthly "metrics" reports released by various Internet tracking agencies re-

---

3. J. Lloyd, "eBay Founder Pierre Omidyar: His Devotion to Community Created a Global Auction House," *Investor's Business Daily* (online), 20 August 2001.

vealed that the typical visitor to *ebay.com* spent approximately 2.5 hours at the site easily making it the "stickiest" site on the Web. Nielsen, one of the most prominent companies monitoring Internet traffic, reported in the spring of 2001 that *ebay.com* had surpassed *Amazon.com* as the most popular retail website.[4]

Whitman and her lieutenants believe that eBay's incredible growth will continue for the foreseeable future. By 2005, the company expects to have websites operating in 25 countries and total revenues surpassing $3 billion annually. Like most successful Internet-based companies, eBay suffered "guilt by association" when hundreds of dot-coms collapsed during 2000 and 2001. The company's stock price dropped sharply during that debacle but then recovered nicely. In the summer of 2001, Henry Blodget, one of the most prominent Internet financial analysts, remarked that eBay "is executing well in a horrendous environment. . . . Investors are paying up for numerous positives in the business—strong expansion and growth opportunities, great margins, and likely upside to [earnings] estimates."[5]

Margaret Whitman easily ranks among the most visible and most frequently interviewed Internet executives. A common question she faces from business reporters is why eBay's business model has been so successful. "It was a business model and a concept uniquely suited to the Web and took advantage of the characteristics of the Web."[6] Since Whitman has had significant experience overseeing both Old Economy and New Economy companies, she is also frequently asked to compare and contrast the skills needed by corporate executives in those seemingly very different business sectors. Whitman insists that despite the differences in the two types of companies, the same skill sets are required of their executives. She typically identifies three skills that are particularly critical for all corporate executives to possess: an ability to recognize and react to customers' needs, the discipline to make difficult choices involving the allocation of scarce economic resources, and an ability to hire and retain highly qualified subordinates who are extremely well suited for the responsibilities they will assume.

The September 1998 IPO of eBay showered riches on Pierre Omidyar, Margaret Whitman, and other eBay executives and employees. Just a few months following that IPO, Omidyar's stock in the company had a market value approaching $7 billion. In reflecting upon Omidyar's wealth, a former co-worker noted that it was an "accidental fortune," a fortune that was never a driving goal of the quiet and unassuming software technician. Instead, Omidyar had simply wanted to experiment with some of the most basic concepts of the supposedly dismal science of economics . . . and, at the same time, help his girl friend track down that elusive Zorro Pez dispenser.

CHALLENGES PAST AND PRESENT

New businesses, especially a firm such as eBay that relies on an unproven, if not revolutionary, business model, face a wide range of challenges. Recurring shut-

---

4. *AFX News Limited* (online), "eBay Overtakes Amazon to Become Most-Visited E-Commerce Site," 30 April 2001.

5. Bloomberg News, "Internet Stocks Help Raise NASDAQ," *Los Angeles Times* (online), 21 June 2001.

6. S. B. Shepard, "A Talk with Meg Whitman," *Business Week*, 19 March 2001, 98.

downs to eBay's website triggered by the unexpectedly large traffic at the site and by occasional breaches of its security controls by hackers and viruses posed a major headache for the company's management team. In its early years, eBay relied on one server to manage its online auction site. When that server failed, eBay immediately went offline since the company did not have a back-up or emergency system in place. Particularly damaging to eBay's credibility was a nearly 24-hour shutdown that occurred on June 10, 1999, referred to by company insiders as the "day eBay stood still." Scott McNealy, the CEO of Sun Microsystems accepted partial responsibility for that crash since it stemmed from a defect in the large server his company had installed for eBay. However, he reminded eBay officials that his company had provided a "patch" to remedy the defect more than one year earlier. eBay officials failed to comment on why that patch had not been installed in their system.

A series of shorter but well-publicized shutdowns plagued eBay during the remainder of 1999. Following each shutdown, the stock market pummeled eBay's common stock. Over the two trading days immediately following the June 10, 1999, shutdown, eBay's stock price plummeted nearly 40 percent. After the company invested in a back-up system, shutdowns became less common but still occasionally "bugged" the company's heavily trafficked website. In early January 2001, *ebay.com* was knocked out of service for nearly 12 hours when a hardware failure "crashed" both its primary and back-up systems.

Despite tough measures taken by Margaret Whitman to ban certain items from eBay listings, the company continued to face criticism for various weapons, tasteless memorabilia, and other questionable or objectionable items that appeared occasionally in its Web pages. In early 2000, embarrassed eBay executives removed listings for items that promoted certain hate groups.[7] A few months earlier, eBay expelled a member who listed a human kidney for sale on its website. In responding to criticism prompted by those listings, eBay's corporate spokesperson noted, "It's the responsibility of each user to familiarize themselves with our user agreement."[8] Such disclaimers failed to placate eBay's critics. One reporter noted that online auction houses were no longer "experiments" and that policy statements similar to eBay's that prohibit certain listings "pack zero punch in the online marketplace" unless they are supported with strong deterrents and an effective compliance system.[9] Legal experts warned that eBay and other online auction houses assumed enormous legal risks by not eliminating illegal or morally reprehensible items from their auction listings. "By not doing a better job to limit such auctions . . . the auction houses are playing a dangerous game. If an illegal weapon purchased online were to be used to seriously injure or kill someone, it could lead to a public relations nightmare, not to mention potentially disastrous lawsuits."[10]

The nature of e-commerce exposes online businesses and their customers to a wide range of fraudulent schemes. *Fortune* magazine profiled the story of a

7. In May 2000, a French court ruled that Yahoo! violated a French law that prohibited the sale of any item that incites racism. The lawsuit stemmed from neo-Nazi materials that had been listed for sale on the company's online auction site.

8. T. Wolverton, "Despite New Policies, Illegal Goods Still on Big Auction Sites," *CNET News.com*, 26 April 2000.

9. J. King, "Web Sites Crack Down on Fraud," *Computerworld*, 13 September 1999, 1.

10. Wolverton, "Despite New Policies, Illegal Goods Still on Big Auction Sites."

young boy who was the winning bidder for a DVD player in an online auction.[11] After wiring the appropriate amount of money to the seller, who happened to be a resident of Moldova, the young man waited for weeks for his DVD player to arrive. Eventually, he realized that the seller had duped him. In fact, the same individual had victimized several other parties in online auctions. Many of these latter individuals belatedly warned the young man not to wire money to the swindler. Moldovan officials were less than sympathetic with the young man's complaints that he filed through the U.S. embassy in that country. Worst of all, he had to suffer from teasing insults subsequently e-mailed to him by the alleged DVD owner.

Among the most embarrassing frauds that tarnished eBay's credibility was a phony $10 million bid on the domain name *Year2000.com*. That popular domain name had been listed by its owners for sale on eBay. When the bid was proven to be bogus, the owners of the domain name publicly criticized eBay officials. "We contacted eBay and they didn't do anything to help. As far as I'm concerned, this kind of thing is a huge black eye for them."[12]

Collusion ranks among the most common fraudulent schemes that online auction houses face. By working together, a group of conspirators can jack up the price of an item being sold by one of their compatriots. Likewise, artificially high bids made by one individual and later retracted before the close of an auction may chase off legitimate buyers and allow a co-conspirator to purchase the item at an artificially low price.

To detect fraudulent schemes perpetrated on eBay members, the company created a fraud unit headed up by a former federal prosecutor and developed a software program to monitor unusual activity in bids, particularly those placed on large ticket items. These efforts failed to reduce the number of fraud complaints filed by eBay members. Critics suggested that eBay refused to take adequate measures to minimize fraud because it feared that those measures would drive users away from its website. The company is "trying to present a minimum barrier to entry for users because they want to grow."[13] A frustrated Margaret Whitman responded sharply to the allegation that her company was "soft" on fraud and related misconduct by eBay users. "Listen, we have zero tolerance for this stuff . . . [but] eBay has grown from being a village to the size of New York City. With that many people, you are going to have some problems."[14]

By the end of the millennium, allegations of auction fraud swamped the Federal Trade Commission (FTC). In 2000, the federal agency received nearly 11,000 complaints related to online auction fraud. Three years earlier, the FTC had received just slightly more than 100 such complaints. In the summer of 2001, the National Fraud Information Center reported that auction fraud was easily the most common type of fraud on the Internet. According to that independent agency, various online auction frauds account for 76 percent of all fraud complaints reported

---

11. N. Parker, "Mom, Moldova, and How a Boy Lost His Innocence," *Fortune*, 29 May 2000, 274, 276.

12. J. Carlton and P. Tam, "Online Auctioneers Face Growing Fraud Problem," *The Wall Street Journal*, 12 May 2000, B6.

13. J. Carlton and K. Bensinger, "Phony Bids Pose Difficulties, Putting eBay on the Defensive," *The Wall Street Journal* Interactive Edition, 24 May 2000.

14. *Ibid.*

each year by Internet users.[15] Largely because of the failure of online auction houses to take an aggressive approach to eliminate fraudulent schemes, the FTC stepped in and implemented project "Safebid" to address this problem. Under this program, the federal agency has identified, investigated, and prosecuted hundreds of frauds involving online auction services.

The most serious challenge that eBay faces is not posed by technical glitches, critics, or con artists. Instead, the biggest threat looming in eBay's future is competition—competition on several fronts. eBay's success spurred several companies to launch competing online auction houses. The two most formidable competitors that entered this new market were Yahoo! and Amazon.com. Initially, Yahoo! targeted Internet users in foreign countries, such as Japan, where eBay did not have a strong presence. A few months after Yahoo! Japan Auctions went online, that site ranked as the leading online auction house in Japan.

The CEO of Amazon, Jeff Bezos, made a huge financial commitment to developing an auction site that would rival eBay's dominant position in the online auction industry in the United States. Market research identified several features of eBay's auctions that frustrated its users. Amazon designed its online auctions to remedy those alleged flaws. For example, Amazon instituted a money-back guarantee for purchases made up to $250. Since the large majority of online auctions involve transactions smaller than that dollar amount, this policy was intended to convince potential users that they would not be adversely affected by fraud, collusion, or simply irresponsible buyers or sellers. Soon after Amazon announced its money-back guarantee, eBay was forced to adopt a similar policy.

Amazon also designed its online auctions to provide a wider array of options to users than those available at *ebay.com*. While eBay sellers were required to run their auctions over three, five, seven, or ten days, Amazon permitted its users to run auctions with durations ranging anywhere from one to fourteen days. Amazon also attempted to limit the "sniping" problem pervasive at eBay's site. Sniping involves an effort by a bidder to "steal" an item in the final few moments of an auction by placing a bid slightly above the previous maximum bid. The new Amazon auction site included a "Going, Going, Gone" feature that extended an auction by ten minutes each time a bid was placed in the final ten minutes of an auction. Initially, at least, Amazon's aggressive campaign to attack eBay's dominant position in the online auction industry appeared to be succeeding. Within a few months after going online, Amazon's auction house had nearly one-half as many item listings as eBay.

Conventional retailers and wholesalers pose an even larger threat to eBay. The company's success caused many of these companies to begin exploring the possibility of selling selected merchandise online. End-of-season or closeout merchandise is particularly well suited for "disposal" through online auctions. In fact, much of the merchandise listed for sale on the eBay site has historically been close-out merchandise bought by liquidators for the express purpose of reselling it on eBay. Conventional retailers that were among the first to establish their own online auctions included JCPenney, Sharper Image, and Lands' End.

Some marketing experts believe that online auctions may become a standard marketing tool used by most companies. That is, we may eventually see the de-

---

15. R. P. Libbon, "What's the Most Common Internet Scam?" *American Demographics*, July 2001, 26.

velopment of an "eBay economy." Ironically, in such an environment, rather than becoming a dispersal agent for a wide range of goods, as envisioned by Margaret Whitman, eBay might find itself relegated to filling the role that it first assumed: an online disposal service for low-priced, miscellaneous "everyday stuff."

REVISITING PAM AND PIERRE

Few of us will ever struggle with the "what now" dilemma posed by having a fortune measured in the billions "imposed" on us. That dilemma did face Pam and Pierre Omidyar after eBay went public in 1998. In commenting on their newly acquired riches, Pam noted that it felt "weird" to be so wealthy, while Pierre once remarked that "it's more of a burden than anything else."[16]

Soon after Pierre walked away from being involved in eBay's day-to-day operations, he and Pam tackled the issue of what to do with their fortune. The two decided to act on their sense of social responsibility and give most of their wealth away. On several occasions, Omidyar has indicated that during their lifetimes, he and Pam intend to give away 99 percent of their net worth. In fact, the Omidyars hope to accomplish that goal by 2020.

Not surprisingly, the methodical Omidyar decided to study the history of philanthropy before becoming a philanthropist. In particular, he studied the charitable efforts of former corporate titans such as John D. Rockefeller and Andrew Carnegie, as well as the philanthropic activities of more contemporary business scions such as Microsoft's Bill Gates and Jerry Yang, one of the two co-Chief Yahoos of Yahoo!. Pam was a full partner in Pierre's effort to develop a gift-giving strategy. She quickly decided that they would not concentrate their charitable giving on what she referred to as MOBS—music, opera, ballet, and symphony. "As much as I love the arts, there are just more pressing problems."[17]

In settling on a basic strategy for giving away their wealth, Pierre recalled the role that Benchmark Capital had played in eBay's early history. Benchmark's several million dollar investment in eBay had provided the company with financial leverage. That leverage had allowed eBay to catapult itself to a much higher level in the business world. The Omidyars decided that they would become venture capitalists within the philanthropic world. They developed a plan to provide seed money (venture capital) to a wide range of charities in which they had an interest. They hoped that the organizations they funded would use this seed money to leverage themselves into more substantive entities.

The Omidyar Foundation created by Pam and Pierre focuses its gift-giving activities on the education of underprivileged children, health clinics in urban areas, environmental problems, and various scientific causes. Within three years of creating the foundation in 1998, Pam and Pierre had made sizable donations to more than 75 nonprofit organizations. One of the Omidyars' initial contributions was a $10 million donation to their beloved Tufts University. That donation came with a promise of more gifts . . . if Tufts demonstrated that it used the money wisely.

---

16. Sachs, "The e-Billionaire Nobody Knows," 234.

17. Q. Hardy, The Radical Philanthropist," *Forbes*, 1 May 2000, 119.

QUESTIONS

1. Identify the five factors that you believed contributed most significantly to the success of eBay. Rank order these factors from most to least important and defend this ranking.

2. Pierre Omidyar's interest in "market efficiency" contributed to his decision to create eBay. In your opinion, are online auction markets efficient? Explain. What factors determine whether or not markets are efficient?

3. Should online auction houses be legally responsible for the sale of illegal goods on their websites? Defend your answer. Should these auction houses accept listings for morally questionable items as long as the sale of such goods does not violate any law? How should online auction houses determine what items qualify as "morally questionable"?

4. To what extent, if any, should online auction houses be held responsible for fraud perpetrated on the users of their services? Besides the measures identified in this case, what policies or strategies could online auction houses implement to address this problem?

5. In your view, do entrepreneurs that "strike it big" in e-commerce or other fields have a responsibility to donate a portion of their wealth to "worthy causes"? Explain.

6. Visit both the eBay website and that of another online auction house. Prepare a list of key differences between the two sites. Which site is easier to use? Defend your answer.

7. Research recent economic, competitive, and technological developments involving or affecting the online auction industry. Summarize those developments in a bullet format and briefly explain their significance to eBay.

Abracadabra, Inc.

Life is either a daring adventure or nothing.

Helen Keller

For decades, the staff of *Time* magazine ended each year by announcing its "Man of the Year." As the end of the twentieth century approached, political correctness caught up with the legendary publication and it began selecting a "Person of the Year." Each December, the press and millions of *Time* readers worldwide anxiously await the announcement of the famous, or infamous, individual who will grace the cover of the magazine's year-end edition. Prior winners of this distinction include Winston Churchill, Josef Stalin, Pope John XXIII, Ronald Reagan, and Mikhail Gorbachev.

In 1999, *Time* shocked many of its readers by choosing a 34-year-old Internet entrepreneur as the most newsworthy individual of the year. Only four individuals who had previously claimed the title had been younger than the 1999 winner, Jeffrey P. Bezos, the founder and chief executive officer (CEO) of Amazon.com. Those individuals included Charles Lindbergh—the youngest winner at age 25 when he was selected in 1927, and Martin Luther King. Most likely, Bezos also qualified as the least-known winner of *Time's* annual title. Outside of Wall Street and the Internet subculture, few individuals were familiar with Bezos [pronounced bay-zoes] whose previous claim to fame had been his cousin, George Strait, a country-western singer.

Time selected Bezos because Amazon.com was among the firms leading the Internet revolution within the business world. According to *Time*, Bezos unquestionably ruled as the "king of cybercommerce" in the late 1990s.[1] In his typically, off-the-cuff manner, Bezos told a newspaper reporter that being introduced to Regis Philbin, the perky host of television's *Who Wants To Be A Millionaire?*, was the most impressive outcome of the *Time* award. Over the next few months, the media would become well acquainted with Bezos's disarming candor that contrasted sharply with the tight-lipped, buttoned-down persona exuded by the top executives of most major corporations. An individual who wrote an early biography of

---

1. J. C. Ramo, "Jeffrey Preston Bezos: 1999 Person of the Year," *Time.com*, 27 December 1999.

Bezos referred to him as a "brilliant, charming, hyper and misleadingly goofy mastermind."[2] In describing himself, Bezos was more blunt and less flattering, noting that he was "dorky" and "nerdy."[3]

Despite Bezos's often casual attitude toward the press, journalists soon discovered that he was totally dedicated to transforming Amazon.com, a company less than five years old, into an online retail powerhouse that would challenge Old Economy companies that had existed for decades. Rather than being a flash-in-the-pan opportunist who intended to "make a quick buck" off the Internet euphoria gripping Wall Street, Bezos insisted from the inception of his revolutionary business that he wanted to build something lasting, "something the world has never seen."[4] The individual he chose to model himself after was Walt Disney. Bezos admired Disney's innovative skills and his hard-nosed approach to doing business. "The thing that always amazed me was how powerful his vision was. He knew exactly what he wanted to build and teamed up with a bunch of really smart people and built it."[5]

SKY HIGH ASPIRATIONS

In the summer of 1994, Jeff Bezos walked away from a plush Manhattan office and an impressive six-digit salary to strike out on his own and create an Internet-based company. The job he gave up was a vice-president's position with the Wall Street hedge fund, D. E. Shaw & Co. Family members and friends questioned his sanity, including his father. Miguel Bezos fled Cuba in the early 1960s as a teenager with three worldly possessions: two shirts and a pair of trousers. The young immigrant struggled to teach himself English and then relied on a varied assortment of menial jobs to work his way through college. Thirty-five years later, Miguel Bezos was an executive officer of the massive oil company, Exxon. Although the senior Bezos doubted the wisdom of his son's unexpected career move, he still supported that decision. He realized that his son's intellect, serene self-confidence, and extraordinary work ethic would serve him well in whatever venture, adventure, or misadventure he chose to pursue.

Jeff Bezos was born on January 12, 1964, in Albuquerque, New Mexico. As a young boy, he never dreamed of being an entrepreneur or a Wall Street executive, for that matter. He wanted to be an astronaut. During his teenager years, Jeff entered a contest sponsored by NASA, the national space agency. The paper he wrote for that contest, entitled "The Effect of Zero Gravity on the Aging Rate of the Common Housefly," won him a free trip to the Marshall Space Flight Center in Huntsville, Alabama. A few years later, during his valedictorian speech at his high school graduation, he urged the federal government to begin colonizing outer space.

---

2. R. Spector, *Amazon.com* (New York: HarperBusiness, 2000), 185.

3. *Ibid.*, 30.

4. *Business Week*, "Jeffrey P. Bezos, Founder of Amazon.com," 27 September 1999, EB 24.

5. J. Quittner, "An Eye on the Future: Jeff Bezos Merely Wants Amazon.com to Be Earth's Biggest Seller of Everything," *Time.com*, 27 December 1999.

Bezos enrolled in Princeton University and chose to major in theoretical physics, a field of study that he believed was ideal for an aspiring astronaut. During his first year at Princeton, Bezos came face-to-face with a jarring realization: he would likely never be a top-notch physicist. Why? Because many of his Princeton classmates consistently outperformed him in his physics classes. After considerable reflection, Bezos changed his major and discarded his dream of becoming an astronaut, deciding instead to pursue another field that intrigued him, computing and information technology.

In 1986, Bezos left Princeton with a degree in electrical engineering and computer science. For the next several years, he held various jobs in which he relied on and enhanced his expertise in computers and information technology. His superiors quickly recognized their young subordinate's extraordinary skills and granted him "fast-track" status. During a two-year stint at Bankers Trust, a metropolitan bank in New York City, Bezos became the youngest vice-president in the organization's history at the age of 26. At D. E. Shaw & Co., he helped develop computer-based models to identify investment opportunities across a wide range of industries but with a particular focus on high-tech lines of business, including those related to the rapidly developing Internet.

While researching Internet companies for D. E. Shaw & Co., Bezos tripped across a fact that he found fascinating. In early 1994, traffic on the World Wide Web, which was still in its infancy, was increasing at an astounding annual rate of 2,300 percent. Bezos could not drive that statistic out of his mind. He reasoned that any technology growing that swiftly almost certainly presented a large number of lucrative business opportunities.

Among the traits that characterized Jeff Bezos as a young businessman was his analytical approach to addressing challenges and problems. In fact, the intensely methodical Bezos developed an explicit strategy for arriving at important decisions impacting his professional or personal life. This "regret minimization framework" required him to analyze every major professional and personal decision against a common benchmark: "You project yourself to age 80 and then minimize the number of regrets you have in your life."[6] Although happy with his position at D. E. Shaw & Co., Bezos recognized that if he failed to pursue the opportunities posed by the Internet and World Wide Web, he might experience significant regrets much later in his life. "I knew that I might sincerely regret not having participated in this thing called the Internet, which I thought was going to be a very big deal. I also knew that there was no way when I was 80 that I was going to regret having tried and failed. In fact, I thought if I had tried and failed, I would look back at 80 and feel proud."[7]

David Shaw, Bezos's close friend and superior at D. E. Shaw & Co., tried repeatedly to persuade his young protégé to remain with his firm. But, those efforts failed. Once Bezos's personal decision model had determined the appropriate course of action for him in a given situation, he became resolutely opposed to considering any other "inferior" decision alternative. So, in mid-1994, Bezos left his cushy Wall Street job, forfeited a large year-end bonus he would have received by

---

6. M. Granberry, "Amazon.com's CEO Is Not Content to Relax in the Face of Success," *The Dallas Morning News* (online), 11 August 1999.

7. *Ibid.*

remaining with D. E. Shaw & Co. for a few more months, and committed himself to becoming an Internet entrepreneur. However, one key unresolved issue remained for Bezos to address, namely, exactly what product or service would he sell over the Internet.

CADABRA, INC.

Jeff Bezos relied on his analytical skills to choose the line of business for his new venture. He began by identifying approximately two dozen products and services that he believed were at least reasonably well suited for being marketed online. Next, he analyzed those lines of business in reference to several decision criteria. One of those criteria was his personal interest in the given field. Bezos realized that if he was to dedicate several years, or possibly the rest of his life, to an industry, he had best have a strong personal interest in that field. After several weeks of intensive study, Bezos narrowed his choices to two lines of business: marketing music over the Internet and selling books online.

Additional research by Bezos revealed that six large record labels dominated the music industry. He doubted that those companies would readily cooperate with upstart businesses on the Internet that wanted a "piece of the action" in the music industry. The bookselling industry, on the other hand, was highly fragmented. In the mid-1990s, there were more than 4,000 firms publishing books and tens of thousands of book retailers. Barnes & Noble and Borders, the two largest bookselling chains, accounted for less than 12 percent of annual book sales. The absence of any "800-pound gorillas" in the bookselling industry convinced Bezos to establish an online bookstore. The fact that Bezos was a lifelong bibliophile made him even more comfortable with his decision. He often spent hours hanging out in bookstores, browsing randomly through the latest books on a wide variety of subjects. A final factor that cemented his decision was the absence of any substantial or even modestly successful online booksellers. By mid-1994, several companies sold books online. But, none of those firms had generated much interest among Internet users.

Bezos did not expect that his company or other online booksellers would drive conventional bookstores out of business. He believed that the large and growing retail book industry, which had approximately $80 billion in annual worldwide sales in the mid-1990s, could easily support existing physical retailers and at least one major online bookseller. If his firm could capture only 2 percent of the industry's market share, it would generate annual revenues of more than $1.5 billion.

Online booksellers would have several competitive advantages over physical bookstores. An online bookstore could offer potential customers access to an enormous database of books and related materials. Bezos recognized that the technology of the Internet and World Wide Web would allow individuals to track down specific books that they wanted to purchase in a matter of seconds in the comfort of their homes or during a brief break at work. The availability of a large online inventory of book titles would also allow customers to browse through books in their general areas of interest. To assist customers, online bookstores could provide capsule summaries of individual books, comments from authors, and online book reviews, including voluntary reviews submitted by Internet users.

Bezos also realized that existing technology would allow an online bookseller to maintain a record of not only the books purchased by each customer but also those that caught their attention as they roamed the virtual aisles of the online bookstore. Since Bezos intended to obtain e-mail addresses from his customers, his marketing staff could periodically zap those customers electronic messages to notify them of new books published in their areas of interest and to alert them to sales promotions. In Bezos's estimation, this personalized database would be among the most valuable assets of an online bookseller and provide the firm with a huge marketing advantage over its landlocked competitors.

Another important competitive advantage of an online bookstore would be the minimal inventory it would be required to maintain. Bezos expected that most books purchased by his customers would be shipped directly to them from book publishers or from one of the two large book distributors that served the retail bookselling industry. As a result, his firm could avoid the bulk of insurance, storage, handling, and other inventory-related costs that accounted for a major portion of physical bookstores' operating expenses.

The central plank of Jeff Bezos's business model for his proposed company was rapidly achieving "scale," that is, economies of scale. Bezos intended to develop a "business model based upon managing a fast-turning inventory from a centralized, low-overhead operation."[8] He recognized that significant, upfront expenditures would be required to get his business "off the ground," including large investments in hardware and software for the company's website. However, those costs were largely one-time or nonrecurring expenditures. Once the company began operating, he expected that its recurring expenses would be relatively modest and largely unaffected by sales volume. In brief, Bezos's company "was going to be built on the altar of scale, with a core belief that as it increased the number of customers, costs would not increase."[9]

By being the first online bookstore to achieve scale, Bezos expected that his firm could drive most other online bookstores out of business. Why? Simply because his firm's size and cost structure would provide it with the ability to sell books more cheaply than those competitors. Throughout the first few years of his company's existence, Bezos adopted the motto of "Get big fast" to rally his employees to meet and exceed revenue forecasts he had established. But, his underlying purpose was to get his company to "scale" as quickly as possible.

Another important feature of Bezos's business model for his new company was customer service. Given his familiarity with the Internet, he expected that word-of-mouth communications would be particularly critical for e-commerce businesses. A few bad experiences by an online business's customers would likely ricochet in the form of disparaging e-mail messages across the length and breadth of the Internet, driving away potential customers in droves. Bezos pledged that his company would adopt the axiom used for decades by many of the most successful Old Economy retailers, namely, "the customer is always right." In later years, he would frequently claim that he had created the most "customer-centric" company in either the New or Old Economy.

Once he had decided to sell books online and had developed a sketchy business plan for his proposed company, Jeff Bezos faced a slew of other decisions.

---

8. Spector, *Amazon.com*, 89.

9. *Ibid.*, 90.

One of those decisions was choosing a name for his new company. His first choice was "Abracadabra." He liked the sound of the word and the fact that it alluded to a mystical or magical ability to ward off bad luck, if not attract good fortune. But, that name was too long, in his opinion, so he shortened it to "Cadabra." A few months after incorporating his company, Bezos had another change of heart. He decided that he wanted a company name that began with the letter "A"—another reason he had initially selected Abracadabra. After poring over the "A" section of a dictionary, he finally settled on "Amazon." That name seemed appealing phonetically to Bezos, plus it would likely create a positive mental image of the new company in the minds of Internet users, triggering an association with the wild and untamed South American river that easily ranks as the longest in the world. Although journalists typically refer to the firm as "Amazon," Bezos prefers its more complete name "Amazon.com" since that name clearly indicates the company's connection to the Internet.

Another decision confronting Bezos was where to locate his company. He considered only those major metropolitan areas that would provide his company with ready access to a large pool of highly qualified information technology (IT) professionals. Bezos concluded that one city was ideally suited for his business: Seattle, Washington. Microsoft's headquarters in nearby Redmond had acted as a magnet for high-tech companies and the large army of IT professionals needed to support those companies. After choosing Seattle as the headquarters for his company, Bezos and his wife vacated the Manhattan apartment they had called home for several years and headed west.

What's Cool? Amazon.com!

After Bezos and his wife, MacKenzie, settled into a modest home in a Seattle suburb, he quickly went about the task of putting together the core of employees who would help him create his new company. MacKenzie was one of those individuals. An aspiring novelist who had worked for the award-winning author Toni Morrison, MacKenzie found good use for her accounting degree since she became Amazon's *de facto* accounting department. During his first several months in Seattle, Jeff Bezos spent much of each workday interviewing job candidates; he insisted on interviewing applicants for even the most mundane jobs. Bezos searched for individuals who possessed two traits: superior intelligence and an interest in "making a difference." He reasoned that such individuals would be productive employees whatever the job role they assumed.

Because he knew very little about the inner workings of the retail bookstore industry, Bezos attended a four-day seminar in nearby Portland, Oregon, shortly after he began organizing his new company. The seminar, sponsored by the American Booksellers Association, was designed for new bookstore owners and dwelt on the most basic elements of a bookstore's operations, including such rudimentary tasks as placing book orders. On returning to Seattle, Bezos shared his "wealth" of expertise in bookselling with his co-workers, who were also newcomers to the bookselling business. Ironically, Bezos held his early employee conferences in a meeting area of a Barnes & Noble superstore.

After more than one year of preparation, Jeff Bezos launched his company's website on July 16, 1995. Internet surfers who visited the new site discovered more than one million book titles to choose from, approximately five times the number of titles available from a typical retail superstore. For well over one year, Bezos relied almost completely on satisfied customers to promote his new company. That strategy worked well for Amazon as the company's sales grew steadily each month. Also responsible for much of that early success was a quirky request Jeff Bezos received three days after the launch of his company's website. An employee from another new Internet company, a company with the strange name of Yahoo!, requested permission to list Amazon.com on its "What's Cool" page. "What's the harm?" thought Bezos as he approved the request, not realizing that the Web search engine would soon become one of the stalwarts of the Internet economy. Thanks to the 12 months that Amazon.com appeared on Yahoo!'s What's Cool page, throngs of Internet surfers became acquainted with Jeff Bezos's online business. One month following the launch of Amazon's website, the company had already sold books to residents of all 50 states and citizens of 45 countries.

Amazon's early months of operations placed a huge strain on Jeff Bezos and his loyal band of employees who referred to themselves as "Amazonians." Computer glitches, frequent panic attacks triggered by the need to track down hard-to-find and out-of-print books, and a shortage of individuals who had the requisite traits to qualify as Amazonians forced Bezos and his colleagues to routinely work 80 or more hours per week. Another shortage, a shortage of funds, proved to be the biggest problem the new company had to overcome. Within a few months, the cash that Jeff and MacKenzie Bezos had invested in Amazon was gone, effectively making them broke and, even worse, a poor credit risk in the eyes of local bankers. Jeff Bezos turned to his friends, family members, and employees for the funds needed to keep Amazon operating. Although he was not shy about asking acquaintances for cash, Jeff Bezos did warn his company's early investors that Amazon would struggle financially for several years. Even more pointedly, he told them there was a significant likelihood that Amazon would fail, totally wiping out their investments.

Despite the odds against Amazon's survival, Bezos managed to keep the company afloat until the spring of 1996. By that point, Internet fever was beginning to grip many large investors, including the partners of major venture capital firms. Then, another lightning bolt of good luck struck Amazon, a stroke of good fortune comparable to Yahoo! listing Amazon on its What's Cool page. In May 1996, a reporter for *The Wall Street Journal* wrote a front page article that praised the *Amazon.com* website and commented on the large underground following the company had amassed on the Internet over the previous ten months.[10] Shortly after that article appeared, Bezos closed a deal with Kleiner Perkins Caufield & Byers, a venture capital firm that provided early financial backing for several successful high-tech companies, including Netscape, Sun Microsystems, and Intuit. In exchange for a 13 percent ownership interest in Amazon, Kleiner Perkins invested $8 million in the company, more than enough funds to meet the company's cash needs for the coming year.

The Kleiner Perkins investment allowed Jeff Bezos to shift from a survival mode of management to concentrating instead on expanding Amazon's revenue

---

10. G. B. Knecht, "How Wall Street Whiz Found a Niche Selling Books on the Internet," *The Wall Street Journal*, 16 May 1996, A1.

base. For all of 1996, Amazon would post sales of nearly $16 million, an impressive figure since the company had managed only $500,000 of sales during the approximately five months it was open for business the previous year. In 1997, Amazon would post another large increase in revenue, registering total sales of $148 million. By the spring of 1997, Jeff Bezos had convinced Wall Street that his company was ready for "prime time." With the help of one of Wall Street's most prominent investment bankers, Morgan Stanley, Bezos took his company public on May 15, 1997. Bezos and each of his early employees and investors were suddenly multimillionaires. But, Bezos was not satisfied. In his mind, his company had many more goals to accomplish. One of those goals was to report a profit.

Mary, Mary, Quite Contrary

The Internet mania of the late 1990s drove the stock prices of Amazon, Cisco Systems, Priceline, and hundreds of other companies closely linked to the information superhighway to astronomical levels, creating the now infamous Internet Bubble within the stock market. That mania produced numerous Internet billionaires, among them Jeff Bezos. By March 1999, the soon-to-be "Person of the Year" was worth more than $8 billion, thanks to the more than 40 percent of Amazon's stock that he owned. Wall Street analysts agreed that a key factor prompting the massive run-up in Internet stock prices was the dramatic increases in revenues reported each period by Amazon.com, which easily qualified as the highest profile and most celebrated online retailer. In 1998, the company's sales rose to $610 million and then topped $1.6 billion the following year. By the late 1990s, dozens of Internet entrepreneurs had copied Jeff Bezos's "Get big fast" business plan for Amazon. Bezos became widely recognized as the "poster boy of e-commerce." So fanatical was the interest in Amazon on Wall Street that the company's board authorized three stock splits between June 1998 and September 1999 to keep the price of Amazon stock at a "reasonable" level. An investor fortunate enough to own 100 shares of Amazon stock in early June 1998 owned 1,200 shares of that stock fifteen months later.

Amazon's prime competitors in the online segment of the bookselling industry proved to be Barnes & Noble and Borders, the two leading conventional book retailers. In the late 1990s, each of those companies established websites to compete with Amazon.com. Barnes & Noble, the leading firm in the industry, adopted a particularly aggressive approach to repel the competitive threat posed by Amazon. One tactic Barnes & Noble used to attack Jeff Bezos's company was litigation. Just a few days before Amazon's IPO in May 1997, Barnes & Noble launched its own retail website and filed a civil lawsuit charging that Amazon.com was misleading the public by claiming to be the "Earth's Biggest Bookstore"—Barnes & Noble insisted that Amazon was not a bookstore at all. That lawsuit also charged that several other statements included in Amazon's advertisements and other promotional materials were false. Bezos responded to the lawsuit by filing a countersuit against Barnes & Noble. Eventually, the two companies agreed to settle their differences outside of court and dropped the lawsuits.

Amazon's rapid growth and the threat it posed to Barnes & Noble and Borders introduced a new word into the lexicon of business: "amazoned," as in, "don't allow your company to be amazoned." Many corporate executives feared that

Amazon look-a-likes popping up in their industries would erode their company's market share, if not drive it completely out of business. Largely discounted within all of this hubbub over Amazon was the fact that the company had yet to post a profit. More to the point, Amazon had posted increasing losses each successive year. The $1.6 billion in revenues that Amazon reported in 1999 seemed impressive, but, in the minds of many long-time investors, the company's $720 million loss for that year was the more telling figure.

While being showered with accolades and awards during the late 1990s, Jeff Bezos increasingly faced pointed questions from the business press regarding his company's schizoid financial results. Bezos typically responded to such questions by reminding journalists that he had predicted from Amazon's inception that the company would struggle financially for several years before it achieved "scale." Another strategy used by the young billionaire was to point to the example set by *USA Today*, the nationwide newspaper founded in the early 1980s, which required 11 years to begin turning a profit. When pressed, Bezos readily acknowledged that Amazon would have to produce profits at some point to be a viable business. And, he pledged that the company *would* become profitable without committing himself to an actual date when that would occur.

Amazon's dazzling revenue trend and Jeff Bezos's rising stature in the business community were not the only factors responsible for the spectacular increase in Amazon's stock price during the final two and one-half years of the 1990s. Another factor, possibly an even more important factor, was the optimism of several leading Wall Street analysts who tracked and regularly issued reports on the company's stock. Principal among these analysts was Mary Meeker, who was assigned to follow the stock in September 1997, a few months after the company's IPO. From the beginning, Meeker extolled the virtues of Amazon's business plan and Jeff Bezos's extraordinary business intellect. Although the company's stock price had surged well beyond its IPO price of $18 by the fall of 1997, Meeker coaxed investors to make a strong commitment to the stock. She cautioned her large army of followers that they certainly did not "want to miss this one."[11]

One journalist complained that Meeker's reports on Amazon's financial health and future prospects were overly "breezy" and "upbeat" and short on substantive analysis.[12] Meeker clearly appeared to craft her reports in a style that even the most naïve investors could understand. "This [online] market is just so immature with oh-so-much growth ahead. I mean, 45 million Web users! They are all literate, and they all could be buying books at Amazon.com."[13] Such blissful reports prodded large numbers of the new, do-it-yourself investors who had established online trading accounts during the late 1990s to pour billions of dollars into Amazon's stock. As these investors drove Amazon's stock ever higher, Mary Meeker became recognized as an "Internet visionary" and, arguably, the highest profile financial analyst on Wall Street.

As time passed, a few skeptics began questioning Meeker's motives in strongly recommending Amazon's common stock. Why? Because she was employed by Morgan Stanley, the Wall Street investment banking firm that had managed Amazon's IPO. Morgan Stanley earned fees running into the tens of millions of dollars

---

11. N. D. Schwartz, "Inside the Market's Myth Machine," *Fortune* (online), 2 October 2000.

12. *Ibid.*

13. *Ibid.*

for managing that IPO and for subsequently providing a long list of additional services to Amazon. An analyst employed by another major Wall Street investment firm admitted that financial analysts are often disinclined to issue negative reports on an important client, such as Amazon, out of fear of driving such clients to another investment banker. "There was significant competition from [investment] bankers for Amazon's attention. And when banking competition is fierce, analysts tread more lightly."[14]

In defense of Mary Meeker, other financial analysts unaffiliated with Morgan Stanley also wrote rave reviews regarding Amazon.com. Another cheerleader for Amazon on Wall Street was Henry Blodget, a young financial analyst who eventually accepted a position with Merrill Lynch. Blodget startled Wall Street in 1998 when he projected that Amazon's stock price would reach $400 per share in the near future. That forecast triggered a frenzied buying spree among investors. Within a short time, Amazon's stock price, adjusted for a stock split, had reached and surpassed Blodget's target price. Blodget later commented that the impact of his forecast on Amazon's stock price was comparable to "touching a match to a bucket of gasoline."[15]

Meeker and Blodget's enthusiasm for Amazon was not shared by all members of the business press or by every analyst tracking the company. Amazon's principal antagonist within the business press was *Barron's*, which referred to the company as Amazon.bomb, on occasion, because of its large losses. At approximately the same time that Henry Blodget released his $400 target price for Amazon, another analyst, Jonathon Cohen, claimed that the stock was worth no more than $50 per share. Without naming names, Cohen charged that many analysts were "playing to Wall Street" and were "logically corrupt." "Amazon has become the victim of supporters eager to endorse its shares at almost any valuation."[16] Cohen warned that the aggressive price targets established for Amazon by analysts placed undue pressure on company management. Under such circumstances, corporate executives may take whatever steps are necessary to reach those price targets over the short term, while being diverted from making optimal economic decisions in the long-term interests of their firm and its stockholders.

The bursting of the Internet Bubble in early 2000 caused Internet stock prices to plunge, including Amazon's. Suddenly, the unpopular views of analysts, such as Jonathon Cohen, who had long argued that most Internet stock prices were grossly inflated, became more credible with investors. The downturn of Amazon's stock price soon compelled other analysts to begin writing negative assessments of the company's long-term prospects. Ravi Suria, a financial analyst with Lehman Brothers, one of Morgan Stanley's major competitors, wrote the most critical of these reports. Suria pointed out that certain analysts tracking Amazon were using unconventional financial measures to justify the high valuations they assigned to the company's stock. One of those metrics was the "the lifetime value of a customer." Suria argued that such New Economy metrics were unproven and highly unreliable. He argued that conventional, time-proven measures should be used to determine a defensible market valuation for Amazon and other Internet companies. Principal among those measures in Suria's mind

---

14. *Ibid.*

15. *Ibid.*

16. *Ibid.*

was a company's ability to generate positive cash flows from its core, profit-oriented activities.

Suria warned investors that Amazon was hemorrhaging cash. Amazon's May 1997 IPO provided the company with a large inflow of cash. But, that cash was soon expended. To raise additional funds—funds desperately needed to finance Amazon's incredible growth—Bezos and his fellow officers borrowed large sums by selling debt securities to the general public. Eventually, Amazon would borrow well in excess of $2 billion. Suria pointed out that Amazon was "burning" through this borrowed cash at an alarming rate and questioned whether Amazon would ever produce sufficient positive cash flows from its operations to retire that debt. An analyst for Moody's, a revered Wall Street company that issues credit reports on major corporations, seconded Suria's concern. This analyst charged that Amazon was effectively running a 1920s era "Ponzi" scheme. Amazon's "bondholders are in effect being paid cash [interest] from money they lent to the company."[17]

Suria speculated that the problem facing Amazon was very basic: the company's business model was flawed. Although steadily growing numbers of Americans made purchases from Amazon's website, the revenues produced by the company's sales were simply not sufficient to cover its more rapidly growing expenses. In other words, there was a positive correlation between the company's revenues and operating losses: the more the company sold, the larger its losses. Suria suggested that the dilemma facing Amazon stemmed primarily from a long series of ill-advised decisions by the company's management team, principally *Time's* 1999 Person of the Year, Jeff Bezos. Unless Amazon's management made major changes in the company's business model, the 29-year-old analyst believed that the only possible outcome was bankruptcy. Suria's initial report on Amazon caused the company's stock price to quickly drop 20 percent, imposing large losses on the company's stockholders.

Ravi Suria's report infuriated Amazon's supporters. Even Jeff Bezos, who was known for his genteel and courteous manner in dealing with his company's detractors, came unwound after reading that report. An angry Bezos characterized Suria's research as "complete, absolute, pure, unadulterated hogwash."[18] One of Amazon's directors, a Kleiner Perkins partner who had approved his firm's $8 million investment in Amazon in 1996, allegedly attempted to persuade Suria's superiors at Lehman Brothers to "tone down" the young analyst's negative attacks on Amazon. Lehman Brothers' top brass was reportedly unhappy with Suria's rhetoric in its own right. Scathing reports filed by an investment banker's analysts, even when those reports involve non-clients, tend to offend potential clients. Companies planning to sell debt or equity securities prefer investment bankers whose analysts are prone to placing favorable or upbeat "spins" on their reports.

Concern over the role that financial analysts were playing in the increasingly volatile stock market prompted a congressional committee to launch an investigation of Wall Street's analyst community in the summer of 2001. A principal focus of that investigation was the apparent conflict-of-interest posed by allowing

---

17. R. Hof, D. Sparks, E. Neuborne, and W. Zellner, "Can Amazon Make It?" *BusinessWeek Online*, 10 July 2000.

18. M. Helft, "The Amazon Slasher," *The Industry Standard*, 5 March 2001, 54.

individuals such as Mary Meeker, an employee of Morgan Stanley, to file research reports on Amazon, one of Morgan Stanley's most important clients. One congressman spearheading that investigation implied that financial analysts routinely filed favorable reports on clients of their employers and that such reports induced naïve investors to purchase highly speculative securities at inflated prices. "I am deeply troubled by evidence of Wall Street's erosion of the bedrock of ethical conduct. It is one thing for one shark to eat another. It is quite another thing for the shark to eat the minnows."[19] Among the Wall Street analysts the congressional committee wanted to interview in its initial hearings were Mary Meeker and Henry Blodget. Both of those analysts reportedly declined to appear for personal reasons.

Mounting criticism of investment bankers spurred by the congressional investigation caused Merrill Lynch to announce a new policy in July 2001. The investment banking and brokerage firm prohibited its financial analysts from owning stock in companies they were assigned to monitor. That decision was met with a lukewarm response by critics who wanted more rigorous measures implemented to promote the integrity of financial analysts' reports. On the other hand, certain members of the investment community maintained that the criticism of investment bankers and their analysts was misdirected and that Merrill Lynch's new policy was unnecessary and even counterproductive. "I like the idea of an analyst owning the stock because theoretically that means he really believes in it. If his recommendations have no consequence to his net worth, he's less likely to catch onto reality about a company fast enough."[20]

ONWARD THROUGH THE FOG

Throughout 2000, the price of Amazon's common stock tumbled lower and lower, eventually losing more than 80 percent of its market value. The company's declining stock price sliced more than $6 billion off Jeff Bezos's personal fortune. Even harsher than those monetary losses was the stinging criticism Bezos faced only months after being named the most newsworthy person in the known universe. With a few exceptions, most notably when he was blindsided by Ravi Suria's initial report on Amazon, Jeff Bezos put up a brave front when accosted by his critics. Bezos stubbornly continued to insist that once his company achieved scale, profits and positive cash flows would soon follow.

Despite Bezos's stance, growing scrutiny of Amazon's finances cast increasing doubt on the soundness of the company's business plan and the prudence of key strategic decisions made by its CEO. Many critics began pointing out that key features of Amazon's business model had been invalidated, forcing Bezos to discard them. An example? Bezos's notion that the company could operate with a minimal amount of inventory. As Amazon's sales ballooned during the late 1990s, Bezos finally admitted to himself that his company could not rely on the two major book distributors and the industry's publishers for timely delivery of the

19. G. Morgenson, "Hearings Begin on Analyst Conflicts," *The New York Times* on the Web, 15 June 2001.

20. G. Morgenson, "Brokerage Puts Limits on Stock Analysts," *The New York Times* on the Web, 11 July 2001.

enormous volume of books being ordered by Amazon's customers. The company was forced to borrow huge amounts to acquire a large network of warehouses and distribution facilities. In 1999, alone, Amazon opened seven new warehouses. Operating expenditures linked to those new properties and interest payments on the related loans added two new layers of expenses to Amazon's income statement and increased the company's negative cash flow. When analysts and reporters questioned the decision to invest in the new warehouses and distribution facilities, Bezos reverted to the all-encompassing "scale" issue. He maintained that although those new assets were expensive, they would allow Amazon to keep sales volume increasing and thus more quickly achieve "scale."

Contributing to Amazon's large and growing need for warehouse space were many questionable inventory management decisions. To obtain volume discounts from publishers, Amazon often purchased large quantities of books that Bezos and his colleagues believed would be in high demand. Amazon also tended to purchase more inventory than it needed to achieve Jeff Bezos's customer service goals. For example, to accomplish his objective of creating the nation's most customer-centric company, Bezos wanted to minimize inventory stock-outs that resulted in customers not receiving books they ordered on a timely basis. He would later admit that inventory management and purchasing decisions were often made informally, by the "seat of the pants"—quite an admission for an individual renowned for his analytical decision-making style. Those informal decisions caused the company's warehouses to become stuffed with merchandise that could only be sold at distressed prices, far below even the discounted prices Amazon had paid for the merchandise. In early January 2000, as Amazon was closing the books for its 1999 fiscal year, the company wrote off $40 million of surplus inventory.

Amazon's customer-centric policy produced other inefficiencies in the company's operations as well. The *Amazon.com* website consistently ranked among the top retail sites in terms of customer satisfaction due largely to the company's excellent customer service department. By early 2000, Amazon employed hundreds of full-time customer service representatives who responded to a daily flood of phone calls and e-mails from customers who wanted to receive up-to-the-minute status reports on their orders, change their orders, recommend modifications in the company's website, file a complaint regarding a tardy shipment, and so on and so forth. Customer service reps routinely waived shipping charges, awarded gift certificates, and bestowed other "bribes" on disgruntled customers to keep them visiting Amazon's website. Although Jeff Bezos and his colleagues could brag about the high quality of service provided to customers, that first-class service contributed significantly to Amazon's cash flow and profit problems.

Following Amazon's IPO in May 1997, the company was awash with cash. Because the company did not have an immediate need for all of those funds, Jeff Bezos and his management team decided to invest much of it in other companies. Not surprisingly, they chose to invest almost exclusively in other Internet companies, principally other e-tailers or dot-coms. After purchasing sizable ownership interests in such firms, Bezos often arranged business deals with them. Many of these arrangements involved Amazon's new "e-commerce partners" agreeing to pay large sums to place banner ads and other promotional materials on the heavily trafficked *Amazon.com* website. Amazon's e-commerce partners included *Living.com, drugstore.com, homegrocer.com, kozmo.com,* and *pets.com*. By early 2000, most of Amazon's e-commerce partners were encountering severe financial problems. By the end of that year, several of the companies had failed, imposing large investment losses on Amazon and exacerbating the company's own financial problems. In commenting on these losses, Jeff Bezos acknowledged that, like many other investors, he had been swept up in the "land rush mentality" associated with the Internet boom of the late 1990s and invested in many undercapitalized and poorly managed concerns.[21]

As Amazon's financial condition steadily weakened during 2000 and beyond, Jeff Bezos and his closest associates placed increasing emphasis on a strategic initiative they had been pursuing on a smaller scale over the previous few years. That two-prong initiative involved establishing new *Amazon.com* websites in overseas markets and expanding Amazon's product line to include a wide range of merchandise in addition to books. Shortly after he created Amazon.com, Jeff Bezos began considering the possibility of converting his company's website into an "electronic commerce destination." Bezos reasoned that once he developed a hardware and software infrastructure for an online bookseller and obtained a database of personal information on its customers, his firm could use those assets to market a wide array of other products and services.

In March 1999, Amazon organized an online auction service to compete with eBay and other Internet auction houses. In July 1999, Amazon began selling consumer electronics and toys directly from its website. By late 2000, Amazon was marketing dozens of unrelated products and services from its massive website, including home improvement products, software, video games, and tools. If you suddenly needed a 500-pound table saw, you could buy one from Amazon. And, the company would subsidize the shipping fee, charging you only a modest $4.95 to deliver the monstrous saw. In describing his expansion strategy, Bezos observed, "We at Amazon.com want to build a place where customers can find and discover anything they may want to buy."[22]

LOOKING TO THE FUTURE

While Jeff Bezos and his top lieutenants struggled to put Amazon on solid financial footing during late 2000 and early 2001, a new problem blindsided the company. Within a period of a few months, the company became the target of two investigations by federal law enforcement authorities. In the fall of 2000, a quarterly financial report filed by Amazon discreetly revealed that the Securities and Exchange Commission (SEC) had begun an inquiry into key accounting and disclosure decisions made by the company. At the heart of this investigation were several large transactions involving Amazon and its e-commerce partners.

In early 2000, Amazon had announced marketing agreements with four of its e-commerce partners, agreements that would "pump as much as $130 million a year in high-margin marketing fees into Amazon."[23] At approximately the same

21. M. Rapoport, "Amazon.com CEO Bezos Remains Upbeat About Internet Retailing," *The Wall Street Journal* Interactive Edition, 13 April 2001.

22. K. Li, "Amazon Sales Up 230% from All-Time High, Stock Battered," *Daily News*, 29 April 1999, 79.

23. M. Veverka, "What Might the SEC Be Probing at Amazon?" *Barron's Online*, 30 October 2000.

time, Amazon's leading analyst, Mary Meeker, reported that the company had received "multiyear cash commitments" from several of its e-commerce partners.[24] These reports were released shortly, and opportunistically, before Amazon sold a large issue of new debt securities. *Barron's* suggested that these announcements allowed the company to sell those debt securities on much more favorable terms than had been previously expected.[25] Several downgrades of Amazon's common stock by financial analysts had caused many members of the investment community to question whether the new debt securities could be sold at all.

The SEC was apparently concerned by Meeker's suggestion that the compensation received by Amazon from its four e-commerce partners would be in the form of cash, an asset desperately needed by Amazon since it was once again facing a liquidity crisis. In fact, that compensation would not be in the form of cash. Instead, each e-commerce partner would compensate Amazon by giving the company additional shares of its common stock. Since the stock prices of those companies were plummeting during 2000—one of those e-commerce partners, *Living.com*, actually filed for bankruptcy during that time frame—the ultimate economic value of those marketing agreements was very much in doubt. One investment services firm that specializes in investigating questionable accounting practices of public companies maintained that Amazon should not have recorded any revenues on those contracts since those revenues were so tenuous.[26] *Barron's* made an even more disparaging allegation, charging that both Amazon and its principal financial analysts were attempting to obscure the company's deteriorating financial condition at the expense of its stockholders and potential stockholders.

> But at a time when Amazon's first 'commerce network' partners are either struggling or going bankrupt—and when one of the nation's top accounting watchdogs, Howard Schilit's Center for Financial Research & Analysis, concludes that Amazon is basically booking bogus revenues from such partners—all we get from a legion of brokerage analysts and scribes are candy-coated pronouncements telling a story that may be little more than fiction.[27]

The second federal investigation of Amazon focused squarely on Jeff Bezos. In March 2001, *The New York Times* reported that the SEC was investigating the sale of 800,000 shares of Amazon stock by Bezos the previous month.[28] Prior to that sale, Bezos had only sold 500,000 shares of Amazon stock since the company's IPO in May 1997. The SEC was concerned by Bezos's February stock sale since approximately one week earlier Amazon had received an advance copy of a soon-to-be released analyst's report. That report, prepared by the company's nemesis, Lehman Brothers' Ravi Suria, suggested that Amazon's financial condition was deteriorating so rapidly that the company might not survive through the end of the year. A Lehman Brothers' executive acknowledged that his firm provided companies with advance copies of negative analysts' reports so that their management teams would be prepared for any adverse reaction to such reports. What

24. *Ibid.*

25. *Ibid.*

26. M. Veverka, "Is It Amazon.com? Or Obfuscation.com?" *Barron's Online*, 25 September 2000.

27. *Ibid.*

28. G. Morgenson, "S.E.C. Said to Be Investigating Amazon Chief's Stock Sale," *The New York Times* on the Web, 9 March 2001.

concerned the SEC was that, unlike Bezos, other Amazon stockholders and potential stockholders did not have early access to Suria's new critique of the company and, thus, did not have an opportunity to unload their stock prior to his comments being released publicly.

A spokesperson for Amazon insisted that Jeff Bezos's sale of stock shortly after he received a copy of Suria's new evaluation of the company was purely coincidental. "Mr. Bezos sold the shares to raise money and to diversify his holdings. . . . The sales had nothing to do with the release of the Lehman Brothers report."[29]

The new report issued by Suria on Amazon's worsening financial condition was just one of many critical commentaries examining the company's management team and financial condition that circulated in the investment community during late 2000 and early 2001. In December 2000, *Fortune* published a lengthy investigative article on Amazon, focusing particular attention on Bezos's effort to convert the company into an online "flea market" that would sell almost anything to anybody, anywhere. *Fortune* questioned the wisdom of that strategy. The periodical also questioned Bezos's assertion that Amazon's operating expenses would rise only modestly as it continued to expand its product line and the number of geographical markets that it served. "This year, Amazon launched sites in France and Japan. So it has to pay to build two new distribution centers, hire two new staffs on two continents, puzzle through different sets of tax codes, and so on. . . . Indeed, just like real-world retailers, Amazon's costs seem to grow with sales."[30] *Barron's* provided a more broad and blunt assessment of Amazon's financial health in January 2001, when it declared that the company's "business model is breaking down."[31]

Throughout 2001, an increasing number of analysts and major institutional investors recommended that Jeff Bezos consider merging his firm with another major company, similar to Steve Case's decision to merge AOL with Time Warner. The most common merger candidate mentioned was Wal-Mart. Another frequent recommendation was that Amazon develop working relationships or alliances with companies across several sectors of the retail industry. In these arrangements, Amazon would manage the partner's online sales effort, or Internet sales "platform," in exchange for a share of the resulting revenues. One such alliance that Bezos had already negotiated, with the large toy retailer Toys 'R' Us, had proven to be beneficial for both companies. In late 2001, Bezos announced two more major "platform services" deals, one with Circuit City and another with Borders. In the latter deal, Amazon effectively took over the operations of Borders' retail website, *borders.com*.

By early 2001, even some of Amazon's most ardent supporters were beginning to lose faith in the company. When asked to comment on Ravi Suria's prediction that Amazon could be facing a solvency crisis by the end of that year, a beleaguered Henry Blodget disagreed, but only half-heartedly. "I think he's wrong. . . . I hope he's wrong."[32] As always, Jeff Bezos gamely stood his ground. Two

29. *Ibid.*

30. K. Brookner, "Beautiful Dreamer," *Fortune* (online), 18 December 2000.

31. M. Veverka, "Amazon Bulls Pull in Their Horns," *Barron's Online*, 15 January 2001.

32. Helft, "The Amazon Slasher," 55.

months after Suria's dire prediction, he told the company's stockholders that Amazon was "in a stronger position now than at any time in the past."[33]

Regardless of the eventual fate of Amazon.com, Jeffrey P. Bezos, *Time's* 1999 Person of the Year, can rest assured that one of his ultimate fears will not be realized. During the early months of Amazon's existence, Bezos warned his colleagues that despite the company's quick start, it could eventually wind up being only a footnote in the history of Internet commerce. That will certainly not be the case, at least according to one business journalist. "What happens to this company, with its highly recognized brand and its weird economics, is certainly going to be a great Internet saga."[34]

QUESTIONS

1. Jeff Bezos often refers to the "regret minimization framework" that he has relied upon to make major decisions. Do you believe that decision-making strategy is an appropriate one for a CEO to use in making judgments that will affect the future of his or her company? Explain. Identify general rules or principles that you believe CEOs should follow in making key strategic decisions for their firms.

2. Compare and contrast the apparent strengths and weaknesses of *Amazon.com's* website with the website of another major online retailer. List what you believe are the three most critical features of a retail website.

3. Accountants often use the terms "fixed costs" and "variable costs" when referring to a company's expenditures. Define each of those terms. How are these two types of costs relevant to a company's ability to achieve economies of scale?

4. Inventory management is an important issue for retail and wholesale companies. List three to five inventory-related business risks that such companies face. For each risk you listed, identify a control policy or procedure that companies can implement to eliminate or mitigate that risk.

5. Customer service can be a very costly but also very beneficial feature of a company's operations. What general rules or principles should a company follow in deciding how extensive its customer service function should be?

6. Compare and contrast the following three financial statement items: net income (net loss), cash flows, revenues. Briefly describe what each of these items reveals about the financial health of a given company. Do you believe that investors should use the same general rules of thumb in evaluating the financial health of Internet-based companies and "Old Economy" companies? Explain.

7. Should financial analysts employed by investment banking firms be permitted to issue reports on companies that are important clients of their employers? Defend your answer.

8. Research recent developments involving Amazon.com. List and briefly describe these developments in a bullet format.

---

33. Rapoport, "Amazon.com CEO Bezos Remains Upbeat."

34. C. J. Loomis, "Amazon," *Fortune*, 1 May 2000, 132.

Mark Cuban: Internet Maverick

Anybody who is any good is different from anybody else.

Justice Felix Frankfurter

As a youngster growing up in Pittsburgh, Mark Cuban had several passions. Most of all, young Mark enjoyed sports, all sports. Hockey, basketball, football, baseball—you name it—he liked it. He particularly idolized the professional sports teams based in his hometown. Predictably, many of Mark's classmates in the public school he attended had a similar interest in sports, but Mark also had other interests that set him apart from his peers, for example, dancing. Mark inherited a fondness for ballet and Russian folk dances from his father's side of the family. His grandfather had immigrated to the United States from Russia around the turn of the century. On arriving, immigration authorities had Americanized the young Russian's surname from Chobanisky to "Cuban."

Adolescents can often be unkind. Despite the strong interest in sports that he shared with most of his male classmates, Mark Cuban's enthusiasm for dancing—ballet, in particular—made him the butt of many jokes and the target of considerable ridicule on the playground. Not helping matters was the fact that Mark was overweight and wore thick glasses to correct his severe nearsightedness. As a young teenager, Mark easily tipped the scales at more than 200 pounds, which spurred less-than-empathetic classmates to hang the nickname "Pudgy" on him.

A turning point occurred in Mark's life in 1971 when he asked his father for a new pair of sneakers. The elder Cuban, who earned a modest income as an auto upholsterer, told his 12-year-old young son that he did not need a new pair of shoes. When Mark persisted, his father struck a deal with him. Mark could buy anything he wanted with money that he earned. Most 12-year-olds would have been disappointed with that offer, but not Mark. After making certain that his father was serious, he was off in search of a job. Recognizing that he faced limited job opportunities given his age, Mark considered his options. Instead of signing up for a paper route, he decided to become a salesman—a door-to-door salesman. Why? Because he had heard that there was a lot of money to be made in sales.

Mark launched his career in sales by hawking garbage bags to residents of his neighborhood. Years later when asked why he chose to sell that item, Cuban looked incredulously at his questioner and remarked, "Who doesn't need garbage bags?"[1] Mark soon expanded his product line to include fire extinguishers, magazines, greeting cards, and even powdered milk. Despite his physical appearance, Mark's gleeful and vaguely charming personality allowed him to rack up impressive sales. True to his word, Mark's father allowed him to buy whatever he wanted with his earnings. Soon, the young entrepreneur's closet sported a collection of new sneakers.

Buying "things" was a pleasure that Mark Cuban learned as a pre-teen but perfected as an adult. Nearly three decades after he purchased his own sneakers, Mark's buying habits were legendary among his friends and family members. In the late 1990s, the avid sports enthusiast decided that he wanted to purchase a professional sports team. First, he set his sights on buying the Pittsburgh Penguins, the National Hockey League team that played in his childhood hometown. When that deal fell through, he made an offer for the Dallas Mavericks, the National Basketball Association (NBA) team that represented the hometown he had adopted as a young adult. This time, he was successful, paying the princely sum of $280 million to purchase a majority interest in the Mavericks from H. Ross Perot, Jr. Could Mark Cuban afford this luxury? Easily. Thanks to a fairly brief but successful foray into the "New Economy," the former garbage bag salesman's net worth at the time hovered somewhere between $2 and $3 billion.

YO QUIERO TACO BELL

When Mark Cuban reached high school, he had a strong desire to be "cool," not unlike most teenagers. But, he apparently never achieved that objective. A friend recalled that in high school Mark's hair looked like it was cut with toenail clippers. He also was known for his fashion *faux pas*, particularly the pair of skintight, turquoise Versace pants that he liked to wear. While in high school, he shook the demeaning nickname he had acquired several years earlier but was soon tagged with another. His new nickname, "Boris," was an apparent reference to Boris Karloff, the movie star who played the big screen's original Frankenstein.

Throughout high school, Mark continued earning his own spending money, principally as a Jack-of-all-products salesman. When it came time for him to go to college, Mark was responsible for paying his own way. He decided that he wanted to major in business and that he wanted to attend a university whose business school ranked among the nation's top ten. He chose Indiana University—the university whose top ten business school had the lowest tuition. Shortly after arriving in Bloomington, Indiana, Mark resolved to make significant changes in his life. One of his personal goals had always been to be different: "I wanted to stand out."[2] At college, Mark decided that he wanted to stand out in a different way, in a positive way. So, he undertook a complete self-improvement program "to control my destiny."[3] Within a few months, Mark had lost a signifi-

---

1. R. Hoffer, "Dallas Maverick: Iconoclastic Dotcom Billionaire Mark Cuban Thought It Might Be a Lot of Fun to Own an NBA Franchise—Even the Woeful Team in Big D—and Guess What? He Was Right," *Sports Illustrated* (online), 6 November 2000.

2. M. Sager, "Yeaahhh baa baaaaabyy!" *Esquire* (online), April 2000.

3. Hoffer, "Dallas Maverick: Iconoclastic Dotcom Billionaire."

cant amount of weight, become an avid rugby player, and been elected president of a freshman dorm. For the first time in his life, Mark was surrounded by supportive friends.

To finance his first two years of college, Mark sold off a large coin and stamp collection that he had accumulated during his high school years. When that collection was gone, he resorted once more to being an entrepreneur. He sold dancing lessons, hosted "retro" disco parties at a local National Guard armory, and eventually opened a very popular and profitable nightclub that catered to Indiana University's 30,000 students.

Upon graduating from IU with a business degree, Cuban returned to Pittsburgh to work in the banking industry. After a brief stint with a large bank, he decided to join several of his college buddies in the sunny, rapidly growing, and, in his opinion, very "hip" city of Dallas, Texas. When he arrived in 1982, he took a job as a software salesman. Cuban quickly realized that computer software and hardware were beginning to revolutionize the business world and he wanted to be involved in that revolution. After spending one year learning as much as he could about computer software, hardware, and related business applications, Cuban created his own company, MicroSolutions. His firm provided a wide range of computer-related consulting services to businesses, but Cuban specialized in integrating the growing number of personal computers being acquired by his clients into local area networks (LANs). Ironically, when he founded MicroSolutions, Cuban did not own a personal computer, nor had he ever taken a computer programming class during college or afterwards.

Cuban's firm faced long odds against being successful. The firm had a minimum amount of capital, a small staff with limited experience in the field, and had to cope with a hostile economic environment. During the 1980s, scores of computer whizzes in each major metropolitan area established consulting firms to accommodate the computing needs of local businesses. Cutthroat competition prevailed among these firms as they struggled to capture their fair share of the consulting engagements within their limited geographical market. Despite the long odds he faced, Mark Cuban succeeded in making MicroSolutions one of the best-known and most profitable computer consulting firms in the Dallas-Fort Worth Metroplex. From 1983 through 1990, Cuban did not take a vacation, working nonstop to make certain that the needs and expectations of his clients were being fully met. To motivate his employees to do the same, Cuban encouraged them to become part owners of MicroSolutions, which many of them did.

By 1990, MicroSolutions had more than 80 employees, annual billings of $30 million, and boasted several high-profile clients, including Neiman Marcus and Zales. MicroSolutions also ranked among *Inc.* magazine's top 500 fastest growing, privately held firms in the nation. At the age of 31, an exhausted Cuban decided that it was time to retire and enjoy the "good life." So, he sold his firm to CompuServe, netting several million dollars, and headed west to Los Angeles. For the next four years, Cuban reports that he played the "the wild and crazy guy" role that Steve Martin made popular on *Saturday Night Live*.[4] He lived on Manhattan Beach a few miles west of downtown L.A., increased his personal fortune by joining the first generation of online day traders, dated several Hollywood starlets,

4. Sager, "Yeaahhh baa baaaaabyy!"

and took acting lessons. The former computer geek won small roles in a couple of forgettable movies. Not long after he failed to win a coveted spot in a Taco Bell commercial, Cuban decided it was time to return to Dallas and reunite with several of his old friends.

KINGS OF THE INTERNET

One of the first friends that Mark Cuban looked up when he returned to Dallas was Todd Wagner, a lawyer and CPA who had attended IU with him. Wagner and Cuban shared several interests but the most passionate was a love for the Hoosier basketball team of Indiana University—a team coached by the irrepressible and irascible Bobby Knight. Wagner was well aware of Cuban's strong computer skills and asked him if it would be possible to listen to IU basketball games over the Internet. Both men had been to parties where radio transmissions of IU games had been "broadcast" to partygoers with the help of a telephone line connection and a set of improvised speakers. Always up to a challenge and with plenty of time on his hands, Cuban set about the task of bringing IU basketball to Dallas. After studying the problem for a short while and then applying his rusty software development and integration skills, Cuban was soon inviting his friends over to enjoy crisp and clear radio broadcasts of IU basketball games delivered by his personal computer via the Internet. Cuban liked to joke that he converted his powerful $4,000 personal computer into a $6 radio, all for the love of his red-clad Hoosiers.

The ease with which Cuban was able to divert radio transmissions from several hundred miles away through his personal computer caused Todd Wagner to begin pondering whether this new "technology" could be exploited for business purposes. Wagner reasoned that there were literally millions of orphaned and rabid sports fans around the nation who were hundreds or thousands of miles away from their Philadelphia Phillies, USC Trojans, Green Bay Packers, or Oklahoma Sooners. Just like Mark Cuban and himself, those fans relied on *ESPN Sportscenter* to keep them in touch with their favorite teams but hungered to hear live radio broadcasts of those teams' games. Wagner discussed the idea with Cuban. Soon, the attorney/CPA and the retired computer consultant were mapping out a new business to deliver radio broadcasts of sporting events to Internet users scattered far and wide across the United States.

Cuban and Wagner believed that the largest market for their online service would be the millions of white-collar workers who spent eight or more hours per day cooped in an office with an Internet-connected computer sitting an arm's length away. No doubt, tapping into the radio broadcast of a sporting event would shorten the workday and reduce the stress level of that army of workers, many of whom were addicted to sports programming. Cuban and Wagner also realized that over the following few years there was projected to be a large increase in the number of home-based, Internet-linked computers, which would create another sizable market for their service. Although they initially intended to deliver only radio transmissions over the Internet, they expected that technological developments in coming years would allow them to provide video transmissions of sporting events over the Internet as well. In short, the two unlikely business pioneers set out on a mission to convert the Internet from a static, text-based medium to a medium that would deliver audio and video transmissions on a real-time basis.[5]

One critical plank was missing from the sketchy business plan mapped out by Wagner and Cuban, namely, how would the proposed business generate revenues? While Todd Wagner studied that issue, Mark Cuban went about the task of creating a prototype of their online service, which they named AudioNet. With an investment of a few thousand dollars, Cuban soon had a skeletal version of AudioNet up and running. An unused bedroom in Cuban's apartment served as the production room and corporate headquarters for the new company. The two owners launched AudioNet by reaching an agreement with a local radio station to broadcast its programming over the Internet. In the early days of AudioNet, Cuban and Wagner enjoyed telling their listeners that, "We are the Kings of the Internet," a declaration that typically produced a batch of sarcastic e-mails to their royal highnesses.[6] Cuban and Wagner enjoyed receiving those tacky responses. Why? Because those e-mails proved that at least some Internet surfers were tuning in to their broadcasts.

As more and more radio stations signed up for the AudioNet service, Mark Cuban's bedroom became a cluttered maze of computer equipment and cables. On one occasion, Cuban tripped over a cable, sending AudioNet into a prolonged blackout. When Cuban's bedroom could no longer contain the company, he and Wagner moved AudioNet's operations to a vacant warehouse in the trendy Deep Ellum section of downtown Dallas. Within a few months, the roof of that warehouse was crammed with an impressive crop of satellite dishes. Collectively, those dishes gave AudioNet the second largest satellite downlink capability in the state of Texas, second only to NASA, the federal space agency.

By the fall of 1996, AudioNet was broadcasting more than 80 radio stations' programming over the Internet. If Internet surfers tired of listening to sporting events or music, they could use AudioNet to tune into the BBC to find out what was going on around the world, snoop on police scanner transmissions from Los Angeles or New York City, or listen to flight control communications from Dallas-Fort Worth Airport. In exchange for broadcasting a radio station's programming over the Internet, AudioNet typically received on-air time slots from that station—slots that they then sold to advertisers. The company also sold to advertisers short time slots that Internet surfers listened to before they joined AudioNet programming and online banner ads that surfers viewed while tuned to AudioNet.

As the Internet grew in popularity, the term "webcasting" was often applied to several online services, including AudioNet and the screensaver service marketed by PointCast. In fact, in the mid-1990s, journalists often referred to AudioNet and PointCast as the two leading webcasters on the Internet, although the services provided by the companies were very different. PointCast relied on "push technology" to deliver news, sports, weather, and other information in a screensaver format to Internet users. Like AudioNet, PointCast targeted office workers. Various technological problems and poor management decisions quickly led to the demise of PointCast and several other first-generation webcasters during the mid- and late 1990s.[7]

---

5. *Ibid.*

6. J. N. Patoski, "Mark Cuban and Todd Wagner," *Texas Monthly*, September 1999, 122.

7. For a discussion of the life and times of PointCast, see Case 3.1, "PointCast, FallFast."

Despite the many companies that helped pioneer one or more approaches to webcasting, Mark Cuban insists that his company was the original webcaster. "Broadcasting on the Internet was an industry we invented."[8] Rather than the term "webcasting," Internet financial analysts and journalists often refer to the line of business founded by Cuban and Wagner as the "streaming audio and video industry." *Business Week* provided the following description of the "streaming" technology that was developed in the 1990s and is an indispensable feature of webcasters' operations. "A method of compressing multimedia information so it can be sent over the Internet in a continual stream. With streaming, PC owners can start seeing and hearing [audio or video] clips within a few seconds instead of waiting for an entire file to download."[9]

Revealing Victoria's Secret

Mark Cuban and Todd Wagner changed their company's name to Broadcast.com in the late 1990s not only to capitalize on the dot-com mania sweeping Wall Street but also to provide a more accurate description of the business since it had become involved in video webcasting in addition to audio webcasting. By that time frame, several companies, such as Sun Microsystems and Cisco Systems, had engineered significant improvements in network infrastructure, storage capacity, and compression technology. These technological advancements enhanced the feasibility and quality of online broadcasts. Likewise, these advances, when coupled with the growing interest in the business opportunities presented by webcasting, drew increasing attention to Broadcast.com within the rapidly evolving world of e-commerce, despite the fact that the young company had yet to produce a profit.

Several large venture capital firms hoping to purchase a sizable ownership interest in Broadcast.com courted Mark Cuban and Todd Wagner. The two young businessmen rebuffed those overtures. They realized that by accepting such investments, they would forfeit some degree of their autonomy. Venture capital firms nearly always demand to have input into key strategic and operating decisions made by the firms in which they invest. Instead of accepting investments from venture capital firms, Cuban and Wagner sought major investors that would allow them to continue directing the development of Broadcast.com. Eventually, Motorola and Intel, two high-tech heavyweights, agreed to invest in the company under those general terms. Not only did those two companies provide Broadcast.com with much needed financing, they also gave the firm a much needed measure of credibility with Wall Street, major banks, and potential business partners.

Cuban and Wagner used the funds provided by Motorola and Intel to expand Broadcast.com's existing services and to add additional services. By 1998, Internet surfers could use Broadcast.com to listen to live audio broadcasts from nearly 350 radio stations and to view the programming of 17 televisions station. Surfers who visited the *Broadcast.com* website could also access an audio book library, a

---

8. Patoski, "Mark Cuban and Todd Wagner."

9. R. D. Hof and E. Lesly, "Don't Surf Us, We'll Surf You," *Business Week*, 9 September 1996, 108.

large library of music CDs referred to as the CD Jukebox, and a variety of special events broadcasts. These latter broadcasts included President Clinton's video-taped grand jury testimony during 1998 and live transmissions from cameras posted on Bourbon Street during New Orleans' Mardi Gras celebration.

Broadcast.com entered the B2B or business-to-business sector of the Internet economy by offering audio and video conferencing capabilities to large corporations and other organizations. Webcasting gave large corporations, particularly the growing number of multinational companies with operations scattered across the globe, a readily available and relatively inexpensive way of reaching a large number of their employees and other groups simultaneously. Corporations could use Broadcast.com's services for online broadcasts of shareholder meetings, earnings announcements, financial analysts' reports, product launches, and other important events. In the words of a *Forbes* reporter, webcasting is "a way of offering businesses their very own TV stations."[10] Companies, such as Texaco, paid as much as $350,000 for one Broadcast.com webcast. By 1998, Mark Cuban and Todd Wagner were convinced that corporate broadcasting, rather than webcasts of sporting events, would likely be their company's primary source of revenue, at least for the foreseeable future. Cuban served as an enthusiastic spokesperson for his company's B2B broadcasting services. "Every company is a potential customer for us, because every company can benefit from real-time communications."[11]

Corporate webcasts accounted for nearly one-half of Broadcast.com's 1998 revenues. During the fourth quarter of that year alone, the company signed up 114 new corporate clients, a 75 percent increase over the prior quarter. Despite the growing number of B2B clients reeled in by Broadcast.com's aggressive sales staff, its revenues were still modest by most corporate benchmarks and the company continued to post operating losses each quarter. For all of 1998, the company reported a net loss of $16.4 million on revenues of $22.4 million. The entire webcasting industry had revenues estimated at only $288 million for 1998. Nevertheless, the existing and potential business applications of webcasting continued to fuel strong interest in Broadcast.com within the investment community. Media Metrix, an Internet market research firm, has conservatively estimated that webcasting in its various forms will produce nearly $3 billion of annual revenues by 2005,[12] while a media industry expert has predicted that by 2008 annual webcasting revenues will approach $20 billion.[13]

In July 1998, Cuban and Wagner took their company public. The prominent Wall Street investment banker, Morgan Stanley, managed the Broadcast.com IPO. Morgan Stanley assigned its highest profile financial analyst, Mary Meeker, to issue periodic reports on the company's future prospects. The stock sold initially at $18 per share but reached an intra-day high of $68 on the first day it was traded. At the time, that huge one-day increase was the largest ever recorded by a newly issued stock. Within six months, the stock had zoomed to $200 per share. Mark Cuban reigned as Broadcast.com's largest stockholder, owning 28 percent of the company's stock. On July 16, 1998, the date Broadcast.com went public, Cuban went from wealthy to super-wealthy in a matter of hours. A few months later, he

---

10. A. L. Penenberg, "Infomercial.com," *Forbes*, 8 March 1999, 116.

11. *Ibid.*

12. D. Bloom, "Playing for Keeps," *Red Herring*, 15 August 2001, 44.

13. N. Gross and S. V. Brull, "The Net's Next Battle Royal," *Business Week*, 28 June 1999, 108.

joined a very elite club, the billionaire's club. Cuban revels in telling journalists, friends, and new acquaintances the exact minute he became a billionaire, which, for the record, was 1:16 P.M.., January 8, 1999.

Motivating employees by making them part owners of their employer was a strategy that worked well for Mark Cuban at MicroSolutions. He and Todd Wagner used that same strategy at Broadcast.com. They regularly offered their employees an opportunity to invest in the company. Many of those employees purchased Broadcast.com stock at $0.50 per share well before Cuban and Wagner had any thoughts or aspirations of taking the firm public. Approximately 300 of Broadcast.com's 330 employees, including dozens of clerical and other workers with modest salaries, would eventually become millionaires thanks to the stock they purchased in the company.

The year 1999 proved to be an exciting one for Broadcast.com. In February of that year, the company hosted the most hyped webcast to that point on the Internet, a Victoria's Secret fashion show. An estimated two million Internet surfers from around the globe viewed that online extravaganza. Technical problems caused by the unexpectedly huge audience for the webcast prevented throngs of other frustrated surfers from logging on to the free exhibition. Although the press focused on the recurring technical glitches that disrupted the Victoria's Secret webcast, the show triggered widespread interest in webcasting within the general public and the business community. Investors expected that the technological problems that hampered webcasting would eventually be resolved, creating huge revenue potential for companies such as Broadcast.com.

The second and more dramatic development involving Broadcast.com during 1999 was the purchase of the company by Yahoo!. In August 1999, Yahoo! bought the company from its existing shareholders by issuing them shares of Yahoo!'s common stock in exchange for their Broadcast.com stock. Following the buyout, Mark Cuban's fortune rose to an estimated $3 billion. Todd Wagner, who had invested considerably less than his partner in Broadcast.com during its early years, received a comparatively modest three-quarters of one billion dollars for his ownership interest in the company.

In looking back on the brief history of Broadcast.com, scads of business journalists and analysts have studied the company to uncover the factors most responsible for its success. According to Mark Cuban, a few readily obvious but typically under-appreciated factors led to the rapid rise of Broadcast.com. The critically important "first-mover advantage" is one of those factors. By definition, the company that invents a new line of business, such as Broadcast.com, has a "head start" on its competitors. Another important factor contributing to Broadcast.com's success was the company's refusal to "worship" technology. Cuban notes that he and Wagner "were agnostic about technology."[14] Unlike many founders of Internet companies, Cuban and Wagner did not become tied to any one feature or aspect of technology that their firm pioneered. If they found that an element of their technological infrastructure was inferior to an innovation developed by a competitor, they quickly discarded their concept and integrated the competitor's enhancement into their business's operations. Cuban also stresses that he and Wagner focused intently on "staying ahead of the technology curve." Internet and information technology was changing so rapidly during the late

---

14. Patoski, "Mark Cuban and Todd Wagner."

1990s that they had to continually anticipate how those technologies would evolve. Based on those anticipated changes, Cuban and Wagner adjusted their firm's business model to take advantage of the business opportunities they expected to arise as a result of those evolutionary changes.

When asked to pinpoint the reason why Broadcast.com was a success, Todd Wagner does not disagree with the observations made by his friend and colleague. But, he also suggests that Mark Cuban's fiery personality and refuse-to-lose attitude easily rank among the key factors responsible for Broadcast.com's success. Despite the wild and crazy guy persona that Mark Cuban has cultivated, Todd Wagner insists that his friend is a disciplined and intellectually gifted businessperson who simply outhustles his competitors. "What people don't understand about Mark is how brilliant he is. He will outwork and outthink you every time."[15]

WEBCASTING: CHALLENGES, OPPORTUNITIES AND THE VIRTUAL MATERIAL GIRL

In November 2000, the "Material Girl," otherwise known as Madonna, crushed the previous record for a webcast audience when she drew more than nine million Internet surfers to an online concert. That webcast demonstrated once more the tremendous potential webcasting had as an entertainment medium. But, the Madonna webcast also confirmed that after several years of intense research and development activities, the technology underlying webcasting had not advanced to the point that this new medium was ready for "prime time viewing." Many Internet surfers who viewed the concert complained that the video was coarse and jerky at times, while other viewers had their online connections repeatedly crash.

In commenting on Madonna's concert, an executive of the Internet service provider that co-hosted the event observed that webcasting is "a promotional tool now. . . . Making money in the long term will be about pay-per-view as in any non-free-to-air station."[16] Several months later, a webcasting specialist employed by a leading Internet firm echoed that same sentiment. "There is a lot of talk about pay-per-view on the Internet: that people would go online and subscribe to this, that and the other. The reality is the quality is not good enough to charge for yet."[17] This latter individual quickly added, however, that although no one had paid to view Madonna's online concert, her record company estimated that the concert generated an additional 80,000 sales of her new CD.

Another problem impeding the development of entertainment webcasting has been the unexpectedly slow spread of broadband Internet access into the home PC market. Early forecasts that projected rapid growth in entertainment webcasting hinged on the assumption that home Internet users would pay the higher access charges for broadband Internet links when they became available. That

15. Hoffer, "Dallas Maverick: Iconoclastic Dotcom Billionaire."

16. A. O'Connor, "Material Girl Brings Material Gains to MSN," *Financial Times*, 30 November 2000, 5.

17. A. Ward, "While Multinational Companies Are Starting to Use Live Webcasting for Presentations and Video-Conferences Between Offices, Real-Time Webcasting on a Mass Scale Is Still Some Way Off," *Financial Times*, 4 April 2001, 8.

prediction has not been borne out. Even after broadband access comes to their neighborhoods, most home Internet users refuse to sign up for the new service, choosing to rely instead on their notoriously slow modems that cope poorly with streaming transmissions. Those sluggish modems create a troublesome roadblock for entertainment companies and other firms that want to use webcast programming to reach home PC users.

Despite the persistent challenges facing video webcasters following the turn of the century, industry insiders continued to maintain that pay-per-view entertainment programs over the Internet would soon become a reality. In fact, an executive of one of the leading media companies in the entertainment industry, HBO, reported that his firm was pursuing a wide range of initiatives involving the webcasting of entertainment programming. In April 2001, the NBA became the first professional sports league to webcast a professional sporting event live when it broadcast online a game between the Sacramento Kings and the Dallas Mavericks, the team owned by Mark Cuban. That free webcast was hosted by RealNetworks, which developed the software that made audio and video streaming possible on the Internet. Initially, RealNetworks had served strictly as a technology supplier to Broadcast.com and other webcasters and Internet-based companies. But, when RealNetworks' executives recognized the business opportunities created by their technology, they decided that their company would become a webcaster in its own right.

As the webcasting industry struggled to make online entertainment programming technologically feasible and economically viable, most webcasting companies focused their business development efforts on two types of services. One of those services was the old standby—the service that prompted the creation of the webcasting industry by AudioNet, namely, radio broadcasting over the Internet. By early 2001, more than 4,000 of the 14,000-plus radio stations in the United States beamed their transmission signals through the virtual corridors of the Internet. The dominant audio webcaster at the time was WebRadio, which webcast the programming of more than 2,000 radio stations, easily surpassing the number of stations serviced by Yahoo! Broadcast Services, the Yahoo! division that absorbed Broadcast.com.

The steady revenue stream that many webcasters received from their radio clients was threatened by a new federal statute passed by Congress in 1998, the Digital Millennium Copyright Act (DMCA), which was subsequently signed into law by President Clinton. This new federal statute mandated that radio stations and other businesses rebroadcasting music over the Internet pay royalties to the copyright owners. These royalties would be funneled through a consortium of organizations within the music industry, most notably the Recording Industry Association of America (RIAA). Since the early days of the radio industry, radio stations had paid royalties on music they broadcast. Radio stations that transmitted their signals over the Internet would be required to pay two royalties on their music broadcasts if federal authorities enforced the DMCA, serving to narrow further the already modest profit margins of most radio stations. In late 2000, the federal agency responsible for enforcing the DMCA, the U.S. Copyright Office, ruled that the statute's stipulations were legally enforceable and began making arrangements to collect the mandated royalties from webcasters.

The DMCA promises to be detrimental to not only radio stations but webcasters as well. Many radio stations have warned that they may be forced to drop their webcasts, which would eliminate an important source of revenues for webcasters. When asked to comment on the DMCA, Mark Cuban blasted the new federal statute and encouraged webcasters to "move your servers to Canada" where they would be outside of the DMCA's purview.[18] Webcasters ignored Cuban's recommendation and instead chose to put their faith in several industry experts and lobbyists who believe that either the federal courts or regulatory authorities will eventually grant online broadcasters some degree of relief from the onerous requirements of the DMCA.

The controversy over the DMCA and the potentially mortal impact that it might have on audio webcasting caused many webcasters to concentrate more heavily on their other major service and revenue producer, video webcasting for business applications. The technological restraints that have hampered the development of video webcasting for entertainment purposes have been less of an issue for video webcasting for business applications since these latter applications do not require television-quality transmissions. Streaming audio and video have proven to be particularly well suited for new advertising applications on the World Wide Web. For example, advertisers have developed creative methods for weaving advertisements and even online shopping options within webcasts. Advertisers have also used streaming technology to develop creative and eye-catching e-mail promotions.

In the fall of 2000, webcasters specializing in business applications of streaming technology received an enormous boost when the Securities and Exchange Commission (SEC), the federal agency that oversees the capital markets and the financial reporting practices of public companies, adopted a new rule known as Regulation Fair Disclosure. This new rule, commonly referred to as Regulation FD, dictates that when public companies release important financial information, that information must be released simultaneously to the investing public and other interested parties. In the past, public companies had routinely disclosed such information to financial analysts and other powerful parties within the investment community before the information was released to the general public. To comply with this new rule, companies needed a cost-effective method of widely and instantaneously disseminating their financial disclosures. They found what they were searching for in webcasting. "To comply with the law, companies are looking for ways to get the word out to everyone at the same time when they make an announcement. Webcasting is an easy and cheap way to comply with the rule."[19]

In fact, the SEC adopted Regulation FD with webcasting in mind. A representative of that federal agency pointed out that, "Technological limitations no longer provide an excuse for abiding the threats to market integrity that selective disclosure represents."[20] During the fourth quarter of 2000, more than 3,500 public companies used webcasting to comply with Regulation FD while reporting their quarterly financial results in conference calls to analysts. Two years earlier, only four companies had webcast their conference calls. Industry observers expect that the revenues produced by business webcasting, particularly the windfall of revenues stemming from Regulation FD, will lead to enhancements in

---

18. J. Mack, "Streaming Industry Headed to Canada," *ZDNet News* (online) 7 December 1999.

19. K. Hoover, "Companies Using Web to Spread the News, New SEC Rule Is Fueling the Trend Toward 'Webcasting,'" *Investor's Business Daily*, 26 October 2000, 1.

20. *Ibid.*

streaming technology that should promote the further development and economic feasibility of entertainment webcasting.

A Few Shades South of Handsome

Mark Cuban's status as one of the newest members of the New Economy's Billionaires Club attracted considerable publicity, not all of which was positive. A lengthy biographical article in *Esquire* provided an often less-than-complimentary view of his personal life and described him as being "a few shades south of handsome."[21] Cuban seemed unaffected by his bad press, including the comments on his personal appearance. No doubt, a few billion dollars makes it much easier to dismiss critics.

Unlike many of the billionaires created by the Internet, Cuban sold the source of most of his newly found wealth as soon as possible. Federal regulations prohibited Cuban from selling his Yahoo! stock during the six months immediately following the buyout of Broadcast.com. But, when that period elapsed, Cuban quickly disposed of most of his Yahoo! stock. Cuban later explained that he recognized most Internet stocks, including Yahoo!'s, were "preposterously" overpriced and would almost certainly fall sharply at some point. As he predicted, the Internet Bubble popped in early 2000, shortly after he sold most of his Yahoo! stock, sending the stock prices of Yahoo! and other Internet companies into a dramatic and prolonged nosedive.

Following Yahoo!'s buyout of Broadcast.com, Mark Cuban and Todd Wagner accepted executive positions with Yahoo! Broadcast Services. However, a few months later, both chose to leave Yahoo! to pursue other interests. Wagner became involved in several philanthropic projects, while Cuban focused most of his time and energy on his new hobby, NBA basketball, after acquiring the Dallas Mavericks in January 2000. Cuban also spent considerable time flying around the country and the globe in the $41 million jet that he purchased on the Internet, which reportedly still qualifies as the largest B2C (business-to-consumer) transaction ever consummated on the Web. Cuban killed time as well by partying with friends in the 25,000 square-foot mansion that he purchased in a ritzy section of Dallas and by zapping "brainstorming" e-mails several times per day to Don Nelson, the curmudgeonly but likable coach of the Mavericks. Apparently, those e-mails suggested personnel changes and other recommendations to improve the win-loss record of the hapless Mavericks. Nelson simply ignored most of the e-mails. But, the team did act on one recommendation made by Cuban, signing NBA "bad boy" and sometimes cross-dresser Dennis Rodman to a contract. In fact, Cuban personally coaxed Rodman out of retirement. Rodman's combustible personality proved to be even too much for the notoriously open-minded Cuban. After a few weeks, Cuban released Rodman.

Despite his tremendous success as a businessperson, Mark Cuban is probably best known for his courtside antics during Mavericks games. He has often appeared on *ESPN Sportscenter* berating referees, belittling opposing players, and even rushing onto the court to defend a Maverick threatened by an opponent.

---

21. Sager, "Yeaahhh baa baaaaabyy!"

Such antics have resulted in the NBA's front office levying several stiff fines on Cuban. Those fines have had little impact, financially or otherwise, on the self-assured Cuban who is known not only for his ostentatious spending habits but also for being extremely generous to others. He often jokes that the massive wealth dumped on him by the Internet craze of the late 1990s insulates him from any further money worries during his lifetime, even if he behaves "moronically" at times. During an interview with a *Sports Illustrated* reporter, Cuban remarked, "Say . . . through a series of incredibly moronic moves, I lose $100 million. Oh, gee! What does that leave me?"[22]

QUESTIONS

1. Many companies use streaming audio and video on their websites and in on-line advertisements and promotional materials. Find an example of an online use of streaming technology by a company. Identify that company and describe the given application of streaming technology. What do you believe the company was attempting to accomplish by using streaming technology? Do you believe that objective was accomplished?

2. One of the keys to the success of Broadcast.com, in Mark Cuban's view, was the "first-mover" advantage that it gained in the webcasting industry. Briefly discuss the potential disadvantages that a first mover in a new line of business may face.

3. "Staying ahead of the technology curve" was another factor that contributed to the success of Broadcast.com, in the opinion of Mark Cuban. Identify an Internet company that you believe failed to stay ahead of the technology curve. (Do not choose a company that is the primary focus of one of the cases in this text.) Defend and explain your choice.

4. Companies involved in the webcasting industry typically fall into one of three categories: technology suppliers, content creators, and distributors (webcasters). Broadcast.com was considered a "distributor." Identify one technology supplier and one content creator within the webcasting industry. Describe each of these companies with a particular focus on the types of services they provide or the products they develop.

5. Do you agree with Mark Cuban's position that the DMCA unfairly penalizes radio stations that rebroadcast copyrighted music over the Internet? Why or why not? Briefly describe or explain the intent of federal copyright laws.

6. Mark Cuban believes that an effective method of motivating employees is allowing and encouraging them to purchase an ownership interest in their employer. Identify other methods that companies can use to motivate employees. Relying on your own judgment, list these methods from most to least effective in terms of their motivational value.

7. Research online or hard copy databases to identify recent technological developments involving streaming media. List these developments in a bullet format and explain their significance to webcasting firms and companies that utilize webcasting services.

---

22. Hoffer, "Dallas Maverick: Iconoclastic Dotcom Billionaire."

E-BUSTS

PointCast, FallFast

*"In information technology . . . being the
next big thing is no sure thing."*

Ken Auletta

As the owners of PointCast sat around the conference table glumly mulling over the buyout offer made for their company, no doubt two words reverberated silently in each of their minds: "If only. . . ." Less than two years earlier, the son of media mogul Rupert Murdoch had offered to purchase PointCast for $450 million. The present offer was less impressive. Some $443 million less impressive, to be exact.

In early 1996, PointCast, Inc., launched the PointCast Network. Utilizing "push" technology, this new Internet service delivered streams of personalized news and other information to its subscribers in a screensaver format. Seen as a killer app by many technophobes, PointCast never fulfilled its great expectations. In filing an obituary for the company, one business reporter noted that PointCast "fell victim to management missteps, poor execution, and frenetic technological change."[1] PointCast's founder and former chief executive officer (CEO), Christopher Hassett, provided a different spin on the company's demise. "We had a lot of luck. . . . We just never had enough to get us over the top."[2]

BRINGING ORDER TO CHAOS

In 1984, Christopher Hassett graduated from the University of Massachusetts at Lowell, a small state-supported institution located in northeastern Massachusetts just a few miles from the New Hampshire border. Trained as an electrical engineer, Hassett was an entrepreneur at heart. Shortly after graduation, Hassett established a small company to develop a computer chip to increase the speed of

---

1. L. Himelstein, "The Rise and Fall of an Internet Star," *Business Week*, 26 April 1999, 88.

2. *Ibid.*

laser printers. The product worked very well and Hassett soon accepted a lucrative offer to sell his company to Adobe Systems. Hassett also accepted a top-level job with Adobe but became restless within a few months and decided to strike out on his own again.

Like many computer enthusiasts, Hassett was both fascinated and frustrated by the Internet and the World Wide Web. The treasure trove of information buried within the Web and the complex and often tediously slow process required to retrieve that information triggered Hassett's entrepreneurial genius. Rather than Internet users being forced to extract or pull information from the information superhighway, why not have information they needed or wanted delivered or "pushed" directly to them online? Hassett's concept of changing from a "pull" to a "push" mode of accessing information served as the foundation for a new company he formed in 1992. Hassett, his wife, and his brother pooled their resources and created a small company that would provide a personalized newspaper to Internet users. He chose to locate the new company in Cupertino, California, in the Silicon Valley region of the Golden State. The young entrepreneur wanted his colleagues and subordinates to be immersed in Silicon Valley's vibrant, high-tech culture.

During the early 1990s, Hassett and his associates refined the concept of an online newspaper, developed the necessary technology to support that service, and searched for deep-pocketed parties to finance the venture. Several investors quickly bought in to a key premise underlying Hassett's new service: the need to help Internet users cope with, and sort through, the huge amount of information they were being bombarded with on a daily and even hourly basis, thanks to the information superhighway. Increasingly, Internet traffic suffered from logjams and frustrated users complained of their inability to track down and access relevant websites. To many Internet surfers, the familiar prefix "www" no longer referred to World Wide Web but instead stood for "World Wide Wait."

Among the early investors in Hassett's new enterprise was the prominent venture capital firm Benchmark Capital. Benchmark and other investors funneled $12 million to Hassett and his partners to get their business off the ground. On February 13, 1996, PointCast, Inc., formally initiated operations with a public announcement that its "pinpoint" or personalized news and information service was available free of charge to Internet users. Any Internet user could simply log on to *www.pointcast.com* and download the PointCast software. Within a few months, PointCast boasted more than one million subscribers and had obtained nearly $40 million of additional capital from investors.

The PointCast Network served as a news and information aggregator. PointCast collected news and other information from more than 700 sources scattered across the globe, including such media behemoths as CNN, *The New York Times*, *The Wall Street Journal*, and Reuters. At PointCast's Silicon Valley headquarters, the company's broadcast facility downloaded information fed to it by satellites on a 24-hour basis. PointCast employees then compressed and formatted this information for rebroadcast on the PointCast Network by utilizing the company's trademarked Smart Broadcast technology.

When PointCast subscribers registered with the company, they were asked to provide background information, including their geographic location, the industry in which they worked, and special interests, such as sports in which they participated or that they followed. PointCast used this information to develop a customized broadcast or webcast for each subscriber from its content databases. The six categories or channels of information available to construct these webcasts included companies, news, industries, sports, lifestyle, and weather. Subscribers were also asked to indicate how often they wanted their personal webcast database updated. The PointCast Network transmitted the personalized information requested by each subscriber over the Internet and downloaded it to the subscriber's hard drive. At periodic intervals selected by the subscriber, streams of PointCast information appeared in a screensaver format on the subscriber's personal computer.

The PointCast Network predated personalized information and news delivery services later developed by Yahoo!, AOL, and other Internet companies, which helps explain the enthusiastic response to this new service's arrival on the Internet. Initially, PointCast targeted business professionals as its primary user group. Market research indicated that business professionals ranked among the savviest Internet users and the most likely to be "first wave" adopters of new Internet services. PointCast targeted this group for another reason as well. Hassett's business plan called for PointCast to begin developing webcasts geared specifically for Internet users within individual large companies. These webcasts would include information specific to each of these companies, such as price and volume data for a company's stock, sales and production data, descriptions of new products, customer complaints, internal communications from management, etc.

A critical element of Hassett's business plan for PointCast was including electronic advertisements in the personalized webcasts. In fact, the company's principal revenue source was expected to be advertising—again, subscribers received the PointCast service free of charge. While scanning their personalized webcasts, PointCast subscribers would also view advertising messages in the form of eye-catching banners and other graphics. These advertisements would encourage subscribers to click on them to receive additional information regarding the services or products being marketed. Hassett predicted that PointCast's primary users would have "great demographics." Business professionals tend to be better educated and have higher disposable incomes than other segments of the consumer market.

The demographic profile of PointCast's subscribers lived up to Hassett's prediction. One study revealed that the average household income of a typical Point-Cast subscriber exceeded $100,000 and that nearly 70 percent of the subscribers were college graduates. That same study indicated that PointCast subscribers were nearly three times more likely than the typical Internet user to purchase a product or service online. Most important, the company reported that the average subscriber was exposed to PointCast screens for 2 hours per day. That statistic compared very favorably with the 1.2 hours per week that the typical *Business Week* subscriber spent perusing that periodical.

PointCast's excellent demographics allowed Hassett to attract a bevy of high-profile companies who wanted to market their goods and services on the Point-Cast Network. Microsoft, Kodak, Hewlett-Packard and many other prominent firms were soon flying advertising banners on the PointCast Network in hopes of catching the attention and tapping the pocketbooks of subscribers to Hassett's innovative new service.

GREAT EXPECTATIONS

As PointCast's first full year of operations came to an end, the company and its founder basked in widespread and favorable publicity. CNET, a technology-oriented media company, named Christopher Hassett its newsmaker of the year for 1996. A list of that award's previous winners read like an honor roll of high-tech CEOs: Bill Gates of Microsoft, Marc Andreesen of Netscape, Larry Ellison of Oracle, and Scott McNealy of Sun Microsystems.

Although no companies offered a service directly comparable with the Point-Cast Network, several offered products or services impacted by Hassett's new service. Tim Koogle, the CEO of Yahoo!, worried that PointCast might diminish the public's use of his firm's Internet search engine. Many analysts for the software industry forecast a sharp decline in sales for conventional screensavers, such as the After Dark screensavers marketed by Berkeley Systems. Firms that operated Web browsers were certainly concerned when the March 1997 cover of the high-tech magazine *Wired* announced "Push! Kiss Your Browser Goodbye," suggesting that PointCast's push technology would soon make Web browsers obsolete.

PointCast's technology caught the attention of leading executives in both the software and media industries. Microsoft approached Hassett with a plan for bundling PointCast with the next edition of its Internet Explorer browser. In early 1997, Rupert Murdoch, the top executive of a worldwide media empire that included Australia-based News Corporation and Fox Studios, arranged to have his son, James Murdoch, meet with Christopher Hassett. The younger Murdoch offered to purchase PointCast for $450 million. Hassett did not accept that offer and it was soon rescinded.

Throughout 1996 and early 1997, PointCast's subscription rolls and monthly advertising revenues continued to swell. The popularity of PointCast and push technology were inextricably intertwined. Push technology was being hyped at trade shows across the nation, in the leading media outlets for high-tech industries, and in thousands of Internet chat rooms. "The hysteria around push is mind-boggling. Everywhere you turn, there is an article on the topic or one of 40 vendors hyping their plans."[3] Another commentator suggested that Hassett and his colleagues had stumbled across a killer app that almost certainly would help shape, if not determine, the future of the Internet. The only stumbling block that might prove to be PointCast's undoing, in this observer's mind, would be "aggressive stupidity" on the part of the company's top executives.

> PointCast's insight is so powerful, and its marketing so ahead of that of its competitors, the company has attained an enviable state known as "inertia." In technology, at least, inertia is a wonderful thing—it's a condition in which a company sits atop the heap regardless of logic or reason. This doesn't mean that the people who run PointCast can be saved from any stupidity they might display. But it does mean that they would have to be aggressively stupid. . . .[4]

BUGS AND BUGABOOS

Storm clouds began gathering on PointCast's horizon shortly after James Murdoch's takeover bid for the company failed. During mid-1997, PointCast's man-

---

3. K. Auletta, "Push Comes to Shove in the Valley," *Management Today,* February 1999, 58.

4. S. Alsop, "PointCast and Its Wannabees," *Fortune,* 25 November 1996, 181.

agement came face to face with two monumental challenges that threatened to tarnish the company's superstar status in the Internet services industry. The first challenge resulted from a growing number of complaints filed by PointCast subscribers and their employers. The second challenge stemmed from the sudden appearance of a wave of new Internet-based services that competed directly with PointCast for the attention of Internet users.

Many PointCast subscribers soon tired of the frequent interruptions to their online work time caused by the service's updates being downloaded to their hard drives. Even more problematic for Christopher Hassett's firm was the growing number of complaints filed by companies charging that PointCast's updates "hogged" a large portion of their computer resources. PointCast offered to sell companies a PointCast server that received the periodic updates and then parceled them out to individual users' computers over a PointCast channel created for internal use. Ironically, as large companies began investigating the technical issues posed by PointCast, a related issue arose: did these companies really want their employees spending a considerable portion of their precious 9 to 5 time viewing PointCast screens? The fact that the typical PointCast subscriber spent two hours per day viewing PointCast screens shocked many corporate executives. In fact, many companies purchased a PointCast-blocking software program marketed by a small firm that had recognized the addictive quality of PointCast.

Although PointCast continued to sign up new subscribers during 1997 at a rapid pace, the turnover rate of its subscribers was huge. Two of every three new subscribers discontinued the PointCast service within a few weeks. Eventually, this high turnover rate jeopardized PointCast's ability to recruit companies to advertise over the PointCast Network. One of PointCast's largest advertisers, Hewlett-Packard, stopped advertising on the PointCast Network after learning of the technical glitches posed by the service and users' high turnover rate.

By early 1997, several companies were creating personalized news services that would compete directly with the PointCast Network. Unlike PointCast, most of these new services were Web-based. PointCast had invested millions of dollars to develop an infrastructure to collect information from content providers around the world and to reconfigure that information for distribution on the Internet. Competitors bypassed this tedious process by collecting the news and information content for their personalized news services directly from Web-based sources. In fact, many of PointCast's content providers by this time had established websites to disseminate news and information over the Internet. By relying on Web-based sources, new entrants in the personalized news field enjoyed significant cost and technological advantages over PointCast.

The technical problems posed by the PointCast service for subscribers and growing competitive pressures from external sources created tension among PointCast executives and management personnel. Two factions soon arose within the company. One faction insisted on raising the necessary funds to convert PointCast to a totally Web-based information service. The other faction, led by Christopher Hassett, staunchly defended the existing PointCast Network and refused to consider "trashing" the company's expensive technological infrastructure to move to the Web. One former PointCast executive noted that the debate over this issue became a "religious war" within the company. As the company entered its second year of operations, PointCast management opted to retain the PointCast Network. In effect, Hassett and his subordinates placed a bet on the

PointCast Network, observed a former company insider. "In hindsight, it was a poor bet because the Web allowed people to innovate more quickly than we could."[5]

THE CEO SHUFFLE

Christopher Hassett's failure to accept James Murdoch's takeover offer and his stubborn insistence that the company continue to use the PointCast Network rather than move to a Web-based information service caused members of Point-Cast's board of directors to begin doubting his skills as a CEO. Key members of the board included representatives of the venture capital firms that funded the early development of Hassett's company and that had continued to support its operations since PointCast was not yet profitable. Although recognized as an entrepreneurial visionary by industry analysts, Hassett had never served as the top executive of a major company, particularly a company experiencing severe growth pains and internal dissension. Critics, including key company insiders, complained that Hassett had become swept up in the favorable publicity that accompanied the introduction of PointCast to the marketplace. One former PointCast executive bluntly suggested that all of the attention Hassett received grossly inflated his ego. "The problem was that for Andy Warhol's 15 minutes Chris was the most famous guy on the Internet. He didn't always deal well with the attention."[6]

In the spring of 1997, several PointCast board members approached Hassett and demanded that an experienced CEO from outside the company be brought in to replace him. After several months of goading by PointCast's board, Hassett agreed to step down as the company's CEO. Hassett's resignation sparked an intensive and nationwide search for a new chief executive for PointCast. The company's board hoped to recruit a leading executive in the media industry.

In October 1997, David Dorman, the former CEO of Pacific Bell, accepted an offer to become PointCast's new CEO. Dorman, who was 44 years old at the time, had 17 years of experience in the telecommunications industry but very limited exposure to the media industry or the Internet services industry. Culture shock, no doubt, greeted Dorman upon his arrival at PointCast. His previous company had 50,000 employees, sported strong financial statements, and operated in a highly regulated environment. At PointCast, Dorman would oversee fewer than 300 employees, immediately face a financial crisis due to the company's need for additional capital, and be forced to cope with a freewheeling, development stage industry characterized by limited and sporadic regulatory oversight.

PointCast's workforce also experienced culture shock during the first few weeks of Dorman's tenure. Accustomed to the perpetual optimism of Christopher Hassett, PointCast's employees faced a CEO in Dorman who insisted on a candid and open discussion of the challenges facing the company. Dorman publicly acknowledged the technical glitches that had plagued PointCast from its inception and the competitive pressures posed by new Web-based information services. Most important, Dorman suggested that PointCast had been "overhyped," re-

5. Himelstein, "The Rise and Fall of an Internet Star," 90.

6. Auletta, "Push Comes to Shove," 60.

sulting in unrealistic expectations on the part of both company insiders and external parties.

The first major problem Dorman tackled was PointCast's weak financial condition. By the time Dorman arrived, PointCast's poor operating results had resulted in an accumulated deficit of nearly $50 million for the company. Even more problematic was the minimal cash the company had on hand. To raise funds desperately needed by PointCast, Dorman decided to take the company public with an IPO (initial public offering). PointCast filed the appropriate documents with the Securities and Exchange Commission (SEC) to sell $50 million of its stock to the public in the early summer of 1998. The PointCast stock allocated to the company's executives stood to make them multimillionaires overnight. Dorman alone, stood to reap a windfall of $20 million when PointCast went public.

The SEC's strict disclosure rules required PointCast to provide detailed financial information concerning its operating results over the previous two years and a candid assessment of the risk factors faced by the company. Potential investors were alarmed by PointCast's poor operating results and the ominous technological problems and competitive conditions that the company faced. The public's poor response to PointCast's disclosures caused Dorman to cancel the IPO in July 1998. Dorman then approached executives of several large firms including Time Warner, NBC, and Yahoo!. None of these executives expressed an interest in investing in PointCast the large amount of funds that Dorman believed the company needed to remedy its financial problems.

In the fall of 1998, Dorman struck upon another idea to salvage PointCast. He developed a plan to convert PointCast into a comprehensive online network comparable to America Online (AOL). His plan required several hundred million dollars of capital and a new technological infrastructure for PointCast. Dorman turned to former colleagues in the telecommunications industry to obtain the technological resources needed to implement his plan. Initially, several large telecommunications companies agreed to become partners in the venture. These companies would contribute the hardware and telecommunications elements for the new online network. Next, Dorman approached Microsoft. His plan called for Microsoft to provide much of the software support for the new project and the bulk of the initial investment to finance the project. Dorman's high hopes for the project were dashed in early 1999 when Microsoft suddenly pulled out of the venture. Following Microsoft's decision to withdraw from the project, the syndicate of telecommunications companies quickly lost interest in the project and withdrew as well. Frustrated and disheartened, Dorman resigned as PointCast's CEO in March 1999.

GOODBYE TO POINTCAST

Dorman's departure in early 1999 left PointCast in a more desperate lurch than the one that greeted his arrival in the fall of 1997. The company had almost no cash, its quarterly revenues had fallen to one-half of the previous year's level, and several of its largest clients had canceled their advertising campaigns on the PointCast Network. While the company's remaining executives urgently searched for a well-heeled party to invest in PointCast, they were forced to deal with another distressing problem facing their company.

By early 1999, push technology was being widely ridiculed within the Internet community and by the business press. Technical problems with several push-based services, including PointCast, when coupled with the grossly inflated expectations that had accompanied the introduction of push technology just a few years earlier prompted industry and financial analysts to write articles scorning most push applications. Suddenly, companies such as PointCast went to great efforts to distance themselves from the p-word. "Push technology has become everyone's favorite punching bag. PointCast now runs screaming from the p-word."[7] PointCast dropped all references to push technology from its brochures, other promotional materials, and press releases. "Push" was replaced with phrases such as "knowledge distribution," "information delivery service," and "relevant personalized content delivered seamlessly to a viewer."

By the spring of 1999, scores of services that served essentially the same purpose as PointCast were widely available, most at no cost to users. For example, many media companies began providing daily e-mails to their subscribers that contained hyperlinks to relevant news items. Yahoo! gave Internet users the option of developing their own personalized My Yahoo! that they could use to access daily news and information features of interest to them. The proliferation of these types of services left PointCast with a dwindling number of subscribers each month.

In mid-1999, idealab!, an Internet "incubator," purchased PointCast for the relatively nominal sum of $7 million. idealab! integrated PointCast into its Entry-Point news information service. At the end of March 2000, PointCast's 400,000 remaining subscribers were notified that the service would be discontinued at the end of that month. A little more than four years after PointCast debuted with a huge media splash, it quietly disappeared in an unceremonious exit that went mostly unnoticed and overlooked by the Internet community.

Christopher Hassett's unhappy and unwanted departure from PointCast in 1997 left him free to pursue other ventures. His next big project was PrizePoint, a Web-based business that featured interactive single-player games. Players accumulated points based on the amount of time they spent playing these interactive games, points they could redeem for prizes. Not surprisingly, the principal revenue stream this venture relied upon was payments from advertisers who marketed products and services on the PrizePoint site. In late 1999, Hassett sold Prize-Point to another Internet firm for a reported $40 million.

QUESTIONS

1. Identify what you believe was the key factor that led to PointCast's demise. Defend your answer. In your view, what factors are generally most responsible for the failure of individual companies? Use specific examples to support your choices.
2. List current examples of personalized news delivery services. Do you use any of these services? Choose one of these services. How does this service apparently produce revenue or other economic benefits for the given company or sponsoring organization?

---

7. K. Nash, "Push Me, Pull This," *Computerworld*, 16 November 1998, 93.

3. As noted in this case, many corporate executives became concerned when they discovered the amount of time their subordinates spent viewing PointCast screens. Identify other work-related issues posed by the Internet. How, and to what extent, should companies limit or control the time spent by their employees on the Internet?

4. "Demographics" is an important term to companies that advertise their goods and services. Identify three products or services marketed over the Internet. Indicate the demographic market or markets to which online advertisements for each of these products or services would likely be targeted.

5. PointCast executives often found themselves searching for sources of additional capital for their company. What alternatives do companies have when they need to raise significant amounts of capital? Identify the advantages and disadvantages of each of these alternatives.

6. The phrase "business plan" was used in this case. Define the meaning of that phrase. What items should be documented in a company's business plan? Briefly explain how the business plan of a retailer that markets its merchandise strictly over the Internet would differ from the business plan of a conventional "bricks and mortar" retailer.

Millennium Mania

*It is a much better policy to prophesy
after the event has already taken place.*

Sir Winston Churchill

Each generation uses memorable events as important mileposts to mark the passage of time. The sinking of the Titanic, the attack on Pearl Harbor, and the untimely death of President John F. Kennedy each left a lasting impression on a generation of Americans. For decades to come, the tragic events of September 11, 2001, will produce "where were you when . . ." anecdotes in the minds and shared remembrances of not only Americans but most citizens of the world. Another common milestone that will trigger more-pleasant memories for most of us is the dawning of the new millennium on January 1, 2000.

Peter de Jager can easily recall where he was when Year 2K arrived. The Canadian citizen was flying over the Atlantic bound for his mother's home in Ireland where he intended to celebrate the new year, new century, and new millennium with his family, singing traditional Irish tunes and enjoying Irish home brew. Some seven years earlier, an article that de Jager wrote for the high-tech publication *Computerworld* had sparked a worldwide Y2K mania. Entitled "Doomsday," that article warned of dire consequences posed by an innocuous "bug" lying dormant in computers.[1] When the internal clocks of computers rolled over to 01/01/00, that bug would spring to life and wreak havoc on computer systems worldwide. This digital time bomb threatened to disrupt the operations of large corporations, disable military defense systems, and impact in some way almost everyone on the face of the earth.

As the fateful day approached, de Jager gradually softened his alarming predictions even as many of his doomsday colleagues prepared to retreat to underground bunkers to ride out the impending disaster. To prove that he had experienced a change of heart, de Jager planned to welcome the new millennium aboard a transoceanic flight. Other Y2K alarmists saw that as an imprudent decision since they believed a large jet's computer systems might shut down shortly after

---

1. P. de Jager, "Doomsday," *Computerworld*, 6 September 1993, 105–109.

midnight on December 31, 1999, sending the plane plunging to earth. Despite such warnings, de Jager and his family boarded the charter flight for Europe.

Although he was confident that the plane would survive the millennium date rollover, de Jager did admit that he scheduled the flight so that the plane would be over the mid-Atlantic at the stroke of midnight. That would give technicians at the airport where the plane would be arriving several hours to correct any Y2K-triggered computer malfunctions.

Dates, Digits, and Disaster

In testimony before the U.S. Senate in 1997, Ed Yardeni, a leading economist, observed that the Y2K problem was both "trivial and overwhelming." The problem was trivial because any one instance of it could be easily corrected in a matter of moments; the problem was overwhelming because Y2K bugs were embedded in billions of lines of computer code that had to be searched line by line so that software technicians could find and then eliminate the pesky nuisances. To save computer storage space, early day computer programmers coded calendar dates in an mm/dd/yy format, meaning that they used two digits to represent the four digits of a given calendar year. Because the Year 00 represented 1900, computers would recognize 01/01/00 as January 1, 1900, instead of January 1, 2000, when internal computer clocks rolled over to greet the new millennium.

An untold number of mathematical calculations and other computer functions stood to be impacted by the Y2K computer bug. Some computers might simply refuse to accept the seemingly invalid date and crash. Most software programs were expected to treat the first day of the millennium as January 1, 1900, and plant corrupt data in millions of bank statements, customer bills, statistical reports produced electronically by government agencies, and countless other computer-generated documents. de Jager cautioned that companies in three important industries, what he referred to as the "iron triangle," were particularly vulnerable to the Y2K bug since they relied extensively on "date data" produced or collected by computers. Those industries included telecommunications, financial services, and electric utilities.

Officials within the federal government worried that the Y2K bug would pose national security problems by causing computer malfunctions in military control systems and other so-called "mission critical" systems. Many experts reasoned that even if the Y2K problem was eliminated in most computer systems, the small minority in which the problem remained would trigger a domino effect of computer system failures worldwide.

Doom and Gloom Predictions

Peter de Jager was born in South Africa in 1955 but as a child traveled from country to country with his family, including an extended stay in his mother's homeland of Ireland. When de Jager was a teenager, his family settled in Canada. Intrigued by computers as a young man, de Jager decided to pursue a career in computer technology. He began his career as a computer programmer and later became a systems consultant specializing in the impact of technology changes on organizations.

In the early 1990s, de Jager began writing and lecturing in Canada on the Y2K problem. With the exception of information technology (IT) experts and other technophobes, few people paid much attention to de Jager and other Y2K doom-sayers, at least initially. By the mid-1990s, journalists in the print and electronic media began investigating and reporting on the Y2K problem. Because of the simplicity of the Y2K issue, the general public, even non-computer types, could easily understand the nature of the two-digit problem that the new millennium posed for computers.

Although the crux of the Y2K problem was easily understood, a large segment of the public had an insufficient knowledge of computers to grasp the true scope of the problem and the likelihood that it could be cured before January 1, 2000. As a result, many computer neophytes began accepting at face value the worst-case scenarios circulated by Y2K prophets. de Jager actually ranked among the more restrained of these prophets. Nevertheless, in his best-case scenario he predicted that the Y2K bug would bankrupt a significant number of businesses and that these business failures would create a pervasive "ripple effect" throughout economies around the globe, leaving a "huge" number of people unemployed.[2] As late as 1997, de Jager insisted that many companies and organizations could not avert the impending crisis. "For some organizations, it is definitely too late. These businesses have no idea how big their problem is: every company which has gone into this and looked at it seriously has come back with one simple message—'I didn't know that it was this big.'"[3]

Other soothsayers made more ominous predictions regarding the potential impact of the Y2K bug. Michael Hyatt, author of the best-selling nonfiction book *The Millennium Bug* (Regnery Publishing, 1998) and the popular novel *Y2K: The Day the World Shut Down* (Word Publishing, 1998), warned of an "impending computer catastrophe." Hyatt encouraged the public to take immediate measures to prepare for the dismal and chaotic post-Y2K era. Among other recommendations, Hyatt urged individuals to learn to "set a broken bone, deliver a baby, distinguish edible plants from those that are deadly, dress a deer, butcher a pig, and pluck a chicken."[4] To make sure the public prepared adequately for the Y2K catastrophe, Hyatt marketed the "Countdown to Chaos Protection Kit" at a cost of $89 (plus $4.50 for shipping).

As concern mounted over the approaching crisis, major consulting firms, such as Andersen Consulting, EDS, and Ernst & Young, created small armies of specially trained technicians and began offering Y2K "remediation" services to businesses and other organizations. Many entrepreneurial types resigned their positions with consulting firms to establish their own firms whose principal, if not only, line of business was scouring computer code to identify and then correct Y2K glitches. By late 1999, an estimated 600 Y2K firms existed, more than one-half of which were located in the United States. In March 1997, the American Stock Exchange established a new index for companies that marketed Y2K-compliant

2. R. Newing, "Rod Newing Talks to Peter de Jager," *Financial Times*, 2 April 1997, 6.

3. *Ibid.*

4. M. Hyatt, *The Millennium Bug* (Washington, D.C.: Regnery Publishing, 1998).

products and services. At its height, the aptly named "de Jager Index" included 113 companies.

Among the more prominent Y2K companies was CCD Online Systems, Inc., which referred to itself as "a worldwide provider of Year 2000 remediation and validation tools." Jim McGovern, CCD's president and chief operating officer, became a self-appointed spokesperson for the new Y2K industry. McGovern often commented on the need for companies to obtain "independent validation" of their efforts to correct Y2K problems. McGovern predicted that computer crashes and the consequent disruptions to business operations caused by the millennium bug would prompt a tidal wave of large class-action lawsuits filed by disgruntled stockholders against corporations and their top officers. Plaintiff attorneys would predicate these lawsuits on the failure of corporations and their executives to take appropriate measures to prepare for Y2K. As late as December 1999, McGovern bluntly stated that many corporations were not adequately prepared for Y2K and the litigation likely to follow.

> It is very clear that there will be significant problems on and after January 1, 2000. . . . In addition to business failures caused by Y2K program errors, corporate executives must also be prepared to handle Y2K lawsuits. Y2K has received more early warnings and widespread public awareness than any other disaster, and companies will need to prove that they went the extra mile.[5]

Not surprisingly, McGovern's principal sales pitch to potential clients was that *his* firm could help companies identify stubborn Y2K bugs still lurking in their computer systems. At the very least, obtaining a Y2K audit would help corporate executives prove that they had make a good faith effort to rid their computer systems of Y2K problems. McGovern was so confident that CCD technicians could find Y2K defects in any company's computer code that his firm promised to pay $50,000 to a school system chosen by a client if CCD failed to discover at least 50 Y2K glitches per one million lines of computer code audited.

Media coverage of the Y2K issue intensified as the turn of the millennium approached. Many journalists in fringe publications chose to ignore leaders of the IT profession and top executives of several important high-tech firms who were issuing press releases and other statements attempting to persuade the public that the Y2K bug would not prove catastrophic or even particularly troublesome. Instead, these journalists repeated and often embellished the most dire predictions made by Y2K prophets, which induced a growing sense of anxiety and, in some cases, panic among individuals unfamiliar with computers, particularly older citizens. One nationwide opinion poll in early 1999 revealed that more than one-half of the public feared that Y2K would cause nuclear power plants to malfunction, spawn electrical blackouts across the nation, and result in plane crashes due to instrument failure. Thousands of Americans converted their basements into underground bunkers and stocked them with food supplies and other essentials in hopes of surviving the lawless, fend-for-yourself society to be ushered in on January 1, 2000. A leading candidate for the Year 2000 Preparedness Award was one of Peter de Jager's fellow Canadians. This gentleman built an elaborate underground shelter consisting of 42 buried school buses that he linked together with a maze of tunnels.

---

5. *Business Wire,* "Y2K Expert Jim McGovern Warns That World's Largest Companies Are Unprepared for Business Failures," 2 December 1999.

Even some of the most prestigious weekly periodicals and major metropolitan newspapers printed articles that heightened the public's uncertainty regarding the millennium bug. Many of these articles provided objective assessments of the potential for extensive Y2K problems but were accompanied by apocalyptic headlines intended, no doubt, to increase "walk-by" sales at newsstands. Among these articles was a *Newsweek* cover story, "The Day the World Shuts Down: Can We Fix the Computer Bug Before It's Too Late?" (June 2, 1997); a *Business Week* article, "Y2K Is Worse Than Anyone Thought" (December 14, 1998); and an article in *The Washington Post* entitled "Y2K Could Bring D.C. to a Halt, Report Says" (February 19, 1999).

BIG BUCKS FOR LITTLE BUGS

Tommy Lee Jones and Will Smith starred in the sci-fi thriller *Men in Black* that packed theaters nationwide in the summer of 1997 and eventually became the year's top-grossing film. These two courageous G-men had one goal: eradicating unfriendly aliens visiting the Earth from points elsewhere, aliens that morphed into a human form although they were actually giant bugs.

Confusion and concern over the potential for extensive, if not catastrophic, Y2K problems spurred businesses, government agencies, and other organizations in the United States to spend massive amounts to find and eliminate Y2K bugs in billions of lines of computer code. Squads of bugsquashers reminiscent of Tommy Lee and Will marched into corporate offices from Bangor, Maine, to Burbank, California. For ten or more hours per day, often for seven days a week, these weary and bleary-eyed technicians searched line by line the computer code of every business application imaginable to find evidence of program code that might trigger a computer malfunction come January 1, 2000.

Economists estimate that U.S. businesses and government agencies spent somewhere between $100 billion and $300 billion on the enormous, multi-year Y2K search-and-correct project. That price tag included $3 billion alone for the salaries paid to throngs of computer technicians, Y2K specialists, and last-minute Y2K draftees who spent the long weekend of Friday, December 31, 1999, through Sunday, January 2, 2000, standing guard over computer systems, watching and waiting for computer crashes induced by bug infestations. Among the highest reported Y2K outlays by U.S. companies were the $650 million and $500 million of expenditures rung up by Citicorp and AT&T, respectively.

The human resource and monetary commitments made to the Y2K mission by most major companies and organizations left limited funds available to finance a wide range of other important IT projects. In particular, hundreds of companies postponed e-commerce projects while they dealt with Y2K issues. The director of research for the Gartner Group, a major IT consulting firm, noted that "The whole [business] world is dying to dive into e-business, but it's stuck in the mire of Y2K."[6] Many business analysts questioned whether companies would budget the necessary resources to complete previously planned e-commerce projects after corporate executives realized how much their firms had spent on the Y2K distraction.

---

6. M. Stepanek, "Y2K Will Affect Everyone, from the Ready to the Clueless," *Crain's New York Business*," 25 October 1999, 38.

OneOne OhOh Comes and Goes

Elaborate and festive celebrations around the world welcomed the new millennium on January 1, 2000. As the day progressed without any widespread computer malfunctions reported by the media, the public quickly dismissed the Y2K bug. A few major but isolated computer glitches did strike third world countries. Computer crashes traced to Y2K bugs shut down Pakistan's Islamabad Stock Exchange and a computer network operated by the central government of Swaziland. However, even large countries that spent relatively nominal amounts on the Y2K problem suffered few Y2K-related incidents. For example, government officials and corporate executives in Russia, who essentially crossed their fingers and whistled in the dark at the Y2K crisis, reported no widespread computer breakdowns or related problems.

News reporters had to search long and hard to find even a few examples of individual citizens significantly affected by the Y2K bug. A Miami, Florida, CPA discovered that the balance of her online investment account had soared by $36 million over the Y2K weekend. Unfortunately for the CPA, her brokerage firm quickly retrieved those funds from her account. The prototype January 1, 2000, news story involved a camera-shy survivalist peering out of a concrete-reinforced bunker while being snidely asked by a brassy reporter, "So, what do you plan to do with all of that Spam?"

Within a few days, hordes of journalists in the print and electronic media were castigating the Y2K doomsayers that had allegedly conned U.S. companies into spending $100 billion or more on a phony crisis. One journalist writing for *Fortune* compared the doomsayers' alleged impertinence to a severe case of medical malpractice. "If you went to a doctor who made you get a bypass when all you required was a roll of Tums, you'd be in a bad mood about it. Well, look what these bozos made us do!"[7]

A few thick-skinned individuals attempted to engage the press in a debate over the necessity of the mammoth Y2K expenditures. One former doomsayer argued that large companies in the United States had faced a much higher risk of Y2K-triggered disasters than comparable firms in other countries. "Did we do more than we needed? My answer is, 'We're never going to know.' But the United States has more embedded technology in its infrastructure than any other country, so we faced the biggest risk."[8] Such arguments were quickly dismissed or simply ignored by the press.

Instead of debating what problems U.S. companies might have faced in the absence of huge Y2K expenditures, journalists singled out the ringleaders of the Y2K campaign for repeated and harsh tongue-lashings. These targeted individuals included top executives of Y2K firms that had relentlessly hawked "bug repellent" services through late 1999 even as most computer experts insisted that the Y2K problem had been grossly overhyped and exaggerated. The press also routinely berated individuals who had authored Y2K doomsday books and preparation kits. For example, one journalist labeled best-selling author Michael Hyatt a

---

7. S. Bing, "Oh, Sure. Now They're Sorry: Y2K Idiots Cost Business $500 Billion! Is No One to Be Punished?" *Fortune*, 7 February 2000, 61.

8. M. Roush, "Y2K Disasters? Never Mind; Glitch Fixers Head for E-Commerce Opportunities," *Crain's Detroit Business*, 17 January 2000, 11.

"scaremonger." As you might expect, Peter de Jager, the founding father of the Y2K mania, received his fair share of media criticism in the early days of 2000. Initially treated as a cult hero in many circles, de Jager forfeited his credibility when most computer systems worldwide easily sidestepped the Y2K bug. Besides being derided by the press, de Jager received a torrent of hate mail. One journalist noted that de Jager seemed despondent in an interview granted during the first week of January 2000.

In the face of widespread scorn following January 1, 2000, Peter de Jager could take comfort in the bonanza that he reaped on his odyssey as a Y2K prophet. At the height of his popularity, de Jager was granting an average of five interviews per day and charging from $4,000 to $7,000 for public appearances and speeches. His speaking engagements included presentations made to the executives of the world's most prominent companies and to political leaders in world capitals around the globe. By the end of 1999, *Forbes* magazine reported that the fees for hundreds of such engagements had earned de Jager a "fortune."[9] Before assuming the role of Chief Y2K Prophet, de Jager had lived modestly on a modest income. The financial windfall that he reaped during the 1990s dramatically changed his lifestyle—for the better. By mid-1998, de Jager had three homes, including a sizable farm outside of his hometown of Toronto that he and his family used as a vacation getaway.

Near the end of 1999, de Jager decided to sell his website, *Year2000.com*, that he had used to help broadcast his forecasts for the third millennium. He registered the site at eBay to be auctioned off to the highest bidder—the minimum initial bid was listed as $1 million. De Jager appeared to have struck gold when he received a $10 million bid for the site. After eBay revealed that the bid was a hoax, de Jager decided to cancel the auction and sell the site privately. To expedite matters, he offered a $10,000 finder's fee to anyone who could help him locate an authentic buyer.

Y2K MAKES WAY FOR E-COMMERCE

The preoccupation with mud-slinging attacks on former Y2K prophets in the early days and weeks of 2000 caused the press to overlook an impressive array of significant, if unintended, benefits that the massive Y2K remediation program produced for U.S. companies. The Y2K crisis forced many companies for the first time to take pause and comprehensively examine and challenge their information technologies. "Even if you believe the Y2K bug was the biggest scam of the century, all the time and money spent on debugging and reprogramming was definitely not wasted. . . . Y2K preparation efforts forced companies and government agencies all over the world to get rid of buggy old software and aging hardware and invest in new technology."[10]

Many major U.S. companies used their Y2K projects to take complete inventories of their computer code, to develop more complete documentation for their computer software, to prepare or update disaster contingency plans for their

9. A. M. Virzi, "In Search of the Post-Y2K Gravy Train," *Forbes.com*, 19 May 2000.

10. M. Stepanek, "The Y2K Bug Repellent Wasn't a Waste," *Business Week*, 17 January 2000, 35.

computer systems, and to rethink the role that information technology should play in their futures. The large automaker DaimlerChrysler spent $260 million over several years to identify and correct Y2K problems. During that process, company technicians discovered 15,000 computer programs that were either redundant with other programs or no longer necessary. Daimler executives also used the Y2K remediation effort to streamline and reconfigure the computer networks that connected the company's hundreds of operating and administrative facilities.

Another unintended but significant outcome of the Y2K crisis was the enhanced respect and stature granted IT professionals within the business world. That crisis gave IT specialists an opportunity to demonstrate firsthand the important role they play within large organizations. Corporate executives finally realized that "information technology is the lifeblood of an organization. It took the crisis to bring that to the forefront,"[11] maintained one IT academic. An Internet business consultant voiced a similar point of view. "The Y2K bug made executives realize that IT is not just an overhead item but an important segment of a company's business strategy. Y2K brought IT into the corporate fabric and into the executive offices and corporate structure, a stature IT had not seen in the past."[12]

After a huge and collective sigh of relief on January 1, 2000, corporate executives and their subordinates focused their attention on the future. Concerns expressed by many business analysts that the enormous Y2K expenditures might choke off funding for more productive IT endeavors were short-lived. The rapidly changing economic environment dictated that companies move quickly to take advantage of new technologies, particularly those facilitating e-commerce that had been shunted to the side by Y2K concerns. A consultant with PricewaterhouseCoopers (PWC) noted that his firm expected an explosion in e-commerce initiatives by companies. "Companies are concerned that they will be left behind. Word is coming from the top: 'We need to do this, find the money!'"[13] Scores of other business analysts echoed that same sentiment:

> Companies spent so much time and money fixing Y2K problems that they put off spending money on e-commerce projects, developing Web sites and other IT projects. But now that the computer kinks brought on by the dawning of the new century are largely behind us, companies will probably free up those millions of dollars to get up-to-date on the latest and greatest technology to boost their productivity and efficiency.[14]

In fact, the Y2K crisis and the effort to eliminate Y2K bugs significantly raised the "IT quotient" of many companies by introducing them to a wide range of new IT technologies. A Hewlett-Packard manager noted that "Y2K, kind of coincidentally, was the compelling event that forced companies to take advantage of new [information] technology."[15] She went on to observe that the IT awareness

11. C. Goforth, "Millennium Bug Specialists Ponder Life After New Year's," *Akron Beacon Journal*, 26 December 1999, 24.

12. C. Marshall, "Y2K Industry in Transition," *Forbes.com*, 13 December 1999.

13. J. Ende, "Consultants Re-Tool for E-Commerce: Switch Focus After Y2K Work," *Crain's New York Business*, 28 February 2000, 28.

14. *Houston Chronicle* (online), "Houston Companies Invest in Technology Improvements After Y2K," 21 January 2000.

15. L. G. Everitt, "De-Bugged Year 2000 Fears Forced Companies to Replace Outdated Computers," *Denver Rocky Mountain News*, 10 January 2000, 4B.

sparked by Y2K projects has made many companies "more prepared for competing in the Internet-based economy."

Company after company indicated that with Y2K out of the way, they planned to move aggressively on a wide range of e-commerce projects made feasible by the more sophisticated and reliable computer systems in the post-Y2K era. As a leading computer consultant observed, "With new, more robust networks in place, companies can take full advantage of the Web and e-commerce to streamline their businesses and reach new markets."[16] The chief information officer of Mellon Bank, one of the largest financial institutions in the nation, expressed a similar point of view. "We want to get things moving along the priority chain, things that were supplanted by Y2K. The electronic commerce infrastructure is really important to us."[17] A top IT executive of one of Mellon's principal competitors, Chase Manhattan Bank, revealed that the $400 million spent to correct Y2K problems was not deterring Chase from devoting a large portion of its post-2000 operating budget to "Web-enabling" IT projects. Investment banking and brokerage services were other examples of industries that made major commitments to strengthen and extend their e-commerce capabilities beginning in early 2000.

> Nowhere is the drive to expand IT in the post-Y2K era keener than on Wall Street. . . . Brokerage houses will launch or accelerate e-commerce projects to offer clients everything from on-line trading to investing in mutual funds to buying insurance. The investments that companies have made in recent years to replace or fix core systems because of Y2K have paved the way for building on-line services for consumers.[18]

Computer consultants welcomed the opportunity to move away from the typically tense and tedious Y2K remediation projects to more challenging e-commerce projects. "Not only will e-business be bigger than Y2K ever was, it will also be less boring. Y2K was about remediation. With e-business, we're helping to change the structure of business,"[19] remarked a top executive of Ernst & Young's consulting division. In 1999, e-commerce projects accounted for approximately 20 percent of that firm's consulting revenues. Ernst & Young officials expected that figure to leap to 80 percent within three years given the substantial commitments companies were making to e-commerce initiatives.

Other major consulting firms expected similar growth in their revenues from e-commerce projects. Andersen Consulting reported that e-commerce projects would soon account for 75 percent of its revenues and that more than 70 percent of its new hires would be trained as e-commerce specialists. A competitor of Ernst & Young and Andersen Consulting, Deloitte & Touche, created an e-business "boot camp" that all 13,000 members of the firm were required to complete. Deloitte officials reported that they expected e-commerce revenues to be by far the fastest growing component of their firm's revenue stream.

All in all, most of the business world was happy to bid farewell to Y2K and its annoying stepson the Y2K bug. Granted, there were exceptions. As you can imagine, Y2K prophets are not much in demand these days. Several journalists joked

16. Stepanek, "The Y2K Bug Repellent Wasn't a Waste."

17. C. Power, "Y2K Out of the Way, Focus Is on E-Commerce Projects," *The American Banker*, 11 January 2000, 12.

18. M. Walsh, "Tech Dollars to Keep Flowing in Y2K's Wake; Wall Street Diverts Budgets to Systems, E-Commerce," *Crain's New York Business*, 25 October 1999, 1.

19. Ende, "Consultants Re-Tool for E-Commerce."

that the Y2K doomsayers would likely be out of circulation until the years leading up to 10000 when the Y10K bug would menace society.

QUESTIONS

1. In your view, did the Y2K doomsayers behave "ethically"? Make any assumptions you believe are necessary and defend your answer.
2. The business press plays an important role in the business world. Briefly describe the nature of that role and the key responsibilities that members of the business press assume. Do you believe the business press covered the Y2K issue properly? Ethically? Again, make any assumptions you believe are necessary and defend your answers.
3. Identify the website of a major e-commerce consulting firm. Briefly describe the primary e-commerce consulting services offered by that firm. In your answer, document the location of the firm's website.
4. Search the Web or other sources for a news report describing a major company that has recently initiated a significant IT project. Provide a brief overview of that project, including its purpose, scope, and intended outcomes. Document the source or sources of your information.
5. Y2K failed to trigger a huge number of lawsuits as predicted by many parties. Nevertheless, there were numerous lawsuits related to the Y2K issue. Search online or hard copy sources to identify one such lawsuit. Briefly describe the nature of that lawsuit and its outcome, if available.

Toby's Toys

We're losing money fast on purpose, to build our brand.

Toby Lenk (*Advertising Age*, June 1, 1998)

In the spring of 1997, Frank Han took a large gamble on a career change. The 33-year-old businessman gave up his secure, well-paying job with Union Bank of California to help a friend organize a new company that would market toys over the Internet. Han encouraged his friend, Toby Lenk, to "think small," at least initially. Han believed that Lenk's new company, eToys, should concentrate on one niche of the huge, retail toy industry, such as educational toys. But, at the urging of a venture capitalist, Lenk decided against the conservative business plan recommended by Frank Han and set out to build an online company that would eventually rival Toys 'R' Us. At the time, Toys 'R' Us dominated the toy industry, accounting for approximately one-half of the industry's more than $20 billion of annual sales.

A banking journal interviewed Frank Han shortly after he resigned from Union Bank. In that interview, Han seemed to be having second doubts about his decision to leave his 9 to 5 job with a large metropolitan bank to become the first employee of an upstart dot-com. "One of the great things about working for a bank is we were able to build a business, but we didn't have to starve and we didn't have to do it on a shoestring."[1] Eighteen months later, Han seemed pleased with the decision he had made to leave Union Bank. By the fall of 1998, eToys reigned as the largest and best-known toy e-tailer. Han, who by this time served as eToys' chief operating officer, proudly told a reporter for the high-tech publication *InfoWorld* that we have "holistically built a fully-integrated, scalable Web-commerce community to meet the needs of today's online retail customers."[2]

Any remaining doubts Han had regarding the wisdom of his decision to leave the banking world for eToys were likely erased in May 1999 when Toby Lenk took the company public. Sold originally at $20 per share, eToys' stock quadrupled in

1. J. K. Bloom, "Banker Runs Off to Play Online with New Toy Marketing Venture," *The American Banker*, 24 April 1997, 16.
2. *InfoWorld* (online), "I-Commerce Online," 9 November 1998.

price during the first few hours it was publicly traded. Thanks to their sizable ownership interests in eToys, Lenk, Han, and the firm's other early employees and investors became instant multimillionaires. Following eToys' initial public offering (IPO), Toby Lenk ranked among the forty richest self-made Americans under the age of 40.[3] The large wad of eToys shares owned by the 35-year-old Han placed him somewhere on the outskirts of Lenk's pricey neighborhood.

Unfortunately, many rags-to-riches stories in the short history of the Internet have become rags-to-riches-to-rags stories. Less than two years after Frank Han became fabulously wealthy thanks to his eToys' stock, he unloaded more than 1.7 million of the shares he controlled. Collectively, those shares had once boasted a market value exceeding $135 million. Han received considerably less than that figure when he sold the stock in late 2000 and early 2001. His total proceeds? A relatively paltry $325,000. But, other eToys investors fared even worse. The once high-flying eToys' shares became worthless when the company filed for bankruptcy in early 2001.

SHOPPING FOR ANNA

Similar to his friend Frank Han, Toby Lenk held a high-paying job with a prominent company when he decided to make a career change. Lenk oversaw the strategic planning function for the theme park division of Walt Disney Company. In 1987, Lenk had received an MBA from Harvard University a few years after earning an economics degree from Bowdoin College, a small liberal arts school in Brunswick, Maine. After spending nine years working his way up Disney's organizational chart, Lenk decided that he was not cut out for the role of corporate soldier. Instead, he had a "burning desire to start my own thing."[4] For several months, Lenk considered a wide range of new career options, including developing and operating a series of driving ranges in golf-crazy southern California. Lenk eventually turned his attention to the Internet. The business plan put together by Jeff Bezos, the founder and chief executive of Amazon, especially fascinated the former Disney executive. After studying Amazon and several other online business ventures for several weeks, Lenk made up his mind. He would become an e-tailing entrepreneur modeled after Jeff Bezos.

The next decision Lenk faced was what product to sell on the Internet. He believed that for an Internet-based retailer to be successful, there had to be a compelling reason to purchase the given product online rather than from a conventional retailer. Largely by accident, Lenk discovered what he was searching for. In December 1996, while shopping for a Christmas gift for his young niece, Anna, Lenk suffered through what he later referred to as a "death march" through the crowded aisles of a Toys 'R' Us store. Midway through that experience, Lenk had an epiphany: he would create a company to market toys on the Internet. "There's a compelling reason for consumers to get out of the toy stores: they're self-service, no sales support, horrible parking, and structurally not built for kids."[5]

3. S. Miller, "Toy Wonder: Net Mogul Toby Lenk's Biz Is Kid Stuff—But That's Not Monopoly Moolah the 38-year-old Bachelor Is Rolling in," *People Weekly*, 1 November 1999, 141.

4. *Ibid.*

5. J. Jensen, "Toby Lenk: eToys," *Advertising Age*, 1 June 1998, S16.

Lenk's "Anna anecdote" became a major feature of eToys' corporate culture. The Anna story typically surfaced each time a reporter interviewed Lenk or one of his key subordinates regarding eToys' history, strategies, or objectives. Toby Lenk served as the point person in eToys' campaign to convince the public that a visit to the local toy store ranked right up there with a visit to the local dentist. "People hate shopping at toy stores, and I know because they kept saying, 'If you liberate me from toy stores, I will be your friend for life.'"[6] To remind consumers that they could avoid the hassle of a crowded Toys 'R' Us store, eToys' marketing department incorporated the phrase "We bring the toy store to you" in the company's early promotional materials. Among eToys' early investors and first members of its board of directors was Michael Moritz, a partner with the venture capital firm Sequoia Capital and an individual who had provided early financial backing for Yahoo!. In a *Fortune* article, Moritz observed, "The premise of eToys is that you never have to go to Toys 'R' Us again. That's one of the most compelling premises I've ever heard."[7] Even the former banker, Frank Han, contributed to the anti-Toys 'R' Us spin campaign. "Parents don't like going to Toys 'R' Us. We've done focus group testing, and that comes through loud and clear. When you take kids to toy stores, their eyes light up, they become uncontrollable, and you end up coming away with more than you went in for."[8]

Toby Lenk's firm belief that the public would jump at the chance to use the Internet to purchase toys served as the founding premise of his company. But, another factor also contributed heavily to his decision to create an online toy company. In early 1997, FAO Schwartz, an upscale toy retailer, was the only major toy company making even a token effort to sell online. Because Lenk expected eToys to be successful from the beginning, he anticipated that many entrepreneurs would copy his firm's business plan. He also assumed that the major toy retailers would stampede to the Internet, led by Toys 'R' Us. Despite those anticipated challenges and his lack of experience in the toy industry, Lenk knew that by establishing the first major toy e-tailer he would gain the "first-mover" advantage that many commercial pioneers on the Internet believed was a critical success factor for an online business.

READY, SET, . . . LAUNCH

After settling upon the idea of selling toys on the Internet, Toby Lenk went about the task of raising funds for his new venture, which he chose to headquarter in Santa Monica, California. Lenk quickly raised $1 million of seed capital from friends and family members. Because he had never started a company and was largely unfamiliar with Internet-based business operations, Lenk approached Bill Gross, the chief executive officer (CEO) of the Internet incubator idealab!, for help in creating his new firm. Gross responded enthusiastically to Lenk's business plan. With Gross's assistance, Lenk raised an additional $4 million. The technological expertise and organizational skills that idealab!'s staff provided Lenk and

---

6. R. Beck, "Web Site Helps to Calm the Frenzy of Toy Shopping," *St. Louis Post-Dispatch*, 11 November 1998, C7.

7. *Fortune*, "Inside the First e-Christmas," 1 February 1999, 70.

8. Bloom, "Banker Runs Off to Play Online."

his small band of employees allowed them to rush the new firm into operation in a matter of months. In exchange for the resources idealab! committed to eToys, Bill Gross's firm received an ownership interest of approximately 20 percent in the new company.

On October 1, 1997, Lenk launched eToys into cyberspace by opening the firm's website for business, just in time for the Christmas holiday season that historically produces 50 percent of annual toy sales. Lenk and his subordinates had few expectations for eToys' first Christmas selling season. Instead, they used that season to fine tune their new firm's website, to gain a better understanding of the toy industry, and to become more familiar with large toy manufacturers and several Internet companies with whom Lenk wanted to establish working relationships.

Despite the meager $500,000 of sales produced by eToys during the Christmas 1997 season, Lenk believed that season was a tremendous success for his new firm. During the first several weeks that eToys' website was fully operational, 250,000 Internet users browsed the virtual aisles of the online toy store, checking out the approximately 1,000 individual items offered for sale. By the end of 1997, Lenk had established relationships with more than 100 toy manufacturers, including such industry leaders as Mattel, Hasbro, Little Tikes, and Lego. Those manufacturers welcomed eToys to the industry and hoped that the new company would boost overall toy sales.

Among the most important strategic relationships that Toby Lenk established in eToys' first few months of operation was an arrangement he negotiated with the Internet service provider AOL. The two companies agreed to a two-year deal that required eToys to pay AOL $3 million for the right to become the sole toy retailer featured on the *AOL.com* Shopping Channel. AOL also agreed to run promotional materials for eToys throughout its large website. By the spring of 1998, Lenk had made similar arrangements with several other websites that served as gateways to the Internet, including Yahoo!, Excite, and Infoseek. Lenk also created the eToys' Affiliates Program in late 1997. Under this program, companies that directed Internet surfers to the eToys' website received a 25 percent commission on the purchases made by those surfers. This generous commission prompted a mad rush by companies to sign up as eToys' affiliates. By late 1998, more than 2,000 companies that operated websites had become participants in the program, including hundreds of Old Economy firms. Lenk vigorously defended the affiliates program when critics suggested that he was "crazy" to pay such large commissions to participants in the program. "This business is all about getting customers. If we sell $40 worth of toys, $10 is a reasonable acquisition cost."[9]

Throughout 1998, Lenk and his top lieutenants prepared for the first major challenge that eToys would face, the Christmas 1998 season, the first true "e-Christmas." In March 1998, eToys purchased its principal online competitor, toys.com, an acquisition that increased eToys' customer base by nearly 40 percent. The next strategic initiative Lenk aggressively pursued was raising more capital for his fledgling firm. By the late summer of 1998, Lenk had raised an additional $10 million of capital from several large investors, including a major venture capital firm. Lenk used some of those funds to update the technology infrastructure for the eToys' website in anticipation of the approaching holiday season when he

---

9. *Fortune,* "Inside the First e-Christmas," 70.

planned to have 10,000 individual toy items available for sale, a 1,000 percent increase over the previous holiday season.

Lenk devoted the largest chunk of the capital raised during 1998 to a nationwide advertising campaign developed by a major Los Angeles advertising agency. Attracting large numbers of Internet users to eToys' website was one goal of that campaign, but the more important goal was simply making the public aware of eToys. In commenting on the significant cost of the campaign, Lenk observed matter-of-factly, "We're losing money fast on purpose, to build our brand."[10] A reporter for *The Washington Post* provided a more in-depth description of Lenk's aggressive marketing strategy. "eToys has followed a hellbent-for-growth strategy and spent lavishly on marketing. This follows on the theory that brand recognition is half the battle of Internet commerce: Once a brand is established, especially in the early stages of online migration, customers will surely swarm, and profitability follow."[11]

eToys' advertising agency wove two key themes into the company's national advertising campaign during the fall of 1998. One theme was the hassle-free nature of online shopping. No more long lines at checkout stands, no more traipsing from store to store searching for popular toys only to be greeted by bare shelves, no more chasing boisterous five-year-olds down the crowded aisles of packed toy stores. The other key theme central to eToys' advertising campaign was a corporate tag line often used by Toby Lenk to describe the company's principal operating strategy: "Just kids, just the Web." Lenk wanted consumers to recognize that his company was dedicated exclusively to one line of business: selling toys online. If he accomplished that objective, Lenk believed that as more and more consumers logged on to the Internet to make toy purchases, they would instinctively go to the eToys' website rather than general merchandise sites such as *Walmart.com*.

Ten months after eToys launched its website on October 1, 1997, Toys 'R' Us began selling toys online. Toby Lenk chastised his major competitor and favorite "whipping boy" for being so slow in responding to the competitive challenge posed by eToys. He had predicted on several occasions that Toys 'R' Us would launch its own website within a few weeks after eToys set up shop on the Internet. Initially, the Toys 'R' Us site seemed anemic compared to the eToys' website. Although Toys 'R' Us had been operating for nearly four decades and had much stronger ties to toy manufacturers than its brassy new competitor, the company's website stocked a much smaller variety of toys than the eToys site. eToys' affiliates program gave Lenk's company another important competitive advantage over Toys 'R' Us.

The weak entry that Toys 'R' Us made into the online toy market caused financial analysts to question whether the company was committed to its new Internet strategy. *Fortune* reported that the industry's leading bricks and mortar retailer suffered from a severe case of "cannibalization inertia."[12] The executives of Toys 'R' Us agonized over the difficult problem of developing a strategy to compete effectively with eToys while, at the same time, protecting their company's dominant position in the offline toy market.

10. Jensen, "Toby Lenk: eToys."

11. M. Leibovich, "Building a Toy Chest on the Internet: New Stock Offering Gives eToys the Cash to Fuel Its Concept," *The Washington Post*, 25 May 1999, E01.

12. *Fortune*, "Inside the First e-Christmas."

During the first several months of eToys' existence, the management team of Toys 'R' Us ignored the potshots taken at their company by Toby Lenk, his fellow officers, and the venture capital firms that provided much of eToys' early financing. But, as eToys became a fixture in news releases for the toy industry and as the press began referring to Lenk as the "Toy Wonder," Toys 'R' Us executives decided to respond to the verbal attacks launched on their firm by Mr. Lenk. After complimenting eToys for making consumers aware of the benefits of shopping for toys online, a top Toys 'R' Us executive claimed that his firm, not eToys, would reap the economic benefits produced by that awareness. He predicted that once consumers realized they could buy toys online, they would gravitate to his company's website to make their purchases.[13] That same executive also suggested that Lenk and his subordinates lacked a sufficient understanding of the volatile retail toy business to make their company a major force in the industry.

TOYING WITH SUCCESS?

Following the Christmas 1998 holiday season, Toby Lenk declared that the first e-Christmas had been an unmitigated success for his firm. Actually, he was a little more graphic: "We just kicked butt."[14] During the fourth quarter of 1998, eToys generated $23 million in sales, a 4,000 percent increase compared to the company's sales during the final three months of 1997. Nearly 3.5 million Internet users visited eToys' website during the 1998 Christmas holiday season, making it the fifth most-visited website during that time frame. In terms of online traffic, the eToys' website easily swamped the struggling, glitch-prone site of Toys 'R' Us that attracted approximately 1.5 million Internet users during the holiday season. For all of 1998, eToys reported sales of $30 million. Among e-tailers, only Amazon and barnesandnoble.com reported higher sales.

eToys' huge increase in revenues during the fourth quarter of 1998 and the large number of Internet users that visited the company's website during the 1998 Christmas season gave Toby Lenk reason to be upbeat regarding his company's future. Adding to his confidence was a forecast released by Forrester Research that indicated online toy sales would surge from $68 million in 1998 to nearly $1.5 billion by 2003.[15]

Despite the optimism of eToys' executives, many critics charged that Lenk and his colleagues were improperly downplaying, if not totally ignoring, the fact that their firm's 1998 financial performance was dismal by practically any conventional benchmark. eToys suffered a net loss for 1998 of nearly $29 million, meaning that the company lost approximately $0.96 for every $1 of sales that it produced. Although eToys' sales leaped spectacularly in 1998, critics and competitors pointed out that the company's sales accounted for just slightly more than 0.1 percent of industry-wide sales for the year. The CEO of Toys 'R' Us provided a more explicit benchmark for eToys' 1998 sales when he noted that some of his company's large stores individually produced that dollar volume of sales each year.

---

13. Leibovich, "Building a Toy Chest on the Internet."

14. *Fortune*, "Inside the First e-Christmas."

15. Leibovich, "Building a Toy Chest on the Internet."

Toby Lenk's stubborn refusal to predict when eToys would begin producing profits also troubled financial analysts. Lenk tersely rebuffed those analysts by insisting that his primary short-term goal remained building brand awareness not generating profits. Lenk's long-term goal was to overtake Toys 'R' Us as the dominant company in the toy industry. To accomplish each of those objectives, Lenk realized that his company needed to raise additional capital, much more capital than eToys' existing investors were willing to provide. To raise those funds, Lenk took his firm public in May 1999. The huge increase in the price of eToys' common stock on the first day it was traded vaulted the company's net worth past the total market value of Toys 'R' Us. eToys' market capitalization of nearly $8 billion was 35 percent higher than the value assigned to Toys 'R' Us by the stock market. The higher market cap of eToys shocked many long-time Wall Street investors given the impressive operating results posted by Toys 'R' Us during 1998: $11 billion of revenues and a $372 million profit.

Following eToys' IPO, Lenk began pursuing several initiatives to prepare his company for the next holiday sales season. He used some of the funds raised by the IPO to acquire a warehouse in Danville, Virginia. To that point, eToys' only warehouse had been located in Los Angeles, which created a logistics problem for the company since 70 percent of its sales came from states east of the Mississippi. Lenk also announced plans to add two new distribution centers—one in Utah and another in Minnesota—to the company's distribution network, a major upgrade of the software used in the company's warehousing and distribution functions, and the acquisition of a sophisticated database management system developed by Oracle Corporation. Lenk's final new initiative was to expand internationally. eToys would begin selling merchandise in a few selected countries with the eventual objective of expanding into international markets across the globe.

As Christmas 1999 approached, *Business Week* reported that eToys' nationwide advertising efforts and the company's other aggressive marketing strategies had drawn the attention of consumers and competitors alike. Despite eToys' modest revenues to that point, those competitors decided not to underestimate the threat posed by Toby Lenk any longer. "There's a single target in their [established toy retailers] crosshairs: eToys, Inc."[16] Leading the charge against eToys was Toby Lenk's old nemesis, Toys 'R' Us. That company's top executives revealed that they planned to invest $80 million in their website to make it more competitive with the widely heralded and award-winning eToys site. Another competitive challenge faced by eToys was a sudden surge in the number of "pure-play" online toy retailers. These companies included ToyTime, Red Rocket, SmarterKids.com, and toysmart.com, a site financed largely by Lenk's former employer, Walt Disney Company.

From Toby Lenk's perspective, the most menacing development for eToys during 1999 on the competitive front was Jeff Bezos's announcement that Amazon intended to enter the online toy market. Lenk had modeled eToys' business plan after the e-commerce model developed by Bezos. Now, the teacher would have an opportunity to emulate his pupil. On July 13, 1999, Amazon began selling toys online. According to one reporter, the front page of Amazon's toy site "looks as if it were taken directly from eToys'"[17] website. One week later, Internet measurement

---

16. *Business Week,* "The Toy War Is No Game," 9 August 1999, 86.

17. *Ibid.*

agencies reported that Amazon's daily toy sales were surpassing those of eToys, making Jeff Bezos's company the leading online toy retailer.

A PROFIT-PROOF BUSINESS PLAN?

Christmas 1999 proved to be a mixed blessing for eToys: the company's sales increased dramatically compared to the previous holiday selling season, but the company's operating losses rose even more sharply. For all of 1999, eToys reported sales of $151 million and a net loss of $190 million. The first quarter of 2000 produced similar results: sales quadrupled during that period compared to the first quarter of the previous year, while the company's losses grew ever larger.

Toby Lenk continued to stonewall Wall Street analysts who pressed him to predict when eToys would finally reach the break-even point. In the spring of 2000, one analyst insisted that the company was unlikely to "turn the corner" until 2002, meaning that it would almost certainly need to raise additional capital to survive. The nosedive in Internet stock prices that began in earnest in March 2000, made the task of raising capital a difficult chore for reasonably healthy Internet firms and an epic undertaking for an e-tailer such as eToys that was piling up enormous losses. By April 2000, eToys' stock, which had traded as high as $86 per share, had fallen to less than $5. Contributing to the downward pressure on eToys' stock price was a flood of shares that company insiders sold when the post-IPO "lock-up" period expired—federal securities laws prohibit company insiders from selling their stock for several months following a company's IPO. Among the insiders that unloaded their stock were executives of idealab!, the Internet incubator that helped Toby Lenk organize eToys. In late 1999, idealab! sold more than four million shares of eToys' common stock, producing a gain of almost $200 million for Bill Gross, idealab!'s CEO, and his colleagues.

In late April 2000, Toby Lenk capitulated to the demands of the business press and named a target date when he believed eToys would become profitable. Lenk projected that his company would finally turn a profit during the fourth quarter of 2001. At the same time, he admitted that his firm was running short of cash and that he was searching for new sources of capital. Two months later, Lenk announced that eToys had raised an additional $100 million from several large investors. As 2000 progressed, eToys continued to struggle, which prompted growing criticism of Toby Lenk, his subordinates, and their key policies and strategic decisions. *Fortune* observed that Lenk faced the distinct possibility of being labeled as one of the many "young Internet opportunists whose only serious business plan was to make a fortune off dot-com-dazzled investors."[18]

Lenk and his subordinates were perplexed by their company's poor operating results since leading business publications consistently ranked eToys' website among the best e-tail sites in terms of overall online shopping experience. Market researchers eventually uncovered the reason why the company's website could attract millions of potential buyers but persuade only a small percentage of them to make an actual purchase. Those researchers found that although eToys scored high in terms of brand awareness or name recognition among consumers, Toys 'R'

---

18. E. Kelly, "The Last e-Store on the Block," *Fortune*, 18 September 2000, 214.

Us had something more important working for it: brand loyalty. Over several decades, Toys 'R' Us had accumulated a huge amount of goodwill with toy shoppers. That goodwill did not prevent those shoppers from cruising eToys' impressive website to identify potential gifts for their children or other youngsters, but when it was time to make an actual purchase, shoppers were prone to go to a nearby Toys 'R' Us store. In fact, one marketing research study found that an online search for toys produces only $1 dollar of online toy purchases for every $8 of offline toy purchases.[19] A financial analyst used that data to take a not-so-subtle jab at the "Anna anecdote" widely circulated by Toby Lenk and his confederates. "eToys may help me figure out which talking doll I should buy for my niece, but I'll likely make the purchase at the Toys 'R' Us store around the corner."[20]

Another problem faced by eToys and other e-tailers was the efficiency of online shopping. Individuals who actually intended to use the Internet to make toy purchases could search through several online toy stores with a few clicks of their mouse to find the site that offered the best price for a Radio Flyer wagon, or an Etch-A-Sketch, or a Jam 'N Glam Barbie. This ready access to pricing information by online shoppers triggered cutthroat pricing among online toy stores. In turn, this cutthroat pricing attracted large numbers of consumers who marketing experts refer to as "bottom feeders," that is, price-fixated individuals who only make a purchase when they can find a "great deal." This vicious cycle meant that the gross profit margins realized by online toy retailers were considerably smaller than those produced by their offline counterparts.

Online toy retailers were also poorly prepared to cope with one of the most problematic features of the toy industry: the very seasonal nature of toy sales. Most toy stores ring up approximately one-half of their annual sales during the six-week period preceding Christmas. Online toy stores produce an even larger percentage of their annual sales during the Christmas season, in some cases as high as 70 percent. Because of their minimal experience with the toy industry, the management teams of online toy companies were unfamiliar with many of the tactics that conventional toy retailers had historically used to control or mitigate their costs during the industry's long off-season. As a result, from early January through mid-November, the new toy e-tailers simply had to absorb the large expenditures required to maintain their physical distribution facilities, their technology infrastructure, and their payrolls.

Analysts charged that the key mistake made by Toby Lenk and the executives of other online toy companies was their failure to obtain a thorough understanding of the types and magnitude of costs associated with their businesses. "The San Andreas Fault in eToys' model is the sheer implacable mass of costs involved in running an online retail business."[21] Online retailers benefit from key efficiencies inherent in their operations, but conventional retailers also have important cost advantages over their online competitors.

> For starters, their [conventional toy stores] technology costs are more reasonable. They don't have to pick merchandise from the shelves and pack it. . . . Even the costs of store construction and salespeople, which eToys mostly avoids, aren't crushing. The average

19. L. Witt, "E-Tail Shares: Shop with Caution," *BusinessWeek Online*, 3 July 2000.

20. *Ibid.*

21. Kelly, "The Last e-Store on the Block."

brick-and-mortar retailer specialty store spends about 7 percent of sales on its property and equipment, and less than 15 percent on personnel. In fact, when you compare revenues per employee, Toys 'R' Us and eToys look very familiar.[22]

A comprehensive analysis of eToys' cost structure by *Fortune* in fall 2000 painted a bleak picture of the online company's operations. *Fortune's* number-crunching report revealed that for every $100 of sales produced by eToys, $81 was absorbed by cost of sales, that is, the cost of purchasing toys from the company's suppliers. Technology expenditures—the costs required to develop and maintain a state-of-the-art website—consumed $29 of every $100 of sales, while distribution costs ate up another $33 of each $100 of sales.

A surprisingly large component of eToys' distribution costs was the expense of dealing with customer inquiries and complaints. Most early e-tailers had assumed that customers would browse their websites, place their orders online, and then wait to receive the purchased items from UPS or FedEx—all with little or no human interaction. That assumption was quickly discarded. "One of the unexpected—and expensive—features of online retail is that it often demands much more human contact than the offline world."[23] Gartner Group, a major market research firm, estimated that each time a customer calls an online retailer it costs that business $20, principally because of the large number of customer representatives that must be available to deal with such inquiries.[24]

According to *Fortune*, advertising was the deadliest cost faced by eToys. "The killer cost was $37 per $100 of sales that eToys spent on advertising. Steep advertising costs are unavoidable when you're an upstart trying to grab customers and when you don't have stores planted at major intersections reminding customers to shop there."[25] By comparison, the advertising expenditures of conventional retailers typically equal only 3 to 5 percent of their annual sales.

Toby Lenk became increasingly defensive as the business press relentlessly questioned his strategic initiatives, operating policies, and the basic business model he had developed for eToys. Particularly galling to Lenk was an allegation that he had constructed a company that was "profit-proof."[26] Lenk implied that his critics did not understand the basic economics of his business plan. "I couldn't read a financial statement either in my first year of business school."[27] The besieged CEO told *Fortune* that a large proportion of the costs of operating eToys were "fixed and would shrink in relation to sales as revenues increase. . . . This is a business of scale."[28] Few of his critics questioned that assertion but had serious doubts whether eToys could survive long enough to take advantage of the economies of scale enjoyed by Toys 'R' Us and other large toy chains.

As the Christmas 2000 selling season approached, many of eToys' online competitors had already closed down their websites, including ToyTime, toy-smart.com, and Red Rocket. To avoid the same fate, Toby Lenk and his subordi-

22. *Ibid.*

23. D. Streitfeld, "At eToys Site, It's Service with a Nervous Smile; Dot-com Pins Future on Customer Hand-Holding," *The Washington Post*, 3 December 2000, A1.

24. *Ibid.*

25. Kelly, "The Last e-Store on the Block."

26. *Ibid.*

27. *Ibid.*

28. *Ibid.*

nates decided to adopt a make-or-break attitude toward the holiday season. Either the company would produce a huge increase in revenues accompanied by much reduced operating losses, or eToys would call it quits. Key changes Lenk implemented to improve eToys' operating results included accepting advertisements on the company's website for the first time and focusing promotional efforts on high-margin toys, particularly a series of toys carrying the company's private brand. In commenting on his newest turnaround strategy and the approaching Christmas season, Lenk observed, "We're so well prepared, in operational readiness, in merchandising readiness, in marketing. We just need to deliver."[29] One leading Wall Street analyst predicted that for eToys to survive, the company needed to produce $240 million of revenues during the final quarter of 2000, more than double the revenues the company realized during the fourth quarter of 1999.

One initiative Lenk refused to consider was negotiating a strategic alliance with a conventional retailer, an alliance in which eToys would give up some of its autonomy in exchange for much-needed financial support and highly skilled management personnel with considerable experience in retailing. Reportedly, several major merchandisers, including Wal-Mart, were more than willing to collaborate with eToys to take advantage of the online company's technology infrastructure and its high brand awareness. Many analysts believed that such an alliance was the only way eToys could survive. In August 2000, Toys 'R' Us and Amazon announced a cooperative arrangement to market toys online. Under the terms of this agreement, Toys 'R' Us was responsible for inventory purchasing decisions, while Amazon assumed responsibility for processing sales orders, customer service, warehousing, and shipping operations.

Toby Lenk insisted that he was happy to hear of the new working relationship between Toys 'R' Us and Amazon. "I'm pleased as punch. They recognize that neither can compete alone against us."[30] In commenting on the suggestion that he strike a cooperative arrangement of some sort with Wal-Mart, Lenk quickly dismissed that possibility by noting that, "Our merchandising skills are distinct from Wal-Mart's."[31] Instead of pursuing an alliance with a major bricks and mortar retailer, the headstrong Lenk chose to bet his company on Christmas 2000 and on his management team's ability to convince holiday shoppers to purchase their Christmas gifts from the eToys' website.

FAREWELL TO ETOYS

Midway through the 2000 Christmas selling season, Toby Lenk realized that eToys would not come close to reaching the $240 million of fourth-quarter sales the company needed to attract large investors. In fact, by the end of the fourth quarter, the company would ring up total sales of less than one-half that amount. Retail experts believed that negative publicity regarding eToys' financial health persuaded a larger than normal number of online shoppers who accessed the

---

29. L. Bannon and J. Pereira, "Two Big Online Toy Sellers Gear Up for Another Holiday Cyber Battle," *The Wall Street Journal* Interactive Edition, 25 September 2000.

30. Kelly, "The Last e-Store on the Block."

31. *Ibid.*

company's website to purchase their gifts elsewhere. "If everyone talks about how beleaguered eToys is, do you trust it to send you a package?"[32] was a sentiment apparently shared by many Internet surfers.

On Christmas Day 2000, *InfoWorld* reported that eToys' management had asked the large Wall Street investment firm Goldman, Sachs & Co. to explore "end-of-the-road alternatives" for the company.[33] In less than four years after he founded eToys, Toby Lenk would be forced to pull the plug on the company's award-winning but highly unprofitable website.

When the news of eToys' imminent demise began circulating in the business press, closet critics of Toby Lenk began publicly chiding the former "Toy Wonder." A commentary column appearing in *BusinessWeek Online* in February 2001 criticized Lenk for refusing to develop a partnership with Wal-Mart or another conventional retailer. "Those [e-tailers] not willing to partner with market leaders are better off focusing on small niches that may not generate massive sales but can at least produce a profit."[34] Another toy industry executive suggested that eToys' grandiose vision of rivaling Toys 'R' Us had never been a viable goal. "Small is sustainable. You have to come to grips with reality. I don't think eToys ever did."[35] The business press was particularly critical of Lenk's decision to pour huge amounts of capital into a campaign to build a nationwide brand for his company instead of first developing a business model likely to produce profits. "A strong brand can't compensate for a business model that becomes ineffective."[36]

In early March 2001, eToys ceased operations and filed a bankruptcy petition with a federal court to stave off its creditors, which the company owed $274 million. One week earlier, Toby Lenk had resurfaced in the news when eToys announced that it was planning to reduce by one-third severance payments to be made to its former employees. At the same time, the company reported that three top executives would receive a total of $1 million as "retention bonuses," payments meant to compensate those executives for their efforts to liquidate the company in the following weeks. One-half of that total was earmarked for Toby Lenk.

The failure of eToys and hundreds of other e-tailers during 2000 and 2001 had little impact on the optimism of key business leaders who continued to insist that the Internet would eventually revolutionize the business world. Those individuals typically blamed inept business models and management teams for the rash of failures among dot-com retailers. These critics included Richard Schmidt, an investment advisor and publisher of a widely read investment letter. "If they [executives of failed e-tailers] had been operating a book store, a factory, a clothing store or an accounting firm, they would have been out of business just as fast. . . . It takes hard work to build a business, and these people aren't interested in that. They're interested in making a statement."[37] Schmidt went on to suggest that the

---

32. L. Fox, "Among the Walking Dead," *Business2.com* (online), 14 November 2000.

33. J. Davis, "eToys' Holiday Shortfall Sends Message to E-Tailers: A Solid Business Plan Helps," *InfoWorld*, 25 December 2000, 52.

34. A. Weintraub, "How eToys Could Have Made It," *BusinessWeek Online*, 9 February 2001.

35. *Ibid.*

36. D. A. Aaker and R. Jacobson, "What Separates Web Winners from Losers," *The Wall Street Journal* Interactive Edition, 12 March 2001.

37. J. Elvin, "www.Bust.com," *Insight on the News*, 26 March 2001, 10.

"Internet is a phenomenal tool" that, when mastered by those individuals who employ sound business strategies, will increase productivity, slash operating costs, and stimulate the profits of individual firms and the economy as a whole.

QUESTIONS

1. Search the World Wide Web to identify two companies that sell toys online. Visit the website of each company. Write a brief summary that compares and contrasts the strengths and weaknesses of the two websites. Which website do you believe is "better"? Explain.
2. Toby Lenk emphasized the importance of building strong "brand awareness" for eToys. Identify two retail companies, one company that operates principally online and another company whose principal operations are offline—these firms do not have to be in the same industry. Research these companies and write a brief summary of the measures each uses to develop or to reinforce their brand awareness.
3. Under what circumstances do you believe it is clearly acceptable for corporate executives to criticize their firm's competitors? Are there any circumstances under which you believe corporate executives should definitely not criticize competitors? Explain.
4. Business journalists frequently asked Toby Lenk to predict when his company would reach the break-even point. Do you believe that corporate executives should be required to issue profit and revenue forecasts for their firms? Defend your answer.
5. A low "buy rate" among Internet users who visited eToys' website was a major problem for the company throughout its existence. eToys' buy rate typically hovered below 10 percent, meaning that fewer than one of ten individuals who visited the company's website actually purchased an item. Identify the key factors that you believe influence a retail website's buy rate.
6. eToys' management faced a very seasonal industry. Identify another industry subject to significant seasonal fluctuations in sales. List specific strategies companies in that industry could use to cope with the highly seasonal nature of their businesses.
7. Among the key objectives of Toby Lenk and his fellow executives was achieving sufficient sales so that the firm could take advantage of "economies of scale." Explain how many small firms survive and actually thrive in industries that are dominated by a few large competitors that have significant "scale" advantages.

Internet Bubble, Part I: Party Time

Few of us can stand prosperity. Another man's, I mean.

Mark Twain

During the latter decades of the twentieth century, William Shatner became a television icon. Throngs of dedicated "Trekkies" knew by heart the story line of every episode of *Star Trek*, a sci-fi television program of the 1960s that featured Shatner as Captain James T. Kirk. Shatner, with the help of Spock, the enigmatic Vulcan, and an assorted cast of other intriguing characters, guided the Starship Enterprise through dozens of intergalactic adventures and misadventures. Unfortunately for Shatner, the notoriety he gained on the popular television show failed to sustain his acting career once *Star Trek* was taken out of production and began a decades-long stint as one of the most commercially successful television series in syndicated reruns.

In 1998, the advertising agency for Priceline.com approached Shatner and asked him to serve as the company's pitchman in a nationwide advertising campaign. Priceline, a name-your-own-price online intermediary between airlines hoping to fill unsold seats and bargain-happy travelers, wanted to find a corporate spokesperson having a high "recognition quotient" with the public. The company's advertising campaign would consist of approximately ten television commercials and a series of related radio and print ads. Reportedly, Priceline could not afford its first choice, Bill Cosby, so the company's advertising agency turned to Shatner. After considering the offer a few days, Shatner agreed to film the commercials that would spoof his dubious singing skills. Earlier in his career, Shatner had produced a few memorable music albums, memorable because for several years they were featured on "The Annoying Music Show" broadcast by the National Public Radio network.

Instead of accepting cash compensation reported at approximately $500,000 for the commercials, Shatner insisted on receiving 125,000 options to purchase the yet-to-be issued Priceline stock. The former Captain Kirk faced the risk that Priceline's stock would never surpass the option "striking" price, that is, the price at which he could purchase the stock over the three-year term of his stock options. In that case, the stock options would be worthless and Shatner would receive zero payment for his role as Priceline's media spokesperson.

Shatner later admitted that his decision to accept the Priceline stock options was a gamble. But, Shatner, who majored in business not acting at McGill University in his native Montreal, believed the gamble was a good one given the soaring prices of dot-com stocks. Shatner was right; his gamble paid off handsomely. The market value of the stock options he received soared to well over $10 million as Priceline's stock rose from an initial offering price of $16 per share to more than $150 per share. Reportedly, Shatner cashed out his options for approximately $8 million.

William Shatner became a trendsetter for dot-com spokespeople. After he wrangled his stock-option deal with Priceline, a long list of other celebrities negotiated similar compensation contracts with dot-coms that wanted to use those individuals' fame to become better known with the public. Cindy Crawford, Whoopi Goldberg, Tori Amos, Jason Alexander, and Ice-T were among the many well-known personalities who accepted stock options in lieu of cash to help establish a recognizable brand name for a new Internet company. Singer Alanis Morissette easily claimed the grand prize in the dot-com stock option sweepstakes. Morissette received stock options from the Web-based music site MP3.com that were eventually worth $30 million.

AN OKLAHOMA LAND RUSH IN CYBERSPACE

In the late 1990s, the investing public's fascination with Internet-based companies prompted the cyberspace equivalent of the Oklahoma Land Rush, according to one prominent investment analyst. "In a land rush, you suspend rules because your perception is that time is of the essence."[1] That perception caused many anxious investors who feared missing out on a once-in-a-lifetime investment opportunity to bid the prices of Internet stocks to ever-higher levels. Those investors easily discounted the fact that most Internet companies were reporting minimal revenues and sizable, if not staggering, operating losses. Over a 15-month stretch between late 1998 and March 2000, the dot-com-laced NASDAQ stock exchange rose by more than 150 percent. By comparison, over the same time frame, the largely Old Economy Dow Jones Industrial Average managed a much less impressive 15 percent gain.

Dot-com fever prompted many investment services and publications to create new stock indices dedicated strictly to Internet companies. On June 30, 1999, *USA Today* launched the *Internet 100* to track the stock prices of 100 companies whose primary lines of business were directly or exclusively related to the Internet. Within a few months, the collective value of that index had risen by more than 60 percent. Other Internet stock indices realized similar increases. By early March 2000, the 300 companies included in the *Forbes Internet Index* had a collective market value of $1.2 trillion, which was approximately equal to the total value of all publicly traded U.S. stocks a little more than one decade earlier.

Thousands of founders, executives, and employees of dot-com companies became multimillionaires in a period of a few hours when their companies sold stock in initial public offerings (IPOs). Scores of leading Wall Street analysts,

---

1. G. Ip, S. Pulliam, S. Thurm, and R. Simon, "How the Internet Bubble Broke Records, Rules, Bank Accounts," *The Wall Street Journal* Interactive Edition, 14 July 2000.

politicians, and celebrities also realized huge profits from those IPOs, thanks to their ties to dot-com insiders. The typical individual investor is precluded from purchasing a new stock at its IPO price, at least new stocks that are in heavy demand, which was true of dozens of dot-com securities issued in the late 1990s. Instead, most individual investors must wait until such stocks hit the market to purchase them. Individuals with ties to company management or with the investment banking firm sponsoring an IPO are permitted to purchase the new securities at their initial offering price. Pent-up demand for these stocks often causes their prices to leap dramatically when they are finally released for public trading, resulting in a quick windfall for the privileged investors who owned the stocks at the market's opening bell.

In November 1998, Theglobe.com, a company that created online communities of Internet surfers who shared common interests, saw the price of its stock leap from $9 per share to nearly $90 in the first few hours the stock was traded. Jimmy Johnson, at the time the head coach of the Miami Dolphins and a friend-of-a-friend of Theglobe.com's chief executive, was allowed to purchase 2,000 shares of the stock at its IPO price of $9. Shortly after the stock began trading, Johnson sold or "flipped" those shares for a reported profit of $150,000.[2]

Investors in Internet stocks soon introduced a new term into investment parlance, namely, the "ten-bagger." Amazon, AOL, eBay, Yahoo!, and dozens of other Internet-related companies produced at least ten-fold, that is, 1,000 percent, investment gains for tens of thousands of stock market mavens. Many individual investors who formerly had been more than pleased with modest, two-digit annual increases in the collective values of their investments were embarrassed to admit to friends and colleagues that their portfolios did not include at least one ten-bagger.

The public's feeding frenzy for Internet stocks eventually produced numerous paper billionaires among dot-com bigwigs. Dot-com billionaires making appearances in the *Forbes 400*, a list of the 400 "richest people in America," included, among several others, Jeff Bezos (Amazon), Stephen Case (AOL), Mark Cuban (Broadcast.com), David Wetherell (CMGI), Pierre Omidyar (eBay), Andrew Mc-Kelvey (Monster.com), Jay Walker (Priceline), and Jerry Yang and David Filo (Yahoo!). As you might expect, the New Economy added an even larger number of new members to the millionaires' club. By early 2000, one publication reported that in northern California's Silicon Valley alone, the Internet revolution was creating 64 new millionaires each day.[3]

As the prices of Internet stocks continued to rally, many Wall Street analysts and business journalists began referring to the huge run-up in those prices as the "Internet Bubble." These parties equated the public's frantic efforts to acquire Internet stocks with several other speculative and spectacular investment crazes of the past including the tulip mania that gripped Holland during the late nineteenth century, the infamous South Sea Bubble that emptied the pockets of British investors during the 1730s, and Wall Street's fascination with radio stocks several generations earlier. In the early 1920s, the introduction of the radio took Wall Street by storm. Investors scrambled to purchase ownership interests in dozens of

2. *The Miami Herald* (online), "Internet-Related Public Offerings Continue to Reap Huge Gains," 15 December 1999.

3. *The Economist* (online), "The Country-Club Vote," 20 May 2000.

new firms in the burgeoning radio industry that many business leaders believed would revolutionize society and the business world. Most of those investments soured when the majority of the hastily organized companies failed to develop sustainable business models and quickly went out of business.

As the end of the millennium approached, an increasing number of economists, politicians, and investment analysts began warning the public that the Internet Bubble would likely burst, causing huge losses for investors who had purchased the securities of Internet companies at prices inflated by the rampant speculation in those stocks. One investment analyst noted in *USA Today* that the skyrocketing prices of Internet stocks "was insanity on top of more insanity."[4] No doubt, Federal Reserve Chairman Alan Greenspan had Internet stocks in mind when he cautioned the public regarding the "irrational exuberance" plaguing the stock market during the late 1990s. A best-selling book entitled *The Internet Bubble* identified 133 Internet stocks that were allegedly overvalued by the stock market. In December 1999, the authors of that book bluntly warned investors to sell those stocks before it was too late. "If you hold any of these stocks, it's time to sell."[5]

Most Internet investors easily shrugged off such warnings. In their minds, the Internet revolution was effecting a fundamental change in the business and investment worlds. These investors reasoned that conventional investment yardsticks and benchmarks could not be applied to companies bold enough to develop revolutionary business plans designed to take advantage of new Internet-based technologies and opportunities.

> So, should canny investors take the Internet phenomenon as proof that the equity markets are out of control and heading for a fall? Internet enthusiasts say no. They argue that the valuations of these companies are entirely reasonable, even without current profits, because they have the potential to revolutionize whole industries—and reap the rewards. . . . The valuations are very high by traditional measures, but on the other hand the Internet is not a traditional phenomenon.[6]

FIVE DOT-COMS THAT WANTED TO CHANGE THE (BUSINESS) WORLD

A new generation of innovative entrepreneurs created thousands of new businesses designed to take advantage of Internet technology and the access it provided to the World Wide Web. Several hundred of those businesses evolved into large companies. Ownership interests in many of these companies were eventually offered to the public in initial public offerings. This section provides a brief profile of five Internet-based companies organized in the 1990s. Although these companies operated in different lines of business, their founders and executives generally shared two common goals: changing the basic structure and nature of the industry in which their company operated and accumulating a large personal fortune.

---

4. S. Block and J. Waggoner, "Net Frenzy Surges on; NASDAQ Hits New High," *USA Today*, 20 January 1999, 3B.

5. S. Tompor, "Big Returns Make Internet Stocks Popular, but Chance for Losses Looms Large," *Detroit Free Press* (online), 27 December 1999.

6. *Financial Times* (London), "Is the Internet Bubble Going to Burst?" 17 July 1999, 1.

LIVING.COM

Andrew Busey organized Living.com in the spring and early summer of 1999 from his small apartment in the downtown business district of Austin, Texas, the capital of the Lone Star State. At the time, Austin served as the home base to a growing number of high-tech companies, most notably Dell Computer Corporation. After graduating from Duke in the early 1990s, Busey had worked for a company developing an Internet browser before starting his own Internet company that he initially named iChat but later renamed Acuity. Busey sold his ownership interest in Acuity for nearly $50 million to pursue another dream, namely, creating a company to sell furniture online. Why furniture? Because Busey's father had worked for 35 years as a furniture salesman. The younger Busey intended to merge his knowledge of the Internet with his father's experience in the furniture industry to create the largest furniture retailer in the United States.

Andrew Busey quickly raised nearly $70 million of capital to establish his new business. Benchmark Capital, a leading venture capital firm for Internet start-ups, provided a large portion of those funds. Busey planned to raise additional funds in the spring of 2000 by taking Living.com public via an IPO. The high-spirited Busey quickly went about the task of creating a recognizable brand name for his new company. He used a large chunk of the funds obtained from Benchmark and other major investors to make a down payment on a five-year, $145 million contract with Amazon. That contract permitted Living.com to place a company icon or "tab" on the shopping section of Amazon's popular website. Critics questioned whether Busey paid too much for that right—criticism that the self-assured young entrepreneur easily brushed aside. Busey insisted that, "To really win at this, we need to spend money."[7] That attitude apparently prompted him to invest an additional $30 million in a nationwide advertising campaign for his new company.

When Living.com opened for business in the last few days of July 1999, Andrew Busey believed that the company would soon become an important, if not the dominant, furniture retailer in the nation. Even if his company did not live up to his high expectations, Busey recognized that the firm could be economically viable if it claimed only a modest fraction of the retail furniture market, which had annual sales of approximately $65 billion. Among Living.com's early skeptics was none other than Jay Busey, Andrew's father. When Andrew asked his father whether selling furniture online was a viable idea, Jay Busey replied, "No way, you have to touch it and feel it to buy furniture."[8]

TOYSMART.COM

In 1998, David Lord served as the chief financial officer for a small toy company based in Boston. Lord had encouraged the company's owners to expand their operations by establishing a website to market their merchandise. When the owners

---

7. A. Park, "Austin, Texas-Based Online Home Furnishings Store Dies Tragic Death," *Austin American-Statesman* (online), 18 September 2000.

8. P. Nowell, "Furniture Sellers Becoming E-Commerce Believers," *The Associated Press State & Local Wire*, 15 October 1999.

were slow to implement an aggressive Internet strategy, Lord took matters into his own hands and raised sufficient capital to purchase the company, which he then renamed Toysmart.com.

Lord not only wanted to build his company into a major toy retailer, he wanted to change the toy-buying habits of the American public. The number of toys that had violent or other inappropriate connotations concerned the young chief executive. He decided that Toysmart would exclusively market what he referred to as "good toys." Toysmart would not sell any toys that alluded to violent or other asocial behavior, such as toy weapons. The company would also market a wide array of educational toys.

To make his company competitive with leading toy retailers, Lord realized that he needed to obtain financial backing from a venture capital firm or from another source. During the summer of 1999, Lord pitched his plan to sell good toys to executives of Walt Disney Co. Impressed with Lord's sales strategy and his plan to exploit the Internet, Disney agreed to purchase a 60 percent ownership interest in the small company. Lord and his management team would retain control over the company's day-to-day operations, although Disney would appoint three of the five members of Toysmart's board of directors. Most important, Disney agreed to commit $45 million to Toysmart, $25 million of cash and another $20 million that Lord could use to advertise the company on Disney's media properties, including its *Go.com* and *Family.com* websites.

With Disney's financial support, Lord launched a nationwide advertising campaign intended to help Toysmart seize a substantial share of the large retail toy market. Shortly after finalizing the arrangement with Disney, Lord remarked that, "We're going to champion good toys, and we're going to shout it from the top of every mountain."[9] The young executive began his advertising campaign with a 22-city "good toy" tour in the fall of 1999. During that tour, Lord promoted the concept of good toys in dozens of interviews with the media. Extensive Web-based advertising and a series of television commercials made Toysmart the fourth most visited toy website during the Christmas 1999 selling season, trailing only eToys, Toys "R" Us, and Smarterkids.com. Overall, Toysmart ranked as the twenty-fourth most visited website during the 1999 holiday season.

By affiliating his small company with Disney, David Lord immediately made Toysmart a "player" in the retail toy industry. Lord and the other members of Toysmart's management team believed that the relationship with Disney would have no downside for their company. However, an executive of another online toy retailer disagreed. This individual maintained that Lord and his subordinates would soon realize that Disney's management team could not resist meddling in the affairs of companies in which Disney held a controlling ownership interest. "Disney has a tendency to over-manage its investments. They can go in with the best intentions, but Disney just can't help themselves. They're going to want to do it the Disney way, eventually."[10]

---

9. D. Germain, "Disney Buys 60 Percent of Internet Educational Toy Retailer," *The Associated Press State & Local Wire*, 26 August 1999.

10. *Ibid.*

EVE.COM

Two San Francisco natives, Varsha Rao and Mariam Naficy, established Eve.com in early 1999. The women planned to use their website to market a full range of beauty products. Within a few months, they had raised almost $30 million of capital to finance their ambitious venture. After realizing that they needed help developing and implementing a comprehensive business plan for their new company, Rao and Naficy met with Bill Gross, the chief executive of the leading Internet incubator idealab!. In April 1999, the novice entrepreneurs agreed to sell a controlling interest in their firm to idealab!. Although Rao and Naficy retained their titles of company co-presidents, Gross soon brought in three executives from Barney's, an upscale retailer based in New York, to oversee Eve's daily operations.

Eve opened its website for business in June 1999, becoming the first major online retailer of cosmetics and related beauty products. Although several competing websites would appear in the coming months, Eve remained the most popular Web retailer of its type throughout 1999 and most of 2000, generating more traffic than competing sites and offering a larger number of individual products and brands than any online competitor. Internet experts recognized Eve as one of the most functional and consumer-friendly retail sites on the Web. *Fortune* magazine, for example, named the company one of the ten best online retailers.

As Eve's first anniversary approached in June 2000, press releases issued by company management declared that Eve had changed the way women everywhere shop for cosmetics. In commenting on the approaching anniversary, Mariam Naficy noted that "Eve.com's success in our first year is only the beginning and we are ready to celebrate many more birthdays to come."[11] After reviewing Eve's operations, one analyst predicted that the firm would eventually capture up to 10 percent of the $10 billion annual market for beauty products. Company insiders hoped that such glowing projections would allow Eve to launch a successful IPO in the fall of 2000.

PETOPIA.COM

In May 1999, Andrea Reisman helped found Petopia.com, an online pet supplies retailer. From the company's headquarters in downtown San Francisco, Reisman supervised a small band of dedicated pet lovers who made up Petopia's workforce. Reisman's stated objective was to change "the way pet owners think about shopping for their pet supplies."[12] More specifically, Reisman wanted pet owners to purchase those supplies online, preferably from her company's website. The potential market awaiting Petopia was substantial. Approximately 63 percent of all U.S. households own at least one pet. Industry data reveal that in addition to food and supplies, a large percentage of pet owners also regularly purchase gifts for their pets: two-thirds of dog owners purchase gifts for Fido, while 54 percent of cat owners surprise Tabby with an occasional present. In the late 1990s, the

---

11. *PR Newswire*, "12 Chances to Win Dazzling Diamonds on Eve.com; The Leading Online Cosmetics Retailer Celebrates Countdown to First Birthday," 12 April 2000.

12. *PR Newswire*, "Petopia.com Announces $9 Million Equity Investment," 10 May 1999.

public's annual expenditures for pet supplies, pet food, and, yes, pet gifts topped $25 billion.

Andrea Reisman spent most of the summer of 1999 asking investors to provide financing for Petopia. By the end of the summer, she had obtained commitments of nearly $80 million for her firm. More important, she had inked an agreement to affiliate Petopia with Petco, the second largest pet supplies retailer in the nation. The agreement included Petco purchasing a 20 percent ownership interest in Petopia with an option to increase that interest in the future. Under the terms of the agreement, Reisman remained Petopia's chief executive officer (CEO). The two companies planned to promote each other's operations and to share customer databases and product information. Petco's chief executive saw the alliance with Petopia as an opportunity for his company to establish an e-commerce presence at a modest cost. "This partnership will provide Petco with e-commerce capabilities almost immediately, and at a significantly lower cost than establishing those functions ourselves. . . . We expect Petopia.com to emerge as one of the leaders in the online pet food and supply market."[13]

Petopia's website opened for business in August 1999. By late 1999, Petopia ranked as the most visited pet site on the Web with 800,000 unique visitors each month, according to Media Metrix, a firm that collects and periodically reports Internet traffic data. That feat was no small accomplishment since dozens of websites were hawking pet food and supplies by the end of 1999. The "dog-eat-dog" nature of the online pet supply business forced Andrea Reisman and her colleagues to continually search for new products and services that would attract Internet surfers to the Petopia.com website. Eventually, the Petopia site would offer more than 12,000 products and services, including a line of health insurance policies for pets. Reisman also added "The Internet Pet Paradise" to Petopia's website. More than fifty freelance writers were retained by the company to develop informative articles and stories focusing on pets and pet owners. One feature that appeared regularly in the Pet Paradise was "Famous Cat Lovers and Haters in History."

VALUE AMERICA

Among thousands of entrepreneurs who established retail websites in the late 1990s, Craig Winn easily ranked among the most ambitious. According to a cover page article in *Business Week*, Winn intended to make his new online firm, Value America, the "Wal-Mart of the Internet." Winn, a businessman with political aspirations, served as Value America's chief executive, principal strategist, fundraiser and, most important, the company's public spokesperson and cheerleader. In the late 1970s, well before the public was aware of the Internet and more than one decade before it was opened to commercial use, Winn had devised a master plan for a "frictionless" form of retailing. The simple concept underlying his plan was eliminating the various middlemen or intermediaries that increase the cost of merchandise purchased by individual consumers.

Winn wanted to develop a business that would bring people and products together by linking consumers directly with the companies that manufactured con-

---

13. *Business Wire*, "Petco Announces Strategic Partnership with Petopia.com to Launch the Premier Online Pet Commerce Site," 13 July 1999.

sumer goods. The introduction of the Internet to the business world during the 1990s provided Winn with the technology he had been searching for to implement his grand retailing plan. *Business Week* described Winn's concept of a megacyberstore. "The store would carry no inventory and ship no products. Instead it would pick up orders from consumers and immediately transmit them to manufacturers who would ship IBM computers and Knorr soups, Panasonic televisions and Vicks Vapo Rub, direct to customers."[14]

Craig Winn had a checkered history of success and failure in his business career that caused many skeptics to question his ability to develop the ultimate retail business on the World Wide Web. A 1978 graduate of the University of Southern California, Winn had always thought of himself as a salesperson, like his father, who worked as a housewares salesman most of his life. In fact, shortly after graduating from USC, Winn teamed with his father to create a small firm to sell housewares. That business succeeded and provided Winn with the capital to bankroll another company that marketed lighting products. Despite going public in 1990, this new company struggled throughout its existence before filing for bankruptcy in 1993.

Winn immediately began searching for another business venture to pursue. After studying the potential commercial applications of the Internet, Winn developed an elaborate business plan for a new firm that he named Value America. At the heart of that business plan was his concept of friction-free capitalism. For the next few years, Winn promoted his nouveau brand of capitalism to any journalist or potential investor who would listen. In late 1997, Winn and several colleagues who had helped him establish Value America, which was still in a developmental stage, convinced an insurance company to invest $10 million in the new age business. Executives of that company then introduced Winn to Paul Allen, cofounder of Microsoft. Allen was impressed by Winn's business plan and ultimately invested more than $65 million in Value America.

Paul Allen's support provided Value America with instant credibility and the resources necessary to begin developing the infrastructure needed to implement Winn's business plan. Allen's support also allowed Winn to convince many other high-profile individuals to invest in Value America, including Fred Smith, the founder of Federal Express, and renowned financier Sam Belzberg. Smith not only committed $10 million to the company but also agreed to serve on the company's board of directors. William Bennett, a member of President George Bush's cabinet in the early 1990s, also accepted an appointment to Value America's board.

In April 1999, Value America went public with a successful IPO. The company's stock traded initially at $23 per share but leaped during the first day of trading to $74 per share. The IPO provided a huge amount of funds for Value America and made Craig Winn a billionaire. Over the next year, Winn cashed out much of his ownership interest in the company by selling stock in the open market. Interestingly, Winn sold Value America stock at the same time he was encouraging other deep-pocketed parties to invest in the company.

Winn and his fellow officers used approximately $70 million of the funds brought in by their company's IPO to finance a nationwide advertising campaign intended to acquaint consumers with the benefits of purchasing merchandise from Value America's website. During 1999, Value America ranked

---

14. J. A. Byrne, "The Fall of a Dot-com," *Business Week*, 1 May 2000, 150.

second only to E*Trade as the most prolific advertiser among Web-based companies. Winn's advertising campaign succeeded in making the public aware of Value America and in making himself a recognized leader of the army of new Web-based entrepreneurs. In fact, in early 1999, *CEO Magazine* labeled Winn "the prince of e-commerce."

Business journalists frequently sought out Winn to obtain his opinions on a wide range of issues involving e-commerce, including whether Web retailers should be required to collect state sales taxes—Winn believed that they should. In a May 1999 interview with *The Washington Post*, Winn recalled that when he first began discussing the concept of friction-free capitalism he had been the subject of considerable scorn and criticism. "We have changed the entire mind-set of Internet companies because of the success of Value America. Everyone we talked to [initially] said, 'You're crazy. This is the dumbest idea in the world. It will absolutely fail. Do not do it.'"[15]

Later in that same interview, Winn was questioned regarding the huge operating losses that Value America had been piling up over the previous few quarters. Winn quickly dismissed the reporter's suggestion that those losses were indicative of his company's long-term prospects and focused instead on the overriding strategic initiatives that he and his management team had adopted. "We are not playing this game to be a niche player. We're not in the arena here to do business with a few people. We're in here to change the world. We're literally in business to change the way that people buy and sell products."[16] Winn maintained that Value America's focus on the two "s" words would eventually result in the company becoming profitable. "The two 's' words drive our day-to-day thought processes. We're in business to do two things: build scale and satisfy our customers. If we do those two things well, it will lead us to profitability."[17]

DOT-COM FEVER LEADS TO EXCESSES AND QUESTIONABLE DECISIONS

As the prices of Internet stocks continued to rise in the late 1990s, the riches reaped by founders, officers, and employees of dot-com companies led to increasing levels of smugness among many of those parties. *The Wall Street Journal* profiled the rags-to-riches story of a young man who accepted a job with an Internet consulting firm shortly after earning a graduate business degree.[18] That new position came with stock options, options that could be exercised by the young man at the minimal price of $1.10 per share if the firm went public in an IPO, which it had plans to do. The ambitious young consultant saw his net worth race past $1 million in the few months following his employer's IPO. When the company's stock price topped $90, the consultant was sitting on a paper gain of $89 per share. The young man later admitted that the sudden wealth "went to his

---

15. *The Washington Post*, "Conversation with Value America's Craig Winn," 10 May 1999, F16.

16. *Ibid.*

17. *Ibid.*

18. S. L. Hwang, "From Rags to Riches and Back: Web Craze Whipsaws a Consultant," *The Wall Street Journal* Interactive Edition, 10 July 2000.

head." He began spending freely and extravagantly on vacations and expensive trinkets to decorate his apartment. Most troubling was the impact the newly found wealth had on his personality. To his old friends who had missed out on the Internet investment express, he became "increasingly distant." No doubt, those friends were more than a little offended when he once noted matter-of-factly, "I made another $58,000 while I was sleeping."[19]

Dot-com fever also infected executives of Internet companies. The huge sums of cash that IPOs dumped upon many of those companies often created a sense of infallibility among their executives, which, in turn, prompted them to make unconventional, if not questionable, business decisions. Following Value America's IPO, Craig Winn became renowned for his ostentatious spending on pet projects. For example, the impetuous Winn signed a contract obligating Value America to pay $5 million for a tract of land on which he intended to build a palatial corporate headquarters. A subsequent appraisal placed the land's fair market value at no more than $2 million. To void the contract, Value America was required to pay $400,000.

Northern California's Silicon Valley became known for lavish launch parties thrown by executives of Internet-based companies when they went public with an IPO. The *Los Angeles Times* reported that many companies spent several hundred thousand dollars on such parties to introduce their executives and employees to the "good life."[20] Executives of the online retailer Boo.com can likely lay claim to the prize for the most outrageous spending habits. Two young Swedes in their late twenties, one a fashion model and the other a writer, founded Boo.com in 1999. The longtime friends intended their company to be an online fashion retailer that would cater to the clothing needs of well-to-do consumers around the world. Within a few months, the two well-connected entrepreneurs had raised $125 million of venture capital to finance their new company, including investments from the Benetton family of Italy, the wealthy French investor Bernard Arnault, and the leading Wall Street investment banking firm of Goldman, Sachs & Company. Boo's founders burned through the $125 million in a matter of months, spending an exorbitant amount on a posh corporate headquarters on London's Carnaby Street and a comparable sum to establish a string of luxurious satellite offices in New York, Paris, Stockholm, Amsterdam, and Munich. Much of Boo's cash was absorbed by travel and entertainment expenses for its executives, who reportedly insisted on flying first-class and staying in five-star hotels.

Elaborate advertising campaigns were typically the largest drain on the cash resources of Internet companies that had tapped into the lucrative IPO market. During Super Bowl XXXIV in late January 2000, 17 companies connected to the Internet spent a minimum of $2 million to run one or more television commercials during the game. Included among those firms were Autotrader.com, HotJobs.com, Kforce.com, and Monster.com. Critics questioned the cost-effectiveness of those expensive Super Bowl commercials. One corporate executive noted that, "The Super Bowl epitomized the exuberance and frenzy of the dot-com world. Everybody was throwing Hail Mary passes, but there were no receivers in the end zone."[21]

19. *Ibid.*

20. K. E. Klein, "Your Company: News, Trends, and Help for Growing Companies," *Los Angeles Times*, 2 August 2000, C6.

21. M. McCarthy, "Super Bowl Aftermath: Dot-com Fumbles," *USA Today*, 27 July 2000, 9B.

Dot-com executives became all too familiar with criticism of their firms' advertising efforts, criticism that seemed justified in many, if not most, cases. In 1999, Pets.com, the major online competitor to Petopia and another one of the dot-coms that ran Super Bowl XXXIV commercials, incurred $460 of advertising expenditures for every $100 of sales it generated during the year. A typical bricks and mortal retailer spends only three to five cents of each sales dollar on advertising expenditures.

STORM CLOUDS GATHER OVER DOT-COMS

By early 2000, the investing public's enthusiasm for Internet-related stocks, particularly securities of companies involved in business-to-consumer or B2C lines of business, seemed to be waning. The most common concern cited by sophisticated investors and Internet analysts regarding dot-com stocks was the large number of firms crowding into Web-based lines of businesses.

The barriers to entry for online industries are generally much less imposing than those for Old Economy industries. As a result, copycat entrepreneurs quickly rushed to mimic new online businesses that seemed to have a reasonable business plan. "Virtually every smart idea a dot-com entrepreneur has ever dreamed up has been duplicated by established concerns with deep pockets and staying power."[22] By the spring of 2000, Petopia, for example, was struggling to compete with more than 100 other online businesses marketing pet supplies. Industry experts reasoned that the online segment of the pet supplies industry could comfortably accommodate only two Web-based retailers. The same problem was faced by Eve.com, Toysmart.com, Living.com, and most other online retailers that had established themselves as leading firms in their new Web-based lines of business. Value America, which wanted to become the "Wal-Mart of the Internet," soon found that the *real* Wal-Mart had established its own general merchandise site on the Web.

The overcrowded conditions facing businesses on the World Wide Web began taking a toll on selected dot-com stocks in early 2000. Nevertheless, the NASDAQ stock index, which most economists used as the key barometer to measure the health of the New Economy, continued to trend ever higher in early 2000, posting new record highs every few days, finally breaking the 5,000 barrier for the first time in early March. As the NASDAQ continued its meteoric rise, far outstripping modest increases being posted by the Dow Jones Industrial Average, more and more concerned investors and financial analysts questioned when the Internet Bubble would finally burst. In the words of one business reporter, "Surely, this madness has to end sometime soon . . . doesn't it?"[23]

22. J. Kerstetter, L. Himelstein, R. Hof, and L. Lee, "Finding the Right Net Formula," *Business-Week Online*, 23 October 2000.

23. *The Miami Herald* (online), "Internet-Related Public Offerings Continue to Reap Huge Gains," 15 December 1999.

QUESTIONS

1. Should the federal government prohibit companies that have seemingly weak or, at least, very speculative business plans from marketing their stock to the general public in an initial public offering (IPO)? Defend your answer.
2. What is the role of the federal government in policing the stock markets? Should the federal government intervene when stock prices seem to be significantly overvalued?
3. Comment on the ethical issues raised by the practice of allowing certain individuals to purchase new securities at their IPO prices before those securities are formally released on the market.
4. Economists often speak of "barriers to entry" to given industries or lines of business. Choose a conventional industry and identify and briefly describe three barriers of entry to that industry. Do the same for an Internet-based industry or line of business.
5. Identify what you believe are the three to five most important keys to success for (a) a new online retail business and (b) a new conventional retailer.
6. Craig Winn of Value America founded his company on the concept of "friction-free" capitalism. What weaknesses, if any, can you identify in that concept? Explain.
7. Compare and contrast the five dot-com companies profiled in this case in terms of the principal competitive issues, challenges, and opportunities they faced in their respective lines of business. Identify which of those companies you believe had the best chance of succeeding and which of the companies was most likely to fail. Defend your choices.

Internet Bubble, Part II: Burn, Baby, Burn

*There are two times in a man's life when he should
not speculate: when he can't afford it and when he can.*

Mark Twain

In 1941, 11-year-old Warren Buffett began his investment career by purchasing three shares of stock in a natural gas company. Over the following six decades, the value of Buffett's investment portfolio grew from less than $100 to more than $35 billion, making him one of the wealthiest persons not only in the United States but the entire world, as well.

Buffett earned most of his billions through an investment company that he acquired in the mid-1960s, Berkshire Hathaway, Inc., a firm based in Omaha, Nebraska. As Berkshire's chief executive officer (CEO), Buffett crafted a simple investment strategy for his company predicated on the well-known "value" investing principle. Buffett and his colleagues do an exhaustive amount of research to identify stocks they believe are undervalued by the stock market. Berkshire then purchases large blocks of such stocks and simply waits until the stock market assigns a more appropriate (higher) price to those securities. When stocks in Berkshire's portfolio become overvalued by the stock market, Buffett and his fellow executives typically sell those securities to lock in their profits. Unlike most investment companies, Berkshire limits its major investments to a small number of stocks. To reassure investors who purchase Berkshire's stock, Buffett pledges to keep his huge personal fortune invested in the company. In fact, Buffett has never sold one share of Berkshire Hathaway stock since acquiring the company in 1965.

Warren Buffett's investment strategy made him the most successful investor on Wall Street during the final three decades of the twentieth century. That success caused business journalists and fellow investors to refer to the down-to-earth and self-deprecating Buffett as the "Oracle of Omaha." Through 1998, Berkshire realized an annual average rate of return on its investments of an astonishing 24 percent. For short periods of times, other investment companies or mutual funds could brag of higher annual returns. But, no manager of a major investment portfolio or investment company came close to matching Berkshire's rate of return over a period of several decades.

Another important element of Warren Buffett's investment strategy is investing only in companies that he understands. Buffett believes that he and his colleagues must thoroughly understand the nature of a company's industry and operations before they can place a value on its traded securities. Because of this policy, Buffett has concentrated his investments in large, high-profile companies. Corporations in which Berkshire has invested recently include American Express, Coca-Cola, Disney, Dun & Bradstreet, Gillette, McDonald's, and Wells Fargo & Company.

During the late 1990s, Buffett stubbornly avoided investing in stocks with close ties to the Internet. Why? Because he insisted that he had no way of determining the values that should be ascribed to such securities since most Internet companies were still in a developmental stage and were relying on novel, untested business models that he did not fully understand. Buffett believed that several years of financial data would be needed to identify the Internet companies that had sustainable and profitable business models. In the meantime, conventional measures used to evaluate stock prices, such as the price-earnings and return on equity ratios, suggested to Buffett that the securities of most Internet-dependent companies were likely overpriced, if not grossly overpriced.

Not only did Warren Buffett avoid investing in Internet stocks, he frequently chided investors who did. At one point, Buffett suggested that investing in Internet stocks was based on the same "get rich" principle that underlies chain letter schemes. "Those who bought early and cashed out would gain and later newcomers would ultimately lose."[1] In commenting on the "Internet Bubble," that is, the huge run-up in the market prices of Internet stocks during 1999, Buffett noted that "there is no question that in the past year the ability to monetize shareholder ignorance has never been exceeded."[2]

As the Internet Bubble continued to grow larger, investments funds that would normally flow into Old Economy stocks were diverted into Internet stocks or, at least, that was the argument made by Warren Buffett and other value investors. Sour grapes? Maybe. In 1999, Buffett saw the book value per share of Berkshire Hathaway's investment portfolio eke out a razor-thin increase of only 0.5 percent. That modest increase compared unfavorably to the large double-digit gain posted by the NASDAQ, which includes scores of Internet companies, and triple-digit gains reported in 1999 by several stock indices that track only the stock prices of Internet companies.

Buffett accepted full responsibility for his company's poor performance in 1999, attributing the minimal gain to poor "asset allocation" decisions on his part, in other words, poor investment decisions. Nevertheless, Buffett refused to even consider changing his long-range investment philosophy, insisting that *value* not *hype* would eventually be the driving force underlying stock prices, including the stock prices of Internet-based companies. "Investors in these [Internet] stocks are expecting far too much. . . . The fact is that markets behave in ways, sometimes for a very long stretch, that are not linked to value. Sooner or later, though, value counts."[3]

---

1. M. A. Hofmann, "Buffett Defends Reserves; $275 Million Adequate to Cover Gen Re's Unicover Losses," *Business Insurance*, 8 May 2000, 2.

2. *The Financial Times* (London), "Equity Markets: Taking Stock of the Brave New World," 6 May 2000, 2.

3. J. Schoolman, "Tangled Web for Buffett, Famed Investor Loses Ground in 1999 as He Shies Away from Internet Stocks," *Daily News* (New York), 27 December 1999, 39.

BARRON'S Report Burns Internet Stocks

In the late 1990s, financial analysts tracking dot-com stocks introduced investors to a new measure used to evaluate the financial soundness of Internet-related companies, particularly those companies still in an early stage of development. Analysts use the term "burn rate" when referring to the average daily net cash outflow of a financially troubled company. Dividing a distressed company's existing cash resources by its burn rate yields a rough estimate of the firm's "flame-out" date, that is, the date it is expected to run out of cash. The founders of the popular website for investors "The Motley Fool" publish a syndicated newspaper column in which they answer questions posed by individual investors. Several of those columns have addressed the concept of a burn rate. One such column discussed the cash flow problems facing iVillage, an online company catering to women's issues and needs.

> It's not unusual for firms to lose money in their early years, but it is important for investors to evaluate how much money those firms are taking in and using up. In iVillage's case, at its current burn rate it'll use up its cash hoard in just a few quarters. To stay alive, the firm will either have to reduce spending—possibly resulting in slower growth, or find some more money—perhaps taking on debt or issuing additional stock, which would dilute value for existing shareholders.[4]

As individual Internet stocks and indices began cresting at higher and higher levels, many prominent investment publications began expressing concern at the high burn rates of individual dot-coms. Jack Willoughby, a business journalist, captured the attention of investors worldwide when he published an article entitled "Burning Up" in the March 20, 2000, edition of *Barron's*. Willoughby began that article with a question: "When will the Internet Bubble burst?"[5] The article went on to suggest that the rapid burn rates of many dot-coms could cause an "unpleasant popping sound" before the end of the year.

Willoughby's article contained a large table entitled "Burn Victims." That table reported selected financial data for 207 Internet companies, including many well known firms in the New Economy such as Ariba, DoubleClick, Inktomi, Price-line.com, and VerticalNet. The caption for the final column of that table was "Months Till Burnout." The data in that column revealed that dozens of Internet companies were just a few months away from running out of cash. Peapod, the best known of several online grocers, had two months of cash remaining; the Web-based software retailer Egghead.com had approximately four months of cash on hand; drkoop.com, an online dispenser of medical information, was three months away from running out of cash; while CDNow, an online retailer of music and other entertainment products, had only a few days of cash remaining.

Willoughby maintained that the cash-starved dot-coms would have considerable difficulty raising desperately needed funds for at least two reasons. First, institutional investors, banks, and other deep-pocketed parties were beginning to question the soundness of those dot-coms' business models. Many of these large investors and lenders had already sunk large sums of capital into those companies and were not inclined to "throw good money after bad." Second, Willoughby

---

4. *The Houston Chronicle*, "The Motley Fool: Ask the Fool," 17 July 2000, 2.

5. J. Willoughby, "Burning Up," *Barron's*, 20 March 2000, 29.

pointed out that major investors and lenders were aware that much of the cash that had been raised by dot-coms over the previous six to twelve months had not been used to finance their operations or to improve their financial condition. Instead, those funds had been diverted to the bank accounts of large stockholders who were selling their ownership interests in those firms. In one case, more than one-half of the cash raised by an Internet company's "secondary" or post-IPO sale of stock went to company insiders. By "cashing out," those insiders discouraged other parties from providing financially troubled dot-coms with additional debt and equity capital, which effectively doomed the companies to failure.

> Sure, venture capitalists and other early-stage investors are in the business of selling out at a profit eventually, but large sales of insider stock while a company is reporting losses can choke off that company's access to fresh capital, thereby diminishing the chances of survival. In the investment world, this is akin to men on a sinking ocean liner pushing women and children aside to commandeer the lifeboats.[6]

The *Barron's* article by Jack Willoughby provided the investing public a stark, objective, and comprehensive snapshot of the extremely poor financial condition of most publicly owned Internet companies. Other journalists began citing that article to substantiate their claims that the stocks of most dot-coms were drastically overpriced. Several going-concern opinions issued by independent auditors on the financial statements of dot-coms added to growing apprehension among investors regarding the financial soundness of Internet companies. These audit reports indicated that there was "substantial doubt" the given firms would survive over the coming twelve months. Internet companies receiving going-concern audit opinions included CDNow and drkoop.com.

Another "red flag" that dot-com skeptics pointed to in early 2000 was the slowing revenue growth of many Internet-based companies over the previous few quarters. Since the inception of the New Economy, venture capitalists who financed dot-com start-ups and many Internet analysts who tracked those companies downplayed the significance of their poor bottom-line financial results. These dot-com advocates insisted that the large losses being posted by Internet companies was strictly a short-term phenomenon since these firms' spectacular revenue growth rates would soon translate into sizable profits. As those growth rates began tapering off in late 1999 and early 2000, that theory became less plausible. "Perhaps the biggest chill has come from the slowing of revenue growth. In an industry where earnings are scarce, investors have used revenue momentum as a gauge of value. Take Amazon.com. Revenues are still expanding, but its growth rate has been cut in half."[7]

DOT-COM SELL-OFF

The long-anticipated drop in Internet stocks finally occurred in the weeks following the publication of the "Burning Up" article in *Barron's* on March 20, 2000. From a high of approximately 5,100 in early March 2000, the NASDAQ stock index plunged nearly 2,000 points by late May. In one week alone in mid-April,

---

6. *Ibid.*

7. D. Sparks and J. Laderman, "The Great Net Sell-Off," *Business Week*, 16 August 1999, 32.

the NASDAQ lost 25 percent of its value. Even more damage was done to the pure Internet stock indices. By September 2000, the *Forbes Internet Index* had plummeted by 64 percent from its high six months earlier, meaning that a stubborn investor who held on to a portfolio of Internet stocks worth $500,000 in March likely saw the value of that portfolio shrink to approximately $180,000 by September.

Among the Internet securities pummeled the most were the stocks of companies listed in the "Burn Victims" table of the *Barron's* article. Peapod's stock price dropped precipitously in early April and by early fall 2000 traded at less than $1, down more than 90 percent from its February high. The stock price of drkoop.com mimicked the sharp downturn in Peapod's stock price, falling from a high of $17 per share in February 2000, to less than $1 by early August 2000. High-profile dot-coms unfortunate enough to make Jack Willoughby's "burn list" also saw their stock prices scorched during 2000. From early March to mid-October, the stocks of both Amazon and Inktomi lost nearly two-thirds of their value. Homestore.com, an online real estate services company, experienced one of the largest and most sudden stock price collapses. Homestore's stock price dropped from a high of $138 in late January 2000 to less than $14 per share three months later.

Among the most interesting analyses of the bursting of the Internet Bubble was a study reported in *Fortune* in June 2000.[8] That article listed the average stock price decline over the previous twelve months of Internet companies whose names included one of the distinctive prefixes often used by cyberspace firms: "Cyber," "e," "i," or "Net." "Cyber" and "Net" stocks each dropped an average of 64 percent over that time frame, while "i" stocks slid 68 percent and "e" stocks fell an average of 73 percent.

By mid-2000, several websites had established "death watches" to monitor financially troubled Internet companies. Among many others, those websites included Downside.com, BubbleEconomy.com, and Dotcomfailures.com whose motto was "Kick 'em while they're down." Downside.com listed dozens of Internet companies on its Deathwatch page and reported the dates those companies were expected to flame out or, in some cases, the dates that the firms had actually bitten the proverbial dust. Firms that at some point checked into Downside's intensive care unit included drkoop.com, iVillage, MP3.com, and Peapod.

The financial turmoil that suddenly gripped the Internet sector of the economy during 2000 forced many executives of Internet-based companies to take sweeping and often drastic measures to salvage their firms. Instead of continually attempting to impress financial analysts and potential investors with grand forecasts of future revenue growth, executives of these firms adopted a P2P—path-to-profitability—strategy. Central to this strategy was a rigorous effort to conserve cash resources. Internet companies began cutting back on discretionary expenditures, particularly advertising outlays. In some cases, executives of Internet companies completely reengineered their firm's business model in a desperate attempt to begin producing positive cash flows from its day-to-day operating activities. Many of the companies that adopted such plans were among the firms profiled by Jack Willoughby in his "Burn Victims" article. In fact, in June 2000, Willoughby wrote a follow-up piece for *Barron's* entitled "Up in Smoke"

---

8.   L. Clifford, "eGADS!" *Fortune*, 26 June 2000, 292.

that examined new strategic initiatives adopted by the companies that were the focal point of his initial article.[9] Skeptical financial analysts and investors insisted that most of those initiatives should be relegated to the "too little, too late" department.

REVISITING FIVE DOT-COMS THAT INTENDED TO CHANGE THE (BUSINESS) WORLD

Case 3.4, *Internet Bubble, Part I: Party Time*, profiled five dot-coms whose executives intended to radically change the nature of the industries in which their firms operated. Each of those companies received widespread publicity during the late 1990s. Many analysts and investors expected those five companies to eventually challenge the Old Economy companies that dominated their respective industries. In this section, we revisit those five dot-coms and examine how they fared during 2000.

LIVING.COM

Andrew Busey, the young founder and chief executive of Living.com, an online furniture retailer, convinced his father Jay Busey that he could sell furniture on the Internet. At first, Jay Busey insisted that his son's idea wouldn't work, maintaining that consumers want to "touch and feel" furniture before buying it. Certainly, the elder Busey had inside information on the retail furniture industry since he had spent several decades working as a furniture salesman. After raising millions of dollars of venture capital to finance his project, Andrew finally persuaded his father to join his new firm. One year later, Jay Busey likely wished that he had been more insistent with his son. Living.com easily ranks as one of the most unsuccessful dot-coms organized in the frenzied heyday of the dot-com mania that gripped the business world in the late 1990s.

Living.com filed for Chapter 7 bankruptcy in August 2000, meaning that the company was immediately ceasing operations and would soon liquidate its assets. The IPO that Andrew Busey planned for his company never took place. Despite spending $50 million on advertising, Living.com generated total sales of only $10 million during its brief existence. Within a few weeks after Living.com filed for bankruptcy, another "leading" online furniture retailer, Furniture.com, shut down its operations as well. Initially, the novelty of buying furniture over the Internet produced impressive monthly increases in online furniture sales. However, by the fall of 2000, online furniture sales were reflecting double-digit declines each month according to the National Retail Federation.[10] Apparently, Jay Busey was right. Current Internet technology cannot provide consumers with the up close and personal encounter that they demand before shelling out several hundred dollars for a sofa and love seat.

---

9. J. Willoughby, "Up in Smoke," *Barron's Online*, 19 June 2000.

10. R. Craver, "Bankruptcy of Housewares Web Retailer Prompts Online Furniture Sales Slump," *High Point Enterprise* (online), 24 October 2000.

The *Austin American-Statesman* produced a lengthy and revealing obituary of Living.com in a September 2000, article.[11] Andrew Busey refused to be interviewed by the reporter who wrote that article. Reportedly, he was hard at work on his next project—writing a "how to" book on entrepreneurship. Former employees of Living.com did speak off the record to the reporter. They attributed the downfall of the company to "hubris" on the part of Andrew Busey and his fellow officers. "Out of touch with the realities of life in a start-up company, the executives spent too much and listened too little."[12]

In retrospect, Andrew Busey and Living.com's other executives simply failed to understand the technical problems and challenges that had to be overcome to make an online furniture retailer a viable business operation. "The challenges in making it work were bigger than anyone anticipated. . . . The logistics of shipping furniture around the country were more complex than anyone had thought."[13] Instead of focusing on the less than glamorous aspects of establishing a new retail business, such as creating a distribution network and developing relationships with vendors, Busey and his colleagues apparently concentrated most of their effort on the company's extensive advertising campaign. Unfortunately, the customers of Living.com footed the bill for much of the company's extravagant spending. Hundreds of customers of Living.com who paid for furniture that the company never delivered received only fractional refunds from the court-appointed bankruptcy trustee who liquidated the company.

TOYSMART.COM

David Lord purchased a small Boston-based toy company and immediately renamed the firm Toysmart.com. The central plank of Lord's business plan for Toysmart was marketing "good toys"—educational toys and other toys with no violent connotations—over the Internet. Lord's hopes for making Toysmart a leading toy retailer were buoyed when he sold a 60 percent interest in the firm to the Walt Disney Co. in the summer of 1999. Disney executives gave Lord a $25 million cash horde to spend on advertising and another $20 million of advertising credits to use for commercials and other promotions on Disney's various media outlets. Although three of Toysmart's five directors would be Disney appointees, Disney insisted that Lord would be allowed to make the key operating decisions affecting the company.

Despite Disney's pledge to allow David Lord to continue running Toysmart, he and Disney executives began butting heads almost immediately. One key point of contention involved Lord's definition of "good toys." Disney produced and marketed a large number of figurines and other toy products modeled after characters appearing in many of its popular animated movies, such as the sword-wielding warriors central to the story line of *Mulan*. Lord decided that many of those products were not "good toys." Although certainly miffed, Disney officials eventually agreed to allow Lord to define what he considered to be good toys.

11. A. Park, "Austin, Texas-Based Online Home Furnishings Store Dies Tragic Death," *Austin American-Statesman* (online), 18 September 2000.

12. *Ibid.*

13. *Ibid.*

Disney executives proved to be less compromising in subsequent disputes with David Lord. Known for being conservative and deliberate, Disney executives did not condone Lord's aggressive, off-the-cuff management style, which he believed was necessary given the dynamic, fast-paced Internet environment in which Toysmart competed. Lord also clashed with his Disney bosses over how best to evaluate Toysmart's performance. Like most Old Economy companies, Disney evaluated its divisions and majority-owned subsidiaries based primarily on the financial results they produced. Lord, on the other hand, believed that Toysmart should be evaluated, at least initially, on the basis of such non-financial benchmarks as period-to-period increases in brand awareness. In commenting on this issue, Lord noted, "Disney is a fine institution that runs its business by the bottom line and we're an Internet company, which means we weren't driven by the bottom line at least in year one."[14]

During the 1999 holiday season, Toysmart produced sales of only $6 million, despite more than $25 million of advertising expenditures in the months leading up to Christmas. During the fourth quarter of 1999, Toysmart also spent nearly $3 million of its Disney advertising credits on promotional materials distributed on the *Go.com* and *Family.com* websites owned and operated by Disney. Those marketing efforts produced only $66,000 of sales. Disney number-crunchers also reported that Toysmart spent $200, on average, acquiring an online customer, each of which purchased only $44 of merchandise. According to one embarrassed and sarcastic Toysmart executive, "We could have just sent everyone $50 and asked them to spend it on Toysmart, and we would have done better."[15]

Frustrated Disney executives decided in the spring of 2000 that Toysmart was unlikely to become a viable entity and shut down the subsidiary's website, effectively ending David Lord's dream of bringing "good toys" to American children. Disney's decision also ended Lord's dream of making a fortune from Toysmart. After Disney purchased a controlling interest in Toysmart, Lord's minority interest in the company was valued at nearly $20 million. When Disney chose to close down Toysmart, the value of Lord's ownership interest evaporated.

EVE.COM

On October 20, 2000, Varsha Rao sat on the floor of her office that overlooked San Francisco's busy Market Street. Rao, a co-president and co-founder of Eve.com, was glumly packing items from her desk into cardboard boxes. A few days earlier, Rao had learned that her company would be liquidated by its majority owner, the Internet incubator idealab!. When idealab! became Eve's principal owner in April 1999, Rao had great expectations for her company, the first major online retailer of cosmetics and other beauty products. One analyst projected that the company's annual sales would eventually reach $1 billion. Rao and idealab!'s executives expected to take Eve public with an IPO sometime in 2000, an IPO that would shower Rao, other Eve insiders, and idealab!'s owners with an embarrassment of riches. Unfortunately, none of those expectations were fulfilled.

14. J. Pereira and B. Orwall, "Disney Shutters Its Online Toy Retailer Nine Months After Buying Majority Stake," *The Wall Street Journal* Interactive Edition, 23 May 2000.

15. W. Bulkeley, J. Pereira, and B. Orwall, "Toysmart, Disney Deal Hit Snags in a Web of Conflicting Goals," *The Wall Street Journal* Interactive Edition, 7 June 2000.

What went wrong at Eve? Internet analysts attributed the company's downfall to three key factors. First, company management believed that women would appreciate the convenience of being able to purchase beauty products on the Internet. However, Allen Mottus, a long-time editor of a trade publication for the cosmetics industry, had maintained that cosmetics were not well suited for being sold online. "Mr. Mottus and other people in the industry say they tried to tell the dot-com entrepreneurs of a flaw in their business models: the assumption that huge numbers of mostly female shoppers would readily abandon their decades-old practice of trying out [cosmetics] products in stores."[16]

A second misjudgment made by Eve's management was the assumption that the major cosmetics manufacturers, including industry leader Estee Lauder, would allow online retailers to market their products. Instead, those manufacturers insisted on retaining control over the distribution of their products, meaning that Eve was stuck selling principally "no name" brands. Ironically, during 2000, Estee Lauder purchased the online cosmetics retailer gloss.com to market its various product lines on the Internet. Unlike Eve, Estee Lauder used its new website to provide information to potential customers and to direct them to the nearest "brick and mortar" location where they could purchase the company's products. Estee Lauder executives decided on that particular thrust for their new website because their market research revealed that women were reluctant to purchase cosmetics online.

A final flaw in Eve's business plan was the absence of a comprehensive and reliable forecast of the nature and magnitude of operating expenses the online retailer would likely incur. *The Wall Street Journal* reported that over the 15 months that Eve operated its website, the company apparently sustained a loss on every product shipment delivered to its customers.[17] During Eve's final few months, the company's management team began selling luxury goods, such as jewelry, in a desperate attempt to become profitable. That strategy did not work either. In summing up why Eve failed, Allen Mottus noted that company executives neglected to "do the research to support their thesis [business plan]."[18]

PETOPIA.COM

The Christmas holiday season easily ranks as the most important time of the year for many retailers. Retail establishments in several industries ring up a largely disproportionate percentage of their annual sales during the six weeks prior to Christmas. The Christmas 1999 selling season was the first holiday season for hundreds of online retailers. Executives of these e-tailers hoped that the 1999 holiday season would trigger an avalanche of "click and buy" orders from Internet users. Those executives also hoped that Internet users who purchased merchandise online for the first time during the holiday season would appreciate the convenience and simplicity of online shopping and become loyal customers of their websites throughout the year.

16. J. Carlton, "Fading Beauties: The Tale of Online Cosmetics Start-ups Is Not a Pretty One," *The Wall Street Journal* Interactive Edition, 17 July 2000.

17. R. Quick, "Beauty Retailer Eve.com Will Shut Down in Wake of Withdrawn IPO Registration," *The Wall Street Journal* Interactive Edition, 23 October 2000.

18. Carlton, "Fading Beauties."

Andrea Reisman found herself extremely busy during the Christmas 1999 season. In fact, the CEO of Petopia, at the time the most visited of all pet supply websites, found herself too busy during the holiday season. Petopia's website was overwhelmed by tens of thousands of Christmas shoppers, many more than Reisman had expected and more than her company's computer system could accommodate. Internet users seeking more information on Petopia products, complaining of problems with Petopia's website, or needing help to finalize purchases flooded the company with phone calls and e-mails. Reisman, herself, helped staff the phone lines and computer workstations to respond to angry customers, potential customers, and former potential customers.

Although the volume of traffic on Petopia's website was impressive during the 1999 holiday season, the company's sales were not. During all of 1999, Petopia's sales totaled a meager $3 million, according to company officials. More extensive financial data were available for Pets.com, Petopia's principal competitor and a publicly owned company that periodically released audited financial statements. Pets.com's website opened for business several months before Petopia's website was launched. In 1999, Pets.com produced $5.8 million of sales. Those sales resulted in a $59.7 million loss. In other words, the company lost $10 for every $1 of sales that it produced during 1999. Not surprisingly, Pets.com ceased operating in late 2000.

Petopia's poor sales and high operating expenses quickly depleted the company's cash resources. By the end of 1999, Petopia had burned through much of the $80 million of venture capital that Andrea Reisman raised during the summer of 1999. That figure included a large cash infusion that resulted from selling a 20 percent interest in the firm to Petco, the second largest pet supplies retailer in the nation. In early 2000, Reisman was forced to initiate another fund-raising effort for her company. At the same time, Petopia's executives began an internal study to determine why their new firm had failed to produce significant revenues.

Reisman and her fellow executives decided that a major factor inhibiting Petopia's sales was the customer-service software utilized by the company's website. They reasoned that the slow and cumbersome software had been responsible for the disappointment and agitation experienced by thousands of Internet users who visited the site during the Christmas selling season. To remedy that problem, Petopia invested $10 million to upgrade the software. Unfortunately, the upgrade failed to have a significant impact on Petopia's subsequent sales.

The problem facing Petopia and the approximately 100 other e-tailers that eventually attempted to sell pet supplies online was quite simple: most pet owners did not want to buy pet supplies online. Statistics reported by the *Internet Retailer* in mid-2000 revealed that 75 percent of all pet owners with access to the Internet were aware of online pet stores, such as Petopia.[19] However, only one-fourth of those pet owners had actually visited one or more of those websites. Among these latter individuals, only one in seven had actually made a purchase from an online pet store. More bad news? The most popular products purchased from online pet stores were bulk items, such as large bags of cat litter and dog food. The online pet stores had extremely small profit margins on those items. In

---

19. *Internet Retailer*, "Sock It to Me: Pet Lovers Know the Sites, but They're Not Buying," July 2000, 10.

fact, Pets.com charged a flat fee of $4.95 for 40-pound bags of generic dog food but paid more than that to have the dog food delivered to a customer.[20]

By late 2000, Petopia had raised and spent nearly $150 million of venture capital, but the company had yet to become profitable. The company had been forced to drop plans for an IPO in the spring of 2000 following the collapse of Internet stock prices. A corporate spokesperson reported in October 2000, that the company was searching for additional venture capital.[21] The spokesperson also suggested that with a major cash infusion, Petopia would become profitable by the spring of 2001. Hope springs eternal but reality cannot be denied. Two months later, Petopia ceased operations.

VALUE AMERICA

Value America never became the "Wal-Mart of the Internet" that Craig Winn envisioned. For fiscal 1996, the company, which was still in an early developmental stage, lost $425,000. In 1997, Value America's first full year of operation, the company lost $2 million. During 1998 and 1999, Value America's losses vaulted to $64.8 million and $174.5 million, respectively.

As the company's losses mounted, Winn repeatedly downplayed the significance of those losses and indicated that he would continue focusing on the company's two primary objectives: satisfying customers and increasing revenues so that the company could take advantage of economies of scale. One scheme that Winn developed to address both of his stated objectives was giving "ValueDollars" to customers who purchased merchandise from Value America's website. "To drive revenue and keep the stock inflated, the company introduced ValueDollars, which consumers could use for 50 percent off the cost of purchases. The discounts virtually assured that the company would lose money on every sale it made."[22]

In May 1999, *CNNfn* anchor, Jan Hopkins, questioned Winn regarding his aggressive, increase-revenues-at-all-costs strategy.[23] The slippery Winn refused to admit that his strategy was anything less than a complete success despite Hopkins' suggestion to the contrary.

Hopkins: Has it [Winn's strategy] worked?

Winn: It's worked extraordinarily well.

Hopkins: It's interesting though. Your revenues are up, but your expenses are also up, and the expenses are actually greater than the revenues, and the expenses are getting higher as you go from quarter to quarter. That's not a good thing for investors, I would think.

20. P. Barlas, "Crowded Online Pet Field Dogs Sites Pursuing Sales," *Investor's Business Daily*, 31 March 2000, 6.

21. C. Said, "Online Pet Store on Its Last Legs, Fires 60% of Staff," *The San Francisco Chronicle*, 28 October 2000, B1.

22. J. A. Byrne, "The Rise and Fall of a Dot-com," *Business Week*, 1 May 2000, 150.

23. J. Hopkins, "Capital Ideas," *CNNfn*, 11 May 1999, Transcript #999051103FN-L07.

Winn: Well, actually, our expenses as a percentage of revenue are hugely down. Our expenses were well below what they were forecast to be, and our revenues were hugely ahead of where they were forecast to be. So, our expenses as a percentage of revenues are considerably more favorable than they've ever been.

Hopkins: But, your losses are getting greater.

In November 1999, Value America's board of directors voted to replace Craig Winn as the company's chairman of the board. Winn resigned from the board one month later after it voted to adopt a cost-cutting program intended to reduce the company's operating losses. In March 2000, Value America's independent audit firm, PricewaterhouseCoopers, reported that the company was in danger of failing. Value America filed for bankruptcy in August 2000, when its stock was trading for approximately $0.72 per share, less than 1 percent of the $74 high the stock reached in April 1999, when the company went public with an IPO. Fortunately for Craig Winn, he sold much of his ownership interest in Value America before the company's stock price tumbled. *Business Week* reported that Winn realized cash gains of more than $53 million from the sale of his Value America stock.[24] Among the more blunt observations that the prestigious periodical made in commenting on Value America was the following statement: "Value America's rise and fall is emblematic of an era of unbridled optimism and outright greed."[25]

TIMELESS TRUTHS VS. RAZZLE-DAZZLE

The five dot-coms discussed in the prior section failed to achieve their founders and executives' goals of taking advantage of Internet technology to create viable, if not dominant, New Economy businesses within their industries. Unfortunately, the mistakes made by the management teams of those companies were not isolated incidents. Executives of scores of other Internet-based firms made similar errors in judgments, gaffes, and bonehead blunders.

The hype that surrounded many first-generation Internet firms and the huge financial rewards reaped by their founders and early investors triggered a stampede by hundreds of would-be entrepreneurs anxious to create the next Web-based company that would have a billion-dollar IPO. Many, if not most, of these new age entrepreneurs lacked the business experience and background necessary to develop a viable business plan for their firm and the requisite skills needed to implement that plan once the business began operations. "In the rush, people forgot time-worn principles of what constitutes a good business—things like healthy gross margins, a clear competitive advantage, a solid management team, and a large potential market."[26]

Instead of focusing on the timeless truths and tenets of good business, many new e-commerce executives concentrated on making the public aware of their firms via expensive, nationwide promotional campaigns. Although those campaigns often resulted in impressive brand name recognition statistics for the

---

24. Byrne, "The Rise and Fall of a Dot-com," 154.

25. *Ibid.*, 152.

26. M. Warner, "Fallen Idols," *Fortune* (online), 30 October 2000.

given companies, they generally failed to prompt consumers to buy the advertised products or services. Many dot-com executives also channeled much of their energy and finances into developing various technological "bells and whistles" to draw attention to the new websites of their businesses. Again, those efforts were largely unsuccessful. A top technical officer of AOL suggests that a "razzle-dazzle" website that makes heavy use of the most recent technological gimmicks may attract curious Internet users. But, ease-of-use is the key to building a functional site for an online business. "There are sites out there that are just functional. Look at Yahoo! It's not fancy; it's just gray and blue. Look at us at AOL. We're pretty much a flat site. You want to make buying really fast and easy. No videos, no bells and whistles. Just get to the point."[27]

Arriving at a final tally on the financial losses and misery caused by the bursting of the Internet Bubble will require years, if not longer. *Business Week* reported that by the spring of 2001, the dive in high-tech stock prices had cost investors nearly five trillion dollars.[28] At least 200 large public or private dot-coms filed for bankruptcy, while thousands of other smaller Internet-based companies across the country failed as well. Several founders and large investors of Internet-based companies suffered billion-dollar-plus losses during 2000 and 2001. Membership in *Fortune's* "Billion-Dollar Losers Club," which tracked the financial woes of top Internet executives, had swelled to 20 individuals by June 2001.[29] Even more telling was the unprecedented drop in the number of millionaires due to the dot-com debacle. Between the spring of 2000 and 2001, more than 10 percent of all U.S. millionaires, or approximately 800,000 individuals nationwide, saw their wealth shrink below seven digits.[30]

Most economists and Wall Street analysts believe that the pain caused by the punishing stock market correction of 2000 and 2001 was unavoidable. History proves that a period of excess and lack of restraint in the business world is eventually followed by a period of economic retribution in which loosely organized and poorly managed firms are driven out of business by their more disciplined competitors. A business journalist writing for *Fortune* suggested that the elimination of scores of marginal Internet companies would provide a better opportunity for the well-managed and well-financed companies in the New Economy to survive and eventually thrive. "Internet mania has finally, decisively burned itself out. The future now belongs to companies that can deliver—of all things—real profits."[31] A *Fortune* article reaffirmed that point of view. "The dot.com era is over. The Internet era, by contrast, is just getting started."[32]

As the turbulent and hectic dot-com era came to a close, many financial analysts wondered when risk-averse investors and those investors burned by the bursting of the Internet Bubble would consider purchasing the stocks of surviving Internet companies. Among the most influential Internet stock analysts is Henry Blodget of Goldman, Sachs & Co. During an interview on *MSNBC* in late

27. E. Barker, A. Borrego, and M. Hofman, "I Was Seduced by the Web Economy," *Inc.*, February 2000, 60.

28. R. Sharpe, "After the Wild Ride," *Business Week e.biz*, 16 April 2001, EB 29.

29. J. Boorstin and M. Boyle, "The Billion-Dollar Losers Club," *Fortune*, 11 June 2001, 127.

30. Sharpe, "After the Wild Ride," EB 30.

31. N. Schwartz, "Trial by Fire," *Fortune*, 26 June 2000, 141.

32. J. Useem, "Dot-coms: What Have We Learned?" *Fortune* (online), 30 October 2000.

2000, Blodget suggested that as the volatile market conditions that accompanied dot-com mania in the late 1990s faded in the minds of investors they would gradually gain confidence in those Internet companies having sustainable and profitable business models. Who knows? Maybe even the Oracle of Omaha, Warren Buffett, will buy a few hundred, or few million, shares of an Internet company in the future.

QUESTIONS

1. Warren Buffett relies upon a "value" investment strategy in his role as the CEO of Berkshire Hathaway. Identify and research other general strategies available to investors. Compare and contrast those approaches to the investment philosophy embraced by Buffett. Which of these investment strategies do you personally prefer? Why?

2. The "Burning Up" article that appeared in *Barron's* on March 20, 2000, apparently contributed to the subsequent sell-off among Internet-related stocks. Do you believe that business journalists should selectively collect and report financial data and related statistics for individual companies? Identify what you believe are the key ethical responsibilities of business journalists who analyze the financial health and future prospects of individual companies and industries.

3. Search online or hard copy databases to find examples of cash flow measures, other than "burn rate," that analysts use to assess the financial health of individual companies. List these measures and explain what insight they provide on a given company's financial condition.

4. Review the five dot-com companies profiled in this case. For each company, identify what you believe was the key factor that prevented it from becoming economically viable. Defend your choices.

5. For each of the dot-com companies profiled in this case, identify one key decision that the given firm's management could have made at some point to significantly enhance the company's likelihood of becoming economically viable.

6. Identify three Internet companies that you would describe as "successful" firms. For each of those companies, what factor apparently contributed most significantly to its success? Explain.

THE DARK SIDE OF E-COMMERCE

Free Kevin

Information wants to be free.

Stewart Brand

On Christmas Day, 1994, Tsutomo Shimomura received a rude shock. A co-worker in San Diego telephoned Shimomura, who was spending the holiday with friends in northern California, to tell him that his computer system had been hacked. By the mid-1990s, heavy-duty Internet users were well-acquainted with the growing problem posed by mischief-minded hackers. Cautious Internet users dealt with that threat by purchasing a firewall for their computer system. A firewall easily deflects most attempts by novice hackers to gain access to private computer files linked to the Internet by an online connection. However, firewall products typically present little more than a nuisance to skilled hackers determined to gain access to a computer system.

Recognized as one of the nation's leading experts on computer security, Shimomura worked for a federal agency, the Los Alamos National Laboratory. In late 1994, the 30-year-old computer scientist was on loan to the San Diego Supercomputer Center (SDSC) located on the campus of the University of California at San Diego. The SDSC is one of five supercomputer centers overseen by the National Science Foundation, another federal agency. Shimomura spent most of his time researching computer security and information technology issues for the federal government. The FBI, various branches of the military, and the National Security Agency periodically called on him to help troubleshoot computer security problems. Shimomura was particularly well known for his skills in investigating and thwarting hacker attacks.

Tsutomo Shimomura took the hacker attack on his own network of some 30 computers as a personal affront. Within a few days, he decided that the most likely culprit was none other than Kevin Mitnick, the nation's most infamous computer hacker. In cyberspace, Mitnick went by the code name Condor because he admired the CIA employee portrayed by Robert Redford in the popular movie *Three Days of the Condor*. For more than two years, Mitnick had been a fugitive on the run, successfully evading the FBI and a long list of other law enforcement agencies. A native of southern California, Mitnick earned the distinction of being the first hacker to appear on an FBI Most Wanted poster. Undeterred by the FBI's failure to track down Mitnick, Shimomura decided that he would find the elusive hacker. Shimomura was not sure why Mitnick had hacked into his computer system. But, motives were not an issue. No one broke into Tsutomo Shimomura's computer system and got away with it.

RADIO SHACKER, COMPUTER HACKER

In 1975, at the age of 11, Kevin David Mitnick cut a deal with the manager of a Radio Shack store located in a Los Angeles suburb. In exchange for sweeping the floor occasionally and doing other errands, the manager would allow Kevin to hang out in the consumer electronics store. Kevin's parents had divorced when he was three and he seldom saw his father. The modest income his mother earned working as a waitress barely covered the family's living expenses. To entertain himself and to help while away the hours before his mother came home from work, Kevin often went to a local mall after school and idly wandered from store to store, checking out the latest toys and other merchandise before clerks chased him away. The sympathetic manager of the Radio Shack store gave the young boy a home away from home. Kevin soon became fascinated by the electronic products that lined the shelves of the store. Curious and inquisitive by nature, the young boy would not stop tinkering with an electronic gadget or pestering the store manager with questions until he fully understood the given product's inner workings.

By his mid-teens, Kevin's fascination with electronic gadgets had become the central focus of his life. He and several friends spent night after night on "phreaking" binges. The teenagers used various means to gain access to Pacific Bell's computer network, including stealing computer codes and tricking naïve employees into revealing those codes. Once inside that network, Kevin and his friends entertained themselves by playing pranks on unsuspecting Pac Bell customers. Posing as telephone operators ranked high on their list of hijinks. Individuals who called directory assistance received an unconventional greeting and sometimes bizarre instructions when Kevin or one of his cohorts intercepted their calls. Kevin also used his phreaking skills to annoy what he considered ill-mannered individuals. After being treated rudely by another teenager, Kevin added $30,000 of bogus charges to that individual's telephone bill.

In the early 1980s, Mitnick and his circle of close friends became bored with their phone pranks and began devoting most of their free time to exploring computer networks, particularly the evolving global network of interconnected computers known as the Internet. Mitnick and his friends soon became full-fledged "hackers." (Refer to Exhibit 1 for a glossary of hacking terms.) They spent long hours figuring out how to use the Internet to gain access to the computer systems of large companies and federal agencies. Once they gained access to a computer system, they caromed through its silent corridors, reading and copying secret files, laughing at racy e-mail messages sent by Internet users who had no idea their messages were being read, and occasionally playing a cyber-prank on an unsuspecting corporate executive.

In 1981, Los Angeles police arrested Mitnick for stealing computer manuals from Pac Bell. The 17-year-old received probation for that offense but was not so lucky two years later when he was convicted of hacking into the computer system of the University of Southern California. Mitnick received a six-month jail

EXHIBIT 1
Glossary of
Hacking Terms

- **Back doors** An alternative entry point used by hackers to regain access to a computer system if the original access point is discovered and "closed."
- **Dark-side hacker** A hacker who breaks into computer systems, often at random, to corrupt data files, steal confidential information, and generally wreak havoc on those systems. Often used interchangeably with "cracker."
- **Denial of service attack** A method of disabling a website by clogging it with a huge number of information requests, e-mail messages, or requests for an Internet connection. Sometimes referred to as jamming, flooding, or smurfing.
- **Hacker** An individual who gains unauthorized access to a computer system. The most common motives of a hacker are to use his or her skills to circumvent a system's access controls and to explore the structure, components, and other features of that system.
- **Phreaker** Someone who uses illicit methods to break into telephone systems to make free long-distance calls, to disrupt telephone service to subscribers of those systems, or for some other malicious purpose.
- **Script kiddies** Individuals who have limited or no hacking experience and thus rely on programs available at hacker websites to break into computer systems. Sometimes referred to as "script bunnies."
- **Sneaker** A computer security expert hired by an organization to identify weaknesses in its computer security controls by attempting to hack into the organization's computer system.
- **Sniffer** A device that allows an individual or organization to monitor the traffic flowing through a computer network. Can be used for control or illicit purposes. Typically used by hackers to intercept passwords, logon IDs, and other sensitive information.
- **Social engineering** A method used by hackers to "con" or trick an organization's personnel, typically administrative support personnel, into providing passwords, computer code, or other confidential information that can then be used to gain access to the organization's computer system.
- **Spoofing** Tricking organizations into providing logon IDs, passwords, or other confidential information regarding their computer systems by routing requests for such information through a bogus e-mail address or website address.
- **Trojan horse** Typically, a software program left behind by a hacker that replaces a software program of the hacking victim. These programs generally execute hidden and malicious computer code that disrupts the victim's computer system. One version is a "logic bomb" that "detonates" when triggered by a given computer operation. Activation of a logic bomb often disables an entire computer system.
- **White-hat hacker** Individuals who use the expertise they gained during years of illicit hacking activities to help organizations design or strengthen their computer security controls.

term for that indiscretion. By his early twenties, Mitnick had become obsessed with hacking, spending practically all of his spare time searching the corners of the Internet for entry points into computer systems. Not just any system would do. Mitnick enjoyed the challenge of foiling the controls of well-guarded computer systems. Prime targets of his hacker attacks included banks, telephone companies, computer firms, and other large corporations. In 1987, he was caught hacking into the computer system of a southern California publishing company. The judge in that case gave him a three-year probationary sentence. One year later, Mitnick found himself back in another California courtroom. This time, he was convicted of copying proprietary software of the computer giant Digital Equipment Corporation (DEC).

In 1989, Mitnick began serving a one-year prison sentence in a federal correctional facility for the DEC incident. He spent eight months of that sentence in solitary confinement. A court-appointed therapist recommended that Mitnick undergo treatment for his "addiction" when he was released from the federal prison. Many psychologists and business journalists scoffed at the suggestion that someone could be addicted to hacking. Nevertheless, a federal judge agreed with the therapist that Mitnick seemed to be a hacking addict. The judge ordered Mitnick to enter a residential treatment center in Los Angeles upon his release from prison. At that facility, Mitnick would undergo a six-month rehabilitation program to remedy his hacking addiction.

The rehabilitation program seemed to have a positive impact on Kevin Mitnick. During that program, he shed more than 100 pounds that he had gained over the previous several years. As if to convince himself that he had put hacking behind him for good, Mitnick purchased a personalized license tag for his car that read "XHACKER." The terms of his probation allowed him to work with computers after completing his rehabilitation program, but only if they did not have a modem—the courts did not want Mitnick to have access to the Internet. For a short while, he worked as a computer programmer. Among the computers he programmed were personal computers marketed by DEC. No doubt, Mitnick was very familiar with the programming instructions for those computers since he had "borrowed" those blueprints when he hacked into DEC's computer system in 1988.

In the early 1990s, Mitnick's personal life began to crumble. He had to deal with the death of his brother due to a drug overdose and work through the difficult aftermath of a brief marriage that had quickly disintegrated. A brief reconciliation between himself and his father also failed to pan out. Mitnick had accumulated a wealth of knowledge regarding the Internet, computer networks, and computer security thanks to his years of hacking, but the terms of his probation precluded him from using that knowledge. So, he drifted from one unfulfilling job to another. Finally, loneliness and despair drove him back to hacking.

While working with a private detective agency in Los Angeles, Mitnick allegedly hacked into the computer system of a credit-rating database to gain information relevant to a case being pursued by the agency. After obtaining a search warrant for Mitnick's apartment, police detectives discovered evidence that he had violated the terms of his probation by accessing the Internet. When federal agents returned to Mitnick's home to arrest him, he was nowhere to be found. Over the next few months, Mitnick remained in southern California. On several occasions, stakeouts and undercover surveillance efforts almost led to his capture. A few days before Christmas 1992, police detectives spotted Mitnick outside a shopping mall in a Los Angeles suburb. After realizing that he was being followed, Mitnick slipped into a crush of holiday shoppers and eluded his pursuers.

Over the next two years, Mitnick crisscrossed the country to avoid capture. All the while, he fed his voracious appetite for hacking, routinely breaking into computer systems, studying the high-level policies and procedures of large organizations, reading the e-mail of complete strangers, and copying important proprietary information of his victims. Although Mitnick illegally obtained a huge amount of confidential information from dozens of large companies and thousands of credit card numbers of individual Internet users, he apparently never attempted to sell that information or to profit from it in any other way. Nevertheless, the publicity attracted by his daring hacker attacks, including front-page articles in *The New York Times*, and his uncanny ability to avoid arrest prompted the FBI to label Kevin Mitnick the nation's "most wanted computer criminal."

After nearly two years of traipsing around the country, Mitnick decided to find an out-of-the-way place where he could "lay low" for a few months. He chose a nondescript apartment complex in Raleigh, North Carolina. Each night, the seldom-seen resident of Apartment 202 went online to scour the Internet for information. Those regular, late night hacking sessions eventually proved to be the downfall of the "Condor." Tsutomo Shimomura tracked Mitnick through cyberspace by learning his habits and by collecting the smallest tidbits of information that he left behind after hacking into a computer system. Most computer security experts would have overlooked the meager trail of telltale signs Mitnick left in his wake. But, the patient, determined, and meticulous Shimomura tediously collected those shreds of evidence and pieced them together.

After tracking Mitnick to Raleigh, Shimomura put together a homemade Geiger counter to find the exact location of the cell phone he was using each night to access the Internet through a modem. Shimomura then notified the FBI of Mitnick's location. In the early morning hours of February 15, 1995, a squad of federal agents surrounded Mitnick's apartment complex. A few minutes after 2:00 A.M., an FBI agent knocked on the door of Apartment 202. Moments later, Mitnick was placed under arrest.

At an arraignment hearing the next morning, Kevin Mitnick came face to face with his nemesis for the first time. When he first saw Shimomura, a startled Mitnick remarked, "You're Tsutomo." Later, as he was being led from the courtroom, Mitnick stopped and briefly addressed Shimomura. "Tsutomo, I respect your skills." Shimomura only nodded politely in response.

E-COMMERCE: DEATH BY HACKING?

Several books and two movies documented the life and times of Kevin Mitnick, including his pursuit and capture by federal agents thanks to the cyberspace detective skills of Tsutomo Shimomura. Companies pioneering the development of electronic commerce rank among the parties most interested in Mitnick and the growing number of hack-happy Internet surfers. The executives of those companies recognize the pervasive implications that highly publicized hacker attacks have for their revolutionary business ventures. Headline-grabbing hacker attacks make Internet users hesitant to shop online. Particularly unsettling to potential cyberspace shoppers are the number of hacking incidents that result in credit card numbers being stolen. Ironically, much of the blame for such incidents must be shouldered by companies that have been too eager to join the New Economy. "In the race to develop websites and jump into e-commerce, many companies have skimped on security measures, leaving gaping holes in their electronic armor."[1]

The prevalence of hacker attacks on Internet-linked businesses and organizations has created several challenging problems and issues that e-commerce companies must address. First, online businesses need to obtain an objective assessment of the threat that hackers actually pose for their operations. Some Internet experts believe that threat has been overstated by the business press. Those experts caution regulatory authorities not to overreact to the problems posed by

---

1. K. Fitzgerald, "Companies Set Sites on Security; Systems Are Vulnerable to Hackers, Employee Breaches," *Crain's Chicago Business*, 15 May 2000, SR 24.

hackers. Robert Frankston, a noted computer scientist and co-inventor of the electronic spreadsheet, suggests that, "the real danger of any terrorism is not so much in the act itself as the overreaction."[2] Frankston and other computer scientists warn that the "state of panic"[3] among e-commerce executives that has been prompted by hacking incidents could trigger overly aggressive intervention by regulatory authorities. Such intervention would likely stifle the innovation and creativity that have been the principal factors responsible for the Internet's incredible popularity and success to date.

> This is a story about clashing cultures. Americans exaggerate the dangers of hacking, while hackers underestimate Americans' technophobia and sense of vulnerability to computer crime. Law enforcement tramples cyberspace norms largely because of a few renegades who claim to be accountable to no one.[4]

E-commerce businesses also need to become familiar with the basic approaches and techniques for dealing with hacker attacks and closely related computer crimes such as denial of service attacks. This seemingly simple task can be overwhelming for e-commerce executives and their subordinates given the widely divergent recommendations made by the growing number of online security experts. All too often, those "experts" simply tout online security control strategies, services, or products marketed by their firms.

Before addressing the two previous issues, e-commerce businesses and other parties wanting to develop a rational strategy to cope with hacker attacks should attempt to obtain a better understanding of the individuals responsible for those attacks. What factors motivate hackers? Do most hackers share a common psychological profile? Are there discernible trends in hacking activities in recent years? Answers to those questions and related questions should allow e-commerce businesses, regulatory authorities, and even casual Internet surfers to deal more effectively with the threats posed by hackers.

THE HACKER PSYCHE

Kevin Mitnick easily qualifies as the most well-known computer hacker of the past two decades. But, tens of thousands of teenagers, young adults, and older men and women have also become hackers. Some of these hackers apparently ply their trade only occasionally, while others become obsessed with forcing their way into computer systems. In many documented cases, that obsession has taken over and wrecked the lives of individual hackers. One bright high school student interviewed by a reporter for *The New York Times* explained that hacking had taken control of his life when he was only 13. "It was like a rush. I couldn't think about anything else."[5]

---

2. J. Markoff, "The Strength of the Internet Proves to Be Its Weakness," *The New York Times* on the Web, 10 February 2000.

3. S. Ninan, "Why Hackers Hack," *NewsEdge* (online), 23 February 2000.

4. A. L. Shapiro, "CyberScoop!" *The Nation*, 20 March 1995, 369.

5. A. Lappe, "New York Hackers See Breaking into Computers as a Healthy Thing," *The New York Times* on the Web, 14 June 1998.

What motives underlie the hacker psyche? In the early days of the Internet, an underground cult of hackers evolved. These individuals communicated regularly with each other, swapping the latest techniques they had discovered to "crack" the online security controls of large corporations and government agencies. These early hackers subscribed to a set of shared beliefs commonly referred to as the "hacker ethic." This set of shared beliefs established a mindset or culture among hackers that bound them together in a shadowy and loosely knit community.

Early-day hackers included many of the current leaders of the Internet Revolution. Bill Gates, Paul Allen, and Steve Wozniak, among many other high-tech titans, were drawn to the mysterious world of the Internet in its early days.[6] Exploring that world and obtaining an understanding of its nature often required these young computer enthusiasts to hack their way into computer systems linked to the Internet.

The central theme of the hacker ethic is a quote attributed to Stewart Brand, an early hacker and the individual who coined the phrase "personal computer." Brand insisted that "information wants to be free." Many hackers use that assertion to justify their hobby. The hacker ethic precludes hackers from destroying, altering, or profiting from the information they have accessed, according to Emmanuel Goldstein, editor of *2600 Magazine, The Hacker Quarterly*, the leading periodical within the hacking "industry."[7] "A true hacker doesn't get into the system to kill anything or to sell what he gets to someone else. He gets in there to satisfy his curiosity."[8] Kevin Mitnick has repeatedly echoed that point of view. He maintains that the key factor that drove him to break into computer systems was pure and simple curiosity. "My case was a case of curiosity. I wanted to know as much as I could find out about how telephone networks work and the ins and outs of computer security. There was certainly no intent on my part to defraud anyone or anything."[9]

Dozens of formal hacker organizations have developed over the years including Black Hand, Cult of the Dead Cow, the Electronic Disturbance Theatre, the Legion of Doom, the Legion of the Apocalypse, and LOpht (pronounced "loft"), to name just a few. Some of these organizations have explicitly embraced the hacker ethic by developing their own written code of ethics. Among the basic tenets of the Legion of Doom's code of ethics are the following guidelines for its members:

Do not intentionally damage any system.
Do not alter any system files other than ones needed to ensure your escape from
    detection and your future access.
Do not hack government computers.

---

6. J. Markoff, "A Strange Brew's Buzz Lingers in Silicon Valley," *The New York Times*, 26 March 2000, Section 3, 1.

7. The four-digit number "2600" is the frequency of a dial tone used by early "phreakers" to gain access to telephone networks. "Emmanuel Goldstein" is a pseudonym borrowed from George Orwell's novel, *1984*. Goldstein was the supposed leader of The Brotherhood, an underground freedom movement featured in Orwell's most famous work.

8. Ninan, "Why Hackers Hack."

9. M. Brunker, "Mitnick Goes Free, but Must Remain Totally Unplugged," *MSNBC* (online), 21 January 2000.

Many hacker groups and hacker publications, including the *2600 Magazine*, maintain that hackers actually promote the development of the Internet and e-commerce. If not for hackers, businesses and other organizations would fail to find and correct on a timely basis fatal flaws in their computer systems and Internet-based facilities.

> If hacking did not exist, people would not discover the mistakes, the basic ways that a system can be compromised until it was too late, until someone with an agenda had actually gotten in there and done something bad for a purpose. Hackers get in there and they tell everybody what they did.[10]

Internet historians maintain that the hacker ethic began to erode during the 1990s. Key factors responsible for that erosion included the dramatic growth of the Internet and the World Wide Web, the corresponding leap in the number of Internet users and, most important, a rapid increase in the number of individuals involved in hacking. The hacker community had always been fragmented and loosely organized given the nature of the Internet and the obvious importance of secrecy for hackers in general. As more Internet users became involved in hacking, the hacker community became even more fragmented. Many of the community's newest recruits did not subscribe to the hacker ethic, while others were unaware of its existence.

During the late 1990s and into the new century, the number of attacks launched on websites by "dark-side hackers" increased dramatically. These attacks often involve efforts to disable websites, to post obscene materials on websites, to profit from stolen credit card numbers, and to benefit in other ways from stolen information. To create even more mischief, some dark-side hackers post "scripts" to their own websites that novice hackers, principally young teenagers and even pre-teens, can then use to become familiar with the basic tricks of the trade. By 2001, an estimated 65,000 websites had been created by hackers or hacking organizations. In most cases, individuals who use hacking scripts, referred to as "script kiddies," are seeking a cyberspace thrill and have no intention of making a statement to society regarding the freedom of information. Because script kiddies are seldom well-versed in hacking techniques, they are much more likely than experienced hackers to be apprehended by law enforcement authorities.

Among the most troubling Internet trends in recent years has been a noticeable rise in extortion cases linked to hacker attacks. A consultant of a leading Internet security company noted that cyber-extortion cases were becoming "more common" and probably totaled "in the low thousands" worldwide by the year 2000.[11] One such case involved Bloomberg LP, a prominent Internet-based financial services firm. Two hackers reportedly e-mailed information obtained from the company's computer system to the firm's founder and CEO, Michael Bloomberg. The hackers offered to help Mr. Bloomberg correct the alleged flaws in his company's computer system in exchange for a $200,000 "consulting" fee. No doubt, the hackers believed that the billion-dollar company would pay the relatively nominal fee they were demanding. Michael Bloomberg reinforced that belief when he agreed to fly to London to personally deliver the $200,000. But, the sly executive double-

---

10. M. Bruner, "Hackers: Knights-errant or Knaves?" *MSNBC* (online), 23 July 2000.

11. A. Salkever, "Cyber-Extortion Deserves No Quarter," *Business Week*, 18 September 2000, 94.

crossed the "consultants" by tipping off the London police. Plain-clothes officers arrested the two hackers shortly after Bloomberg handed over the $200,000.

DAMAGE ASSESSMENT: WHOSE OX IS BEING HACKED?

In full-page advertisements run during the late summer of 2000 in major business periodicals, including *The Wall Street Journal*, PricewaterhouseCoopers reported that losses linked to hacker attacks had reached $45 billion. In fact, law enforcement authorities struggle to obtain reliable statistics documenting the nature, extent, and losses stemming from hacker attacks. The FBI estimates that possibly as high as 95 percent of such attacks go undetected.[12] Even more troubling, only 17 percent of hacker attacks and related computer crimes detected by online businesses and other online organizations are reported to a law enforcement agency.[13] Companies hesitate to report hacker attacks because of fear that such disclosure might prompt additional attacks and cost them credibility among their customers and potential customers. "A big concern is loss of public trust and image—not to mention the fear of encouraging copycat hackers."[14]

An annual "Computer Crime and Security Survey" sponsored jointly by the FBI and the Computer Security Institute (CSI) easily qualifies as the most widely quoted source of statistics regarding the impact and frequency of hacker attacks and other types of computer crime. CSI is a worldwide association of information security professionals based in San Francisco. Large corporations and government agencies account for most of the several hundred respondents to the annual CSI/FBI survey. In 2001, 85 percent of the respondents to the confidential survey reported that they had detected breaches of their computer networks during the previous year. Those breaches included hacker attacks, denial of service attacks, sabotage of data or networks, and computer viruses.

Two-thirds of the respondents to the CSI/FBI survey indicated that they suffered significant losses resulting from unwanted intrusions into their computer systems. The average loss reported by respondents was a staggering $2 million. Theft of proprietary information ranked as the most costly type of security breach experienced by the respondents, followed by financial fraud, and sabotage of data or networks.

A CSI official reported that "hacking is considered one of the top three methods for getting trade secrets and it's only increasing in importance."[15] In one such case reported by a computer consulting firm, two large manufacturing companies were competing to obtain a contract valued at nearly $1 billion. Employees of one of the companies hacked into the other's computer system. Those employees stole e-mail in which the competing firm's executives had discussed the details of

---

12. Financial Accounting Standards Board, "Business Reporting Research Project: Electronic Distribution of Business Reporting Information," (Stamford, Connecticut: FASB, 2000).

13. J. Guinto, *Investor's Business Daily* (online), 4 April 2000.

14. I. Sager, "CyberCrime," *Business Week* (online), 21 February 2000.

15. M. McKay, "Companies Increasingly Use Cyber-Hacking as Corporate Espionage Method," *The Record* (online), 20 February 2000.

the bid they intended to submit for the large contract. That information allowed the first company to obtain the contract by undercutting the bid submitted by its competitor. Fortunately for the "hackee" company, its computer security professionals found "electronic fingerprints" left by the other firm's personnel during the hacker attack, which led, in turn, to the discovery of the stolen e-mail.[16]

Among the most publicized hacker attacks on individual companies was an intrusion into Citibank's computer system by a Russian computer programmer in the mid-1990s. After gaining access to New York-based Citibank's computer system, the programmer stole $10 million from the bank. Citibank eventually discovered the theft and recovered all but $400,000 of the stolen funds. Cooperation of Russian authorities resulted in the hacker being extradited to the United States where he was convicted and received a three-year prison term.

A former federal official noted that such attacks on large metropolitan banks are not rare, although they are seldom publicly reported. "This sort of thing happens often but is hushed up. The federal government requires banks to report losses, but banks avoid potentially bad publicity by reporting such losses as 'accounting efficiency errors.'"[17] Another former federal official who served for the Secret Service noted that he was "shocked to discover the magnitude of hacker losses that banks were swallowing."[18] That individual, who became a security consultant for the banking industry upon leaving the Secret Service, revealed that some hacker "hits" on individual banks have resulted in losses of several million dollars.

Recent history proves that no company is immune from hacker attacks. Even Microsoft, the acknowledged leader of the Internet Revolution, has suffered financial losses and a loss of credibility at the hands of hackers. In late 2000, reports circulated in the business press that hackers had broken into the company's computer systems and accessed the source code of existing software applications and applications under development. An irate and embarrassed Steven Ballmer, Microsoft's CEO, eventually confirmed those rumors and responded to reporters' questions regarding the impact on his firm. "They [hackers] did in fact access the source codes. . . . You bet this is an issue of great importance."[19] In investigating the incident, *The New York Times* noted that the most alarming feature of the attack was that the intruders did not use "highly sophisticated" means to gain entry to Microsoft's systems.[20]

Monetary losses linked to hacking incidents are difficult to quantify but even more difficult to peg is the emotional trauma hackers inflict on their victims. Individuals occupying positions representing the complete range of the employment hierarchy of online organizations have been victimized by faceless, hit-and-run "cyber punks." A chief executive of a computer security firm reported his firsthand encounters with such victims.

---

16. *Ibid.* The identities of the companies involved in this case were not revealed, nor was the eventual resolution of the case.

17. D. H. Freedman, "How to Hack a Bank," *Forbes ASAP*, 3 April 2000, 57.

18. *Ibid.*

19. T. Bridis, R. Buckman, and G. Fields, "Microsoft Said Hackers Failed to See Codes for Its Most Popular Products," *The Wall Street Journal* Interactive Edition, 27 October 2000.

20. J. Markoff and J. Schwartz, "Microsoft Says Online Break-in Lasted 6 Weeks," *The New York Times* on the Web, 28 October 2000.

This isn't fun stuff. There is real damage. You get some system or network manager who works up on Wall Street and his systems have been broken into by one of those barely post-pubescent hackers and they're scared for their jobs, they're afraid they're going to lose their careers, they're worried about their mortgages. I've seen grown men reduced to tears by this kind of thing.[21]

AN OUNCE OF PREVENTION VS. A TON OF CURE?

In the face of mounting concern over hacker attacks and other cyber crimes, President Clinton called an Internet summit in February 2000, to address the important issue of online security. That summit included nationally recognized computer security experts, top executives of major e-commerce firms, and leading academics in the fields of computer security and information technology. In addressing these individuals, President Clinton noted that "vulnerabilities at one place on the Net can create risks for us all."[22] A few months later, U.S. Attorney General Janet Reno reiterated that theme. "We must share information about vulnerabilities, so that we can each take steps to protect our systems against attack. We have a common goal: to keep the nation's computer networks secure, safe and reliable for American citizens and its businesses."[23]

Among specific measures that the Clinton administration encouraged the American public to take were educating children and teenagers that hacking was not an acceptable pastime. Additionally, federal officials strongly urged American businesses to report hacking attempts made on their websites to the appropriate law enforcement authorities and to cooperate in efforts to prosecute the individuals responsible for such attacks.

Despite the widespread publicity focusing on hacker attacks in recent years, a survey released by an Internet industry group revealed that nearly 20 percent of businesses with websites had not taken any steps to protect their computer systems from hacker attacks.[24] On the other hand, many businesses, particularly smaller firms and those with limited in-house Internet expertise, have exhibited a knee-jerk reaction to the problem of hacker attacks. These latter businesses engage in overkill by purchasing an impressive—and excessive—number of costly software and hardware products to fend off hackers. "At the end of the day, a lot of people buy a lot of security that they don't use. There's little point in investing in technology if you don't have the policies and procedures to use it."[25]

Online security experts recommend that businesses connected to the Internet adopt a risk management approach to dealing with the problems posed by hackers. That is, businesses should attempt to reduce the risk of damaging hacker attacks to an acceptable level, while at the same time choosing a mix of control policies and procedures that will allow them to accomplish that objective at a

21. Bruner, "Hackers: Knights-errant or Knaves?"

22. I. Sager, N. Gross, and J. Carey, "Locking Out the Hackers," *BusinessWeek Online*, 28 February 2000.

23. *The New York Times* on the Web, "Americans Worried About Hackers and Cybercrime, Poll Says," 19 June 2000.

24. *NewsEdge*, "Nearly 20% of Firms Have Taken No Anti-Hacker Steps," 29 February 2000.

25. M. Friedman, "Hackers and Security," *eBusiness Journal* (online), April 2000.

reasonable cost. Central to this strategy is the realization that eliminating the risk of hacker attacks is not technologically or economically feasible.

> There are virtually no unhackable sites. The security experts who test systems by doing live penetrations get in 100% of the time. The essential quandary of e-business is how to open up your business to the wild world of the Internet without opening yourself up to attack and, conversely, how to secure your systems without closing yourself to on-line business.[26]

Business periodicals in recent years have been replete with "Top 10" lists that identify control measures e-commerce businesses can use to protect themselves from hacker attacks. Exhibit 2 includes one such list adapted from a series of anti-hacking measures published by the American Institute of Certified Public Accountants.

EXHIBIT 2
Security Measures to Protect E-Commerce Businesses from Hackers

1. Conduct a risk assessment to identify potential weaknesses in a business's computer systems and existing security controls. Make a special effort to identify the links in those controls that expose a business's computer systems to the greatest threat of penetration by hackers.
2. Develop security standards and policies designed to address the threat of hacker attacks by individuals external to a business and by internal parties, such as disgruntled employees. Communicate these standards clearly to all members of the organization and make them aware of the sanctions they face for violating those standards and policies.
3. Retain a computer security expert to review a new system's computer security standards and controls and to test the integrity of the controls. This expert should examine and report upon the integrity of the overall computer system as well as the apparent reliability of individual components of that system, such as firewalls.
4. Periodically test computer security controls to determine that they are operating as intended. These tests should focus on both internal and external points of access, including employee workstations, e-mail, telephone, and the Internet.
5. Employ authentication procedures to restrict the number of individuals who have access to a business's computer systems. Examples of such procedures include passwords, fingerprint scans, and smart cards. Encrypt data to render it unusable to unauthorized parties who gain access to a business's computer systems.
6. Install firewalls to channel incoming Internet messages and data into a computer system through one control point at which the integrity of those messages and data can be verified.
7. Use surveillance tools along with computer logging procedures to monitor and document the users of a computer system. Also use intrusion detection software or services to monitor a computer system for any indications of unusual activity.
8. Communicate with a business's Internet service provider to determine the controls it has in place to prevent hacker attacks.
9. Immediately report significant intrusions into a computer system to the appropriate law enforcement authorities.
10. Review a business's insurance policies to determine whether they provide coverage for losses due to hacker attacks. If not, consider obtaining an insurance policy that covers business interruption losses, theft of proprietary information, and other losses that may result from hacker attacks.

Adapted from the following source: American Institute of Certified Public Accountants, "Best Practices for E-Commerce Self-Defense," *Journal of Accountancy*, April 2000, 12.

---

26. *Ibid*.

Online businesses should study their computer systems and related controls to identify weak points that might allow unauthorized individuals to gain access to those systems. Despite the publicity that has focused on hacker attacks launched by individuals such as Kevin Mitnick, most hacker attacks originate from within organizations. "Sadly, the biggest threat is from within. Law enforcement officials estimate that up to 60% of break-ins are from employees."[27] For this reason, a key element of an online business's anti-hacking policies must be severe sanctions for employees who intentionally gain unauthorized access to the firm's computer systems. Computer security professionals also strongly recommend validation of a business's computer security controls by an independent third party and periodic testing of those controls.

Online companies can employ various authentication procedures and products, such as passwords and smart cards, to limit access to their computer systems. Most online businesses install firewalls to serve as the primary line of defense against unauthorized entry into their computer network via the Internet. Surveillance products and electronic logging procedures are also commonly used by online businesses to monitor and document access to their computer systems by both authorized and unauthorized parties. To provide further protection for their sensitive financial records and other confidential data, e-commerce firms should consider encrypting the information flowing through their computer systems. Encryption renders data unusable by unauthorized parties who successfully break into a computer system—unless they also obtain access to the decryption key.

Major Internet service providers (ISPs) have extensive control procedures to minimize the risk of hacker attacks and other unwanted intrusions into the computer systems of their clients. Smaller ISPs typically place less emphasis on security controls. As a result, organizations that use the services of smaller ISPs may need to implement rigorous intrusion policies and procedures to compensate for any weaknesses evident in the corresponding controls of their ISP.

Businesses should immediately notify appropriate law enforcement authorities when they suffer significant hacker attacks. Such notification allows law enforcement personnel to alert other online businesses and organizations that might be targets of the same hacker. Timely reporting of hacker attacks also helps law enforcement agencies track down and eventually prosecute the parties involved in those attacks.

A final feature that e-commerce businesses should consider integrating into their anti-hacking policies and procedures is insurance. Online businesses should review their existing insurance policies to determine whether they cover potential losses due to hacker attacks, such as lost revenues resulting from disruption of business operations. In most cases, businesses will find that conventional insurance policies do not cover such losses. Only a few major insurance companies offer Internet-specific insurance coverage. These latter firms include Lloyd's of London and U.S.-based American International Group (AIG). Lloyd's of London, the most prominent insurance company worldwide, markets a variety of insurance policies that reimburses companies for losses resulting from hacker attacks. The base policy offered by Lloyd's of London provides $1 million of coverage for an annual premium of $20,000.

27. Sager," CyberCrime."

On the bright side, e-commerce businesses that decide to ratchet up their Internet-related security controls will find a large and growing number of vendors who offer such products and services. By 2004, financial analysts predict that the annual revenues of the computer security industry will top $8 billion, more than double the industry's annual revenues in 1999.[28] Sales of Internet security products and services will account for approximately one-half of those revenues.

KEVIN MITNICK: COMPUTER SECURITY GURU

Federal prosecutors filed a long list of charges against Kevin Mitnick following his arrest in February 1995 in Raleigh, North Carolina. Those charges included allegations that Mitnick had violated various provisions of the Computer Fraud and Abuse Act of 1984. That statute makes hacking into computer systems of the federal government and major financial institutions a federal offense. Mitnick never faced trial on the charges on which he was indicted. After being held for four years in federal prison, Mitnick accepted a plea bargain agreement with federal authorities that allowed him to be paroled in January 2000.

While Mitnick lingered in prison awaiting resolution of the charges pending against him, his colleagues in the hacking underground mounted a spirited crusade to compel federal authorities to release him. That crusade included the distribution of thousands of "Free Kevin" bumper stickers and the creation of dozens of "Free Kevin" websites. Mitnick's supporters also launched damaging hacker attacks on the websites of parties blamed for his arrest, including *The New York Times*.

Defenders of Mitnick targeted *The New York Times* because of front-page articles written by *Times'* reporter John Markoff in the early 1990s that focused on Mitnick. Those articles made Mitnick the most well-known and feared hacker worldwide. Markoff "portrayed Mitnick as a superhacker who could wreak cyberhavoc—and ruin lives—if not caught by the Feds."[29] Friends and supporters of the jailed hacker maintained that Markoff had caused the public and law enforcement authorities to view Mitnick as a menace to society when, in fact, he was simply a "typical" hacker who, with the exception of a few pranks, had harmed no one.

In May 1995, a major publishing company announced that it had paid a $750,000 advance to John Markoff and Tsutomo Shimomura to co-author a book chronicling Shimomura's pursuit of Mitnick. That announcement prompted several reporters to challenge the motives underlying John Markoff's journalistic tirade against Mitnick. One reporter asked whether Mitnick was really "the Darth Vader of the Internet as depicted by Markoff?"[30] Another reporter answered that question. "The reality is a lot less sexy. Kevin Mitnick is a recreational hacker with a compulsive-obsessive relationship to information. He hoarded information, never sold it, and wouldn't even share it with his friends."[31]

---

28. B. I. Koerner, "Desirables, Undesirables," *Business 2.0*, 12 June 2001, 54.

29. A. L. Penenberg, "Mitnick Speaks," *Forbes.com*, 5 April 1999.

30. M. Meyer, "Is This Hacker Evil or Merely Misunderstood?" *Newsweek*, 4 December 1995, 60.

31. Penenberg, "Mitnick Speaks."

The dispute over Kevin Mitnick's criminal status and stature resurfaced in early 2000 when he was released from federal prison. When Mitnick was offered several jobs in the computer security industry, federal officials insisted that the terms of his probation precluded him from accepting those positions. Those officials maintained that Mitnick was still a threat to society and should not be allowed to accept any employment position linked to the Internet or to profit from the expertise he had gained over his long tenure as a hacker.

Despite the controversy over Mitnick's right to work in the computer security industry, few industry insiders questioned his status as an expert on online security issues. In fact, in the spring of 2000, a U.S. Senate subcommittee asked him to testify on that topic. Much of Mitnick's testimony focused on the measures that online businesses can take to protect their computer systems from external hacker attacks. Mitnick surprised the Senate subcommittee when he maintained that a considerable portion of the huge annual expenditures made by companies to deter and detect hacking attacks was being wasted. Mitnick testified that experienced hackers use "social engineering" tactics to circumvent expensive firewall products, authentication systems, and other anti-hacking software and hardware installed by major corporations and government agencies. Social engineering involves cajoling, persuading, or tricking low-level employees of an organization into revealing passwords or other computer codes that allow hackers free access to a computer system.

In a subsequent interview with a business publication, Mitnick warned corporate executives that employees, particularly lower level administrative employees, are the Achilles' heel of an organization's security controls. "The weakest link in the chain is always the human element. You can have the newest security tools to protect your technology, but in the end, if you have a $7 or $8 per-hour person using the equipment, that can be exploited by a hacker."[32]

Kevin Mitnick's struggle to win the right to work in the computer security industry stretched into a protracted court battle in the spring and early summer of 2000. Outside court one day, a contrite Mitnick told reporters that he was "just trying to make a living like the next guy."[33] In July 2000, federal probation officers suddenly and without explanation stopped contesting Mitnick's right to work in the computer security industry. Almost immediately, Mitnick became one of the most sought after experts on computer security. In an interview with the Internet-linked publication *Red Herring* in the summer of 2001, Mitnick confessed that he was living a hacker's dream. "The challenge of figuring out vulnerabilities of the corporate network and coming up with solutions and at the same time getting compensated for it—that's the hacker's dream."[34]

QUESTIONS

1. Find an example of a hacking incident reported recently by the business press. Write a brief summary of that incident. Your summary should identify the vic-

32. *CIO Magazine* (online), "Conversation with Kevin Mitnick," 1 June 2000.

33. A. Goldberg, "The Telegraph.com: Silicon Valley Diary," *The Daily Telegraph*, 6 July 2000, 4.

34. J. Littman, "Reformed Hacker Kevin Mitnick Is Now Using His Powers to Do Good," *Red Herring*, 15 July 2001, 83.

tim of the hacking incident, the impact the incident had on the victim, the party responsible or allegedly responsible for the attack (if available), any charges filed or planning to be filed against the hacker, and related information. In your opinion, what was the hacker's likely motive?

2. Identify a website operated by a hacker organization or that is devoted to hacking activities. Document the Web address of that site and summarize the site's contents in a bullet format. In your view, what is the site's primary objective?

3. Suppose that an employee of a corporation inadvertently discovers a way to gain access to a competitor's computer system. Should the employee report the discovery to his or her immediate superior? To the other company's computer security group? Defend your answer.

4. Now, assume that you are the individual who makes the discovery just described in Question 3. Suppose that after reporting this information to your superiors, they instruct you to access the competitor's computer system and copy key information files. How would you respond? What alternative courses of action are available to you? Identify the parties who will likely be affected by your decision. What responsibility, if any, do you owe each of those parties?

5. Corporate executives are often reluctant to report hacker attacks and the resulting losses suffered by their company. In your view, should publicly owned companies be required to report significant hacker attacks on their computer systems and the related losses? Is it unethical *not* to report that information to stockholders, creditors, and other interested parties? Defend your answer.

6. Should individuals who have been convicted of hacking be allowed to profit from their ill-gained expertise by working in the computer security industry? Explain.

7. Identify a website of a company that markets Internet security products or services. Document the address of that website and describe the principal services and/or products the firm markets.

Master of Their Domains

"What's in a name?
That which we call a rose,
By any other name would smell as sweet."

William Shakespeare

What do Brad Pitt, Sylvester Stallone, and Hillary Clinton have in common? One hint: the same problem shared by Bugs Bunny, Daffy Duck, and the elusive and enigmatic Road Runner. All six of these famous characters suffered the indignity of having their names borrowed, if not outright swiped, by entrepreneurial cyber-enthusiasts. To regain the right to one variation of her cybername, *hillary2000.com*, Hillary Clinton coughed up $6,000.

As the 1990s progressed, a new market suddenly emerged in dot-com names. A growing number of opportunists recognized that certain domain names on the World Wide Web had tremendous economic value. One dot-com domain name, *business.com*, sold for $7.5 million. Particularly sought after were domain names that mimicked the names of famous personalities or that replicated trademarked names, logos, and other identifying marks or symbols of major corporations. Thousands of corporations, professional firms, and organizations that were slow to register their names and trademarks as Web addresses found that those names and trademarks had been co-opted by other parties.

Examples of companies victimized by "cybersquatters" include America Online, Kmart, Volkswagen, and Warner Brothers, the creator of Bugs Bunny, Daffy Duck, and the Road Runner. Most cybersquatters offered to sell their copycat domain names to the companies whose trademarks were duplicated in those names or auctioned those names off to the highest bidder through an online auction house such as eBay. In some cases, copycat domain names were purchased by major competitors of the affected companies. These corporate cybersquatters typically "sat" on the domain names to keep them out of circulation or used them to channel customers of the victimized companies to their own websites. In a few cases, cybersquatters used copycat domain names to establish e-businesses that competed directly with the companies from whom they had "borrowed" those names.

Many companies paid large sums to purchase their cybernames that had been claimed by other parties. But, as the end of the millennium approached, a growing number of large firms refused to pay what they perceived to be ransoms to recover what they believed were their rightful Web names and addresses. By the late 1990s, cybersquatting cases clogged state and federal courts, so much so that the U.S. Congress was forced to take up the issue. In November 1999, President Clinton signed into law the Anti-Cybersquatting Consumer Protection Act (ACPA). Among other provisions, the ACPA extended trademark protection to domain names.

What's in a Name?

So, you have a halitosis problem? What do you do? Those among us who believe that every answer to every problem can be found on the information superhighway might search for relief on the Internet. In fact, if you type in *badbreath.com*, your search engine will quickly whisk you away to a Procter & Gamble site. One more click and you will face a glistening "Feel the Tingle" graphic that invites you to try Scope Mouthwash—Original or Peppermint—one of Procter & Gamble's dozens of successful brand-name products. Unlike many major companies, Procter & Gamble in the early days of the Internet recognized the importance of corralling key domain names on the Web. Besides *badbreath.com*, P&G quickly locked up *laundry.com*, *headache.com*, and the ever-popular *underarm.com*.

In cyberspace, domain names serve as the mailbox addresses for individuals, organizations, and businesses. Domain names allow Internet users to quickly find the proverbial needle in a haystack: the needle being a specific individual or entity a user wants to contact; the haystack being the hundreds of millions of Internet users around the world. Domain names are partitioned into fields or domains separated by periods or "dots." For example, consider the two-level domain name *espn.com*. The alphanumeric data in the far right field of a domain name is known as the top-level domain. So, "*com*" serves as the top-level domain of *espn.com*, while "*espn*" is referred to as a second-level domain. (Of course, e-mail addresses always include a specific domain name. An individual's online *nom de plume* appears immediately to the left of the ubiquitous @ sign that precedes the lowest-level domain included in an e-mail address.)

Every Internet site has a designated Internet Protocol (IP) address. An IP is simply a string of numeric data that allows one Internet-connected computer to find another. Since IP's are strictly numeric, they are comparable to electronic telephone numbers. The early pioneers of the Internet recognized that users would find it difficult to remember long and unwieldy IP addresses. To alleviate this problem, each IP address is assigned a corresponding mnemonic domain name.

The magic of the Internet quickly converts a domain name entered by an online user in a search window to the underlying IP address. An electronic routing system then takes over to zap the user's request through the maze of interconnected networks that make up the Internet to locate the appropriate website. For example, when you type in *badbreath.com*, that domain name is translated into the corresponding and prodigious IP address, which the Internet then uses to connect your computer with Procter & Gamble's website. The Internet's electronic routing system consists of interconnected "root servers" or "root zone files" that contain huge databases of domain names and corresponding IP addresses.

> When asked to translate an unknown domain name into an Internet Protocol number, a computer will ask its Internet Service Provider's server if it knows the domain name and corresponding Internet Protocol number. If that server lacks the information, it will pass the query to a "root server," also call a "root zone" file, the authoritative and highest level of the domain name system database. The root zone file directs the query to the proper top-level domain zone file, which contains the domain names in a given domain and their corresponding Internet Protocol numbers.[1]

During the early years of the Internet, domain names were assigned by one individual, a graduate student at UCLA. At the time, UCLA had a contract with the U.S. Department of Defense to assign domain names and to maintain a registry of those names. When that graduate student, Jonathon Postel, left UCLA to accept a position at its fierce cross-town rival USC, he retained his job as the domain name kingpin. Recognize that Postel's responsibilities were not particularly time-consuming. In 1981, only 300 computers were linked to the Internet. As the Internet grew in size, the federal government realized that a more formal system was needed to assign and keep track of domain names.

By 1992, the U.S. Department of Commerce had assumed the primary regulatory responsibility for overseeing the assignment of new domain names. In that year, the federal agency contracted with a small private company, Network Solutions, Inc. (NSI), to assign domain names and maintain a registry of those names. This contract gave NSI the exclusive right to assign domain names ending in one of four top-level domain designations: *com*, *edu*, *net*, and *org*. By far, the most popular top-level domain classification is *com*, which is intended for use by business entities.

Between 1992 and 1997, NSI registered approximately one million domain names, most of the dot-com variety. NSI charged registrants $70 for the standard two-year registration period. By the late 1990s, the tremendous growth in domain name registrations translated into huge profits and revenues for NSI, which went public in 1997. During 1999, NSI registered five million new domain names, compared to only 100,000 in 1995, and posted a record profit of $27 million on $220 million of revenues. Near the end of 1999, the market value of NSI's stock approached $15 billion. In 1995, an astute investor had purchased the company for a little more than $4 million.

Criticism of NSI's government-mandated monopoly for assigning domain names prompted the federal government to once again restructure the domain-name assignment process beginning in late 1998. The federal government created an international non-profit organization entitled the Internet Corporation for Assigned Names and Numbers or ICANN to manage the process of assigning Internet domain names not only in the United States, but worldwide as well. The Department of Commerce subsequently brokered an agreement between NSI and ICANN that led to the creation of a new name-assignment system for websites, the shared registry system. Under this new system, ICANN would open the domain name registration process to other companies, meaning that NSI would no

---

1. *William Thomas, et al. v. Network Solutions, Inc., and the National Science Foundation*, 276 F.3d 500 (U.S. App., 1999).

longer be the sole registrant of new domain names. However, NSI would serve as the managing agent of the shared registry system. In this role, NSI would be paid an annual fee of $6 for every new domain name registered by other companies.

By late 1999, dozens of companies had entered the newly created domain name registration industry. Register.com soon became the largest rival to NSI in this industry, although NSI was expected to remain the industry leader for the foreseeable future. Approximately one year after the shared registry system was launched, NSI still registered approximately 85 percent of all new domain names. During 2000, the large Internet firm Verisign acquired NSI in a $20 billion corporate takeover. Verisign assumed responsibility for the shared registry system created by ICANN—a system it renamed Verisign Global Registry Services.

DOMAIN NAME MANIA

Businesses moving into e-commerce recognized that having just any old domain name was not adequate. A key to success on the Internet is an ability to "grab" eyeballs. One method for channeling eyeballs to a site is the strategy used by Procter & Gamble. Someone suffering from recurring headaches might naturally use "headache" as the key word in an Internet search for relief from that malady. Another approach is to use a "snappy" or distinctive domain name that easily embeds itself into an Internet user's memory. Fogdog.com, a sports equipment retailer, used its distinctive domain name and a series of equally memorable television commercials to capture the attention of potential customers. "Catchy addresses are as important to online merchants as prime retail space is to conventional merchants. It's easier to order jewelry from a business that can be reached by typing 'gold.com,' for example, than it is to buy it from another vendor with a forgettable address."[2]

Understandably, existing companies with large customer bases wanted to use their own corporate logos, brand names, and other trademarks to flag down consumers motoring on the information superhighway. High-tech companies such as Dell Computer, Intel, and Cisco Systems quickly realized the significance of domain names for establishing a presence on the increasingly crowded Main Street of electronic storefronts. These companies did not hesitate to pay the nominal annual registration fees to stake claims to the domain names linked directly or indirectly to their corporate identities, products, and services. Some of these companies went one step further and registered dozens of domain names that Internet surfers might inadvertently use in attempting to access their websites. This strategy was intended to derail so-called "typosquatters." Books.com, an early competitor of Amazon.com, registered the domain name *Amazom.com*, realizing that an occasional weary or careless Internet shopper would use that domain name in a wayward attempt to access the king of online booksellers. Internet users who typed *amazom.com* into a search window were delivered to the *books.com* website.

Less Internet-savvy companies were much slower to stake claims to the e-world equivalents of their corporate identities. In the mid-1990s, thousands of opportunists snapped up domain names that duplicated, or at least were suggestive

---

2. S. Higgins, "What's in an Internet Name? To Online Merchants, Lots," *Investor's Business Daily,* 17 October 1995, A10.

of, the names of well-known individuals, companies, products, and services. Thus, when Warner Brothers finally got around to registering appropriate domain names for Bugs, Daffy, and Road Runner, the company found that those names had already been taken.

NSI assigned domain names strictly on a first-come, first-served basis. If you were the first to pay the $70, two-year registration fee for a given domain name, that name was yours. NSI did not assume any responsibility for verifying that registrants had a legal right to use the domain names they were claiming. Many individuals and companies registered thousands of domain names, both generic names such as *drugs.com* and trademarked names such as *porsche.com*. One up-start company alone, registered more than 12,000 domain names at an initial cost of nearly $900,000.

The stampede to register domain names spawned a secondary market in those names. Investors could speculate in domain names by purchasing them in electronic marketplaces created by eBay and other online auction houses. Many domain names changed hands several times before they became associated with an actual business, either a virtual business or a "conventional" business intending to make a foray into e-commerce. GreatDomains.com quickly established itself as a leading domain name auctioneer. For example, the owner of *america.com* listed that name on the *greatdomains.com* website at an "asking price" of $10 million. In an advertisement appearing in *The Wall Street Journal* for the domain name *fly.com*, GreatDomains chided Continental Airlines: "Hey Continental, *fly.com* is for sale. Don't let one of your competitors take off before you."

The $7.5 million price paid for *business.com* by the Internet incubator eCompanies in November 1998 produced a frenzy of speculative activity in the domain name market. Soon, dozens of domain names were being offered, and some purchased, in the seven-digit price range. Examples of other dot-com names that broke the million-dollar price barrier include *autos.com*, *bingo.com*, *drugs.com*, *korea.com*, and *wine.com*. By the late 1990s, hundreds of individuals had left their jobs to become "name brokers" and to search for the Holy Grail of domain names—the first domain name to bring an eight-digit price. "It's an addiction. . . . You find a name. It costs you $70. You sell it for 10 times more than that. You're like, 'that's unbelievable.'"[3]

CYBERSQUATTERS EVERYWHERE

Angry corporate executives coined the term "cybersquatters" to refer to individuals and companies that registered domain names infringing on existing corporate trademarks. Many of these executives reluctantly paid prices ranging into six digits to purchase domain names that they viewed were rightfully their company's property in the first place. By the late 1990s, as the asking prices for domain names skyrocketed, most corporate executives refused to negotiate with cybersquatters, choosing instead to take them to court. The lawsuits provoked by cybersquatting incidents were typically predicated on one simple premise: corporations, other businesses, and not-for-profit organizations had a legal right

---

3. S. Cummings, "Free-for-All on the Name Exchange," *The New York Times* on the Web, 29 March 2000.

to any domain names derived from their trademarked names, products, and services.

Trademarks have existed since medieval times. Noted craftsmen of the Middle Ages used unique symbols to identify their products for the purpose of protecting their reputations. In the United States, Congress passed the first federal trademark law in 1870. In 1946, Congress unified a hodgepodge of federal trademark statutes when it passed the Federal Trademark Act, commonly referred to as the Lanham Act. Although amended several times, that law still serves as the principal federal statute that dictates the rights and privileges associated with U.S. trademarks held by businesses, other organizations, and individuals. Two principal objectives underlie the Lanham Act and the case law that has developed around that statute. The first objective is to protect the public from deceitful practices perpetrated by individuals and entities attempting to trade on the "good name" of another party. The second objective is to protect the goodwill and other resources trademark holders have invested in their business's names, symbols, and other identifying marks.

To paraphrase the Lanham Act, a trademark consists of any word, name, symbol, or device, or combination thereof, that is used to identify and distinguish goods and services of an entity from those manufactured or sold by others. In the brouhaha over domain names and corporate trademarks, corporate lawyers alleged that cybersquatters impaired or diluted the value of a pre-existing trademark by replicating it or embedding it in a domain name.

The NSI's stubborn refusal during the mid- and late 1990s to accept any responsibility for determining whether individuals filing claims for given domain names had a legal right to those names served to embolden cybersquatters. Anyone with $70 and a few minutes to spare could "squat" on an unclaimed domain name that included a registered trademark of an existing business or organization. Consider a few of the higher profile cases of cybersquatting or alleged cybersquatting.

MTV

Adam Curry worked as a video disk jockey for MTV during the 1990s. While employed by MTV, Curry developed a website with the domain name *mtv.com*. At that site, Curry reported daily tidbits of news and gossip pertinent to the entertainment and music industries. Although MTV granted Curry permission to establish the website and apparently encouraged him to maintain it, Curry personally paid the bi-annual registration fee to NSI for the site and registered it in his own name. After being released by MTV in the early 1990s, Curry continued to operate the very popular *mtv.com* website. At the height of its popularity, the site received upwards of 35,000 "hits" each day.

In 1994, MTV sued Curry, charging that the domain name for his website infringed on company trademarks. Curry claimed that MTV filed the suit only after it discovered the popularity of the site and its potential commercial value to the firm. Eventually, the two parties settled the case out of court. The key stipulation of that settlement required Curry to turn over the *mtv.com* website to his former employer.

Stanley Kaplan Keeps His Beer

At approximately the same time that MTV and Adam Curry were skirmishing over the rights to the *mtv.com* website, a similar dispute arose between two companies that offered test preparation services to the public, Stanley Kaplan and Princeton Review. In the early 1990s, officials of Princeton Review registered a website with the domain name *kaplan.com*. Princeton Review used this site to distribute unflattering assertions regarding the quality of Kaplan's services and instructional materials. Most galling to Kaplan executives was that the *kaplan.com* website did not reveal it was actually owned and operated by Princeton Review.

Not surprisingly, Kaplan sued Princeton Review. To settle the matter, Princeton Review offered to sell the website to Kaplan for a case of beer. Unamused by the offer, Kaplan failed to respond. After both parties agreed to settle the case in arbitration, the arbitrator who presided over the case ruled that Princeton Review had to relinquish the *kaplan.com* site to Kaplan.

I Don't Have a Clue . . . Website

Clue Computing, Co., a firm based in Boulder, Colorado, registered the domain name *clue.com* in 1994. Two years later, Hasbro, Inc., the large toy manufacturer that markets the popular *Clue* board game, learned of the *clue.com* site and immediately sued Clue Computing. Hasbro charged that Clue Computing was guilty of cybersquatting and had infringed on the trademark it owned on the *Clue* game.

The owner of Clue Computing insisted that given the name of his company and the fact that his company was in a totally different industry than Hasbro, his *clue.com* domain name could not dilute the value of Hasbro's trademarked *Clue* game. Just as pointedly, the Clue Computing owner reminded the court that he had taken fair advantage of NSI's first-come, first-served policy and registered the *clue.com* domain name two years before Hasbro considered laying claim to that name. After incurring several hundred thousand dollars of legal expenses, Clue Computing prevailed when a federal judge ruled that the company had an exclusive right to the *clue.com* domain name.

By mid-1999, more than 500 lawsuits involving cybersquatting or related allegations were pending in state and federal courts. Thousands of other companies, organizations, and individuals had fallen victim to cybersquatters and had either paid to recover domain names containing their trademarks or were still considering their legal options. An industry trade publication deplored the extortion schemes that some cybersquatters were using to extract huge sums from large, prominent companies.

> Cyberpirates are ruling high technology much the same way their infamous counterparts once ruled the high seas. The booty these pirates seek are the reputations and financial resources of internationally renowned businesses, who are discovering that they have to buy, barter or sue for the rights to use their own name on a Web site because cyberpirates and cybersquatters already own their Internet domain designation.[4]

---

4. B. Janoff, "Scuttling the Cyberpirates," *Progressive Grocer*, November 1999, 61.

In 1998, a federal appeals court ruled that "cyberpiracy" violated federal trademark laws. In that case, an individual had purchased a domain name that contained a company's trademarked name and then offered to sell the domain name to the company for $13,000. In making that offer, the individual suggested to the company that it would be much cheaper to simply pay the $13,000 rather than take him to court. The rapid growth in the number of cybersquatting cases that amounted to cyberpiracy forced the U.S. Congress to tackle this issue in 1999.

CONGRESS ATTEMPTS TO EVICT SQUATTERS

The Anti-Cybersquatting Consumer Protection Act (ACPA) became law on November 29, 1999, when signed by President Clinton. A leading expert on cyberlaw provided a concise overview of the new federal statute.

> The Act establishes a new framework which provides companies with more effective and expanded legal recourse against domain name piracy than existed under previous trademark law. The new law takes a common sense approach, based on a number of factors, that balances the rights of trademark owners with the fair use of domain names which encompass someone else's trademark.[5]

The ACPA generally mandates that cybersquatters who attempt to profit from a domain name that is identical or confusingly similar to another party's distinctive or famous trademark will be forced to relinquish the domain name to that party. Plaintiffs that successfully pursue a claim filed under the ACPA are also entitled to recover damages from the defendant, including profits that the defendant earned from employing the domain name in question. Instead of actual damages, courts may award successful plaintiffs statutory damages from $1,000 to $100,000 for each illicit domain name used by the defendant.

Legal experts in intellectual property rights believe that the outcome of most cases filed under the ACPA will hinge on whether a plaintiff can establish "bad faith intent to profit" on the part of the defendant. The ACPA identifies several specific factors that courts should consider in addressing this issue. Listed next are some of these factors.

1. Does the defendant have any bona fide intellectual property rights to the trademark included in the disputed domain name?
2. The extent to which the domain name consists of the defendant's legal name or a name that is commonly used to identify that person or entity.
3. The defendant's prior use, if any, of the domain name in connection with a legitimate business or venture.
4. Did the defendant intend to divert consumers from the plaintiff's online location to its own online location?
5. Did the defendant attempt to sell the domain name to the plaintiff or any other third party without first using or intending to use the domain name in connection with a legitimate business or other venture?

---

5. *Business Wire*, "Congress Passes Anti-Cybersquatting Consumer Protection Act, Changes to Federal Trademark Law Seen as Potent Weapon Against Domain Name Piracy," 14 December 1999.

6. Did the defendant acquire multiple domain names that duplicate or resemble the trademarks of parties other than the plaintiff?

The first major test case involving the ACPA came before a federal appeals court in early 2000 and involved a trademark infringement lawsuit filed by Sportman's Market, Inc., a mail-order catalog company that specializes in selling aviation merchandise to pilots and aviation enthusiasts. The defendants in that lawsuit were Omega Engineering, Inc., and a wholly owned Omega subsidiary, Sporty's Farms.

Sportman's Market began using "sporty's" as an identifying logo for its aviation products and catalogs during the 1960s. In 1985, Sportman's established a legal right to "Sporty's" when it registered that trademark with the U.S. Patent and Trademark Office. Since registering the *Sporty's* trademark, Sportman's has used the trademark in its catalogs, advertising brochures, and other promotional materials. In fact, the company's toll free number for customer orders is 1-800-Sportys. During the late 1990s, Sportman's spent $10 million annually promoting products that sported the *Sporty's* trademark.

In early 1995, the owners of Omega Engineering, Inc., a mail-order catalog company that sold scientific instruments, decided to establish an aviation catalog business. Omega's principal owner was a pilot who was very familiar with Sportman's Market and the *Sporty's* logo. Omega's owners named their new business Pilot's Depot. In April 1995, the owners registered the domain name *sportys.com* with NSI. Several months later, Omega's owners formed another business venture, Sporty's Farm, and transferred the *sportys.com* domain name to this new business. The principal operations of Sporty's Farm involved the growing and marketing of Christmas trees.

Sportman's Market filed the trademark infringement lawsuit against Omega and Sporty's Farm before the ACPA was signed into law in November 1999. After that law was enacted, a lower court ruling in the Sportman's lawsuit was appealed to the Second Circuit of the U.S. Court of Appeals. Since Congress mandated that key provisions of the ACPA were to be applied retroactively, the appellate court relied heavily on the ACPA in resolving the Sportman's lawsuit.

The first issue addressed by the appellate court was whether the *Sporty's* logo was distinctive or famous. A related issue was whether the *sportys.com* domain name was confusingly similar to the *Sporty's* logo. The appellate court quickly decided that the *Sporty's* logo was distinctive and recognized nationwide by parties involved in the aviation merchandising industry.[6] Next, the court ruled that the *sportys.com* domain name, although not identical, was confusingly similar to the *Sporty's* logo.

The key issue that the appellate court had to resolve in the Sportman's lawsuit was whether the owners of Omega Engineering acted with a "bad faith intent to profit" from the *sportys.com* domain name. First, the court ruled that neither Omega nor Sporty's Farm had any intellectual property rights in the *sportys.com* domain name when Omega registered that name. In fact, Sporty's Farm didn't exist when Omega acquired that domain name. The court noted that the Sporty's Farm subsidiary was formed by Omega only after Sportman's filed the trademark

---

6. The appellate court noted that the *Sporty's* logo likely qualified as "famous" as well. However, since the ACPA requires only that plaintiffs prove that the trademark in question is distinctive or famous, the court did not explicitly rule on this issue.

infringement lawsuit. Ostensibly, Omega had transferred the ownership of the *sportys.com* domain name to the Sporty's Farm venture in an effort to prove that the domain name was connected with a legitimate commercial venture. The most credible evidence that Omega acted with "bad faith intent to profit" in registering the *sportys.com* domain name was court testimony that the company eventually intended to link the domain name to an aviation merchandising business that would compete directly with Sportman's business.

In the opinion handed down in the Sportman's lawsuit, the appellate court ruled that Omega's use of the *sportys.com* domain name had violated Sportman's statutory right to the *Sporty's* logo under federal trademark law as amended by the ACPA. The court then ordered Sporty's Farm to transfer the *sportys.com* domain name to Sportman's.

LOOKING TO THE FUTURE

The ACPA left many issues in the ongoing war over Internet domain names unresolved. For example, in many situations two or more companies or organizations have a shared name in their trademark, a name that each wants to attach to its website. Which company should have an exclusive right to the *ritz.com* domain name? Ritz Crackers, one of the sumptuous Ritz Hotels, or any of dozens of other "ritzy" businesses? In such cases, the courts have generally held that the first-come, first-served policy of NSI, Verisign, and other domain-name assigners determines who has the right to use the contested domain name.[7] That was the outcome of a lawsuit that CBS filed against The Network Network. The latter company registered the domain name *tnn.com*, only to have CBS insist that because of its TNN (The Nashville Network) Channel it had an exclusive right to the *tnn.com* domain name. A federal judge disagreed.

> The fact that Nashville [CBS] missed its opportunity to select the domain name it would now like to have is not sufficient to state a claim of infringement under the federal trademark law, particularly where, as here, there can be no genuine risk of confusion— initial or otherwise—by any consumer of reasonable prudence, and no argument that Network [The Network Network] has sought or is now seeking to trade on Nashville's good name.[8]

At approximately the same time that the ACPA became law, ICANN established its mandatory Uniform Domain Name Dispute Resolution Policy to help parties involved in domain name disputes avoid the costly litigation often required to resolve those disputes. When a domain name dispute arises, one of four independent arbitration agencies is assigned to the case by ICANN. After studying the circumstances of the case, the arbitrator issues a ruling that grants one party an exclusive right to the contested domain name. If this ruling is not challenged in court within ten days by one of the parties involved in the dispute, the ruling becomes final. The fee for this service generally ranges from $1,000 to

---

7. Apparently, the Ritz Paris won the *ritz.com* derby since it operates the website having that domain name.

8. *Business Wire* (online), "CBS Loses Internet Domain Name Dispute in Federal Court," 22 February 2000.

$3,500, an amount that is a small fraction of the legal expenses that parties incur when they insist on settling their dispute in the courts.

Soon after ICANN instituted its dispute resolution policy, the organization was flooded with domain name disputes. By the end of 2001, nearly 4,000 of those disputes had been resolved by ICANN arbitrators. More than 90 percent of these cases were decided by the two largest arbitration agencies used by ICANN, the Arbitration and Mediation Center based in Geneva, Switzerland, and the U.S.-based National Arbitration Forum. The bulk of these disputes involve cyber-squatting charges filed by large companies alleging that one or more of their corporate trademarks have been infringed upon by a domain name registered by another party. In more than 80 percent of such cases, the corporate "plaintiffs" have prevailed and been granted the right to the disputed domain name.[9]

Despite the ACPA and the efforts of ICANN, domain name piracy remains a major problem and an impediment to e-commerce, particularly international e-commerce. Internationally, there are approximately 250 different top-level domain designations for individual countries. The top-level domain designation for the United States, *us*, is not nearly as popular in this country as the all-powerful *com* designation. But, in many other countries, the top-level country domain designation is widely used.[10] In some of these countries, cyberpirates have used trademarked U.S. names and phrases as second-level domain names just to the left of the top-level domain name for their given country. For example, in Russia an anti-smoking organization established the *marlboro.ru* website to distribute information condemning the tobacco industry.[11] Even more domain-name headaches for multinational corporations were created during 2001 when Verisign began registering domain names in dozens of languages, including Chinese, Korean, and Japanese. Suddenly, U.S. companies found that foreign-language versions of their trademarked names had been claimed by a new generation of cybersquatters. In the People's Republic of China, one name merchant quickly laid claim to the Chinese equivalent of *coca-cola.com* and many other domain names replicating valuable trademarks of U.S. companies.[12]

In the United States, ICANN inadvertently touched off a new siege of cyber-squatting when it approved seven additional top-level domain designations in late 2000. Those designations include *info, name, pro, museum, aero, coop,* and *biz.* Many Internet insiders expected that *biz* might eventually prove to be a rival to *com* in the online business world. Not surprisingly, that expectation prompted a flurry of interest in *biz* names on the part of nouveau cybersquatters. Since ICANN intends to add additional top-level domain designations in the future, there appears to be no end to the potential mischief that cybersquatters can pose

9. S. Bonisteel, "Law Expert Charges Bias in Domain-Dispute Arbitrations," *Global News Wire* (online), 20 August 2001.

10. Two of the more popular top-level domain classifications for individual countries are Moldova's *md* and Tuvalu's *tv.* (For the geographically impaired, Moldova was formerly a province of the USSR, while Tuvalu is a small Polynesian country.) A U.S. company purchased *md* domain names from Moldova and markets those names to physicians in this country. Tuvalu signed a $50 million deal with the Internet incubator idealab! to auction off *tv* domain names.

11. G. Manuel, "Domain-Name Grab by 'Cybersquatters' Is Setting Off Big Turf War with Firms," *The Wall Street Journal* Interactive Edition, 23 February 2001.

12. *Ibid.*

for companies, other organizations, and individuals fortunate enough to control valuable trademarks.

As new dimensions and mutations of the cybersquatting plague arose during 2000 and 2001, major U.S. companies faced the increasingly daunting task of protecting their trademarked names, products, and related assets in cyberspace. To date, many multinational companies have pledged to fight cybersquatters on all fronts. Coca-Cola, which owns one of the most valuable brand names across the globe, has adopted that strategy. In February 2001, a Coca-Cola spokesperson reported that, "We shall handle any registration by other parties of our trademarks in any language as an infringement, and will attempt to use all legal means necessary to have the domain names returned to us."[13]

Frustration and mounting criticism of the domain-naming process and ICANN's oversight role in that process drew the attention of Congress during 2001. The most vocal ICANN critics were corporate executives who charged that the independent agency was largely responsible for the domain name "mess" that had arisen over the previous few years. More specific complaints leveled at ICANN included that the agency had failed to develop a master strategy to guide the assignment of domain names, worked in secrecy, and did not answer to any government body. During hearings sponsored by the U.S. House Commerce Committee, Representative John Dingell observed that ICANN "appears to be accountable to no one,"[14] while Representative Edward Markey observed that, "Decisions made in the Vatican to select the pope are more clear to the public than how new domain names are issued."[15]

QUESTIONS

1. Choose a large company and identify domain names that it uses. Identify other domain names that the company might find useful. Determine whether those names have been claimed by other parties.
2. Many cybersquatters believe that the ACPA is unfair to them. They argue that the "first-come, first-served" policy for domain name registrations gave everyone an equal chance to register valuable domain names. According to this point of view, the party who first registered a domain name should be entitled to exclusive ownership of that name. Do you agree or disagree with this view? Explain.
3. Cybersquatting is just one example of an abusive practice that complicates e-commerce ventures. Identify several other such practices and the implications they have for online businesses.
4. Identify three examples of corporate trademarks. Are these trademarks "distinctive" or "famous"? Defend your answer in each case. For each example you provided, develop a competing trademark that would be "confusingly similar."

13. *Ibid.*

14. V. Sinha, "Battle for Internet Domain Names Begins to Heat Up," *The Virginian Pilot* (online), 20 August 2001.

15. A. Shadid, "ICANN, Charged with Clearing Up the Murky Water of Domain Naming, Is Under Fire from Every Quarter," *Boston Globe* (online), 9 April 2001.

5. Besides trademarks, identify other examples of intangible assets owned by businesses. Compare and contrast the general strategies that companies use to protect tangible assets, such as buildings and equipment, and intangible assets.

6. Multinational companies encounter numerous challenges and problems that companies domiciled in one country do not face. Identify several such challenges or problems. For each item you list, indicate one strategy that a multinational company could use to deal effectively with that issue.

7. Research recent developments involving Internet domain names, particularly the issues addressed in this case. List and briefly describe those developments in a bullet format.

Debits, Credits, and Dot-coms

"Accounting irregularities" is a nice euphemism for what amounts to the deliberate manipulation of bookkeeping to create desirable illusions, disguising regrettable realities.

Mario Cuomo

Project Uptick, an undercover investigation spearheaded by the FBI, culminated in the largest fraud indictment ever handed down by the U.S. Justice Department.[1] That indictment, issued in June 2000, named more than 120 individuals who had allegedly collaborated to manipulate the stock prices of 19 companies, many of the dot-com variety. Ironically, one of the companies targeted by the fraudsters was FinancialWeb.com, an online company that operated a website, *StockDetective.com*, intended to help online investors spot stocks whose prices were being manipulated by "pump and dump" schemes. In such scams, a group of individuals typically embellishes the projected revenues and profits for a company in messages posted on electronic bulletin boards and during exchanges in investor chat rooms. After the price of the given company's stock rises considerably, the pumpers dump their shares of the stock at a large profit.

Protecting investors from being fleeced has become a much more difficult task in the Internet Age. Federal authorities estimate that the pump and dump frauds uncovered by Project Uptick imposed more than $50 million of losses on investors. Although significant by most standards, those losses pale in comparison to losses suffered each year by hordes of investors hoodwinked by a more common and subtle method of manipulating stock prices.

Over the past several decades, executives of many publicly owned companies have fallen victim to the temptation to "window dress" their firms' financial statements. These financial statements are easily pawned off on unsuspecting investors as authentic. And why not? Such financial statements have been prepared by skilled corporate accountants, scrutinized by reputable audit firms, and stamped with the approval and authorization of a company's top officers and

1. The development of this case was funded by the 2000 McLaughlin Instructional Grant Award. I would like to thank Glen McLaughlin for his generous and continuing support of efforts to integrate ethics into business curricula.

board of directors before being filed with the Securities and Exchange Commission (SEC), the watchdog agency for the nation's capital markets.

In the late 1990s, Arthur Levitt, chairman of the SEC, launched a nationwide campaign against aggressive accounting and financial reporting methods used by publicly owned companies. Levitt's principal objective was to curtail so-called earnings management practices. By taking advantage of the inherent flexibility of generally accepted accounting principles (GAAP), companies can often heavily influence, if not dictate, the reported dollar amounts for key financial statement items such as total sales and net income.

Levitt and his subordinates quickly discovered that the most freewheeling practitioners of earnings management were high-tech firms, including a large number of poorly capitalized dot-com corporations struggling to survive. Particularly troubling to Levitt were revelations by his agency's financial detectives that a company's accountants commonly worked side by side with its executives to design and implement earnings management schemes. By employing what Levitt labeled "accounting gimmicks" and other "sleights of hand," executives and accountants were often able to sculpt favorable impressions of their financially distressed firms in the minds of potential investors.

The earnings management schemes and related accounting frauds uncovered by the SEC and other federal agencies have imposed huge losses on investors—losses several magnitudes greater than those stemming from pump and dump schemes. Disclosure of illicit accounting methods used by a company in the past and their impact on previously issued financial statements can trigger an avalanche of sell orders for the firm's common stock. In the spring of 2000, MicroStrategy, a prominent software company with close ties to the Internet, announced that it was lowering its previously reported 1999 revenues by approximately 25 percent. This after-the-fact revision or restatement of revenues was due to the company's decision to stop applying certain "creative" approaches to accounting for revenues. On the date of the announcement, MicroStrategy's stock plummeted from $227 to $87 per share. Over the next few weeks, the company's stock price continued its free fall, eventually slipping below $20 per share. In December 2000, the SEC announced that two of MicroStrategy's top executives had agreed to pay nearly $11 million in civil penalties to settle accounting fraud charges the federal agency had filed against them.

A series of investigations by the SEC and other federal agencies has identified several factors that tend to predispose dot-coms and other e-commerce companies to engage in accounting hijinks. Next, we examine some of those factors. Then, we consider generic examples of accounting and financial reporting gimmicks available to e-commerce firms and some specific applications of those subterfuges by resourceful executives and accountants. We conclude by examining measures to improve accounting and financial reporting practices within the e-commerce domain and key obstacles that may stymie such efforts.

DOT-COM FEVER AND ACCOUNTING HIJINKS: MOTIVES AND OPPORTUNITIES

Corporate executives have always wrestled with the temptation to misrepresent their firms' reported operating results and financial condition. Recent history suggests that the executives of e-commerce firms may have a stronger motivation to do so than their colleagues with more traditional companies. Motives alone, are not a sufficient condition for misrepresented financial statements. Wayward corporate executives must also have the opportunity to misstate their firms' financial data. In the current financial reporting environment, owners and managers of e-commerce companies often have a greater opportunity than their peers at Old Economy firms to employ abusive accounting and financial reporting practices.

SURVIVAL AT ALL COSTS MINDSET

A few fortunate e-commerce companies, eBay and Yahoo! being prime examples, raised significant amounts of cash in initial public offerings over the past decade. However, most e-commerce companies have struggled to obtain the funds needed to set up their required technological infrastructure, to establish relationships with vendors, and to acquire office space and distribution outlets—even virtual companies need some physical facilities. In many cases, an Internet company's short-term survival totally hinges on its executives' ability to raise those funds from banks, venture capital firms, or individual investors.

Top officers of e-commerce firms recognize that grandiose promises of future financial success are often necessary to attract desperately needed infusions of debt and equity capital. To make such promises resonate with deep-pocketed investors and lenders, the financial statements of an e-commerce company must, at the very least, suggest that the firm is making progress toward achieving its financial goals. Dot-com executives who adopt a survival-at-all-costs mindset may choose to coax needed funds from investors and lenders by inflating their firms' reported revenues and earnings.

STOCK OPTION MANIA

Over the past decade, no phrase has triggered more adrenaline rushes among corporate executives than the two-word zinger "stock options." Because most dot-coms have been chronically short of cash, they have relied heavily on stock option grants to lure skilled management personnel away from well-established firms. Hundreds of executives with e-commerce companies have cashed in lottery-sized sums after exponential increases in their company's stock price. In May 2000, *The Economist*, a scholarly British publication, reported that 64 new millionaires were being made each day in California's Silicon Valley, home to hundreds of dot-coms and other high-tech companies.[2] Stock options were responsible for booting many of those Californians into a higher tax bracket.

Corporate executives who jump from an Old Economy to a New Economy company typically leave behind their huge salaries. If the market price of their new firm's stock languishes, these executives can be "left holding the bag"—a bag of worthless stock options, that is. SEC officials maintain that some e-commerce executives adopt aggressive accounting policies for the sole purpose of producing impressive financial data that will ignite a rally in their company's stock price. A sharp run-up in a company's stock price, even if it is later followed by an

---

2. *The Economist* (online), "The Country-Club Vote," 20 May 2000.

equally sharp decline, provides a window of opportunity for executives to reap a windfall profit by cashing in their stash of stock options.

GAPS IN GAAP

Unsophisticated financial statement users fail to realize that many, if not most, financial statement items are subjectively determined. Naïve investors, for example, are often lulled into a false sense of security by the pinpoint accuracy with which accountants can arrive at a multibillion-dollar company's gross profit or inventory or net income. As a result, they are unaware that specific dollar amounts reported in corporate financial statements may result from professional judgments, rough approximations and, in some cases, pin-the-tail-on-the-donkey guesstimates. Likewise, many investors are unaware of the bias that companies can introduce into their financial statements given the rubber-like quality of GAAP. "The rules governing bookkeeping at public companies, the Generally Accepted Accounting Principles (GAAP), leave plenty of wiggle room for those inclined to dupe unsophisticated investors while remaining within the letter of the law."[3]

Executives and accountants who lose their objectivity may search for accounting methods that cast their company's financial statements in the most favorable light. E-commerce companies often encounter transactions and economic circumstances not specifically addressed by existing accounting standards, which means that the officers and accountants of these firms frequently have the luxury of creating their own "generally accepted" approaches to accounting for their business's operations. All too often, these new accounting procedures, or new twists on old accounting procedures, inject an optimistic bias into the reported financial statement data of e-commerce firms.

Once a company has intentionally distorted financial statements issued to third parties, even if mildly, the temptation to "tinker" with future financial statements becomes almost irresistible. One business journalist suggests that the executives of e-commerce firms often become trapped in an "ethical quagmire" in which they lose sight of right and wrong and begin "stretching" accounting rules to produce the financial data needed to support rosy forecasts for their firm.[4]

TOP LINE FIXATION

Historically, financial analysts and sophisticated investors have focused on the "bottom-line" results of companies. "What was a company's net income in the most recent year compared to its five-year earnings trend? What is the compound growth rate in a firm's earnings per share over the past ten years? How did a company's return on equity for the just concluded fiscal year compare to historical norms and to industry benchmarks?" Hype artists, including overzealous corporate executives and Internet financial analysts, have convinced a large segment of the investing public that the bottom-line fixation evident in fundamental analy-

3. J. Kahn, "Presto Chango! Sales Are Huge!" *Fortune*, 20 March 2000, 90.

4. R. J. Samuelson, "High-Tech Accounting," *Newsweek*, 3 April 2000, 37.

sis of financial statement data is inappropriate for New Economy firms. This point of view allows e-commerce executives to downplay the significance of conventional financial performance measures for their firms—measures that often suggest that their firms are much less than healthy specimens.

Instead of focusing on the profitability of e-commerce firms, many investors now fixate on the "top line" of income statements issued by these firms, namely, sales or revenues. "Over the last several years, investors have all but ignored old-fashioned financial analysis when it came to investing in Web startups or other tech favorites with little or no foreseeable profits. . . . Since many of these companies don't have earnings, investors are relying on revenue growth as a key benchmark."[5]

To accommodate this top-line approach to analyzing the financial statements of e-commerce companies, Internet analysts have developed new financial ratios such as revenue per share, revenue per customer, and revenue per active customer. These and other comparable ratios focus on a company's ability to "grow" revenues, while ignoring other key dimensions of its financial health such as liquidity, solvency and, most important, long-term profitability. This preoccupation with revenue growth allows e-commerce executives to shape perceptions of their firms' future prospects by distorting (inflating) reported revenues by any means possible.

> Never before has the way an entire industry books its sales mattered so much to investors. For a website [stock] trading at 200 times expected [annual] sales, even a tiny increase in reported revenues can translate into a huge increase in market capitalization. That, in turn, has provided Internet executives with a powerful incentive to inflate sales figures through accounting gimmicks.[6]

RECOGNIZE THIS?

In the late 1990s, as revenue growth became the key financial barometer for e-commerce companies, an increasing number of these firms began developing imaginative schemes and scams for enhancing their reported revenues. This trend, in turn, triggered a large increase in litigation cases alleging securities fraud. A research study revealed that 20 percent of all civil lawsuits alleging securities fraud in 1998 stemmed from charges of improper recognition of revenues; the following year, that figure leaped to 50 percent.[7]

Most revenue recognition scams involve artful interpretations, or flagrant breaches, of the accounting profession's "revenue recognition rule." Before revenue is recognized (recorded) in a business's accounting records, the revenue should be both realized and earned.

> Revenues and gains are realized when products (goods or services), merchandise, or other assets are exchanged for cash or claims to cash. . . . Revenues are considered to have been earned when the entity has substantially accomplished what it must do to be entitled to the benefits represented by the revenues.[8]

---

5. C. Yang, "Earth to Dot.com Accountants," *Business Week*, 3 April 2000, 40.

6. Kahn, "Presto Chango! Sales Are Huge!" 92.

7. E. Iwata, "More Firms Falsify Revenue to Boost Stocks," *USA Today*, 29 March 2000, 1B.

8. *Statement of Financial Accounting Concepts No. 5*, "Recognition and Measurement in Financial Statements of Business Enterprises," (Stamford, Conn.: FASB, 1984), para. 83.

CHANNEL STUFFING

As the end of a quarterly or annual reporting period approaches, corporate executives tend to panic if previously published financial targets seem to be out of reach. These executives want to avoid disappointing investors and lenders since they may need to tap their pocketbooks in the near future to obtain additional financing.

To remedy a revenue shortfall as the end of a reporting period approaches, many e-commerce executives have regularly "stuffed" their distribution channels with inventory. For example, a software company may ship a large quantity of products to its distributors and book those shipments as sales even though the distributors already have an excessive amount of the given products on hand. Instead of incurring the delivery and related costs associated with "parking" inventory in distribution channels, some e-commerce companies have simply recorded phantom shipments of product to their distributors or other customers.

SWAPPING PROFITS

E-commerce companies sometimes collaborate with each other to produce much needed revenues. Cash-starved dot-coms have routinely swapped or bartered goods and services among themselves to conserve their cash resources. At some point, executives of these firms realized that barter transactions could be used to "kill two birds with one stone." By booking revenue equal to the dollar value of the goods or services swapped to the other party to a barter transaction, a dot-com company can report a larger revenue figure in its income statement. Granted, since a corresponding expense must be recorded to recognize the cost of the goods and services acquired from the other entity, such transactions qualify as "washes" in terms of bottom-line profitability. But, that is of little concern to dot-com executives given analysts' and investors' obsession with these firms' top-line financial growth.

Online advertising agencies easily rank among the most swap-happy dot-com businesses. In the past, Internet-based ad agencies have obtained legal and accounting services, transportation vouchers, and a wide range of merchandise in barter transactions. By early 2000, barter transactions reportedly accounted for 15 to 20 percent of the total revenues booked by online advertising agencies. Before the dramatic upswing in electronic commerce in the late 1990s, the accounting profession paid little attention to barter transactions since they represented a nominal proportion of all business transactions. Typically, the parties involved in barter transactions recorded the goods and services exchanged at fair market value. Smaller businesses often ignored barter transactions for accounting purposes since they had no impact on their profitability.

As barter transactions became more prevalent with the rise of Internet commerce, the accounting profession focused more attention on this ancient form of doing business. The SEC and other regulatory authorities became interested in barter transactions when they discovered that many online companies were improperly augmenting their revenues by swapping merchandise and services among themselves. Suppose that the fair market value of the goods or services swapped among two online companies is $50,000. The two parties to that transaction might jointly agree to assign an inflated value to those goods or services of

$100,000, $200,000, or even more. Result: more impressive "top line" numbers for each company.

> Bartering has been abused when managers boost reported revenue by marking up the exchanged products or services to greatly inflated amounts. . . . Like all addicts, these managers eventually lose all restraint and inflate the exchange price beyond any approximation of the truth.[9]

"Gross" Revenues

"Grossing up" is a revenue-inflating tactic used by Internet companies that serve as middlemen or intermediaries for transactions between two or more parties. Such firms include dot-coms that operate virtual marketplaces where buyers and sellers can transact business electronically with each other. These companies typically receive a percentage fee or commission for each transaction completed over their website. For example, suppose that one company purchases $50,000 of merchandise from another at such a site. The site operator may receive a 1 percent commission, or $500, as its fee for bringing the two parties together.

To enhance their reported revenues, some companies serving as Internet intermediaries record the gross dollar amount of each transaction consummated at their website as revenue. In the previous example, the given company might have recorded revenue of $50,000, offset by a "cost of sale" item of $49,500, rather than simply "booking" a $500 commission from the given transaction. This strategy makes such companies appear much more substantial than they actually are.

Applying Old Economy Accounting Gimmicks to New Economy Firms

Many e-commerce executives and accountants became acquainted with "traditional" accounting scams in their previous work roles. As you might expect, they sometimes retrofit these scams to their new work environment. "Front-loading" revenue on long-term contracts is among the most common revenue scams used by conventional businesses and one that can be readily adapted to a virtual business environment.

Suppose a construction company signs a contract to build a dam. The project will require three years to complete, including one year to develop the blueprints for the dam. Total cost of the project is estimated at $20 million, while the fee to be paid the construction company is $25 million. The key accounting question raised by this scenario is when the company should recognize (record) the revenue and related profit to be earned on this project. Generally, the revenue and profit on such projects should be prorated over their term on some rational basis, the most common being a "percentage-of-completion" basis. Companies involved in long-term construction projects are often tempted to "front load" revenue, that is, recognize a disproportionate percentage of the revenue in the early stages of these projects.

---

9. J. E. Ketz and P. B. W. Miller, "Pumping Internet Revenues: More e-games People Play," *Accounting Today*, 12 March 2000, 25.

Generally accepted accounting principles encompass both accounting and financial reporting practices. Both Old and New Economy companies may apply the appropriate accounting principles to their transactions but then use clever maneuvers to distort the resulting data reported to the public. High on the list of these subterfuges is selectively reporting or emphasizing financial statement items that reflect positively on a company's financial health, while downplaying any "bad news" financial statement items. Such selective reporting typically occurs in press releases issued to the public or in reports submitted to financial analysts since the required formats for financial statements filed with the SEC leave little room for flexibility.

ACCOUNTING SCHEMES AND SCAMS, E-STYLE

No doubt, many, if not most, e-commerce companies make every effort to apply the most appropriate accounting methods to their transactions and to the other economic events that impact their financial condition and operating results. Then, there are those Internet firms that choose to apply one or more of the questionable accounting and financial reporting methods discussed in the previous section. Here, we consider several of these firms and the specific methods they have used to "massage" financial data reported to the public.

PRICELINE.COM

William Shatner, a/k/a Captain Kirk of the Starship Enterprise, revived his fading television career by spoofing his dubious singing skills in a series of TV commercials promoting Priceline.com. Best known as a source of cheap airline tickets, Priceline underwent the scrutiny of Wall Street and regulatory agencies when several accounting experts challenged the company's aggressive revenue recognition policies.

Priceline serves as a conduit between airlines hoping to fill vacant seats, particularly on low traffic routes, and potential passengers wanting to purchase those seats with lowball bids submitted at the company's website. From its inception, Priceline has recorded the full price of each ticket purchased by an Internet user as revenue in its accounting records although the company keeps only a fraction of the proceeds from such ticket sales as a commission before passing on the remainder to the relevant airline. During one recent year, Priceline's income statement listed gross revenues of $482 million. The company forwarded nearly 90 percent of those "revenues" to the airlines and other parties that had sold goods or services through the *Priceline.com* website.

In an interview on *CNNfn*, Priceline's chief executive officer (CEO) vigorously defended his company's revenue recognition policies, insisting those policies complied with the accounting profession's revenue recognition rule. "We do exactly what we're told to as far as our revenue recognition policies and we have continued to do that ever since we introduced Priceline to the market."[10] Priceline's critics concede that accounting standards do not specifically prohibit the

---

10. P. Sabga and C. Molineaux, "The N.E.W. Show," *CNNfn*, 24 April 2000, 5:20 P.M., ET.

company from "grossing up" revenues in its income statement. "Not that it's illegal, but it's just so gray and borderline."[11] Despite that admission, these parties maintain that the broad concepts underlying accounting and financial reporting practices dictate that Priceline record as revenue only the commissions received on transactions completed at its website.

KNOWLEDGEWARE, INC.

In the early 1990s, KnowledgeWare, Inc., ranked number two on *Business Week's* list of the fastest growing small companies in the United States. At the time, the company's principal line of business was marketing mainframe computer programs. Later, the company began developing software products designed for personal computers, networks, and Internet-related applications. Shortly after *Business Week* focused attention on KnowledgeWare's rapid growth, several key executives of the company collected more than $14 million from the sale of large blocks of the firm's common stock. One of those executives, in fact, the CEO, was none other than Francis A. Tarkenton, a former NFL quarterback and member of the NFL Hall of Fame.

Disappointing financial results in the mid-1990s and rumors of accounting irregularities prompted the filing of several class action lawsuits against KnowledgeWare and its executives. A multi-year investigation by the SEC confirmed that KnowledgeWare's officers had masterminded an elaborate accounting fraud within the company. In late 1999, the SEC issued a series of official reports referred to as *Accounting and Auditing Enforcement Releases* that described the specific methods KnowledgeWare's executives had used to overstate their company's reported revenues and profits.

According to the SEC, KnowledgeWare's executives instructed subordinates to record as bona fide sales large amounts of inventory that had been "parked" with the company's distributors. The distributors agreed to accept the product shipments only after receiving "side letters" from KnowledgeWare. These documents relieved the distributors of any obligation to pay for the product shipments unless they were successful in selling the inventory to their own customers, that is, end users of those items.

> Tarkenton [and six other KnowledgeWare executives] engaged in a fraudulent scheme to inflate KnowledgeWare's financial results to meet sales and earnings projections. In all, KnowledgeWare reported at least $8 million in revenue from sham software sales. . . . As a result of this scheme, KnowledgeWare falsely reported record sales revenues and dramatic increases in earnings in press releases and quarterly reports filed with the Commission [SEC] and disseminated to the public.[12]

INFORMIX CORPORATION

In summarizing the operations of Informix Corporation, the popular Yahoo! Finance website recently noted that the firm "provides a fast, simple and complete

---

11. Kahn, "Presto Chango! Sales Are Huge!" 92.

12. Securities and Exchange Commission, *Accounting and Auditing Enforcement Release No. 1179,* 28 September 1999.

way to bring businesses to the Web." Yahoo!'s more in-depth description of Informix's operations indicates that the high-tech firm "designs, develops, manufactures, markets and supports object-relational and relational database management systems, connectivity interfaces and gateways, and graphical and character-based application development tools for building database applications that allow customers to access, retrieve, and manipulate business data."

Press releases issued by Informix executives in the late 1990s regaled the firm "as the fastest growing company in the database software industry."[13] That assertion was supported by the company's periodic financial statements that reflected rapidly growing revenues each reporting period. Investors' admiration for Informix quickly turned to contempt when the SEC released the results of a lengthy investigation that revealed the source of the company's glossy financial data.

> In reality, its [Informix's] apparent growth in revenues and earnings largely was the result of the use of a multitude . . . of improper practices . . . driven by some former managers' perceived need to meet or exceed the Company's internal revenue and earnings goals. . . . The type of conduct that occurred in this matter strikes at the heart of the financial reporting system established by the federal securities laws. . . . Complete and accurate financial reporting by public companies is of paramount importance to the disclosure system underlying the stability and efficient operations of our capital markets.[14]

Among the "multitude" of improper accounting methods Informix used to sustain its gaudy financial trends was recording revenues for inventory "parked" with its distributors. The SEC noted that Informix used one of its largest customers as a "virtual warehouse" for excess inventory. In fact, Informix employees commonly referred to that customer as a "revenue bank." Near the end of a reporting period when Informix needed additional revenue to reach its financial goals for that period, it could count on this customer to accept large inventory shipments—shipments that Informix's accounting staff recorded as completed sales transactions. The customer was more than happy to cooperate with the scam since Informix made various "side agreements" that effectively relieved the customer from paying for the shipments or economically benefited it in other ways. In one case, Informix induced the customer to accept additional inventory shipments by agreeing to purchase certain worthless assets from the customer.

Informix regularly signed multi-year software maintenance contracts with major customers. GAAP dictate that the revenue produced by such a contract should be prorated over its term. Informix employees did not allow this technicality to prevent them from "front-loading" the revenue on these contracts. Near the end of 1996, Informix customers signed software maintenance contracts valued at more than $11 million. Although this revenue would be earned in future accounting periods, Informix immediately booked the $11 million as revenue for fiscal 1996.

Informix and a computer manufacturer formed an alliance in the late 1990s to develop "joint hardware-software solutions" for their customers. The two companies established demonstration centers or Superstores to display and market these products. Informix contributed software to the joint products, while its part-

---

13. Securities and Exchange Commission, *Accounting and Auditing Enforcement Release No. 1215,* 11 January 2000.

14. *Ibid.*

ner provided the necessary hardware components. To increase its reported revenues, Informix recorded the software committed to the joint products as sales to its partner in the venture. In turn, Informix "purchased" the hardware committed to the joint products by its partner. Internally, Informix employees referred to these mutual transactions as "swaps."

The SEC's investigation revealed that these and other shady accounting practices overstated Informix's revenues by $295 million and its earnings by $244 million over a three-year period. Before these misstatements were disclosed to the public, two company officers unloaded more than $15 million of their Informix stock on investors unaware of the company's accounting chicanery. When the SEC required Informix to issue corrected financial statements to the public, the company's stock price plunged more than 90 percent.

STAPLES, INC.

Public companies are reluctant to publish forecasts of their future sales and earnings since failing to meet projected numbers might goad disgruntled investors to sue the companies and their executives. To fill this void, financial analysts generally prepare and release financial forecasts for the companies they track. Wall Street anxiously awaits the release of forecast data for each major company. Such forecasts may signal a turning point in the health of a company, its industry, or possibly the entire economy.

In recent years, business journalists have coined the term "earnings surprise" to refer to the difference between the consensus forecast for a company's earnings per share and the actual dollar amount for that item subsequently reported by the company. Negative earnings surprises—and negative revenue surprises, for that matter—can cause a company's stock price to be hammered by the stock market. For the first quarter of 2000, Excite@Home missed its forecasted profit figure by a slim $0.02 per share. Within one week, the stock market had slashed the collective market value of Excite's stock by 20 percent or a cool $1.7 billion.

Negative financial forecasts, alone, can have an immediate and drastic impact on a company's stock price. Such forecasts may also affect a company's ability to borrow funds and sell additional equity securities. Given the pervasive implications that financial forecasts can have for a company, it is not surprising that corporate executives often attempt to influence the format and content of those forecasts by cajoling or even coercing the financial analysts who prepare them.

First Call/Thomson Financial collects revenue and earnings forecasts for publicly owned companies from financial analysts, merges multiple forecasts for individual firms into one consensus forecast, and then sells these consensus forecasts to large institutional investors such as mutual funds. In recent years, First Call and similar firms have tangled with financial analysts who attempt to submit nonstandard financial forecasts for the companies they follow. In early 2000, such a dispute arose between First Call and analysts tracking the common stock of Staples, the office supplies retailer.

Similar to many conventional retailers, Staples established an online subsidiary in the late 1990s. In the spring of 2000, financial analysts submitted financial forecasts to First Call for Staples that did not include projected revenue and earnings data for the company's online subsidiary, Staples.com. In fact, Staples' management encouraged the analysts to leave out that data. Since Staples.com's financial data were dismal, the omission of those data resulted in a much more optimistic financial forecast for Staples.

A Staples executive defended his effort to encourage financial analysts to omit Staples.com's data from the parent company's consolidated forecast. "It doesn't make sense for investors . . . to see the development of an Internet business as a negative."[15] The executive went on to note that, as required by generally accepted accounting principles, Staples' subsequently released financial statements would include the financial data of Staples.com.

An official of First Call insisted that it was inappropriate to omit Staples.com from the consolidated financial forecasts for Staples. "Who ever heard of a company excluding the losses of a majority-owned subsidiary?"[16] The chief financial officer of Office Depot, Staples' primary competitor, agreed with that point of view. "We think that the Web is not a separate business. It is an integral part of our business. It is just another way customers order our products."[17] After being pressured by First Call, the majority of the 18 financial analysts tracking Staples agreed to include data for Staples.com in their consolidated forecasts for the company.

The conflict involving Staples, the company's financial analysts, and First Call was not an isolated incident. A *Wall Street Journal* reporter observed that such conflicts are becoming more common.

> The dispute is part of a growing trend by companies to emphasize whatever numbers make them look best—revenue or even the number of Web site visitors, for example, in the case of money-losing Internet start-ups. Established companies with Web businesses, critics say, are trying to have their cake and eat it too—that is, gaining market recognition for having a sexy Internet side, while not being penalized by the losses.[18]

ACCOUNTING FOR THE FUTURE

Efforts to improve the accounting and financial reporting practices of e-commerce companies face several roadblocks. Among the most important obstacles to accomplishing that objective are the economic pressures that predispose e-commerce executives to manipulate their firms' financial statement data. Another key deterrent to improving the quality of financial reports released by e-commerce companies is the belief held by many parties that managing or window dressing reported financial data is a benign and acceptable practice.

A leading columnist for *Forbes* chided SEC Chairman Arthur Levitt for his widely publicized campaign to eradicate earnings management. "The practice [earnings management] has a long—one might almost say proud—history in corporate America."[19] The columnist went on to note that under the leadership of Harold Geneen, the corporate titan ITT reported steady, uninterrupted earnings growth for 58 consecutive quarters. "It was widely assumed that this streak de-

---

15. L. Johannes, "No Accounting for the Net? Profit Issue Sparks Conflict," *The Wall Street Journal* Interactive Edition, 19 May 2000.

16. *Ibid.*

17. *Ibid.*

18. *Ibid.*

19. D. Seligman, "The Crusade Against Smoothing," *Forbes*, 12 June 2000, 338.

pended on a certain amount of gray-area fiddling with the numbers, but Geneen was nevertheless rated a business genius, not a fraud. ITT was in fact growing steadily during his years, and investors were not being misled about the big picture."[20] The *Forbes* journalist wrapped up the attack on Arthur Levitt by suggesting that his "campaign to demonize earnings management seems . . . plain silly."

Such attitudes are not uncommon, even on Capitol Hill. High-tech companies, including several high-profile dot-coms, have spent large sums lobbying legislators in hopes of derailing attempts to adopt more restrictive accounting and financial reporting standards. Recent allegations by political leaders that the SEC is "anti-business" are likely a product of those lobbying efforts. Two prominent politicians, Senator Charles Schumer, a New York Democrat, and Senator Phil Gramm, a Texas Republican, joined together to chastise the accounting profession for insisting on applying "old world accounting standards to the new knowledge economy when everybody agrees they don't make sense."[21]

Despite such attacks, Arthur Levitt refused to yield in his efforts to provide for more "transparent" financial reports by public companies, particularly the go-go growth companies that dominate the e-commerce sphere. Levitt often pointed to the near collapse of several Asian economies during the 1990s as a reminder of what can happen when economic decisions are hampered by the lack of high-quality financial reports. In a 1998 speech made to a leading conference of corporate executives, Levitt noted that the financial crisis in the Far East was "fueled by the lack of transparency in financial reporting stemming from low-quality accounting and disclosure standards."[22]

Throughout the late 1990s and into the new century, the SEC adopted increasingly aggressive measures to thwart misleading financial reports by e-commerce companies and fraudulent investment schemes perpetrated over the Internet. In 1997, the SEC established an Internet Enforcement Office to scour the Web for investment scams targeting Internet users. The SEC also began participating in periodic "fraud sweeps" of the Internet along with the FBI, the U.S. Justice Department, and other federal agencies to nab cyberspace con artists.

In late 1999, the SEC issued a new authoritative pronouncement, *Staff Accounting Bulletin No. 101*, that provides extensive guidance to public companies concerning appropriate and inappropriate revenue recognition methods. At the same time, the federal agency sternly warned that it would begin prosecuting companies that failed to eliminate overly aggressive revenue recognition policies. That warning prompted more than 120 public companies, principally firms engaged in e-commerce, to alter their revenue recognition practices and to restate (revise) financial statements issued in prior years. In some cases, these restatements wiped out a huge portion of the companies' previously reported revenues and earnings, sending their stock prices into a tailspin. Prominent dot-com companies that restated their earnings included drkoop.com, CDnow.com, and Peapod.com.

The efforts of the SEC and other agencies to clean up the accounting and financial reporting practices of public companies, particularly firms involved in e-commerce, have almost certainly improved the overall quality of financial data

20. *Ibid.*

21. J. McTague, "Congress Could Block Move to Sink Pooling," *Barron's Online*, 15 May 2000.

22. S. Burkholder, "SEC Official Warns of Possible Action Against All in the Kitchen if Books 'Cooked,'" *Securities Regulation & Law Report*, 20 November 1998, 1675.

made available to the investing and lending public. Nevertheless, the strong and undeniable incentives of corporate executives and others to mislead the investing and lending public means that the root cause of this problem remains.

Arthur Levitt resigned as SEC chairman in early 2001 when the Clinton Administration left office. Nevertheless, Levitt has continued to be a major spokesperson for various advocacy groups wanting to reform and improve the financial reporting practices of public companies. Levitt and his fellow reform advocates often maintain that the most effective deterrent to unethical financial reporting by public companies is honest, competent, and stiff-backed accountants. Corporate accountants "live in the trenches" with the corporate executives who have the final responsibility for shaping their firms' accounting and financial reporting practices. As a result, corporate accountants have an opportunity to discourage their bosses from taking that first tentative step on the slippery slope of earnings management. Accountants recognize that such efforts are not always appreciated by their superiors. Consider the case of a former chief accountant of a major e-commerce company. She alleges that shortly after being hired by the company, top management insisted on implementing "marginal and even inappropriate accounting practices" that resulted in premature recognition of revenues.[23] When the accountant refused to approve those accounting practices, she was fired.

Unfortunately, during the past decade, many accountants of e-commerce firms have capitulated to top management's demands. A former accountant turned professor observes that unprincipled accountants can easily take advantage of the flexibility of GAAP to ensure that their companies' reach predetermined financial goals. "Clever accountants will always be able to bend the rules. But whether they do is a matter of ethics. The temptation is there, and the question is 'Do I go with it? or, Do I try to do it the right way?'"[24] How that question is privately answered by individual accountants will likely have a larger impact on the future quality of financial reports in the U.S. economy than the huge sums spent each year by the cadre of governmental agencies that police the nation's securities markets.

QUESTIONS

1. The business press, the accounting profession, and the SEC often distinguish between "earnings management" and "fraudulent financial reporting." In your mind, what is the difference between these two practices, if any? Explain. Is earnings management ethical or acceptable in certain situations but not in others?

2. The economic interests of corporate executives are intertwined with the financial health of the companies they manage. What controls or policies should companies establish to minimize the likelihood that corporate executives will take inappropriate measures to enhance their firm's reported financial data?

3. Suppose that you are the top accountant of an e-commerce company and that the end of the current financial reporting period is rapidly approaching. To

---

23. Kahn, "Presto Chango! Sales Are Huge!" 90.

24. *Ibid.*, 96.

sustain your company's impressive growth trend in revenues, the firm's chief executive instructs you to record several recent sales orders as consummated sales transactions. Accounting principles dictate that the sales should not be recorded until the next financial reporting period when the product will be shipped. What factors should you consider in deciding how to respond to this situation? Identify the parties who will be potentially affected by your decision and how they may be affected. Finally, how would you respond to the chief executive's request?

4. Search online or hard copy databases to find a recent example of a financial scandal involving misrepresented financial statements of an Internet-based company. Provide a brief summary of that scandal, including the parties involved, the financial statement items that were distorted, the methods used to distort those items, the magnitude of the distortions, and related information.

5. Sophisticated investors employ a wide range of financial ratios to analyze financial statement data. Identify five such ratios and explain what insights they may provide on a company's financial status. For each ratio, indicate whether you believe it applies equally well to Internet-based companies and more traditional companies.

6. Many financial websites, including Yahoo! Finance, summarize financial forecast data for publicly owned companies. Go to one such website and access financial forecast data for a major public company. Briefly describe the content and format of that data.

7. What is the central role or purpose of the nation's major stock exchanges? How does the SEC facilitate the operation of those stock markets? Do you believe the SEC's recent regulatory efforts discussed in this case are "anti-business"? Explain.

Cyberethics: Means, Ends, and Mean Ends

How can you build a culture of accountability in an ecology of anonymity?

Michael Schrage, *Fortune*, December 6, 1999

In early 2000, the owners of Salesgate.com had their company poised for rapid growth.[1] Salesgate, which began operations in 1996 and was headquartered in Buffalo, New York, served as an Internet-based intermediary for more than 300 clients, primarily small businesses. The company accepted and processed credit card orders for its clients, receiving a commission on each transaction. At the time, Salesgate's owners were attempting to persuade a venture capital firm to invest $5 million in their company. That investment would provide the funds Salesgate needed to finance an ambitious expansion program.

A hacker attack in March 2000, derailed Salesgate's future plans. A teenager from Wales who went by the handle "Curador," Welsh for "custodian," broke into Salesgate's computer system and copied 3,000 credit card numbers belonging to customers of Salesgate's clients. Curador then began methodically posting the credit card numbers on various hacker websites. After being arrested for breaking into Salesgate's computer system and the computer systems of several other companies, the teenager told a British newspaper that he "just wanted to prove how insecure"[2] those systems were. In response, a company spokesperson for Salesgate observed, "I would have appreciated an e-mail from him instead."[3]

---

1. The development of this case was funded by the 2000 McLaughlin Instructional Grant Award. I would like to thank Glen McLaughlin for his generous and continuing support of efforts to integrate ethics into business curricula.

2. F. O. Williams, "The Hacker Called 'Curador' Figures He Did Chris Keller a Favor," *The Buffalo News* (online), 11 April 2000.

3. *Ibid.*

ROBBER BARONS NEW AND OLD

Salesgate's rude introduction to international sabotage cost the firm a large number of clients—a common outcome for online companies victimized by a hacker. More important, the incident highlights the disjointed and misguided ethical behavior that has plagued the pioneers of e-commerce. In the shadowy and largely anonymous world of cyberspace, Internet users such as Curador often develop and apply their own unique, off-the-cuff sense of justice and morality. An academic who oversees an ethics research center at Santa Clara University suggests that the warp speed at which events take place in cyberspace can adversely impact the ethical judgments made by Internet users. "One of the problems is that ethics implies deliberation. It implies periods of contemplation and deliberation, and working through a moral calculus. Who has time for such navel-gazing when everyone is moving at Internet speed?"[4]

Criticism of the new brand of ethics apparent in cyberspace, so-called "cyberethics," extends beyond the sociopathic behavior of individual hackers, cybersquatters, online stalkers, and other cybermiscreants. The business press has documented a wide range of morally questionable judgments made by top executives of some of the most prominent dot-com companies. One reporter bluntly suggested that "Few dot.coms would know a corporate code of ethics if it fell on their heads."[5]

Generations of social critics have routinely disparaged the ethical judgments of corporate executives. To many of these critics, the phrase "business ethics" qualifies as a classic oxymoron, a contradiction in terms comparable to "tough love" or "jumbo shrimp." This impression of the morality displayed by owners and managers of business enterprises stems largely from the Industrial Revolution of the eighteenth and nineteenth centuries when ruthless robber barons carved out huge financial empires by using practically any means possible to trample their competitors.

John D. Rockefeller, who founded Standard Oil in the 1860s, helped create the U.S. petroleum industry and became enormously wealthy as a result. Throughout a business career that spanned eight decades, Rockefeller clung tenaciously to a survival-of-the-fittest approach to doing business. A devoutly religious man who became a philanthropist in his later years, Rockefeller believed it was not only his right but also his obligation to drive weaker competitors out of business. Allowing marginal businesses to sustain their operations was bad for the economy over the long run, Rockefeller reasoned. So, he and his subordinates used a wide range of cutthroat business practices, many of which are now illegal, to dominate the petroleum industry.

Some business journalists suggest that the rapid growth of electronic commerce over the past decade has created a new generation of robber barons who serve as the top executives of dozens of high-tech firms. In fact, several of the firms leading the e-commerce revolution, Microsoft being the prime example, have been charged with predatory business practices, comparable to those employed by Standard Oil in the latter decades of the nineteenth century. Ironically,

---

4.   J. Useem, "New Ethics or No Ethics?" *Fortune*, 20 March 2000, 86.

5.   *The Economist* (online), "Doing Well by Doing Good," 22 April 2000.

similar to Rockefeller, many of the supposed new age robber barons spend their weekends and occasional vacations engaging in their principal hobby, namely, philanthropy.

Has the e-commerce revolution given rise to a new generation of schizoid robber barons? Are the tens of thousands of e-millionaires and the occasional e-billionaire more ruthless than their predecessors who were largely responsible for the economic prosperity sparked by the Industrial Revolution? Maybe. Maybe not. At the very least, the e-commerce revolution has spawned several new twists on old ethical issues and created a new set of ethical issues unknown to earlier generations of business owners, corporate executives, and their subordinates. Here, we examine many of these ethical issues and specific contexts in which they have arisen. We begin our exploration of cyberethics by defining "ethics" and the related term "ethical dilemma." Then, we examine a series of recent ethical dilemmas within the e-commerce world. Finally, we consider several factors that will influence, if not shape, the future evolution of cyberethics.

ETHICS AND ETHICAL DILEMMAS

Random House Webster's College Dictionary provides the following overlapping definitions for "ethics":

> A system or set of moral principles; the rules of conduct recognized in respect to a particular class of human actions or governing a particular culture, group, or individual; the branch of philosophy dealing with values relating to human conduct, with respect to the rightness and wrongness of actions and the goodness and badness of motives and ends.

Most of us would not quarrel with the observation that ethics ultimately involve the "rightness and wrongness" of specific human actions and the "goodness and badness" that motivate those actions. The quarreling would begin when we attempted to determine exactly what conduct is "right" and what conduct is "wrong." Similar disputes would arise if we attempted to reach a consensus on what motives and objectives are "good" and which are "bad."

Since few of us are ethicists, developing elegant theoretical arguments to support the rightness and wrongness of given actions or motives, arguments sprinkled with references to Immanuel Kant and John Stuart Mill, does not come naturally. An alternative approach to examining ethical issues is to study actual contexts in which these issues arise. Ethical dilemmas provide real-world reference points that we can use both to identify ethical issues and to foster productive debates focusing on the rightness and wrongness, goodness and badness of specific human judgments related to those issues.

Now, we have another phrase to define. Exactly what is an "ethical dilemma"? Merging and paraphrasing dictionary definitions of "ethical" and "dilemma" yields the following description of an ethical dilemma: *a situation involving principles of morality that requires a choice between two undesirable alternatives.* The cliché "choosing between the lesser of two evils" seems appropriate here. By definition, an ethical dilemma typically involves one or more individuals who are trapped in a "lose/lose" situation. The ultimate objective in such situations is to somehow identify which of the two undesirable outcomes to the given set of circumstances is at least marginally less objectionable than the other.

Ethical dilemmas often prove to be critical tests of an individual's ethical values or morals. In fact, the resolution of such situations can be instrumental in shaping or redefining an individual's ethical norms. At some point, each us of stands on the edge of that "slippery slope" of which ethicists and political journalists are so fond. One minimally questionable ethical judgment may lead us to step further out on that slope. Another step or so and we are unintentionally "slip sliding away" into an abyss of moral bankruptcy.

Businesses also face that same slippery slope. Accounting and financial reporting issues, in particular, tend to test the ethical temperament of corporations. Suppose that a major company is a few thousand dollars short of reaching its revenue goal for a given quarterly reporting period. What harm is there in "pre-recording" a large sale that is certain to be finalized in the next few days? Granted, those "next few days" fall in the new quarter. If the decision to book the sale early is made by a corporate accountant and approved by his or her superiors, the next time a similar situation arises the decision to pre-record the given sale will be much easier to make. In fact, the accountant may simply go ahead and record the sale without requesting approval of that decision by superiors.

Michael Young is a noted attorney who has been involved in several high-profile lawsuits predicated on allegations of fraudulent financial statements. Young observes that most corporate frauds start small. Companies that take a few tentative, baby steps on that proverbial slippery slope may soon find themselves beyond the equally proverbial "point of no return."

> Massive financial fraud does not start with a grand plan or conspiracy. It does not start with a group of executives in a conference room in which someone volunteers, "Let's perpetrate a massive fraud." In fact, its origin is precisely the opposite. It starts out very small—so small that the one or two participants don't even appreciate that they are stepping over the line. Then, as the need to disguise past performance inadequacies is compounded by the need to make up for new ones, the problem [fraud] starts to grow.[6]

ETHICAL DILEMMAS IN CYBERSPACE

In this section, we examine actual ethical dilemmas that companies and individuals involved in e-commerce have faced in recent years. Some of these dilemmas have been discussed widely in the business press, while others have gone largely unnoticed or unreported. The situations considered here are grouped into three general categories: ethical dilemmas related to disclosure issues, ethical dilemmas linked to new technologies common or unique to e-commerce and, finally, ethical dilemmas closely related to a mindset prevalent in the culture of the Internet.

FULL AND FAIR DISCLOSURE IN CYBERSPACE

Who hasn't faced a situation in which there are two options: telling the truth, the whole truth, versus . . . something else. No doubt, candor can be good for the soul.

---

6.   M. R. Young, *Accounting Irregularities and Financial Fraud* (San Diego: Harcourt, 2000), 11–12.

But, in the business world, truthtelling is not necessarily rewarded by investors, lenders, and other moneyed and influential parties.

Pay Up, or Else!   An important premise underlying our free market economy is that businesses have a responsibility to provide full and fair disclosure of all facts and circumstances that might be of interest to potential investors, creditors, regulatory authorities, and other parties. In fact, "full and fair disclosure" is the governing creed of the Securities and Exchange Commission (SEC), which oversees the nation's capital markets. The SEC does not pass judgment on the investment merits of new securities or business ventures. Instead, this federal agency simply attempts to ensure that publicly owned companies honestly and comprehensively report appropriate financial and nonfinancial information to the public.

Suppose that a hacker compromises a large company's computer system. In exchange for a "cyber-ransom," the hacker offers not to reveal the intrusion or to create havoc within the company's computer system. Executives of two British banks faced that exact scenario recently. Reportedly, the unnamed banks chose to pay a ransom of one million British pounds, the equivalent of approximately $1.6 million at the time, to avoid the public humiliation of revealing the hacker attack.[7] In the United States, the failure of a publicly owned company to disclose a major hacker attack and any accompanying ransom payment might be considered a violation of the SEC's full and fair disclosure principle.

Online Credit Card Fraud: "It's a huge problem." "No it's not!"   Federal authorities cracked an online credit card scam of epic dimensions in the spring of 1999. Over a little more than one year, a California businessman with considerable help from his wife and several subordinates posted $45 million of bogus charges to the credit cards of throngs of unsuspecting Internet users. Most of the defrauded individuals had subscribed to online adult entertainment sites. The prolific con artist operated one adults-only website and had contracts to handle the billing for many similar sites. Several months later, federal authorities discovered another colossal credit card scam. In this latter case, a hacker broke into the customer database of CD Universe, an online business that markets music and video products. The hacker copied more than 300,000 credit card numbers belonging to the company's customers as well as biographical information for those customers.

Such episodes are public relations nightmares for online merchants and major credit card companies. Public opinion polls reveal that the fear of falling victim to credit card fraud deters many Internet users from purchasing goods and services from online businesses. To quell such concerns, major credit card issuers such as Visa and MasterCard insist that the business press exaggerates the extent of online credit card fraud. Credit analysts and many other parties counter those assertions by maintaining that credit card fraud is rampant on the Internet and is actually growing faster than the volume of e-commerce transactions. "There's a great deal of conflicting information about just how much money fraud is costing online merchants. Credit-card companies, which stand to make millions as online

---

7.   B. Braun, D. Drobny, and D. Gessner, "www.commercial_terrorism.com: A Proposed Federal Criminal Statute Addressing the Solicitation of Commercial Terrorism Through the Internet," *Harvard Journal on Legislation*, Winter 2000, 150.

sales increase, say fraud is low. Companies that hawk fraud-protection software say it's rampant."[8]

Even the statistics quoted by the combatants in this ongoing war of words are grossly different. Credit card issuers maintain that the percentage of online credit card transactions that prove to be fraudulent hovers near 2 percent. Credit specialists and fraud protection vendors argue that the overall rate of credit card fraud is much higher and approaches 20 percent in certain industries. In truth, no one knows the actual rate of online credit card fraud since neither public agencies nor private organizations have developed a system to capture reliable and comprehensive data that document the extent of this problem. So, for the foreseeable future, Internet users will be peppered with self-serving arguments and questionable statistics as the great debate over the magnitude of online credit card fraud continues.

CYBERTECHNOLOGY AND CYBERETHICS

Nineteenth century accounting clerks did not have to contemplate the ethical implications of accessing and reading a co-worker's e-mail or of putting aside the general ledger for a few moments to log on to the Internet and download Madonna's or Mettalica's latest hot tune. High technology poses many conveniences for corporate executives and their subordinates and many thorny ethical questions as well.

All the Jokes Fit to Click.   Sharing jokes among friends is a time-honored tradition in the American workplace. What better way to kill a little time and make the day a little shorter than by swapping the latest joke or wisecrack with your buddies at work? In the old days, jokes were shared around the water cooler. Decades later, the copy machine became comedy central. Now, co-workers can share jokes without leaving their desks or workstations. Most bosses don't mind if their subordinates spend a few minutes each day zapping jokes back and forth over the company network. But, what if some of those jokes are a little off-color? What if rather than zapping jokes back and forth, a company's employees begin sharing graphic pictorials downloaded from the Internet?

In late 1999, management personnel at *The New York Times* discovered that almost two dozen of their subordinates had used e-mail to exchange offensive jokes and related materials over the company's computer system. Should hardworking, productive employees be dismissed for engaging in such behavior? Should they be given a second chance? The *Times'* executives answered those questions "Yes" and "No"—in that order. In November 1999, the 22 employees involved in exchanging impertinent materials over the company's computer network were dismissed.

In defending the dismissals, company officials revealed that the offensive e-mails circulated among the fired employees had been discovered during an investigation of an unrelated incident. Those same officials denied that reviewing employee e-mails without the employees' prior approval or knowledge violated their freedom of speech rights under the First Amendment.

---

8.   D. Scheraga, "Lost in Cyberspace," *Chain Store Age Executive*, January 2000, 158.

This is not a First Amendment issue. There is no First Amendment right to transmit pornography over the company's e-mail system or to view pornography in the workplace. [The *Times*] . . . doesn't "routinely" monitor e-mail, but it may do so while investigating a complaint. . . . [The] courts generally have found that companies have a legitimate interest in monitoring the use of their computer equipment.[9]

Here Come the Spiders. Arachnophobia—fear of spiders—affects many online businesses. Recently, eBay discovered that spiders, spiders of a robotic species, were roaming its massive website. Cyberspace spiders are actually software programs that sift through the information on a website and extract data that meet certain specifications. Among the companies releasing spiders on eBay's website was Bidder's Edge, an "auction aggregator." Bidder's Edge and other auction aggregators collect information from websites maintained by eBay, Yahoo!, Amazon, and other online auction services. These businesses then reformat that information and post it on their websites to be used by their own customers.

No doubt, executives of Bidder's Edge recognized that robotically harvesting information from online auction sites posed ethical questions, not to mention a litany of important legal issues—eBay later sued Bidder's Edge for "trespassing" on its website. But, the underlying premise of the business plan developed by Bidder's Edge was to offer customers more complete "market" information than that available on any one online auction site. So, the company forged ahead and released a Web-full of spiders on dozens of unsuspecting online auctioneers.

Target Marketing at Its Best (Worst?). Computer technology provides companies with the ability to analyze a customer database by an almost limitless number of variables. Say a nationwide hardware retailer wants to know the southern boundary of its snowblower market? No problem. That computer science major recently hired from Mankato State can knock out a program to compile that information by lunch.

Many online merchants rely on similar methods to limit their bad debt write-offs. These merchants use software programs to access online databases containing extensive information regarding potential customers. These databases have been constructed by "information brokers" who track and document the buying habits of millions of consumers. Information brokers charge their clients fees for accessing these databases. By applying a "risk-profiling," software-based algorithm to such databases, companies can identify which individuals are not only *potential* customers but also *potential paying* customers.

Risk-profiling algorithms rely on an extensive and diverse set of variables to assign a risk score to each member of a database. Examples of such variables include age, household income, nationality, religious affiliation, the types and number of books ordered from Amazon.com, whether an individual is an eBay member, whether an individual participates in an online fantasy sports league, and the socioeconomic status of an individual's neighborhood. By studying the relationship between such variables and the credit history of millions of individual consumers, credit analysts can convert any combination of these variables into a risk score that indicates how likely or unlikely a given individual is to pay for items he or she purchases. After identifying "low-risk" potential customers, a company

---

9. A. Carrns, "Bawdy E-Mails Were Funny Till Times' Parent Fired 22," *The Houston Chronicle*, 6 February 2000, 3.

can then design its marketing and advertising plans to target those individuals. Risk-profiling algorithms also can be used to assign a risk score in a matter of moments to an individual in an online database who has expressed interest in buying a product or service from a company.

Many potential customers who want to purchase products and services are being prevented from doing so simply because they live in the wrong neighborhood or because they have "joined" the wrong age group or because they are a member of the wrong political party. To thrive, if not survive, companies must take affirmative measures to limit the likelihood of selling goods and services to extremely high-risk customers. But, should online companies be allowed to turn down a potential customer because he or she lives in a neighborhood populated by a disproportionate number of individuals who have skipped credit card payments or because that individual orders the "wrong" books from Amazon.com?

THE WILD WILD WEB

Several business journalists have compared the Web to the wild and wooly western frontier of the nineteenth century. Similar to the Old West, individuals trekking through the Web often have an opportunity to invoke their own personal codes of conduct, while incurring little risk of being held responsible by the "law."

Cybervigilantes. "Pump and dump" schemes have become legendary in the brief history of the Internet. In one case, several college buddies reaped trading profits of nearly $350,000 on four "penny" stocks.[10] The students first purchased several thousand shares of a stock and then posted comments on electronic message boards enthusiastically endorsing that stock. The scheme worked so well that one of the stocks the scammers purchased for slightly more than $1 per share rose to nearly $8 per share in a span of thirty minutes. When the SEC learned of the scheme, the federal agency filed criminal charges against the participants. And how did the SEC learn of the scheme? The college students posted a "how to run a pump and dump scheme" memo on a website. Go figure.

Furious that federal authorities have failed to rid the Internet of pump and dump schemes, many private citizens, most of whom have lost money in such schemes, have taken it upon themselves to track down and expose the con artists. Among the most notorious self-appointed "cybervigilantes" is Janice Shell.[11] Ms. Shell was so offended by the growing number of pump and dump schemes that she decided on a brash, if not rash, strategy to demonstrate to regulatory authorities how easy it is to perpetrate a stock hoax on hordes of gullible Internet surfers. Ms. Shell "invented" a company and then issued a press release on *Business Wire*, an Internet news service, extolling the profit potential of the firm. The response to the press release was overwhelming. Hundreds of potential investors sent e-mail messages to Ms. Shell expressing an interest in purchasing stock in the company. Executives of *Business Wire*, unamused when they learned of Ms. Shell's

---

10. M. Schroeder, "Georgetown Students Draw Web Investors—And an SEC Bust," *The Wall Street Journal*, 3 March 2000, A1, A8.

11. J. R. Emshwiller, "Controversial Cyber-Cop Stirs Wild World of Web Chat," *The Wall Street Journal*, 10 May 2000, C1, C20.

hoax, filed fraud and conspiracy charges against her. The lawsuit was eventually settled out of court for a modest amount.

Cybersting.   Suppose that you are a top-level executive of a high-tech company that is "on the move." One of the most critical decisions you periodically face is which of your subordinates to promote to key management positions that become vacant. You realize that your success largely depends on the competence of the individuals who occupy key positions beneath you in your company's organizational chart. Your many years of experience as an executive have made you a good judge of those individuals who have the potential to be effective managers and those who do not. But, you find it difficult to evaluate the loyalty of subordinates. You do not want to promote an individual who will use that promotion as a stepping-stone in the near future to obtain an even better position with a competitor, which has happened to you many times. What to do, what to do?

A columnist for *Forbes* magazine reported that a business executive facing a situation comparable to the one described in the previous paragraph decided to make use of information technology to help him resolve his dilemma. The executive instructed a computer technician within his company to prepare an e-mail that appeared to be a "personalized inquiry from a prestigious consulting firm." That e-mail asked the recipients to attach a vita to their response, implying that they had been targeted as candidates for positions with the consulting firm. The e-mail was then forwarded to the executive's subordinates who were being considered for promotions. Two of the subordinates responded to the e-mail. The *Forbes* columnist predicted that such cyberstings will become more common in the future. "There has never been a better time or technology for management to use guile, deception, and trickery to catch employees in the act of disloyalty or dishonesty. . . . In other words, we will see a surge of cyberstings as organizations realize that networks make testing human integrity even easier than testing data integrity."[12]

Trick or Treat.   What company doesn't want to probe the business files and future plans of its key competitors? In intensely competitive, high technology industries an ability to predict the next move of your competitors can be the difference between financial success and an express paid ticket to the corporate boneyard.

In recent years, several companies have attempted to gain a sizable share of the expanding market for high-speed Internet service. Firms competing for the Houston region of that market in mid-2000 included Time Warner Cable (TWC) and Southwestern Bell. Each of these firms desperately wanted to learn which specific areas in Houston the other company could serve. Such information could be used to gain an important competitive advantage. For example, knowledge of the other company's market area could be used to make better decisions regarding the allocation of advertising budgets.

To pinpoint the exact neighborhoods within Houston where Southwestern Bell could offer turbo-charged Internet access, managers of TWC came up with an ingenious plan. Employees living in the Houston area were offered a chance to win $100 or free Internet service. To be entered in this contest, the TWC employees

---

12. M. Schrage, "E-Mail or E-Sting? Your Boss Knows, but He's Not Telling," *Forbes*, 20 March 2000, 240.

had to contact Southwestern Bell and ask to sign up for the company's Internet service. Those employees who were told by Southwestern Bell that they could sign up for such service were instructed to "get cold feet" shortly before making a formal commitment to receive the service. Each employee who contacted Southwestern Bell was also instructed to report the outcome of the service request to a TWC administrative assistant in the company's Houston office.

An employee of TWC apparently found the "trick" being played on Soutwestern Bell unpalatable. That employee gave Southwestern Bell management a copy of a flier describing the TWC contest. Angry Southwestern Bell officials immediately filed a complaint with the Federal Communications Commission and the Texas Public Utilities Commission. Much of the anger expressed by those officials was sparked by the $370 that Southwestern Bell spent to process each bogus service request made by a TWC employee.

CYBERETHICS: LOOKING TO THE FUTURE

E-commerce poses numerous and complex ethical issues that cut across a wide range of circumstances and business settings. Those parties wanting to advance the overall moral "goodness" of e-business practices face several major hurdles. Among those hurdles is the mushrooming growth rate of criminal, fraudulent, and unethical behavior in cyberspace. An attorney for the Federal Trade Commission (FTC), one of the federal agencies involved in policing the Internet, recently observed that online fraud is increasing "exponentially." Over a recent two-year period, the number of fraud cases reported to the FTC that involved online auctions leaped from approximately 100 to nearly 11,000. In mid-2001, the FBI announced the results of Operation CyberLoss, a nationwide investigation of online fraud that involved local, state, and other federal law enforcement agencies. That investigation identified nearly 60,000 individuals who had been victimized by Internet scams of various types. In commenting on the results of that investigation, the U.S. Deputy Attorney General observed that, "Internet fraud, whether it's in the form of securities and investment schemes, online auction and merchandising schemes, credit-card fraud or identity theft, has been one of the fastest growing and most pervasive forms of white-collar crime."[13]

Another impediment to "raising the ethics bar" in e-commerce is the difficulty of reaching a consensus on which cultural standards or norms across the globe should be applied to this exciting new frontier of the business world. The multinational and multicultural nature of e-commerce makes it difficult to begin a discourse on major ethical issues, much less arrive at mutually acceptable policies and procedures for addressing those issues. For example, certain efforts to limit e-commerce abuses depend upon the encryption of data transmitted over the Internet. In many Third World countries, in nations ruled by totalitarian regimes, and even in some industrialized democracies, this practice is viewed dimly by governmental authorities. France, a leading member of the European Union and a major trading partner of the United States, did not legalize the encryption of data for transmission over the Internet until 1998.

---

13. Associated Press, "Series of Internet-Fraud Probes Results in Arrests of 62 People," *The Wall Street Journal* Interactive Edition, 23 May 2001.

Investigating and prosecuting Internet abuses often requires the cooperation of law enforcement authorities from two or more nations. Take the case of a credit card fraud perpetrated by a Romanian teenager on several U.S. businesses. Romanian authorities were given concrete and extensive evidence of the teenager's elaborate scam. In response to that evidence, Romanian police observed that the teenager "is clearly guilty." However, no charges were filed against the teenager. Why? Romanian police indicated that they did not have the "time" to concern themselves with Internet-related crimes.[14,15]

Within the United States, a key obstacle to curtailing the unethical practices plaguing e-commerce is the opposition of many advocacy groups to various remedial measures that have been suggested to eliminate or control those practices. For example, vendors of online security services have developed several biometric security systems and technologies. These products grant access to a computer, network, or online files only after identifying unique physical characteristics of potential users that have been scanned into a security database. One such technology relies on identifying 80 "facial landmarks," which are used to develop a unique "face print" for any given individual. Numerous Internet users and activist groups maintain that such technologies violate the privacy rights of individuals.

In March 2000, the SEC revealed that it was developing an automated surveillance system to search the Internet for evidence of fraud, particularly pump and dump schemes. A major focus of this system would be the message boards and chat rooms operated by Yahoo!, AOL, and dozens of other online companies. The federal agency asked several firms having extensive experience in fraud detection to participate in this project. These firms were instructed to submit bids for several facets of the project being contracted out to the private sector. Among the organizations asked to submit a bid was PricewaterhouseCoopers (PWC), one of the Big Five accounting firms that dominate the public accounting profession. PWC officials refused to submit a bid to the SEC. The firm "advised the agency that it would not participate because the endeavor might impinge on the constitutional protection against unlawful search and seizure."[16]

Several members of Congress also questioned the constitutionality of the SEC's surveillance project. U.S. Representative Robert Barr was one of the principal congressional opponents of the SEC's plan. Congressman Barr argued that federal agencies should not make use of the extensive and largely anonymous monitoring technologies made possible by the Internet simply because those technologies are now available.

Most experts agree that the largest stumbling block to achieving a higher overall level of ethical conduct in e-commerce is an attitude shared by many Internet users. The Internet's free-spirited culture has convinced many New Age entrepreneurs, their subordinates, and large numbers of their customers that cer-

---

14. D. Berman, "Card Sharps, the Net Provides Fertile Ground for Credit-Card Scams," *Business Week e.biz*, 3 April 2000, EB 68.

15. In the summer of 2001, the United States, Japan, and the 41 member countries of the Council of Europe approved the first international "cybercrime" treaty. Under the terms of this treaty, these countries agree to cooperate in investigating and prosecuting cross-border crimes involving the Internet.

16. M. Moss, "SEC's Plan to Snoop for Crime on Web Sparks a Debate Over Privacy," *The Wall Street Journal*, 28 March 2000, B1.

tain constraints relevant to the traditional, "physical world" business environment do not necessarily apply to business conducted in cyberspace. "If there's anything that characterizes . . . the Internet boom . . . it's the ineffable sense that old rules no longer apply, that the laws governing the universe have been suspended. From there, is it such a leap to conclude that the old rules of ethics have been suspended?"[17] A professor of business ethics suggests that this problem can be overcome only by a "top-down" strategy. The top executives and managers of e-commerce companies must convey to their subordinates a high sense of commitment to ethical norms, both in policy statements and in observable conduct. "Training in ethics has minimal impact on people. What has a bigger impact is the leadership in organizations."[18]

QUESTIONS

1. Develop a general strategy that an individual could use in resolving ethical dilemmas. This strategy should include three or more specific steps or procedures.
2. Refer to the ethical dilemma entitled "Cybersting." Are "cyberstings" ethical under all circumstances? Under any circumstances? Explain.
3. Do you agree with the implied argument of *The New York Times* that monitoring employee e-mails is a morally acceptable business practice? Are "legal" business practices always "ethical"? Are "ethical" business practices always "legal"? Explain.
4. As a general rule, when should a superior be held responsible for unethical conduct by his or her subordinates? Who should hold large corporations accountable for their ethical judgments?
5. Identify "sensitive" financial or nonfinancial information that you believe corporations should *not* be required to report to the public despite the SEC's full and fair disclosure principle. Defend each item you list.
6. Search the Internet for an example of a corporate code of ethics or conduct. Document the website at which you found this code of ethics and provide a brief summary of the contents of that code.
7. Do you agree with the assertion that "training in ethics has minimal impact on people"? Defend your answer. In your opinion, what is the most effective strategy for reducing unethical conduct within an organization?

17. Useem, "New Ethics or No Ethics?"

18. G. Chapman, "Some Dot-coms Know Value of Stock but Put No Stock in Values," *Los Angeles Times*, 22 May 2000, C4.

MODULE FIVE

STATUS REPORTS

E-Mail: *The* Killer App

I distrust the incommunicable; it is the source of all violence.

Jean-Paul Sartre

Following the collapse of the Roman Empire, bands of Germanic tribes known as Franks dominated much of western and central Europe. During the eighth century, nomadic warriors from northern Europe and from the Iberian peninsula invaded the Franks' homeland. Charles Martel, the leader of the Franks, realized that he needed a new military strategy or tactic to fend off the invaders who easily outnumbered his own armies. Martel found the solution to his problem by relying on a simple contraption that he had noticed certain horsemen using a few years earlier, namely, the stirrup. By adding stirrups to the saddles of his soldiers' horses, Martel converted those soldiers into mounted cavalry. These mounted soldiers could use the leverage provided by the stirrups to deliver crushing blows to the enemy's soldiers, both those on foot and those on horseback. Thanks largely to this simple battleground tactic, Charles Martel repelled the invaders and, in doing so, helped mold the future of Europe for centuries to come. Following Martel's death, his grandson, Charlemagne, would be crowned the first emperor of the Holy Roman Empire by the Pope.

In their 1998 bestseller, *Unleashing the Killer App*, Larry Downes and Chunka Mui documented numerous "killer applications" or "killer apps" that had played prominent roles in the history of mankind, including Charles Martel's stirrup.[1] Prior to collaborating on that bestseller, Downes and Mui worked for more than a decade each as consultants in the information technology field. Both men found their assignments challenging and stimulating but frustrating, as well. Their frustration stemmed from the realization that their efforts and those of their colleagues typically produced only "incremental improvements" in the information, production, or distribution systems of their clients. Eventually, Downes and Mui decided to forego their comfortable salaries and strike out on their own. Their objective? To explore the secrets underlying the processes and circumstances that

---

1. L. Downes and C. Mui, *Unleashing the Killer App* (Boston: Harvard Business School Press, 1998).

result in those rare but dramatic human inventions or discoveries that radically change society.

In a business context, Downes and Mui define a killer app as a "new good or service that establishes an entirely new category and, being first, dominates it, returning several hundred percent on the initial investment."[2] Dozens of other definitions for this phrase can be found including one offered by the online "Jargon Dictionary." This latter source notes that a killer app "makes a sustaining market for a promising but underutilized technology." Other killer apps identified by the two consultants-turned-authors included the arch, the pulley, eyeglasses, elevators, asphalt, and the cotton gin. Downes and Mui observed that killer apps are often very disruptive to pre-existing businesses, business processes, and workers. A new killer app can literally throw an entire industry into upheaval. "In business, killer apps undermine customer relationships, distribution networks, competitive behavior, and economies of size and scale. . . . They give customers, suppliers and new entrants power, upsetting the careful cultivation of competitive advantages that were themselves based on technology, technology that is now suddenly obsolete."[3]

Downes and Mui's book introduced the "killer app" phrase to a large segment of the general public and the press. However, that phrase had been used widely in the information technology field before the Downes and Mui book was published. Apparently, the killer app appellation was first used in the early 1980s in reference to the spreadsheet program, *Lotus 1-2-3*. That software program contributed significantly to the personal computer's explosive growth in popularity during the 1980s, meaning that *Lotus 1-2-3* was a killer application for the personal computer.

During the 1990s, swarms of high-tech entrepreneurs worked feverishly to develop the next killer app, the next technological Holy Grail. Venture capital firms, Wall Street bankers, and other large investors poured billions of dollars into those research and development projects. Contributing to the frantic search for killer apps was the business press. Business journalists wanted to be the first to break the news regarding the "next big thing" in the technology field. Type "killer app" into the search window for an online database of business articles and you will discover scores of new products and services over the past few years that have been assigned that badge of honor—granted, most often the assignors are the self-interested developers or promoters of those products and services. The fascination with killer apps even prompted the creation of an annual "Most Likely Killer App" contest in California, the home of many high-tech firms.[4]

Among the most publicized potential killer apps of the mid-1990s was PointCast, an online information service that delivered headlines, weather reports, sports scores, and other information in a screensaver format to Internet users. Self-appointed Internet experts predicted that PointCast would be the killer app for "push technology." Instead of Internet users being forced to search for information they needed or wanted on the far-flung World Wide Web, push technology promised to deliver that information automatically to their computer screens.

2. *Ibid.*, 4.

3. *Ibid.*, 8.

4. *Business Wire*, "On2's V-Community a Finalist in First Annual 'Bandies' Awards; On2's Suite of Interactive Video Products Nominated in 'Killer Apps' Category," 22 November 2000.

Although PointCast initially proved to be very popular with high-tech trendsetters, operational problems plagued the new service. Within a few years, PointCast disappeared and along with it a slew of other "push" services and applications.[5]

Similar to PointCast, most widely proclaimed killer apps have failed to fulfill their initial expectations. But, there are exceptions. According to one business journalist, two applications have earned the killer app title within the Internet domain. "Ask any techno-pundit to name the 'killer app' for the Internet, and you're likely to get one of two answers: e-mail or the World Wide Web."[6] That journalist went on to suggest that e-mail is *the* killer app for the Internet. "While e-mail may not be as sexy as the Web, it's the most-used and the most useful application. For most folks, it's the one thing that makes them understand the importance of the Internet."[7] The two killer app experts in the high-tech world, Downes and Mui, agree with that assessment. "E-mail, a simple hack invented by scientists whose computers were connected during the early days of the Internet, has reached killer app status."[8]

E-MAIL: A LITTLE HISTORY

Scroll through online chronologies documenting the history of the Internet and you will find that most cyberspace historians report that electronic mail was invented in the early 1970s, most likely 1971. In 1972, e-mail was first introduced to the Advanced Research Projects Agency Network or Arpanet, the forerunner of the Internet. Scientists working on the Arpanet project intended to develop a fail-proof computer network that could be used by government and military personnel in the event of a major national catastrophe, such as atomic warfare. An individual instrumental in adapting e-mail to the Arpanet was Ray Tomlinson, an employee of a Massachusetts-based company that had obtained a contract from the U.S. Department of Defense to help develop the Arpanet. Cyberspace trivia buffs recognize Tomlinson as the individual who selected the now ubiquitous @ sign as the symbol to connect an Internet user's online name and cyberspace address.

E-mail messages sent over the Internet do not travel as one continuous block of information. Instead, these messages are chopped into "packets" by the sender's computer and then routed across various paths on the Internet to the receiver's computer where they are reassembled. This packet technology helps preserve the integrity of a network's communications system in the event that portions of the network are destroyed or otherwise incapacitated.

> Instead of transmitting a single and complete e-mail message over the Internet, the sender's computer replicates each e-mail message and breaks it into numerous packets. Packets and multiple copies were used in the Arpanet in case portions of the network were destroyed: because multiple copies of the message exist and are being transmitted

5. For a more in-depth history of PointCast, refer to Case 3.1, *PointCast, FallFast*.

6. D. Silverman, "Here's Why to Have Eudora Love Affair," *Houston Chronicle*, 2 July 1999, Technology, 1.

7. *Ibid.*

8. Downes and Mui, *Unleashing the Killer App*, 19.

through separate paths, at least one complete copy of the information was more likely to get through even if portions of the network were destroyed.[9]

The scientists working on the Arpanet project did not intend to develop a communications medium that would be widely used by the public. During the first two decades of e-mail's existence, members of the scientific and academic communities were the primary users of this new technology. But, as word spread regarding the ease and speed of communicating by e-mail, the new communications medium crept into the mainstream of society. Downes and Mui suggest that 1993 was a pivotal year for e-mail. During that year, they believe that the number of e-mail users reached "critical mass." "Once a standard has achieved critical mass, its value to everyone multiplies exponentially."[10]

Finding a rigorous definition of e-mail is not an easy task, most likely because it has become a common and often overlooked feature of our everyday lives. *Random House Webster's College Dictionary* provides the following definition of this widely used but often under-appreciated phenomenon: "a system for sending messages via telecommunications links between computers." A business reporter used a little geography to help define e-mail. "An asynchronous and written word-based worldwide electronic system that delivers your messages via wire-line and/or wireless to Naples or Nepal for the same cost as the identical message delivered to your neighbor's place down the street."[11]

Efforts to commercialize the Internet during the early 1990s triggered widespread interest in e-mail within the business world. Business executives initially viewed e-mails as an alternative to faxes. But, those executives and their subordinates quickly realized that e-mail was not only cheaper, more timely, and less intrusive than faxes, but also superior in several respects to long-distance telephone calls and the U.S. Postal Service's so-called "snail mail." The perceived advantages of e-mail over other communications media caused companies large and small to rapidly integrate this new technology into their communications systems.

Consulting firms, government agencies, and Internet measurement services have produced an impressive stream of statistics documenting the massive and rapid shift to electronic communications in recent years. The mind-boggling magnitude of those statistics makes them difficult to grasp. For example, one source estimated that 23.5 quadrillion e-mail messages were sent in 1998 alone in the United States.[12] (For the math-impaired, one quadrillion is equivalent to 1,000 trillion.) A more credible statistic reported widely by the press pegged the annual number of e-mail messages at approximately seven trillion worldwide by the late 1990s.[13] In mid-2001, *The New York Times* reported that the number of business-related e-mails topped six billion each day.[14]

9. D. Hricik, "Lawyers Worry Too Much About Transmitting Client Confidences by Internet E-Mail," *Georgetown Journal of Legal Ethics*, Spring 1998, 459.

10. Downes and Mui, *Unleashing the Killer App*, 5.

11. L. Grant, "The E-Mail Information Carnival Changes with Stupefying Alacrity," *Journal of Commerce*, 21 August 1996, 5C.

12. S. A. Thumma and D. S. Jackson, "The History of Electronic Mail in Litigation," *Santa Clara Computer and High Technology Law Journal*, November 1999, 1.

13. *Business Wire*, "Sandpiper Networks and RadicalMail Team Up to Deliver Streaming Multimedia E-Mail," 8 December 1999.

14. B. Headlam, "How to E-Mail Like a CEO," *The New York Times* on the Web, 8 April 2001.

The most frequently circulated e-mail metric measures the amount of time the typical corporate office worker spends reading, clearing, and writing e-mail messages. *The Wall Street Journal* reported in late 2000 that office workers received an average of 50 e-mails each day and spent an estimated two hours on e-mail-related tasks.[15] By 2002, the latter figure is expected to double to four hours per day.[16] Collectively, the scads of statistics that document the extent of e-mail usage demonstrate that in a brief period from the early 1990s through the end of the decade e-mail became the primary communications medium used by corporations.

Most parties agree that the real-time nature of e-mail revolutionized business communications. No longer could procrastinators take advantage of the time-worn excuse "It's in the mail." During the course of the e-mail revolution in the mid- and late 1990s, most companies invested little time or effort in addressing and resolving several important issues posed by this new technology. Diverting the attention of corporate strategists from these issues was the nearly simultaneous and just as rapid development of the World Wide Web. "Web-based business practices are becoming well-understood if not actually resolved. In contrast, e-mail remains a truly untamed frontier, which has suffered from the comparative lack of attention paid to it over the previous five years."[17]

For corporations, the most important e-mail issue is a simple one: how best to utilize this relatively new communications medium for marketing purposes. As e-mail surged in popularity during the 1990s, corporate marketers quickly recognized that it had an almost limitless number of advertising and marketing applications. However, the dearth of relevant scholarly and scientific research and related hard data on the proper and most effective use of e-mail for marketing purposes forced marketing professionals to adopt a trial and error approach to using this new technology. The rush to integrate e-mail into corporate marketing strategies and plans quickly raised another important issue, namely, whether unsolicited e-mail was an appropriate means of promoting goods and services over the Internet. As a steady stream of unsolicited commercial e-mail messages, or "spam," began pouring into Internet users' in-boxes, many of those users revolted and insisted that legislative bodies or governmental agencies regulate the use of e-mail for commercial purposes.

Another broad set of issues raised by the introduction of e-mail into the business world involves its impact on the workplace. When e-mail suddenly and haphazardly barged into the work environment of millions of business executives and employees, these individuals found that this new method of communicating had pervasive implications for the nature of their work assignments and responsibilities. For example, e-mail posed many new and thorny ethical dilemmas and questions that corporate America had not previously faced.

The following sections of this case address the general issues identified in the previous two paragraphs. We begin by examining the impact of e-mail on the marketing function of businesses. Next, the unpleasant spam "problem" that is so closely linked to online marketing is considered. Finally, we focus on the

15. B. Bright, "E-Mail, a Tool of Efficiency, Sometimes Adds to Overload," *The Wall Street Journal* Interactive Edition, 22 August 2000.

16. C. Hymowitz, "Executives Are Overwhelmed by Overuse, Misuse of E-Mail," *The Wall Street Journal* Interactive Edition, 26 September 2000.

17. E. Goldman and M. P. Ochoa, "Stupid E-Mail Tricks, Stupid E-Mail Laws?" *Boardwatch Magazine*, December 1999, 98.

influence that e-mail has had on the American workplace, particularly on the work roles and responsibilities of the millions of individuals who qualify as "office workers."

IRRESISTIBLE ECONOMICS

In the business world, a well-known expression is that "Nothing happens until someone sells something." The "nothing" in that statement refers to capturing market share, generating positive cash flows, realizing profits, distributing dividends to stockholders, and other objectives that are a primary topic of discussion in corporate board rooms. A business's survival depends upon its ability to attract and retain customers—customers who buy the firm's products or services. An indispensable feature of the selling process is communication. When e-mail burst onto the scene of American business in the 1990s, corporate marketers suddenly had at their disposal a low cost, high-tech communications tool. Not only does e-mail allow businesses to readily contact customers at a lower cost than conventional communication methods, Internet technology provides businesses with the ability to pinpoint those individuals likely interested in their products or services. E-mail advertising also provides businesses with quick and reliable feedback regarding the effectiveness of given promotional materials. In early 2001, Thomas E. Weber, a high-tech guru for *The Wall Street Journal*, observed that "e-mail is delivering on the Net's early promise of advertising that's cheap, targeted, measurable, and effective."[18]

Rather than investing heavily in online advertising programs, several small Internet-based companies struck on the idea of allowing their customers to serve as their online advertising agents. During the mid-1990s, executives of the free e-mail service Hotmail decided to append the phrase "Get Your Private, Free Email at *http://www.hotmail.com*" to every e-mail message sent by the service's subscribers. As that phrase ricocheted across the length and breadth of the Internet, it caught the attention of throngs of bargain-happy Internet users. The result: in a little more than one year, Hotmail accumulated 12 million subscribers, while spending only $500,000 on advertising. Hotmail's large and growing membership roll allowed its owners to sell the e-mail service to Microsoft for a reported $400 million in early 1998.

Understand that so-called "viral marketing" preceded the Internet. But, this tactic seems particularly well suited for cyberspace marketing efforts. The success of Hotmail's viral marketing program and several similar and well-publicized marketing campaigns by upstart and undercapitalized companies persuaded more established firms to plant "viruses" among potential online customers. In May 2000, CBS executives worried that conventional advertising efforts would fail to convince the public to tune in to their new television series, *Survivor*. So, those executives identified approximately 30,000 Internet users that marketing research suggested would be intrigued by the unique nature of the new series.[19] Each of those individuals received an e-mail accompanied with a brief video at-

---

18. T. E. Weber, "Why Companies Are So Eager to Get Your E-Mail Address," *The Wall Street Journal* Interactive Edition, 12 February 2001.

19. R. Meredith, "You've Got Ad-Mail," *Forbes.com*, 18 September 2000.

tachment that featured a clip of the new program and other commercial content. The e-mail encouraged the recipients to forward the video clip to friends and acquaintances. And they did. By "infecting" the public with the *Survivor* "virus," CBS executives created a "buzz" within the television viewing audience that contributed significantly to the eventual success of the *Survivor* series.

To date, entertainment companies have been among the most prolific users of online viral marketing campaigns. In March 2000, the record company of N'Sync sent a video e-mail to nearly 250,000 known fans of the boy band. One-third of those fans forwarded that e-mail to one or more friends or acquaintances. Britney Spears' record producer topped that figure a few months later by zipping more than one million video clips to Internet users. For whatever reason, only 9 percent of Britney's supposed fans forwarded the e-mail to other parties.

The limited research performed to date on online viral marketing provides important insight on why this tactic has been so successful. Recall that Charles Martel added stirrups to the saddles of his mounted soldiers. Why? So those soldiers could gain more leverage to deliver blows to opposing warriors. Leverage also serves as the pivotal feature of viral e-mail marketing. According to the executive of a market research firm, influential individuals have a much greater ability to shape the attitudes and opinions of others in the Internet era. "In the old economy—or the offline world—one person was generally thought to have an impact on the attitudes and behavior of two people . . . [but] one influential online person has an impact on the attitudes and the behavior of approximately eight [other people]."[20] Marketing experts recognize that recommendations by such influential individuals, even if those recommendations are in the relatively subtle form of a forwarded e-mail, rank among the most potent marketing tools. "Viral marketing is a powerful theory. It attempts to harness the strongest of all consumer triggers—the personal recommendation."[21]

A viral marketing campaign carried out with the help of e-mail ads can be a compelling technique to use in promoting a product, but it also has certain limitations. One limitation should be obvious: viral marketing works well only when the given product or service appeals to the target group. A viral marketing campaign has little chance of being successful if the wrong individuals receive the e-mail ad. Likewise, if the members of the target group have a negative reaction to the product or service, a viral marketing campaign can boomerang by spawning a flurry of negative e-mails disparaging that product or service. Viral marketing also seems to work for only a limited number of products and services, namely, those items that have the potential for eliciting some degree of emotional response from consumers. Books, furniture, car accessories, and most other consumer products lack that potential.

Triggering an "epidemic" of forwarded e-mails among Internet users is not the primary objective of most e-mail ad campaigns. Instead, companies that use such campaigns typically intend to produce a desired response only from the initial recipient of an e-mail ad. During the early years of Internet advertising, companies and organizations that chose to advertise on the Internet relied heavily or exclusively on banner ads flown on popular sites such as Yahoo! or AOL. By the late

20. I. Mount, "Ebola. Smallpox. Christina Aguilera. What Do They All Have in Common? They All Spread Virally," *eCompany* (online), October 2000.

21. E. Neuborne, "Viral Marketing Alert!" *Business Week e.Biz*, 19 March 2001, EB 8.

1990s, the "click-through" rates on banner ads hovered at a dismal 0.5 to 1 per-cent.[22] On the other hand, e-mail ads targeted to individuals known to have an interest in a specific product or, at least, a type of product, typically produce a click-through rate of between 10 to 15 percent. Some e-mail ad campaigns have produced a much higher response rate. A common method of inducing favorable responses to an e-mail ad campaign is to pilot test different versions of an ad on samples of consumers drawn from the targeted population. The version of the ad that generates the highest response rate is then distributed to the remaining members of the target audience.[23]

E-mail ads tend to be much cheaper than conventional or offline promotional materials. Data reported in the press suggest that the average cost of an e-mail ad typically ranges from $0.02 to $0.25. For large e-mail "outsourcers" that organize and carry out e-mail advertising campaigns for hundreds of companies, the average cost of an e-mail ad can be as low as one penny, or even less.[24] On the other hand, promotional materials providing comparable information that are distributed via the U.S. Postal Service typically have a per unit cost ranging between $0.50 and $2.

E-mail ads have another important advantage over their offline counterparts: the ability to provide quick and precise feedback on their effectiveness. The executive of a major e-mail outsourcer notes that e-mail is "the most measurable marketing vehicle of all time. You know exactly who you are sending e-mails to, you know how they are responding—did they click, did they buy?"[25] That same executive went on to comment on the timeliness of the feedback provided by e-mail ads. "People respond to their e-mails in a matter of days. So, marketers can determine if their campaign was a success in 48 hours versus the four to six weeks it might take for a direct-mail campaign."

The precise feedback yielded by e-mail ads results from the integration of online tracking devices, principally "cookies," in e-mail marketing campaigns. These tracking devices allow e-mail advertisers to readily collect information that documents with great precision the success of their marketing efforts. "Marketing companies now regularly keep tabs on which prospective customers open their e-mail solicitations, and at what time of day."[26] Privacy advocates rail against this feature of e-mail ads. Advertisers respond that this monitoring feature allows them to develop more personalized ads that will appeal to specific Internet users and to cull individuals who apparently have little interest in their products from their mailing databases.

As e-mail advertising became a widely used marketing technique in the late 1990s, articles began appearing in the press instructing businesses how to fine tune this new marketing tactic to make it more effective. Peter Brondmo, the founder of a company that creates customized e-mail marketing programs, identified the "twelve golden rules for e-mail marketing" in an article that appeared

---

22. E. Schibsted, "Email Takes Center Stage," *Business2.com*, 26 December 2000, 64.

23. Weber, "Why Companies Are So Eager to Get Your E-Mail Address."

24. *Ibid.*

25. J. Schwartz, "Marketers Turn to a Simple Tool: E-Mail," *The New York Times*, 13 December 2000, H1.

26. A. Harmon, "Software to Track E-Mail Raises Privacy Concerns," *The New York Times* on the Web, 22 November 2000.

in the Internet-focused publication *eCompany*.[27] Several of Brondmo's rules were intended to protect the privacy and security of potential customers' confidential information: "develop and post a privacy policy," "guarantee that personal information is secure," and "let customers know what you know." Brondmo also urged e-mail advertisers to be concise and to solicit feedback on their e-mail ads. The most blunt commandment among Brondmo's golden rules was simply "Thou shalt not spam." In explaining that rule, he noted that e-mail advertisers should "contact only those customers who have expressed interest in receiving messages electronically, and who have voluntarily supplied their e-mail addresses."

Unfortunately, despite the insistence of professional marketers such as Peter Brondmo, companies often fall prey to what one Internet expert refers to as the "irresistible economics" of spam.[28] The low cost of e-mail ads when coupled with their relatively high response rates often induces firms that are initially well-intentioned to resort to a "batch and blast" e-mail ad strategy. Instead of investing the time and money required to compile or otherwise acquire databases of potential customers for a given product or service, many companies resort to acquiring large, indiscriminate databases of e-mail addresses and then begin bombarding the electronic mail boxes represented by those addresses with repeated and often redundant e-mail ads. A key factor motivating these "shotgun" marketing efforts is the realization that the more e-mail ads sent out over the Internet, the lower the average per unit cost of those ads.

As e-mail ads have become a more common marketing technique their effectiveness as measured by click-through or response rates has gradually fallen.[29] Given that e-mail expenditures are projected to increase dramatically in the future, the effectiveness of e-mail ads will likely continue to slide. Many online marketing experts believe that the declining effectiveness of e-mail ads may actually encourage more online marketers to resort to a low cost "spamming" strategy.

CAN THE SPAM

In 1994, Sanford Wallace became caught up in the Internet Revolution when he subscribed to America Online. Wallace spent much of his free time interacting with other AOL members on the online service's message boards. Wallace, a college dropout who had experienced minimal success in several business ventures, recognized that the e-mail addresses readily available from AOL's message boards could be potentially valuable to companies wanting to sell products and services to Internet users. So, Wallace "harvested" nearly 10,000 of those addresses by hand and then approached several businesses with the idea of sending online advertisements and other promotional materials to the individuals in his personal database. Within two weeks of signing up his first client, Wallace had earned $10,000. "Spurred by that success, he enlarged his list. Soon his company,

---

27. H. P. Brondmo, "Spam Not, Want Not," *eCompany* (online), September 2000.

28. D. Miller, "The Spam King Is Back, and His New Recipe Clicks," *The Wall Street Journal* Interactive Edition, 13 December 1999.

29. E. Fitzloff, "Email Marketing at a Price," *Business2.com*, 26 January 2001.

Cyber Promotions, was beaming out one mass e-mailing after another for entrepreneurs hawking everything from insurance to vitamins."[30]

Within a matter of months, Wallace's company was releasing a flood of e-mail messages, as many as 25 million per day, onto the information superhighway. Most of those ads were sent to individuals who had little, if any, interest in the products and services being promoted. Wallace's prodigious efforts earned him the title "King of Spam" among irate Internet users who were the unwanted recipients of his ads. Firms that used more legitimate online marketing tactics also frequently berated Wallace since his "batch and blast" strategy diminished the effectiveness of their e-mail marketing campaigns. Although Wallace's company produced impressive profits initially, the firm was eventually forced out of business. "By 1997, he [Wallace] had become a pariah, unable to find a company willing to supply him with the Internet connections he needed to send out his spam."[31]

Although Sanford Wallace reigned as the "King of Spam," his business plan was emulated on a smaller scale by hundreds of other individuals. By the late 1990s, spam was recognized as the "scourge of the Internet" by most cyberenthusiasts. According to one business journalist, "Sending spam is the moral equivalent of jumping in front of a pedestrian, blocking his path, and shouting the advertiser's message in his face."[32] Contributing to the spam epidemic of the late 1990s was the introduction of robotic software that could be used to search online databases and collect information meeting certain criteria. "Bots" provided spammers with a low cost method of electronically prowling online sources of e-mail addresses and harvesting those addresses for their own databases.

By early 2001, an estimated 30 percent of all e-mail messages qualified as spam, a figure that was expected to rise over the following years.[33] As the volume of spam continued to grow, many companies, organizations, and individual Internet users began taking aggressive measures to confront this problem. Among the most vigorous anti-spam crusaders were Internet service providers (ISPs), whose computer circuits were often clogged by unsolicited e-mail, and other online service companies, such as eBay and Yahoo!, whose users' e-mail addresses were commonly confiscated by spammers.

To combat the spam problem, EarthLink, an ISP, installed the "Spaminator" in its computer networks. This filtering program diverts e-mail having spam-like features into a spam storage folder. EarthLink subscribers can review the messages stored in that folder before those messages are purged. Yahoo! protects its e-mail clients with a comparable software program known as SpamGuard. Anti-spam products available to the general public include E-sweeper, marketed by Content Technologies, a British firm; SpamKiller, a product of the U.S. firm Novasoft; and a free online product, Spam Buster, that can be downloaded at the website *www.contactplus.com*. The SpamKiller product, which initially sold for $29.95, applies 2,200 spam-sniffing filters to incoming e-mails. Those filters in-

---

30. Miller, "The Spam King Is Back."

31. *Ibid.*

32. S. Stellin, "Marketers Get Help from E-Mail Experts," *The New York Times* on the Web, 21 August 2000.

33. P. Felps, "Proposals to Stem Junk E-Mail Don't Get Far," *The Dallas Morning News* (online), 4 January 2001.

clude domain names of well-known spammers as well as catch phrases commonly used by spam producers including "earn extra cash" and "Dear Homeowner." When an incoming e-mail triggers one of the filters, a rifle shot sound effect alerts the computer user that another piece of spam has been "fried." Another company that markets anti-spam products, Brightmail, has developed a "spamometer" to monitor the daily volume of e-mail ad activity for the purpose of providing their clients with real-time warnings of anticipated spam attacks.

The anti-spam products installed by Internet service providers and those available to the public work reasonably well. A study funded by one vendor of anti-spam software found that its product captured 73 percent of all incoming spam.[34] On the downside, such filtering products register a sizable number of "false positives," meaning that legitimate e-mails are often diverted to the spam dump. Another limitation of anti-spam products is that canny spammers continuously monitor these products and develop methods to circumvent them, meaning that their usefulness tends to degrade over time. An outspoken critic of spammers suggests that filtering products are not an effective solution to cyberspace's equivalent of junk mail. "Filtering doesn't really address the problem. It's a Band-Aid. Filtering approaches are bad for both consumers and businesses. Filtering is actually more expensive than sending spam itself."[35]

Several not-for-profit organizations sprang up in the late 1990s with the express purpose of protecting Internet users from unsolicited commercial e-mail. Most prominent among these organizations are CAUCE—the Coalition Against Unsolicited Commercial Email, MAPS—Mail Abuse Prevention System, and FREE—the Forum for Responsible and Ethical E-mail. MAPS created a blacklist of known spamming organizations that it provides to ISPs and other online companies and organizations that rely heavily on the Internet. Most ISPs and other online service providers use this list, known as the Realtime Blackhole List, to update their anti-spam filters. Any organization that appears on the Realtime Blackhole List finds it difficult, if not impossible, to deliver messages to e-mail clients of AOL, Yahoo!, and scores of other companies and organizations. By late 2000, more than 4,000 known or alleged spammers appeared on the Realtime Blackhole List.

Several e-mail marketers eventually sued MAPS, insisting that they be taken off the organization's blacklist. These companies typically alleged that (1) they were mass e-mail marketers, not spam producers, and (2) that MAPS' effort to blackball them violated their freedom of speech. In several cases, these lawsuits were successful. For example, Harris Interactive Inc., a company well known for doing broad-based survey research for political organizations including polling for presidential elections, used the courts to prevent MAPS from blocking e-mails that it sent to Hotmail subscribers. In late 2000, a federal judge issued a restraining order that required MAPS to take Exactis.com, an e-mail marketing agency and newsletter delivery service, off the Realtime Blackhole List. In responding to that decision, a spokesperson for Exactis.com noted that "MAPS intentionally harms innocent networks that send legitimate, authorized mail."[36]

---

34. B. Sullivan, "Spam Scams Infiltrate the Internet Just as House Legislation Progresses," *The Wall Street Journal* Interactive Edition, 16 June 2000.

35. *Ibid.*

36. J. Accola, "Judge Restrains Anti-Spam E-Mail Blocker," *Denver Rocky Mountain News*, 18 November 2000, 3B.

The success several organizations had in taking MAPS to court encouraged other blacklisted firms to do the same including Yesmail, a Chicago-based e-mail marketer. Yesmail maintained in federal court that it invoked a "permission-based" policy under which e-mail ads were sent only to those parties who, at some point, had indicated a willingness to accept such ads. MAPS officials maintain that e-mail marketers should be required to use a more rigorous "double opt-in" policy. Under this policy, e-mail marketing agencies can send online ads only to those Internet users who agree to receive such ads in an initial sign-up procedure and then confirm that agreement in a subsequent e-mail. As in the Exactis.com case, a judge issued an order requiring MAPS to take Yesmail off its infamous blacklist.

As the spam wars raged on, CAUCE, MAPS, and other companies and organizations frustrated by the growing volume of spam took their case to the U.S. Congress. In 2000, two major anti-spam bills were introduced in the U.S. House of Representatives, one of which was entitled "Can the Spam." Congress passed neither of those bills. The following year, four anti-spam bills floundered in Congress. Concerns that the proposed measures in those bills limited e-mail marketers' freedom of speech apparently proved to be their downfall. The frustrated co-founder of CAUCE insisted that the spam problem would only worsen in the future and that Congress was the only authority that could remedy the problem. "In the best of all possible worlds, we wouldn't need a law, but people have abused the Internet. We formed CAUCE in 1997, and here, almost four years later, there's almost no fix for it [spam] out there, so it has to become a government issue."[37]

YOU'VE GOT E-MAIL . . . IN THE WORKPLACE

The use of e-mail as the ultimate New Economy marketing tool has grabbed much of the attention that has centered on the Internet's most indispensable killer app. But, the impact of e-mail on the business world has not been limited to viral marketing, e-mail advertising, and spam. The emergence of e-mail has had a dramatic impact on the work roles and responsibilities of millions of individuals who occupy job positions ranging from the lowest to the highest rung on the employment hierarchy within corporate America.

The primary workplace issue posed by e-mail is the impact that this technology has had on the efficiency and productivity of individual employees and executives. During the mid-1990s, most business owners and executives saw few downsides to this new communications medium that was rapidly sweeping through the business world. But, over the following few years, many of those individuals had a change of heart. In late 2000, a corporate executive interviewed by *The New York Times* questioned whether e-mail had actually become more of a burden than a benefit to corporate workers. In commenting on the large number of e-mails that he was forced to deal with each day, that executive noted, "I can't keep up, and can't imagine how executives in larger organizations do."[38] Market

---

37. Felps, "Proposals to Stem Junk E-Mail."

38. Hymowitz, "Executives Are Overwhelmed."

research firms predict that the volume of e-mail will continue to grow in the future, a trend that threatens to "overwhelm executives and employees and suffocate businesses."[39] Many large corporations have issued directives to their members on how to use e-mail more efficiently. Those directives include establishing e-mail accounts that are reserved for high-priority issues, using administrative personnel to screen the e-mail of their superiors, and simply insisting that e-mail messages be concise.

Another important implication of the e-mail culture that has developed within the business world is the impact that it has had on the nature of corporate communications. Several researchers have observed that individuals tend to be less inhibited when they use e-mail as opposed to the telephone. One journalist notes that the "itchy trigger finger syndrome" often results in corporate workers experiencing an immediate sense of regret after zapping a hastily and angrily written missive to a co-worker, a vendor, or some other unfortunate party. "Everyday, thousands of people online get all worked up over what someone somewhere said about something, and, in reaction, compose a quick-and-nasty reply. Before they can holster those itchy trigger fingers, the 'enter' key is whacked and off it goes."[40] Many corporate executives have learned that such hastily written e-mail messages can expose their firm to adverse legal and economic consequences. "E-mail contains spontaneous and unfiltered thoughts, which can be dangerous in a lawsuit. It [e-mail] is also viral and can be sent to many people—there's a loss of control."[41]

To help e-mail users rein in their emotions, one e-mail program, Eudora, has a built-in Moodwatch feature. When activated, this feature monitors e-mail messages for potentially inflammatory statements. If such statements are identified, one or more red hot chili peppers appear on the user's computer screen. An ice cube icon appears on the user's screen as long as the individual keeps his or her emotions in check.

Privacy has easily become one of the most controversial, if not explosive, topics in the Internet era. The technology of the Internet provides many opportunities for hackers, corporate security personnel, and even co-workers to "snoop" on the billions of e-mail messages sent and received each day by unsuspecting corporate employees. As one corporate security expert suggests, when we use e-mail "we think we're whispering, but we're really broadcasting."[42] In early 2001, the Privacy Foundation, a not-for-profit organization that monitors Internet privacy issues, revealed that a sophisticated "e-mail wiretap" made it possible for corporations or individuals to access personal comments appended to e-mails that they had previously forwarded to other parties. A reporter used a hypothetical scenario to illustrate this subversive feature of certain e-mail programs.

> Imagine a large corporation wants to acquire a small Web company. The corporation sends an e-mail with a price proposal to the target—and includes a few lines of invisible computer code. As the target's executives pass the message around, the corporation

---

39. *Ibid.*

40. K. K. Campbell, "Learning to Bite Your Tongue," *The Toronto Star* (online), 10 August 2000.

41. I. Mount, "This E-Mail Will Self-Destruct in 10 Seconds, 9, 8 , 7 . . ." *eCompany* (online), October 2000.

42. S. Singh, "Careful, Computers Have Ears," *Sunday Telegraph*, 21 January 2001, 13.

gets a copy each time it's forwarded—with all the supposedly private comments attached.[43]

To counter this problem and to mitigate other privacy concerns posed by e-mail, many companies have integrated encryption software into their e-mail communication systems.

In recent years, the business press has been replete with articles discussing less sophisticated but just as effective methods that large companies have used to monitor e-mail messages of their employees. In the most publicized of those cases, *The New York Times* released 22 employees found to have circulated offensive e-mails among themselves. Individuals who fail to acquaint themselves with the specific stipulations of their employer's e-mail policies run the risk of violating those policies and facing a variety of sanctions, including discharge. An article appearing in the *Pittsburgh-Post Gazette* listed several stipulations commonly found in corporate e-mail policies, including the following items.[44]

> The electronic mail system hardware is company property. Additionally, all messages composed, sent or received on the electronic mail system are and remain the property of the company. They are not the private property of any employee.

> The use of the electronic mail system is reserved solely for the conduct of business at the company. It may not be used for personal business.

> The electronic mail system is not to be used to create any offensive or disruptive message. Among those which are considered offensive are any messages which contain sexual implications, racial slurs, gender-specific comments or any other comments that offensively addresses someone's age, sexual orientation, religious or political beliefs, national origin or disability.

> The company reserves and intends to exercise the right to review, audit, intercept, access and disclose all messages created, received or sent over the electronic mail system for any purpose. The contents of electronic mail properly obtained for legitimate business purposes may be disclosed within the company without the permission of the employee.

> The confidentially of any message should not be assumed. Even when a message is erased, it is still possible to retrieve and read the message. Further, the use of passwords for security does not guarantee confidentiality. All passwords must be disclosed to the company or they are invalid and cannot be used.

LOOKING TOWARD THE FUTURE

In a span of less than one decade, e-mail has had a huge impact on the nature of business practices, business communications, and the work environment and re-

---

43. *The New York Times* on the Web, "Group Warns Against E-Mail Wiretap," 5 February 2001.

44. T. Ove, "Companies Deal with Issue of Web Surfing, Personal E-Mail Usage at Work," *Pittsburgh Post-Gazette* (online), 19 March 2000.

sponsibilities of millions of Americans. No doubt, e-mail will continue to have a significant impact on the business world in the future. Current trends under way involving e-mail, new developments in communications and computer technology, and the resolution of pending regulatory and legislative issues related to e-mail will determine the extent to which this new communications medium helps shape the future of American business.

One future prediction related to e-mail usage that can be made very comfortably is that the daily volume of e-mails will continue to grow in the foreseeable future. A key factor that will help sustain that trend is a sizable expected increase in commercial e-mail ads, both "legitimate" ads and spam. A study by Forrester Research, a major Internet research firm, revealed that e-mail ad expenditures are expected to triple between 2001 and 2004.[45] Corporate marketing executives also expect e-mail ads to become more sophisticated in the future, relying more heavily on "rich" media, such as personalized audio messages, color photos and graphics, and streaming video. Finally, marketing executives also predict that most major companies will eventually adopt an "opt in" or permission-based e-mail advertising policy.

Among the most important unresolved issues involving e-mail is whether federal regulators will take steps to limit spam. If Congress fails to enact anti-spam legislation, freewheeling spammers will continue to clog the Internet with unsolicited e-mails and, in doing so, cast a shadow on the integrity of all e-mail marketing efforts. Congress' reluctance to act has spurred more than one dozen states, most notably the high-tech havens of Washington and California, to pass anti-spam laws. However, most experts agree that a patchwork of state-level anti-spam statutes will not cure the spam problem. Instead, federal legislation will almost certainly be necessary.

The spam issue is actually one component, one major component, of a broader issue—that issue is how the communications "overload" problem facing corporate executives and their subordinates should be resolved. Study after study suggests that corporate personnel face a growing risk of being swamped by e-mails, voice mails, faxes, and "snail" mail. As a result, corporations and other organizations are insisting that communications vendors and consultants provide them with "communications solutions" that integrate the different types of communications media. Recently, several major vendors have begun offering such solutions in the form of "unified messaging" systems. "A key component of unified messaging is the ability to receive and create messages in any media format and to access those messages through the most appropriate device."[46]

Will unified messaging prove to be the "next big thing" in communications technology? Two journalists recently suggested that "unified messaging really is the killer app"[47] in the communications field that corporations and other large organizations have been seeking. That may be true in the future but, for now, that "simple hack" invented by a handful of scientists more than three decades ago remains the "true" killer app of the exciting world of the Internet.

---

45. Schwartz, "Marketers Turn to a Simple Tool."

46. T. Jennings and S. Miner, "The Message Is Loud and Clear," *Business and Communications Practices*, September 2000, 71.

47. *Ibid.*

QUESTIONS

1. Research online or hard copy databases and identify an article or other publication that refers to a new Internet-related product or service as a "killer app." Document the source of the publication, describe the given product or service, and explain whether or not you believe that item will actually become a "killer app."

2. Research online or hard copy databases and find an article that announces a new e-mail product or service. Identify this new product or service and its key features.

3. Downes and Mui suggest that the number of e-mail users reached "critical mass" in 1993. Define what that phrase implies. Identify another major advancement in the business world and the approximate point in time that it apparently reached critical mass.

4. Identify a specific product for which you believe a viral marketing campaign would be effective. Briefly explain how you would develop such a campaign.

5. List three recent e-mail ads that you have received. Briefly describe the nature of each of these ads, including the specific product or service that each promoted. In your opinion, how effective was each of the ads? Explain.

6. Many "spammers" insist that any legislative, regulatory, or private effort to prevent them from indiscriminately sending e-mail ads to Internet users infringes on their right to freedom of speech. Do you agree with that assertion? Why or why not? In your view, what is the best solution to the spam "problem" that presently plagues the Internet?

7. This case listed several stipulations typically included in corporate policy statements governing the use of e-mail. For each of those stipulations, indicate whether or not you believe it is justified.

To B or Not 2B

To be, or not to be: that is the question.

William Shakespeare

In 1878, the Wizard of Menlo Park, Thomas Alva Edison, founded the Edison Electric Company. A few years later, Edison renamed his company General Electric. Throughout the twentieth century, General Electric (GE) ranked among the elite companies in Corporate America. By continually bringing "good things to life," the several generations of GE executives who succeeded Thomas A. Edison have built a huge and profitable company.

During the last two decades of the twentieth century, Jack Welch served as GE's chief executive officer (CEO). In that position, Welch made several key decisions that allowed GE to remain one of the most respected and prominent corporations worldwide. One of the challenges that Welch faced during his long tenure as GE's senior executive was deciding how his firm should react to the Internet. Although the potential business opportunities posed by the rapid expansion of the Internet in the mid-1990s intrigued Welch and his top subordinates, they delayed acting on those opportunities. Critics charged that GE's deliberate and cautious management style prevented the company from taking a leadership position in the rapidly evolving New Economy. Welch, himself, eventually admitted that he was "slow to embrace the Internet."[1]

In 1994, Glen Meakem worked as an information technology (IT) specialist for GE. The 29-year-old Meakem, who was just a few years removed from an MBA program, developed a proposal to use the Internet as a tool to reengineer one of the most fundamental but unglamorous business processes of a manufacturing company. Meakem proposed to "do no less than reinvent one of the murkiest, most backward, least sexy processes in industry: the purchase of the parts and materials that go into everything from granola to cars."[2] Meakem's plan, which he presented to his superiors at GE, called for his company to develop an online marketplace in which vendors would compete against each other to obtain GE

---

1. J. E. Garten, "The Mind of the C.E.O.," *Business Week*, 5 February 2001, 106.
2. S. Tully, "The B2B Tool That Really *Is* Changing the World," *Fortune*, 20 March 2000, 132.

as a customer. The young IT specialist wanted "to make suppliers compete for manufacturers' orders in live, open, electronic auctions. No more golf-course schmoozing, no more haggling, no more sealed bids."[3] Meakem projected that his plan would eventually save GE's manufacturing divisions billions of dollars by driving down the acquisition cost of production materials, office supplies, and even professional services that those divisions routinely purchased from thousands of external suppliers.

Meakem's proposal also included a recommendation calling for GE to develop electronic marketplaces for other industries. GE would operate those marketplaces and collect commissions from buyers and sellers that participated in them. In effect, GE would become the equivalent of a "bustling bazaar" for all of corporate America. Meakem exuberantly proclaimed, "This idea will transform the global economy!"[4] But, GE's top management did not share his enthusiasm. GE's executives apparently decided that the proposal was too risky and passed on the idea. Within a few months, Meakem left GE to pursue his dream. The persistent Meakem brought his dream to life when he launched FreeMarkets, an Internet-based business-to-business (B2B) marketplace. After taking his company public, Meakem joined the growing ranks of rich Internet moguls. By early 2000, FreeMarkets' common stock had a collective market value approaching $10 billion, while Meakem's personal fortune, thanks to his large ownership interest in that stock, neared $1 billion.

During the mid-1990s, several other Internet visionaries developed grand schemes similar to Glen Meakem's to revamp the purchasing processes of businesses large and small. Like Meakem, these visionaries predicted that their proposals would radically change the business world. Sanjiv Sidhu, who organized i2 Technologies, a company that develops software to operate B2B marketplaces, declared that B2B "is the next Industrial Revolution."[5] Sidhu insisted that many manufacturing companies could easily cut their production costs by 50 percent by joining electronic marketplaces.[6] Larry Ellison, the CEO of Oracle, second only to Microsoft in annual software sales, suggested that electronic B2B marketplaces would wipe out large numbers of companies that failed to integrate this new feature of the business environment into their operations. "These technology transitions are like the Tertiary-Cretaceous boundary. They are extinction-level events."[7]

Even many individuals who had spent their entire careers in the Old Economy became convinced that B2B would revolutionize the business world. Frederick Schulz, a 71-year-old former member of the Federal Reserve, accepted an appointment to the board of directors of a company that organized a large B2B marketplace. In commenting on the trend to establish electronic marketplaces for specific industries, Schulz remarked that "What's happening today is creating much more massive changes than the Industrial Revolution, and is changing things so much faster."[8]

---

3. *Ibid.*

4. *Ibid.*

5. S. V. Brull, "Such Busy Bees in B2B," *Business Week*, 27 March 2000, 50.

6. S. V. Brull, "The 'Velvet Hammer' of E-Commerce," *BusinessWeek Online*, 28 August 2000.

7. J. Fox, "Lumbering Toward B2B," *Fortune*, 12 June 2000, 264.

8. D. A. Blackmon, "eBricks, Gen-X Brainchild, Faces Off with Construction-Industry Barons," *The Wall Street Journal* Interactive Edition, 12 April 2000.

Despite such bold statements and predictions, many executives of leading brick and mortar firms remained unconvinced that B2B would revolutionize their industries, much less the entire global economy. One reporter captured those individuals' state of mind when he observed that only time would tell whether B2B proved to be a "transforming moment in American business" or simply another "fad juiced by manic investors and a trend-obsessed media."[9]

B2B: PREMISES AND PROMISES

The simple premise underlying Glen Meakem's plan that he presented to GE's top brass was that the company could use the Internet to slash its operating costs. Scan any article that discusses a financially distressed firm and you will almost certainly find that the company's management team is implementing "cost-cutting measures." Finding new and innovative methods to reduce costs is a goal shared by all businesses, regardless of the industry in which they operate, their financial condition, their location, or their size. In fact, the efforts of business executives to minimize transaction costs during and following the Industrial Revolution apparently led to the creation of hundreds of megacorporations across the globe.

In the 1930s, a young British scholar traveled to the United States to study several large American companies including Ford, General Motors, Union Carbide, U.S. Steel, and the country's major oil companies. Ronald Coase hoped to discover why large companies increasingly dominated the U.S. economy. Coase eventually found what he was searching for. "Firms are created, Coase concluded, because the additional cost of organizing them and maintaining them is cheaper than the transaction costs involved when individuals conduct business with each other."[10]

Coase defined transaction costs as incremental expenses or inefficiencies that increase the cost of a product or service. There are six general types of transaction costs: search, information, bargaining, decision, policing, and enforcement.[11] Buyers and sellers in a given market, for example, incur travel and communication costs to locate each other. Buyers often incur sizable "information" costs because they have to investigate the quality of products being offered by potential sellers. "Bargaining" costs include legal expenses necessary to negotiate contracts between, or among, the parties to a transaction.

To better understand the impact of Coase's transaction costs on the efficiency of manufacturing operations, consider an extreme example. General Motors can build 1,000 cars much more cheaply than can 1,000 individuals working independently—even if those individuals are mechanically inclined. Each of the latter individuals would be forced to absorb redundant expenditures that would increase the collective cost of the 1,000 automobiles they build. For example, each individual would incur search costs to locate a supplier for the battery needed to give his or her vehicle a "charge." Multiply the cost of one such search by 1,000 and you have the total search cost that would be included in the collective

---

9. A. Diba, "The B2B Boom: What's Real, What's Not," *Fortune*, 15 May 2000, 142.

10. L. Downes and C. Mui, *Unleashing the Killer App* (Boston: Harvard Business School Press, 1998), 39.

11. *Ibid.*, 37–38.

production expenditures of our 1,000 self-styled Henry Fords. On the other hand, the total production cost for the 1,000 cars manufactured in a GM factory would include the cost of only one search for a battery supplier.

Coase realized that the task of minimizing transaction costs posed a much greater challenge for certain companies than it did for others. In particular, companies operating in industries characterized by complex manufacturing activities and numerous suppliers, such as the automobile industry, faced potentially large inefficiencies in their operations. According to Coase, the solution to this problem was the formation of megacorporations. These massive firms could afford to establish internal cost-control mechanisms that would overcome the inefficiencies inherent in their operations. For example, a large firm can create a purchasing department to process purchase transactions uniformly and efficiently.

After completing his doctorate at the London School of Economics, Ronald Coase emigrated to the United States and eventually became an American citizen. He taught at several major universities including the University of Chicago from which he retired in 1981. More than 50 years after Coase began studying the nature of American businesses, his life's work was rewarded when he received the Nobel Prize for Economics. In late 2000, at the age of 90, *The New York Times* interviewed a still spry Professor Coase. When asked to comment on how the Internet would likely impact the future of large American companies, Coase replied that the Internet would allow those firms to become even larger. The Internet "enables you to have more specialization and greater production, because you're more efficient."[12] When pressed by his interviewer, Coase respectfully declined to comment further on that issue. "So much is wrong with economics that I'm trying to correct some other things now. And one doesn't need to study the actuarial tables to know there isn't a lot of time for that." Fortunately, other economists have used Coase's theories to explain in more depth why electronic marketplaces suddenly sprang to life in the late 1990s, with an assist from the Internet, of course, and forward-looking individuals such as Glen Meakem.

Internet-based marketplaces provide the means for businesses to eliminate, or at least significantly reduce, a wide range of transaction costs. By bringing buyers and sellers together in an online meeting place, B2B marketplaces dramatically reduce the search costs those parties incur to find each other. Likewise, by providing centralized databases that aggregate product availability and product quality data, these marketplaces drastically reduce the "information" transaction costs of buyers and sellers within an industry. Electronic marketplaces also promote head-to-head competition among sellers, which typically results in sellers being forced to lower their prices. B2B marketplaces give entire industries the ability to use the Internet as a "kind of central computer system—allowing companies to instantly check the inventories of their suppliers or make huge purchases—all with digital speed and efficiency."[13]

B2B marketplaces are particularly well suited for the large, complex manufacturing industries that Ronald Coase studied. Those industries typically use standardized components and supplies as the key inputs into their manufacturing

---

12. B. Tedeschi, "A Nobel-Prize Winning Idea, Conceived in the 30's, Is a Guide for the Net," *The New York Times*, 2 October 2000, C1.

13. D. A. Blackmon, "Where the Money Is," *The Wall Street Journal* Interactive Edition, 17 April 2000.

processes, items that readily lend themselves to being bought and sold sight-unseen in bulk quantities. Highly fragmented industries that have a large number of geographically dispersed buyers and sellers can also benefit significantly from the creation of B2B marketplaces. By early 2000, new electronic marketplaces were being announced on an almost daily basis. Examples of industries in which fast-thinking opportunists established websites to facilitate B2B commerce included automotive parts, construction supplies, electronic components, industrial chemicals, medical and laboratory supplies, among many others.

Entrepreneurs who created B2B websites promised significant cost savings to lure buyers and sellers to those marketplaces. One Wall Street analyst predicted that integrating the Internet into the procurement process would reduce by nearly $100 the cost to process a typical corporate purchase.[14] Another analyst predicted that B2B purchasing systems would allow General Motors and Ford to shave $3,000 from the production cost of a typical mid-size car.[15] An environmentally conscious B2B proponent noted that by eliminating much of the extensive "paper trail" produced by corporate purchases, electronic marketplaces would allow corporate America to "save a few forests."[16]

B2B: THE CAST OF PLAYERS

To obtain a thorough understanding of the B2B phenomenon, we must first identify the key "players" in this sector of the New Economy. The phrase "B2B" is most commonly used when referring to electronic marketplaces, such as FreeMarkets. Every electronic marketplace has one primary objective: to bring buyers and sellers together. However, there are several different types of electronic marketplaces. Some B2B marketplaces specialize in the "direct" materials used within a given manufacturing industry, while others focus exclusively on the ancillary or "indirect" materials or supplies required by a specific industry. A few B2B sites match buyers and sellers of professional services, for example, IT consulting services. Finally, some electronic marketplaces specialize in relatively low volume or niche markets. The California-based Patent & License Exchange brings together companies wanting to buy intellectual properties such as patents, copyrights, and trademarks. Listed among this B2B firm's clients are several Fortune 500 companies including 3M, Honeywell, and Procter & Gamble.

Numerous labels have been applied to B2B marketplaces including trading exchanges, b-webs (business webs), electronic communities, net markets, vertical hubs, vertical portals or "vortals," among many others. B2B "aggregators" operate websites that bring together a large number of B2B marketplaces across multiple industries. A common approach to classifying electronic marketplaces is by the specific method they utilize to create a market mechanism to prompt interaction between buyers and sellers. The most prevalent of these methods are reverse auctions, forward auctions, and exchanges.

14. N. D. Schwartz, "Playing the Internet's Next Gold Rush," *Fortune*, 15 May 2000, 178.

15. J. Doherty, "Learning the B-to-Bs," *Barron's*, 13 March 2000, 16.

16. M. Trottman, "Airlines Form Internet Marketplace, Following Trend Set by Auto Makers," *The Wall Street Journal* Interactive Edition, 28 April 2000.

In a reverse auction, a buyer indicates a need for a particular material and cites specifications such as size, weight, time it must be delivered and the amount the buyer is willing to pay. Suppliers then respond with quotes geared to that need. In a forward auction, a supplier posts an RFQ (request for quote) for a particular material it is selling. Companies then present their bids to buy it. An exchange, on the other hand, is a site that collects quotes from product suppliers and submits them to buyers.[17]

Most firms that operate B2B marketplaces charge a commission for their services based upon the dollar value of each transaction consummated at their website. Many of these firms also generate revenues by providing various services on a fee basis to their customers. These services include credit checks, quality assurance reports, and industry news services. Some B2B marketplaces rely heavily on advertising placed on their Web pages as a source of revenue. These latter sites include Global Sources, a Hong Kong-based B2B firm that brings together manufacturers, wholesalers, and retailers of consumer products.

The earliest B2B marketplaces were not associated with companies involved in the given industry that they served or professional organizations or other bodies linked to that industry. "Independent" B2B marketplaces that quickly made a name for themselves included Glen Meakem's FreeMarkets, VerticalNet, and Ventro, all of which were aggregators since they operated multiple B2B websites. FreeMarkets would eventually operate more than 100 B2B marketplaces that served companies in more than 50 countries. Most independent B2B sites chose to specialize in a given industry. ChemConnect, a site funded largely by Goldman Sachs, focused on bringing together buyers and sellers of industrial chemicals. As a class project, a group of Harvard MBA students developed a proposal for eBricks, an electronic marketplace for the construction industry. After obtaining a several million-dollar investment from Warburg Pincus, a major venture capital firm, the MBA students converted their group project into a real, if virtual, business.

Professional organizations and dominant companies in given industries soon recognized that they had more expertise and familiarity with the purchasing processes and suppliers within their industries than the companies creating independent B2B marketplaces for those industries. That realization spurred the creation of what some journalists referred to as ISMs—industry-sponsored marketplaces. Six large tire and rubber companies, including Goodyear and Michelin, banded together in early 2000 to form an electronic marketplace for their industry, Rubbernetwork.com. Boeing provided the primary financial support for Aerospan, a marketplace for the aviations industry. The highest profile B2B marketplace organized by an industry was Covisint, the B2B website created by the "Big Three" automakers, General Motors, Ford, and DaimlerChrysler. Analysts for the automotive industry projected that as much as $240 billion of purchase transactions would flow through the Covisint site each year once that marketplace became fully operational. Those same analysts also forecast that the B2B site would produce annual cost savings approaching $50 billion for the large automakers.

The B2B industry also includes hundreds of companies that operate as so-called "enablers" for e-commerce involving business entities. These firms develop the technology to create electronic marketplaces, the software applications

---

17. R. Banham, "The B-to-B Virtual Bazaar," *Journal of Accountancy*, July 2000, 26.

required by such sites, and the software products needed by companies to establish an online B2B capability. Ariba and Commerce One were among the companies that pioneered the development of important B2B software applications during the 1990s. Both companies develop software used to create and operate B2B sites and each markets popular e-procurement software packages that allow companies to link their computer networks with B2B marketplaces. Among other functions, e-procurement packages allow companies to automate their purchase orders and payments, which eliminates "the blizzards of faxes and invoices that conventional purchases inevitably generate."[18] Ariba also operates an online marketplace designed principally for small businesses wanting to purchase goods and services over the Internet.

Although Ariba and Commerce One produce competing software products and services, they have distinctly different operating strategies. Historically, Ariba has concentrated on selling its products and services to B2B clients, charging as much as $2 million for major applications. In lieu of cash payments, Commerce One often accepts a fractional ownership interest in the B2B marketplaces and other B2B businesses that it helps develop. Essentially, Commerce One places a "bet" on the viability and profitability of many of its clients.

Other leading B2B enablers include i2 Technologies, Oracle, and SAP. Besides marketing various B2B software applications, i2 Technologies operates the Trade-Matrix electronic marketplace that allows users to link up with a large number of other online marketplaces. During the 1990s, Larry Ellison built Oracle Corporation into the premier developer of database software. When the stock price of Microsoft's common stock plummeted in 2000, Ellison briefly supplanted Bill Gates as the wealthiest U.S. citizen. Oracle's database software allows major corporations to organize, reshape, and extract needed information from their enormous databases. When B2B e-commerce blossomed in the late 1990s, Larry Ellison recognized that his company could readily develop software products to meet the needs of electronic marketplaces and the companies that wanted to be participants in those marketplaces. Although software firms such as Ariba, Commerce One, and i2 Technologies had a sizable head start on Oracle in the B2B software market, Ellison and his subordinates quickly closed the gap. By mid-2000, *Fortune* magazine reported that nine of the top ten B2B sites used one or more Oracle software products.[19]

Throughout the 1990s, Oracle's principal competitor in the database software market was the German firm, SAP—Systemanalyse und Programmentwicklung—which translates roughly into "system analysis and program development." SAP is best known for its ERP (enterprise resource planning) software products that help companies link together their key functions—such as accounting, sales, human resources, manufacturing, etc.—into one seamless internal network. Like Oracle's management, SAP's executives recognized in the late 1990s that the rapidly growing B2B sector of e-commerce provided an opportunity to create a large and profitable new revenue stream for their company. Those executives immediately put their software engineers to work on new products that would compete with the early generation B2B software developed by Ariba and Commerce One. Within the software industry, SAP is known for being meticulous

---

18. Tully, "The B2B Tool That Really *Is* Changing the World," 133.

19. Schwartz, "Playing the Internet's Next Gold Rush," 180.

when it comes to developing and testing new products. That trait prevented the German firm from getting its B2B software products to market in time to take full advantage of the large spike in B2B software sales during 2000.

In March 2000, another software company announced that it would begin developing software applications for the B2B industry. That company, Microsoft, the leading software company in the world, had essentially ignored the B2B market since its inception a few years earlier. However, Microsoft's top executives promised that the software products their firm produced would pose serious and immediate challenges to existing B2B software products in terms of both overall functionality and price. Microsoft's decision to enter the B2B software market surprised few Internet analysts. The huge size of that market enticed the dozen or so largest software companies across the globe and hundreds of smaller software makers to begin developing B2B products. In the words of one journalist, "There's a war going on over who's going to build the next generation of B2B e-commerce."[20]

B2B Mania

The simple but powerful message that B2B marketplaces would yield huge cost savings and operating efficiencies for a wide range of industries quickly swept through the business world and captured the imagination of the business press, investors, and the general public. Internet "experts" provided eye-popping and, in many cases, largely indefensible predictions regarding the impact that B2B would have on the cost to manufacture specific products, on the profitability of individual companies and industries, and on the health of the national and global economies. Estimates of the revenues and profits that B2B marketplaces would produce in future years ranged widely and wildly from analyst to analyst. In May 2000, *Fortune* magazine reported B2B revenue forecasts issued by several prominent Wall Street investment houses and leading consulting firms, including Merrill Lynch and Forrester Research.[21] Those forecasts predicted that the dollar volume of transactions processed by B2B marketplaces in the year 2003 would be as high as $3.9 trillion or as low as $1.4 trillion. Comparable forecasts released by less prominent firms predicted total B2B transactions approaching $10 trillion by 2003.

The spine-tingling forecasts for B2B marketplaces caused an avalanche of investment capital to flow into companies that had established B2B sites and those that had announced an intention to do so. Among the major investors in B2B projects and stocks were the large venture capital firms that had provided early financing for hundreds of B2C websites. *Forbes* magazine reported that in 1999 alone, ICG, the large Internet incubator, invested more than $2 billion in 70 companies sponsoring or developing B2B marketplaces.[22] Several Wall Street investment firms also sunk enormous sums into new and unproven B2B projects. Gold-

20. M. Coleman, "Business-to-Business E-Commerce: Big B2B Winners?" *Investor's Business Daily*, 16 January 2001, A6.

21. Diba, "The B2B Boom," 143.

22. L. Kroll, "P2P or Bust," *Forbes*, 17 July 2000, 94.

man Sachs, arguably the most prominent Wall Street financier, invested more than $130 million in nearly two dozen B2B ventures during 1999. The common stocks of B2B companies that went public during this time frame soared. In early 2000, Commerce One's common stock reached a split-adjusted $423 per share after having been sold initially six months earlier for $21 per share. FreeMarkets' common stock reached an all-time high of $370 per share in January 2000, compared with an initial offering price of $48 just a few weeks earlier. In fact, FreeMarkets' common stock leaped from that initial offering price to more than $280 per share . . . on the first day the stock was publicly traded.

By early 2000, the mania over B2C companies and common stocks was beginning to die down. Disappointing sales figures reported for the Christmas 1999 holiday season by many leading B2C firms caused analysts and investors to question whether retail e-commerce would be as lucrative as most had originally thought. The waning interest in B2C ventures, when coupled with enthusiastic predictions in the press regarding the potential of B2B, diverted increasingly large amounts of investment capital into B2B projects. Many B2C companies that failed to generate substantial revenues during the B2C craze of the late 1990s hurriedly transformed themselves into B2B companies. These overnight conversions were typically desperate final attempts by those firms to remain in business by raising urgently needed financing from investors.

In July 2000, Deloitte Consulting, a leading consulting firm in information technology, reported that nearly 1,500 B2B marketplaces had been created.[23] Another Internet consulting firm predicted that the number of electronic marketplaces would likely double during 2001 and that 20,000 B2B websites would exist by 2003 if the "birth rate" of new sites continued unabated.[24] Often within a span of six months, or even less, an industry went from having no B2B marketplaces to having several dozen. Those marketplaces competed against each other for the same buyers and sellers, meaning that many of them had few transactions being consummated at their websites. One of the first B2B websites for the industrial chemicals industry was ChemConnect, the site backed by Goldman Sachs. On a worldwide basis, the industrial chemicals industry had total revenues approaching $2 trillion by the year 2000. Given that figure, few analysts doubted that ChemConnect would become a viable and profitable operation. But, after nearly 50 online marketplaces suddenly sprouted in the chemicals industry, ChemConnect's future looked much less rosy.

The overcrowded condition of the new B2B industry quickly began taking a toll on the weaker competitors within the industry. Many B2B sites created during early 2000 failed to survive until the end of the year. In fact, according to press reports, dozens of B2B sites never processed any transactions before being closed down by their founders. Among the first B2B sites shut down were several operated by Ventro, an early B2B aggregator that had planned to establish an electronic marketplace for every major industry. Ventro's decision to shutter Chemdex, a much-hyped site designed to serve the chemicals industry, shocked many Internet observers. According to one business journalist, the Chemdex site

---

23. *Financial Times*, "Internet Rain Puts a Bloom on the Business-to-Business Marketplace," 18 October 2000, 1.

24. *Ibid.*

"had been a veritable poster child for the e-market revolution."[25] A few months earlier, Goldman Sachs and the other owners of ChemConnect had been forced to scrub a planned IPO for that B2B company when its revenues failed to reach projected levels.

As the year 2000 progressed, it became apparent to most e-commerce insiders that the young B2B industry was extremely troubled. That realization caused the stock prices of most B2B companies to come crashing back to earth. From mid-2000 through the spring of 2001, the stock prices of Commerce One and FreeMarkets fell into single digits, reflecting a more than 90 percent decline in the value of each security. Over that same time frame, the Delphi Top 50 B2B Index, which tracks the leading B2B firms, also declined by more than 90 percent.

RETHINKING THE B2B CONCEPT

The failure of hundreds of B2B marketplaces to become viable and the corresponding collapse in the prices of most B2B stocks by early 2001 sent Internet experts, Wall Street analysts, and Main Street investors on a search for answers, answers as to why much of the potential of the B2B Internet sector had gone, at least temporarily, unfulfilled. One problem was obvious to even the most naïve observer of B2B e-commerce: there were simply too many B2B marketplaces created during the manic early days of the B2B craze. In industry after industry, corporate executives and other industry spokespeople insisted that only one or two B2B sites were needed, even in large, worldwide industries such as industrial chemicals.

A further examination of the B2B craze uncovered several additional problems and issues that prevented many electronic marketplaces from becoming viable, among them some of the most heavily capitalized and widely touted B2B sites. Early B2B sites were typically created by groups of IT consultants who did not have strong connections to the industry that their online marketplace was intended to serve. These individuals had the technological expertise to create an online market mechanism for a given industry but did not have personal relationships with key buyers and sellers in the industry nor an in-depth understanding of the industry's key operating features and characteristics. Independent B2B operators "tried to wedge themselves between existing business partnerships" with the objective of obtaining "a piece of the transactions" executed between those buyers and sellers.[26] Instead of attempting to establish relationships with buyers and sellers within an industry and becoming very familiar with the important features and idiosyncrasies of that industry, the developers of most independent B2B sites simply focused on becoming operational as soon as possible. "In their rush to get online, the companies that run the [B2B] exchanges haven't taken the time to study their customers' priorities. . . . They've simply used off-the-shelf software to set up simple auctions as quickly as possible."[27]

25. R. Karpinksi, "Ventro Pulls Plug on E-Marketplaces," *B2B* (Crain Communications), 18 December 2000, 3.

26. *Investor's Business Daily*, "The Stunning Turn of B2B: Boom to Bust," 2 January 2001, A8.

27. R. Wise and D. Morrison, "Beyond the Exchange: The Future of B2B," *Harvard Business Review*, November/December 2000, 86.

Another mistake made by independent B2B sites was defining their role very narrowly as helping buyers reduce the acquisition cost of materials, supplies, and other goods and services they needed in their business operations. In fact, price is not necessarily the most important feature of business-to-business transactions.

> The value proposition offered by most [B2B] exchanges—competitive bidding among suppliers allows buyers to get the lowest possible prices—runs counter to the best thinking on buyer-supplier relations. Most companies have come to realize that getting supplies at the lowest price may not be in their best economic interest. Other factors, such as quality, timing of deliveries, and customization are often more important than price in determining the overall value provided by a supplier. . . . Many companies have spent . . . decades methodically forging tighter, more strategic relationships with suppliers. The online exchanges' focus on arm's-length, price-driven transactions flies in the face of all this hard work.[28]

The critical mistakes made by the managers of independent B2B sites that were hurriedly organized and rushed into operation provided an opportunity for industry-sponsored marketplaces to step in and establish themselves. These second-generation B2Bs were typically organized by the dominant companies in a given industry—companies that were well aware of the multi-dimensional nature of buyer-seller relationships in their industry. More important, these dominant companies recognized that by creating their own B2B exchanges they could capture the bulk of the cost savings produced by the new mode of Internet-based purchasing. As one journalist noted, allowing independent B2B sites to take over an industry's purchasing function was "an exercise in value transfer" not "value creation."[29] In other words, why let interlopers new to an industry pocket the considerable cost savings stemming from the creation of electronic marketplaces?

The prototype for an industry-sponsored marketplace is Covisint, the B2B site organized by the Big Three automakers in early 2000. Covisint gained instant credibility within the automotive industry thanks to the influence wielded by General Motors, Ford, and DaimlerChrysler. The new B2B marketplace quickly signed dozens of automotive parts suppliers and other vendors to participation agreements. Several smaller automobile manufacturers also expressed an interest in becoming involved in Covisint. Peugeot-Citroen and Renault, both of France, and Japan-based Nissan eventually joined the Covisint alliance, while Volkswagen chose to sponsor its own B2B site.

Leading Internet analysts predicted that the move to create industry-sponsored B2B marketplaces would eventually result in the realization of the huge expectations that had surrounded the introduction of the B2B concept by Glen Meakem and other B2B pioneers. The parties that stood to benefit the most from the trend toward industry-sponsored B2B sites were the dominant companies that organized them and their smaller peers within their given industries. Other winners would be the enablers that helped develop the expensive industry B2B sites and that sold the software allowing buyers and sellers to link up with those sites. These so-called "infrastructure" companies included Ariba, Commerce One, i2 Technologies, Microsoft, and Oracle, among many others. Com-

---

28. *Ibid.*

29. J. W. Gurley, "BigCompany.com: Should You Start a B2B Exchange?" *Fortune*, 3 April 2000, 260.

merce One and Oracle scored an early coup in the race to build industry-sponsored B2B marketplaces when they were chosen by the Big Three automakers to oversee the development of Covisint. Reportedly, the Covisint site alone, would require expenditures approaching $400 million, the largest chunks of which would go to Commerce One and Oracle.

The companies that stood to lose the most in the face of the trend toward industry-sponsored marketplaces were those B2B firms that had few, if any, direct links to the industries they served. Many experts believed that the only independent B2B firms likely to thrive or even survive were firms such as FreeMarkets that had gotten a head start on weaker competitors and had managed to develop considerable "domain expertise" and credibility with key players in the industries they served. Throughout 2000, FreeMarkets ranked among the busiest B2B websites. But, FreeMarkets' perch near the top of most B2B rankings was perilous, at best, since it lost one of its largest customers, General Motors, when the Covisint marketplace was created.

Despite the renewed optimism regarding the B2B concept triggered by the move to industry-sponsored marketplaces, these businesses also faced numerous challenges that had to be overcome before they could fully realize their potential. Among the largest of these challenges are the antitrust issues posed by these B2B sites. For example, before Covisint could begin operating, it had to undergo an extensive investigation by the Federal Trade Commission (FTC). The FTC questioned whether Covisint "could lead to collusion, illegal price signaling or other exchanges of sensitive business data, or illegal collective action by the auto makers to suppress prices charged by suppliers."[30] Following a six-month investigation, the FTC granted approval for Covisint to begin operating in late 2000.

Another challenge faced by industry-sponsored marketplaces is the need to establish electronic standards and protocols for all participants to minimize the risk of botched transactions and communications. In 2000, an industry-sponsored marketplace was organized for wholesalers and manufacturers of electronic components and computers. When Arrow Electronics attempted to make a $31,500 purchase from Intel at that marketplace, a glitch in the B2B software caused the transaction to be processed for $31.5 million.[31] Industry-sponsored B2B sites also face several legal issues. For example, who will own the large databases of valuable information accumulated as a by-product of their operations? Likewise, how will these sites ensure that confidential proprietary information of their buyers and sellers is shielded from other participants and from external parties? "Privacy concerns are also sticky. Will company executives that have a seat on the [B2B] exchange's board of directors be privy to confidential information about their competitors?"[32]

No doubt, industry-sponsored B2B sites will continue to struggle with a laundry list of challenges and unresolved issues in coming years. Nevertheless, the FTC's approval of Covisint in the fall of 2000 was seen as a watershed event by most Internet observers. That approval seemed to clear the way for the creation of industry-sponsored marketplaces in most industries.

---

30. J. R. Wilke, "U.S. Antitrust Regulators Approve Car Makers' Online Parts Exchange," *The Wall Street Journal* Interactive Edition, 11 September 2000.

31. D. A. Blackmon, "Where the Money Is," *The Wall Street Journal* Interactive Edition, 17 April 2000.

32. P. Patsuris, "B2B Exchanges Still in the Dark," *Forbes.com*, 12 September 2000.

GE GOES TO B2B . . . FINALLY

By the fall of 2001, several hundred B2B sites had stopped operating, while a large number of others had merged or consolidated their operations. But, leading Internet analysts believed that the turbulent "shakeout" period for the new industry was nearing an end. A key signal of the industry's improving condition was the solid, if not impressive, operating results being reported by many surviving B2B firms. Within the first six months of 2001, ChemConnect processed more than $1 billion of transactions for the chemicals industry. During the same time frame, automakers funneled $33 billion of purchases through the Covisint site. Easily among the busiest B2B websites over the past few years has been EnronOnline, an electronic marketplace designed to bring together buyers and sellers of various energy commodities including natural gas, oil, and electricity. From late 1999 through late 2001, EnronOnline processed nearly $700 billion of transactions. Despite the growing volume of online B2B energy transactions, the future of EnronOnline seems perilous, at best. In December 2001, EnronOnline's parent company, Enron Corporation, stunned the business world and the nation by filing for bankruptcy.

Throughout the period when B2B stock prices were collapsing and large numbers of B2B sites were being dismantled, most Internet analysts never backed off their optimistic projections regarding the revenues and traffic that B2B sites would eventually produce. Instead, those analysts continued to forecast huge revenues for the B2B industry within a few years. Why did analysts remain so convinced that B2B e-commerce would become viable? Because those analysts recognized that well designed and operated B2B marketplaces provided companies the ability to slash and, in some cases, eliminate many of the transaction costs studied by Ronald Coase some six decades earlier.

Despite the volatile ups and downs that the B2B industry has experienced over its short life, the industry's bright prospects almost certainly provide a sense of vindication for Glen Meakem. By the fall of 2001, Meakem's firm, FreeMarkets, had handled millions of transactions and, in the process, saved its clients nearly $5 billion.[33] Ironically, one of the biggest B2B "players" is now General Electric, Meakem's former employer that rejected his grand scheme to create B2B marketplaces. The financial services unit of GE, GE Capital, has helped develop and finance numerous B2B sites for several industries. One of the largest B2B sites around the globe is the multi-industry GE Global Exchange Services or GXS. That B2B site boasts more than 100,000 participants and operates in nearly 60 countries. That statistic alone, provides Glen Meakem with every right to smugly tell his former GE superiors . . . "I told you so."

QUESTIONS

1. Research online or hard copy sources and identify five recent statistics reported in the press that relate to the B2B industry. List those statistics and ex-

---

33. N. Weinberg, "B2B Grows Up," *Forbes.com*, 10 September 2001.

plain the significance of each. Collectively, what insights do those statistics provide regarding the future of B2B e-commerce?

2. Identify two B2B marketplaces that are not discussed in this case. For each of these marketplaces, obtain the following information: its website address, the name of the company or organization that operates the site, the principal market or markets that it serves, its principal source of revenue, and any other information that you believe provides important insight on the nature of the marketplace and/or its operations.

3. Go to the website of a software company that sells B2B software products. Identify three major software products marketed by that company. List those products and the key features of each.

4. Choose two industries that are not referred to in this case. For each of those industries, explain whether or not you believe it is well suited for a B2B marketplace. Your explanations should include a discussion of one or more of Ronald Coase's "transaction costs."

5. Both B2C and B2B e-commerce fell victim to "hype" and the resulting unrealistic expectations that many parties had regarding these two sectors of the New Economy. In your view, what party or parties were responsible for overstating the potential of B2C and B2B commerce? What parties benefited from the unrealistic expectations created for the two types of e-commerce and what parties were adversely affected?

Wapathy and Waplash: Welcome to the Wireless Internet

*All progress is precarious, and the solution
of one problem brings us face to face with another.*

Martin Luther King, Jr.

Be prepared is the two-word motto of the Boy Scouts of America. "Be careful" is a motto that business executives should use when selecting a name for a new product or service. A new product burdened with a bad name may be doomed to also-ran status despite being cheaper and superior in other respects to the old standbys. Many major companies have spent huge sums to select and test market names for a new product only to suffer ridicule at the hands of the business press when it finally hits the market.

Ford Motor Company has a long and proud history within the auto industry. The company's product managers have developed many models that have introduced the public to important new advancements in automotive style and engineering. Contributing significantly to the success of those models have been vigorous promotional campaigns directed by the company's top marketing executives. Those efforts typically include tense brainstorming sessions during the early developmental stage for a model to come up with an appealing and attention-grabbing name. Names such as "Thunderbird," "Mustang," and "Explorer" helped make each of those vehicles bestsellers for Ford.

On the other hand, Ford's marketing staff has tagged a few new vehicles with clunky monikers that triggered years of abuse from late night comedians. For example, what were Ford's marketing gurus thinking when they named a sleek new car the Ford "Probe"? During the 1950s, Ford invested heavily in a new model that sported an array of distinctive features that the car-buying public was apparently not ready to embrace. To make matters worse, the name chosen for the car, Edsel—a Ford family name, turned off potential buyers. Decades later, the term "Edsel" serves as a synonym for a new product that not only fails to capture the imagination of the public but effectively repels potential consumers.

In the late 1990s, a large consortium of technology companies tackled the job of developing a new software product to benefit users of wireless telecommunications services. The consortium intended to develop a set of "open source" technical specifications that could be used uniformly around the globe to connect mobile phones and other wireless devices to the Internet. That consortium of more than 100 companies and organizations included such high-tech and international heavyweights as Alcatel, Ericsson, IBM, Nokia, and Sony, among many others. This new product was named the "wireless application protocol." But, that name was quickly forgotten as industry insiders and novices, alike, adopted the easier-to-remember but vaguely rude-sounding three-letter acronym "WAP."

Corporate marketers are not the only individuals who recognize the importance of catchy tag lines and one-word zingers. Business journalists constantly search for snappy terms, cute expressions, and double entendres that they can embed in the titles to their articles to attract potential readers. Reporters for the *The Wall Street Journal*, *The New York Times*, *Business Week*, and other periodicals could not wait to exercise their poetic license on "WAP" when that term was introduced in the late 1990s. Shortly after WAP began appearing in new wireless products, journalists were condemning the technology to an Edsel-like existence by taking advantage of the numerous plays on words that its abbreviated name offered for the taking. Journalists insisted that the business community was suffering from "Wapathy" well before the new technology had an opportunity to establish itself. Other journalists suggested that the consortium of high-tech companies and organizations that developed the wireless application protocol would soon be experiencing "Waplash" as the public became disenchanted with their creation.

Initially, journalists could not decide whether "WAP" should be pronounced with a hard or soft "a." So, they used both variations, no doubt to double their pleasure. "WAP is a flop," and "WAP is crap" were widely used putdowns. Over time, most members of the business press adopted the hard "a" pronunciation for WAP, as in, "WAP is no killer app." A few fair-minded reporters eventually decided that they and their peers had not given the new wireless technology an opportunity to prove itself. So, these modern-day Longfellows came up with the apologetic tag line, "WAP has gotten a bad rap."

THE BIRTH OF THE WIRELESS INTERNET AND M-COMMERCE

The rapid growth of the Internet and the World Wide Web was not the only high-tech trend evident during the 1990s. That decade also witnessed a surge in the use of mobile phones and other "information appliances," including pagers, beepers, Palm Pilots, and a long list of other PDAs (personal digital assistants). One business reporter noted that the Internet Revolution was being paralleled by the birth of the "era of information appliances."[1] Wireless phones were especially popular in Europe. By 1997, Finland had the highest per capita use of wireless phones in the world, thanks largely to Helsinki-based Nokia, the leading company in the mobile phone industry. Three years later, nearly two-thirds of all citizens of European Union (EU) countries owned a mobile phone compared to only one-third of all U.S. residents.

The growing popularity of mobile phones and other information appliances during the Internet boom of the 1990s prompted many companies to search for

---

1. D. Gillmor, "Here's a Quick Test: When You Imagine the Internet, What Do You See?" *San Jose Mercury News* 9 (online), 11 April 1999.

strategies to take advantage of those parallel trends. The most obvious of those strategies was to provide access to the Internet via wireless devices. Information technology (IT) engineers recognized that extant technology would not allow wireless users to readily surf the World Wide Web with their handheld devices. Instead, a new, condensed version of the Web would have to be created to serve wireless users, the so-called wireless Web.

Interest in developing the wireless Internet and wireless Web was particularly prevalent in those countries where mobile phones were widely used. In addition to EU countries, mobile phone usage was very high in certain countries of the Far East, including Japan, South Korea, and Hong Kong. In both the EU and the major industrialized powers of the Far East, home access to the Internet was not nearly as common as in the United States. Among other factors, unreliable telecommunications lines and the cost of personal computers had prevented large numbers of citizens in those two regions of the world from regularly surfing the Internet.

In the brief history of the Internet, most major technological breakthroughs have been widely heralded and hyped well before their usefulness has been clearly established. That was certainly true of the wireless Internet. In the minds of many self-appointed experts, the combination of the Internet and wireless technology was a "can't miss" proposition. An academic at the Massachusetts Institute of Technology predicted that, "All the things that have happened on the Internet so far are likely to be dwarfed by what happens when the Internet goes wireless."[2] An executive with Sprint PCS, the telecommunications giant, made a similar prediction regarding the wireless Internet. "People will look back on it as they do with the Internet today and say, 'How did we get along without this?'"[3]

Many financial analysts and other parties who track the Internet sector expected the spread of wireless Internet access to trigger a sharp increase in electronic commerce. "You can only attract so many people to PCs. . . . Wireless is almost limitless," observed a CEO of a technology consulting firm who went on to predict that "mobile commerce is going to take us all by storm."[4] "Mobile commerce" soon became the hottest new phrase among business journalists, venture capitalists, and individual investors. As always, in the interest of efficiency, the phrase "mobile commerce" had to be replaced with a zippier, New Age appellation. "M-commerce" became the accepted code word for this new segment of the Internet economy, although a few out-of-step journalists insisted on using the phrase "w-commerce"—wireless commerce.

Off-the-cuff comments regarding the grand potential of m-commerce were soon buttressed by a flurry of hard data and economic forecasts collected and distributed by Internet research firms and other agencies. The Gartner Group reported that nearly 400 million mobile phones were sold worldwide in 2000—70 million in the United States; by 2003, the Internet consulting firm estimated that

2. J. M. Moran, "Web Firms Taking Steps Toward Wireless," *Hartford Courant*, 26 October 2000, E2.

3. G. Creno, "Is M-Commerce Worth the Trouble?; Wireless Shopping Is Calling America," *Arizona Republic*, 3 September 2000, D1.

4. J. Kutler, "Un Wired; Banks Again in Catch-Up Mode as Wireless Devices Widen Net," *The American Banker* (online), 6 August 1999.

nearly 700 million mobile phones would be sold annually, including 150 million in the United States.[5] Since most mobile phones sold in 2001 and beyond would be Internet-ready, the pool of potential wireless Internet users was growing rapidly. Analysts tracking the telephone industry predicted that by 2003, or there-abouts, the annual volume of calls placed on mobile phones would surpass those made on fixed-line networks.[6] Many of those calls would involve what analysts enjoyed referring to as "dialing for dollars," that is, m-commerce. International Data Corporation (IDC), an Internet research firm, projected that 47 million Europeans and 29 million Americans would be m-commerce consumers by 2004.[7] *Investor's Business Daily* reported in June 2000 that total m-commerce revenues would likely reach $100 billion annually within a few years.[8] Such forecasts convinced growing numbers of companies to include wireless technology in their new strategic initiatives.

The companies and organizations tirelessly promoting the wireless Internet realized that several hurdles had to be overcome before m-commerce could become a major contributor to the New Economy. One of the biggest challenges that had to be addressed was the lack of uniformity in Internet access standards and protocols across the dozens of mobile phone and wireless device manufacturers. To resolve that problem, the Wireless Application Protocol Forum was created. This organization set about the task of developing a "vendor-neutral and network-independent open specification [to serve as] the unified worldwide standard for providing wireless Internet access from handheld devices."[9] In simple terms, WAP would serve as a wireless Web browser. "Think of WAP as a new sort of browser fitted to the next wave of mobile phones, allowing them to access specially adapted Web pages. Normal Web pages, the sort you look at on your PC, take an age to download into a mobile and are ill-suited for the handset's small screen. WAP ensures that the pages are configured for mobiles."[10]

A principal objective of the international WAP Forum was to jumpstart m-commerce with the eventual goal of making the wireless Web self-sustaining. Once m-commerce began producing credible revenue streams, companies could more readily justify investing large sums to pursue and develop wireless Internet initiatives. While WAP was being developed, companies began positioning themselves to take advantage of this newest, next big thing involving the Internet. "As wireless technology comes online that lets people access the Internet on the fly, companies positioned to absorb this migration from fixed-line networks will be the big winners of the wireless Web."[11]

---

5. Creno, "Is M-Commerce Worth the Trouble?"

6. W. Boston, "Wireless Auctions Wind Down in Europe. Now What?" *The Wall Street Journal*, 23 August 2000, A17.

7. G. Naik and A. Latour, "Overseas, People Use Mobile Phones to Bank, Buy Wine, and Pay Rent," *The Wall Street Journal* Interactive Edition, 18 August 2000.

8. E. Nash, "Trends," *Investor's Business Daily*, 27 June 2000, 2.

9. *Business Wire* (online), "Wireless Application Protocol Embraced by All Sectors of Worldwide Telecommunications Industry," 11 November 1998.

10. J. Doward, "Internet Unplugged: Wired Up on a PC? Next-Generation Mobiles Will End All That," *The Observer*, 12 December 1999, 9.

11. Boston, "Wireless Auctions Wind Down in Europe."

M-COMMERCE GETS OFF TO A STUMBLING START

In the early days of the wireless Internet, marketing experts and Internet consultants identified several products and services they believed were ideally suited for m-commerce. Consumers were expected to use the freedom and flexibility afforded by wireless Internet connections to do their banking and brokerage transactions while commuting to and from work, while having lunch at the local pizzeria, or even "under the table" during a boring sales presentation or other meeting in their employer's conference room. Merchandise considered "impulse purchase" items—including books, flowers, and software—were also projected to be hot sellers for m-commerce. eBay, Yahoo!, Amazon.com, and other companies operating Internet auction houses expected the spread of wireless technology to boost their traffic and revenues. Finally, Internet-related activities that demand privacy, including Web-based gambling and purchases of adult entertainment materials, seemed perfect for the wireless domain.

Another important source of m-commerce revenues would be the fees collected from wireless users by the telecommunications companies that controlled the airwaves over which those consumers would access the Internet. The telecoms also hoped to collect "rake-offs" or small commissions on transactions completed over their airwaves and to generate revenues from allowing companies to place electronic ads on the mobile handset display screens of wireless users. Internet portals, principally AOL and Yahoo!, also hoped that the wireless Web would provide them with a new source of customers and revenues. One problem these firms faced, however, was that several of the telecommunications companies planned to become *de facto* portals for the wireless Web. Executives of both AOL and Yahoo! launched efforts to persuade major telecommunications firms to work with them to create portals for the wireless Web—and to share the resulting revenues.

M-commerce got off to a slow start in the United States and in most other regions of the world despite the widespread interest in developing and promoting the wireless Internet and the introduction of WAP in the late 1990s. Ground zero for m-commerce was 1999. According to IDC, only 44,000 Europeans and even fewer U.S. citizens used a mobile phone or other handheld device during 1999 to make a purchase on the wireless Web.[12] Those figures rose only modestly the following year. Many of the problems that impeded the development of m-commerce were painfully obvious. For example, the small and monochromatic displays of most mobile phones and wireless devices were clearly not well suited for viewing anything more than basic text. Wireless users complained that their displays presented only "snippets" or "dabs" of the Web content they were accustomed to accessing over their PCs. Entering data on the small keypads of mobile devices also proved to be very cumbersome. Making the process even more awkward was the need to learn the entry code for each letter of the alphabet—for example, depressing the "2" button three times to enter "C" on a handset.

The earliest mobile phones capable of accessing the Internet downloaded information at a tortuously slow pace. Wireless users killing time waiting for a

---

12. Naik and Latour, "Overseas, People Use Mobile Phones to Bank, Buy Wine, and Pay Rent."

delayed flight could run up several dollars in access charges obtaining a weather report for New York City, the final score of the Knicks-Sixers game, and the closing price of Microsoft's common stock. Even more problematic was losing your wireless connection just as you were getting ready to close an important stock transaction. Concerns over security also proved to be a major stumbling block for m-commerce. Most consumers were not reassured by the insistence of security experts that credit card numbers and other confidential data transmitted over a wireless connection were less likely to be intercepted by high-tech thieves than such information transmitted over a phone line.

Despite the efforts of the WAP Forum and other industry organizations, a confusing maze of wireless products and standards plagued the early years of m-commerce, particularly in the United States. Some companies simply refused to cooperate with their competitors and ignored WAP and other industry-wide standards. Problems posed by technical and technological constraints and related issues proved to be significant obstacles to early m-commerce efforts; however, the most significant impediment to early m-commerce was a psychological barrier created by companies involved in the wireless industry. Those companies grossly inflated the public's expectations for the wireless Internet and m-commerce. Telecom companies such as AT&T Wireless and Sprint PCS gave "the impression that cruising the Internet on your mobile phone is a breeze if you just sign up for their services," while the cell phone makers often embellished the benefits of WAP technology "as a way of selling a new generation of pricier Web-enabled phones."[13]

To further their own economic interests, companies promoting the wireless Internet and its various uses, including m-commerce, ignored or, at least, obscured a fundamental reality, namely, that "the wireless Internet is not the Internet wireless."[14] A senior analyst at IDC observed that many purchasers of Web-ready mobile phones were led to believe that "the wireless Web is a PC screen just squished down to a phone."[15] That simply was not true. The wireless Web was an entirely new universe that was still languishing in the Stone Age of the high-tech evolutionary process. "For now the mobile experience is more Flintstones than Jetsons. The devices needed for such transactions are laughably awkward, connection times are maddeningly slow, and only a fraction of retailers on the Internet are set up for shopping through wireless channels, which requires a whole additional set of software and links."[16]

By late 2000, many Internet analysts began scaling back the optimistic forecasts they had made regarding the eventual size and scope of wireless commerce. In December 2000, Forrester Research, among the most prominent and conservative Internet research firms, predicted that worldwide retail sales via m-commerce would amount to no more than $3.4 billion by 2005 or approximately 0.1 percent

13. W. S. Mossberg, "Guide for the Perplexed," *Smart Money*, September 2000, 84.

14. J. Graham, "Cell Phones Giving More and More Traders a Hand," *Investor's Business Daily*, 25 May 2001, A7.

15. A. Petersen, "U.S. Providers Bet More Americans Will Shop via Their Mobile Phones," *The Wall Street Journal* Interactive Edition, 18 August 2000.

16. L. Kaufman, "Shopping in Palm of the Hand Is Making Its Holiday Debut," *The New York Times*, 11 November 2000, A1.

of all retail sales.[17] That figure stunned companies that had invested heavily to develop an m-commerce capability and caused many of them to begin rethinking their wireless Internet strategy.

In May 2001, Barnes & Noble stopped selling merchandise on its wireless website. That same month, Amazon.com reported that it had trimmed the size of its "Amazon Anywhere" mobile initiative. In responding to a direct question by a *Wall Street Journal* reporter, an Amazon spokesperson confirmed that the company's expectations for that initiative had not been fulfilled. "Yes, we did scale the [m-commerce] team back as a lot of companies did when they realized that the bold predictions for penetration [of m-commerce] in the market were not panning out."[18] According to an unnamed company insider, Amazon's m-commerce revenues amounted to a microscopic $1 million for all of 2000.

Another major company that acknowledged in the spring of 2001 that m-commerce had been a major disappointment was AOL Time Warner. The president of AOL Mobile, the company's m-commerce division, candidly discussed its unimpressive financial performance to that point and readily admitted that she expected the unit to continue struggling for some time. "We're really in the early stages [of m-commerce]. It depends, again, on creating a broader audience than exists today. Until we pull a mass market onto the wireless platform to read their e-mail, to look at content, the advertising and mobile commerce revenue isn't going to be very interesting."[19]

Despite the dismal early performance of most major m-commerce initiatives, there were exceptions. The most notable exception came from the Land of the Rising Sun. A company that few Americans was aware of developed a unique and aggressive approach to m-commerce in the late 1990s that proved to be profitable from its inception. NTT DoCoMo's m-commerce business plan was so successful in Japan by early 2001 that company management intended to export that business model to other countries.

GOOD MOJO AT DOCOMO

In 1992, a deregulatory plan adopted by the Japanese government required the nation's largest telecommunications company, Nippon Telegraph & Telephone (NTT), to spin off its mobile phone division. That division went by the name DoCoMo, a shorthand version of "Do Communications over the Mobile network," and a name that roughly refers to the Japanese term for "anywhere." The new company was named NTT DoCoMo, although it is most often referred to as DoCoMo.

The initial goal of DoCoMo's management team in the early 1990s was to become Japan's dominant mobile phone company. By the late 1990s, the company

---

17. A. E. Johnson, "Report Sees Slow Start to M-Commerce," *Financial Times*, 11 December 2000, 28.

18. N. Wingfield, "Amazon.com's 'M-Commerce' Effort Fizzles Along with the Wireless Web," *The Wall Street Journal* Interactive Edition, 7 May 2001.

19. R. Krause, "AOL's Hook: 'You Really Need to Get People Used to It,'" *Investor's Business Daily*, 25 May 2001.

had easily achieved that goal and, in fact, had become the third largest mobile phone company in the world. Company press releases in the summer of 2001 reported that DoCoMo had 63 million subscribers to its mobile phone service, which represented almost one-half of Japan's total population. After conquering Japan's mobile phone market, DoCoMo's executives established another lofty objective for their firm: to become the nation's leading supplier of mobile Internet services. Unlike most mobile Internet service suppliers in Japan and elsewhere in the world, DoCoMo did not adopt WAP technology. Instead, the company developed a proprietary technology known as "i-mode" to provide mobile phone users access to the Internet. At various times, company officials, journalists, and others have suggested that the "i" in i-mode refers to "information," "Internet," "interactive," or "independent."

From its inception, i-mode was extremely popular among Japanese citizens, few of whom had an Internet-linked PC at home. The ability to communicate electronically at a modest cost was the feature most responsible for the Japanese public's immediate and overwhelmingly favorable response to i-mode. To help i-mode users communicate more efficiently via their mobile keypads, the company developed a series of symbols and icons that users could activate with two-digit codes.

Initially, many industry insiders believed that DoCoMo made a serious strategic blunder by designing i-mode to appeal principally to individual consumers rather than developing it as a business-to-business (B2B) service. Company officials made that decision principally because they were aware that millions of Japanese spend as much as three hours per day commuting to and from work. They reasoned that with the help of i-mode, individuals could use that time to complete a wide range of tasks or, alternatively, to more readily and enjoyably "kill time." Shortly following the introduction of the new service, millions of Japanese citizens were using i-mode to access news reports, review movie listings, check on weather forecasts, complete bank transactions, trade stocks and, of course, zap messages to friends and family members. One segment of the consumer market particularly attracted to i-mode was the under-20 crowd. Many Japanese youths quickly became hooked on i-mode and spent several hours per day using the service to download cartoons, play interactive games, and swap electronic notes with their friends.

DoCoMo's i-mode is different in several important respects from mobile phone services based on WAP specifications. First, i-mode offers subscribers the convenience of a constant Internet connection; whenever an i-mode subscriber's phone is turned on, the subscriber is linked to the Internet. Second, unlike WAP services, the computer code used to create i-mode websites is written in compact HTML, a subset of HTML, which is used to create websites for the wired Web. This feature allows "content suppliers" to easily convert their wired websites to i-mode websites. Third, i-mode's technology allows DoCoMo to charge subscribers based upon the amount of data received rather than the time they spend connected to the Internet, a feature subscribers find particularly appealing. Other technical features that make i-mode attractive include larger display screens on DoCoMo's mobile handsets and more impressive graphics than WAP-based applications, including limited color capability. DoCoMo's handsets also have considerably longer battery lives than most competing products.

The dissimilarities between i-mode and other mobile Internet services do not end with technical and technological differences. DoCoMo's executives developed an innovative business model for their wireless Internet service oriented around the consumer market they were targeting. The key to this business model is encouraging content suppliers to develop a large number of high-quality websites that DoCoMo's subscribers will want to visit. Content suppliers are more than willing to cooperate given the ease with which their wired websites can be converted to i-mode websites. By late 2001, DoCoMo's subscribers could access more than 50,000 i-mode formatted websites on the wireless Web.

The most unique, if not revolutionary, facets of DoCoMo's business model are the revenue streams the company has created. Subscribers pay a modest monthly subscription fee that permits them to access most i-mode websites. However, the company has hundreds of "premium" sites that subscribers pay additional monthly fees to access—fees that typically range between $1 to $3 per site. Premium sites tend to be heavily trafficked sites created by high-profile content suppliers, such as the Walt Disney Company. DoCoMo charges its subscribers a small monthly fee for the right to download Disney cartoons, songs, and other information from the Disney i-mode site. The company collects such "micropayments" from its subscribers by simply adding the charges to their monthly phone bills.

DoCoMo profits from the arrangements with its content suppliers by deducting a 9 percent commission or collection fee from the amounts that it periodically remits to those suppliers. Each time a subscriber downloads data from a premium site, DoCoMo also charges the subscriber a fee based upon the volume of information downloaded. Another, more conventional revenue stream for DoCoMo is payments made to the company by premium content suppliers and other firms to advertise their products and services on the mobile handset display screens of DoCoMo's subscribers.

Internet financial analysts and consultants have praised DoCoMo's executives for correcting a flaw in the prototype Internet business model used by content suppliers that rushed to the wired Web beginning in the early and mid-1990s. "i-mode addresses a critical mistake made by Internet [e-commerce] pioneers. Businesses should never have put so much content on the Web for free. Now, it's almost impossible to go back and start charging computer users for news and information. . . . If you make bad content, you get nothing. If you make good content, you get nothing. Quality costs money."[20] These same analysts and consultants also believe that DoCoMo made a wise strategic decision by focusing its m-commerce efforts on "small-ticket" goods and services. Such goods and services will likely be a fixture, if not the lifeblood, of m-commerce since marketing research indicates that consumers will continue to rely on other channels to research and purchase "big ticket" items such as household appliances.

Another feature of DoCoMo's business model central to i-mode's success has been an unrelenting focus on anticipating and serving the needs and interests of customers and potential customers. In recent years, DoCoMo has spent more than $1 billion annually on research and development activities. A primary objective of those R&D activities is to make i-mode more functional and useful for subscribers. That orientation contrasts sharply with the strategic thrust of DoCoMo's

20. A. Goldstein, "Success of Japanese Internet Service Lies in Simplicity," *The Dallas Morning News* (online), 23 August 2000.

competitors. Industry analysts suggest that DoCoMo's competitors aspire to developing the wireless industry's most intricate, sophisticated, or chic service. That strategy has resulted in those firms developing wireless services that include numerous "bells and whistles" most consumers simply do not want. One Internet executive believes that such companies are doomed to frustration and failure. "The wireless business is futile if you know technology but don't know what your customers want."[21]

A subtle but nevertheless critical factor in the success of DoCoMo's i-mode service has been the marketing strategy used by the company. Unlike suppliers of wireless Web services in the United States, DoCoMo has intentionally downplayed the Internet and the "real" Web in marketing its services. Company management did not want i-mode users to expect to receive a "squished down" version of the World Wide Web on the display screens of their mobile handsets. DoCoMo's executives realized that if subscribers had such expectations, they would be disappointed by i-mode. Instead of selling i-mode as an Internet access service, the company's promotional materials typically refer to i-mode as a "mobile multimedia communications" service.

i-mode was launched in February 1999; within one year, the service had nearly 5 million subscribers. In less than three years, 25 million Japanese citizens had signed up for the service. *USA Today* reported in March 2001, that i-mode had become the newest "national obsession" in Japan.[22] Company press releases reveal that over 90 percent of i-mode subscribers access an average of 11 i-mode sites each day. Approximately 80 percent of the service's users pay a monthly subscription fee for at least one of the company's premium sites. The runaway success of i-mode helped DoCoMo report record revenues of $3.3 billion for the fiscal year ending March 31, 2001. That success has created economic synergy for the company. As more and more subscribers sign up for i-mode, increasing numbers of high-quality content suppliers establish DoCoMo websites, which leads to more new subscribers, and so on, and so forth.

To continue its breathtaking growth rates in subscribers and revenues, DoCoMo must turn its attention to markets outside of Japan. "DoCoMo is like a huge sumo wrestler overpowering the [Japanese] market. There's nowhere left for it to go but overseas."[23] And, the company is doing just that. DoCoMo's management has established working relationships with, or direct ownership interests in, several major international firms in hopes of introducing i-mode to those firms' domestic markets. In the United States, DoCoMo is partnering with both AOL Time Warner and AT&T Wireless. Other countries in which DoCoMo is pursuing expansion initiatives include Belgium, China, France, Germany, Great Britain, Hong Kong, Malaysia, and The Netherlands. According to a DoCoMo executive, his firm is on a mission "to prove the viability of the mobile Internet, not just in Japan, but in the rest of the world as well."[24]

21. C. Shirky, "The Real Wireless Innovators," *Business2.com*, 17 April 2001, 50.

22. J. Louderback, "America the Wireless?" *USA Today* (online), 18 March 2001.

23. I. Kunii, M. Johnston, and W. Echikson, "DoCoMo's Mission: World Domination—on the Cheap," *BusinessWeek Online*, 28 August 2000.

24. *The Business Times Singapore* (online), "3G Up and Running in Japan, DoCoMo Says," 21 June 2001.

GENERATION GAP

DoCoMo's tremendous success with its i-mode service soon became the envy of the telecommunications world. Particularly envious of that success were the major telecom companies in Europe and the United States that had invested heavily in WAP-based wireless services. As these companies worked out the "bugs" in those services, they became much more functional. But, even glitch-free WAP services were no match for i-mode. Frustration drove telecom giants such as British Telecom, Deutsche Telekom, France Telecom, Sprint PCS, and Vodafone to look to the future, to the next generation of wireless technology, the so-called "third generation" or 3G wireless services.[25]

3G quickly became the watchword of the telecommunications industry. Unlike WAP-based services utilizing "second-generation" technology, 3G services promise to provide a true multimedia experience over handheld wireless devices, including high-quality streaming audio and video. 3G will also provide that content quickly. Software engineers for telecom companies predict that 3G will be at least 30 times faster than most WAP-based services. Similar to i-mode, 3G services will not require users to dial up but instead will feature an "always-on" connection to the Internet. The ability to provide so-called "location services" to consumers is easily the most anticipated facet of 3G technology.

3G technology will allow telecommunications companies to determine the exact location of each of their wireless users. The telecoms can then sell this information to content suppliers and merchants involved with the wireless Web. "You've got someone who's driving down the street and says, 'Hmm, I want a Starbucks coffee or a McDonald's hamburger.' At that moment, if you can connect that person to the store, you have a much higher probability of capturing that customer."[26] Location-based services will also give m-commerce merchants the ability to locate wireless users who just happen to be "in the neighborhood." By zapping those users a message over their mobile handsets, these businesses should be able to dramatically increase their "drop-in" revenues. "You could walk by the Starbucks and get a message that says, 'If you go in now and give them a code, you can get two lattes for the price of one.'"[27] One industry observer projects that this ability to pinpoint the location of each mobile phone will prove to be "a fundamental strategic asset" for the major telecom companies who develop 3G wireless services.[28]

In the wired world, telecommunications firms rely principally on copper wires and fiber optic cables to transmit messages, data, and other information. Among the biggest challenges facing telecom companies pursuing 3G initiatives

---

25. Many recent articles in business periodicals focusing on the wireless industry provide a historical overview of the evolution of mobile phone services. The industry was launched in the early 1970s with analog wireless services, which later become known as "first-generation" wireless technology. "Second-generation" wireless services, which utilized digital technology, came on the scene in the late 1980s.

26. K. Kaplan, "M-Commerce Gives Shell-Shocked Web a Glimmer of Light," *Los Angeles Times* (online), 12 March 2001.

27. *Ibid.*

28. A. Reinhardt, "Wireless Web Woes," *Business Week e.biz*, 4 June 2001, EB 27.

is obtaining the airwave frequencies or "spectrum" needed to operate a wireless service. "Think of spectrum as the pipes through which wireless voice and data traffic flow."[29] By the turn of the century, spectrum had become a very scarce and valuable commodity, an economic reality that has huge implications for the 3G initiatives of telecommunications firms. "Spectrum cannot be produced endlessly like strands of fiber optic, coaxial cable, or copper wire. . . . Spectrum is, and forever will be, a scarce commodity, and whoever controls it will secure a firm grip on the potentially massive wireless customer base."[30]

Within the telecommunications industry, the major European firms were the most aggressive in pursuing 3G strategic initiatives because of the large number of EU citizens who were already wireless users. During 2000, those firms bid on large blocks of spectrum auctioned off by EU countries. In total, these telecom firms spent well in excess of $100 billion to purchase the rights to use Europe's airwaves for 3G services. Most telecoms headquartered in the United States delayed purchasing 3G spectrum. Executives of these latter firms intended to learn from the successes and failures of their European competitors before making huge financial commitments to developing the very costly 3G wireless networks. Because of this wait-and-see approach, industry insiders predict that 3G wireless services will not be widely available in the United States until at least 2004, and possibly later.[31] On the other hand, most European telecoms expect a full "roll-out" of their 3G services by 2003.

DoCoMo's executives recognized that the 3G development efforts of many of their international competitors posed a significant challenge to their company's i-mode service. If 3G works as promised, i-mode could quickly become outdated. To hedge their bets, DoCoMo's executives launched a large-scale development effort during 2000 to integrate 3G technology with their company's successful i-mode platform and a parallel effort to develop a standalone 3G service. In commenting on these initiatives, a DoCoMo official observed, "We fully expect sophisticated new 3G-based mobile multimedia services, including an advanced version of i-mode, to provide substantial revenue streams and eventually become core to [DoCoMo's] overall revenue."[32]

DoCoMo was the first company to do a large-scale "beta test" of a 3G prototype wireless service. DoCoMo press releases issued in the summer of 2001 maintained that the test, which involved approximately 4,500 wireless users, was a "tremendous" success. Despite that claim, reports circulating within the business press suggested DoCoMo's prototype test was an "embarrassing disappointment," principally because more than one-third of the handsets used in the test consistently malfunctioned.[33]

---

29. E. Schonfeld, "The Wireless Web's Wasted Billions," *eCompany* (online), September 2000.

30. *Ibid*.

31. Federal agencies in the United States, principal among them the Department of Defense, control much of the spectrum suitable for 3G wireless services. Those agencies' reluctance to auction off portions of that spectrum to the private sector also contributed to delays in the 3G initiatives of U.S. telecoms.

32. K. Enoki, "DoCoMo Takes Positive View of New 3G Mobile Networks," *Financial Times*, 20 December 2000, 14.

33. M. M. Yamada, "The Trials of DoCoMo," *The Industry Standard*, 25 June 2001, 42.

Notwithstanding DoCoMo's insistence to the contrary, the poor results of the first major test of the 3G technology concerned the major telecommunications companies that had invested billions of dollars just to acquire the airwaves to deliver 3G services. Besides those huge investments, those firms faced equally large expenditures to develop the actual 3G software and to build the required infrastructure for 3G services, an infrastructure that would include an extensive network of base stations and transmission towers and an array of other equipment and hardware. As the news of the DoCoMo 3G prototype test leaked out, many closet critics of 3G technology began questioning whether this new generation of wireless service would actually deliver on its promises. These concerns ranged from basic technical issues involving 3G technology to the overall economic soundness of 3G strategic initiatives being pursued by several large telecoms.

A Finnish computer science professor startled many 3G proponents when he pointed out a seemingly obvious engineering flaw in handsets that would be used to deliver 3G services.[34] At the high end of the data transmission speeds promised by 3G advocates, this professor insisted that wireless users would find their mobile phones literally too hot to handle because of the extreme heat produced by the batteries in those phones. Additionally, at those promised speeds, the batteries would have an expected life of only a few minutes, according to that expert. Solving these problems would require extensive reengineering of the technical specifications for the prototype 3G mobile handsets. Another solution to these problems would be to reduce drastically the transmission speeds utilized by 3G handsets, which would compromise one of the most significant benefits of 3G technology: rapid-fire delivery of streaming audio and video to users.

Other critics questioned whether the much-anticipated location-based services would appeal to a broad enough segment of wireless users to be economically feasible. No doubt, users of those services would include gadget lovers and other "first wave adopters" who find practically any space-age technology too enticing to ignore. But, would more "real-worldly" types, including CPAs, attorneys, corporate executives, blue-collar workers, and others use those services regularly? 3G skeptics also pointed out that the new technology would not solve the user interface problem that had plagued the wireless Web since its inception. Like earlier generations of wireless services, 3G services would still be delivered on a mobile handset or other handheld wireless device. Even if other technical problems, such as the overheating issue, could be solved, did a large number of individuals want to view high-resolution video on a display screen measured in millimeters?

3G advocates typically responded to such criticism and doubts by insisting that, at the very least, the new generation of wireless services would be an improvement on i-mode, which had been an enormous technological and financial success in Japan. But, skeptics also found that argument unconvincing. One former executive of a U.S. wireless firm suggested that i-mode would not necessarily be a huge hit in the United States or elsewhere in the world—whether or not it was supercharged with an underlying 3G technology. According to that executive, Japan is "the reality distortion zone" for consumer products and services.[35] He doubted that many of the "gee whiz" services used frequently by i-mode

34. J. Ledbetter, "Secrets and Lies," *The Industry Standard*, 25 June 2001, 37.

35. Schonfeld, "The Wireless Web's Wasted Billions."

subscribers, such as downloading animated cartoon characters, would appeal to wireless users outside of Japan.

Before 3G wireless services are widely available around the globe, most consumers wanting to go wireless will be forced to choose from a hodgepodge of devices and technologies with varying features and degrees of sophistication. In the United States, a large percentage of new wireless devices sold over the next few years will be powered by so-called 2.5G technology. Telecommunication companies are developing 2.5G as a transitional technology to bridge the gap between current WAP-based wireless services and 3G wireless services. This transitional technology is three times faster than existing WAP-based services and has the "always on" feature of i-mode and 3G systems. On the downside, 2.5G is only one-tenth as fast as the projected speed of 3G technology.

LOOKING TO THE FUTURE: CHAOS, CONFUSION, AND KILLER APPS FOR THE WIRELESS INTERNET

With the obvious exception of DoCoMo's i-mode service, the wireless Internet and m-commerce were disappointing underperformers during their first few years of existence, at least compared to the great expectations that had accompanied the introduction of each. Industry analysts agree that for the evolving wireless sector of the New Economy to achieve its potential, new applications are desperately needed to lure more consumers to the wireless Internet. According to *Fortune* magazine, "Let's Invent Mobile Internet Killer Apps" is a game that software makers around the globe have been intensely playing in recent years.[36] To date, the only true candidate for killer app status on the wireless Internet is actually a class of related applications that are responsible, collectively, for drawing most current users to this new domain.

Across the globe, various modes of e-mail and messaging services are easily the most common use of the wireless Internet. The wireless communications service that has received the most publicity originated in Europe and is most widely used in Great Britain. By early 2001, an estimated one billion SMS—short messaging service—communiqués were being sent in Great Britain each month. Wireless missives sent via SMS are limited to 160 characters, which has forced clever young Brits to develop a new, shorthand version of English. In fact, SMS's popularity has prompted the publication of several books that serve as dictionaries for the evolving SMS "language."

Wireless messaging services provide a welcome source of revenue for many companies heavily involved with the wireless Internet. But, those companies are searching for ways to generate more lucrative m-commerce revenue streams from the users of those services. DoCoMo followed a similar path with its i-mode service. Most i-mode subscribers began using that service because of its communications features. Effective marketing tactics applied by DoCoMo, however, persuaded most of those subscribers to begin accessing the company's premium websites and other i-mode features. Essentially, DoCoMo used a "bait and switch" marketing strategy for its popular service. According to one Internet executive,

---

36. *Fortune* (online), "The Future of the Internet: Dialing for Dollars," 2 October 2000.

that strategy should work as well for other wireless Internet service suppliers given the habit-forming, if not addictive, nature of SMS, wireless e-mail, and other forms of wireless communication. "You get people hooked on a delivery service, and the commerce will flow naturally from it."[37]

The chaos and confusion that have characterized the wireless Internet will likely continue for the foreseeable future. Nevertheless, Internet analysts agree there is little doubt that the wireless Internet and wireless Web will continue to develop and become important features of the Internet domain. Likewise, although few analysts expect m-commerce to be the dominant segment of the Internet economy, it is expected to eventually produce significant revenues. The key questions are when that will happen and which fortunate companies will receive the lion's share of those revenues. "The wireless Internet remains an exciting new frontier. But who exactly is going to capture the prizes remains very unclear."[38]

QUESTIONS

1. Identify a product or service other than those mentioned in this case that you believe is well suited for being marketed over the wireless Internet. Defend your choice and explain how a company would promote that product or service.
2. Do you agree with the individual quoted in this case who believes that DoCoMo's i-mode service would not necessarily be successful in the United States? Defend your answer. Identify key cultural differences across the globe that can impact the success of given consumer products and services.
3. Identify three mobile phones or other wireless devices that can be used to access the Internet. Research and then critique the key features of each of these products.
4. The members of the WAP Forum included many companies that were direct competitors in the telecommunications, information technology, or other high-tech industries. Under what general circumstances do competing companies have an incentive to cooperate? Is such cooperation always in the public's interest? Explain.
5. This case suggests that DoCoMo uses a "bait and switch" marketing strategy for its i-mode service. Do you believe that such a strategy is ethical? Why or why not? Identify comparable marketing strategies used by other companies.
6. "Planned obsolescence" was a phrase that came into vogue in the business press during the latter decades of the twentieth century. What does that phrase imply and do you believe that it is relevant to the telecommunications industry?
7. Research hard copy or online databases to find recent articles discussing developments involving 3G wireless technology. List those developments in a bullet format and briefly describe each.

---

37. G. Lindsay, "An Answer in Search of a Question: Who Wants M-Commerce?" *Fortune* (online), 10 October 2000.

38. J. Hakim, "Who Will Win on the Wireless Web?" *The Wall Street Journal* Interactive Edition, 27 November 2000.

Online Brokers:
Going for Broke on the Internet

It is not the return on my investment that I am
*concerned about; it is the return **of** my investment.*

Will Rogers

Among the most prized commodities in the business world is information. Nowhere is information more highly sought after than in the fast-paced, rough and tumble environment of the stock market. Wall Street brokers, portfolio managers of huge mutual funds, self-employed individuals seeking to build a retirement nest egg, and rabid day traders constantly search for more information to plot their next investment move. That information may include "hot tips" from anonymous sources, third-party rumors from a friend of a friend, "insider" disclosures provided confidentially—and illegally—by a corporate executive or other corporate insider, or any of a wide array of other slivers or tidbits of previously undisclosed, undiscovered, or uncorroborated data. Why do investors crave such information? Because they realize that any given piece of information might be the key to making that elusive "killing" in the stock market.

On the morning of April 18, 1906, a young Wall Street stockbroker came into possession of important, "market-moving" information that his competitors would not have access to for several hours. That brief window of opportunity allowed Edward F. Hutton to pile up large trading profits for his firm and his customers. Thanks largely to that windfall, E. F. Hutton & Co. eventually became one of the most prominent Wall Street brokerages of the twentieth century.

Edward F. Hutton was born into a poor family in New York City in 1876. Fatherless at the age of ten and lacking a high school education, Hutton drifted from one job to another in New York City's financial district until his mid-twenties. The fortunes of the self-confident and charming but shallow-pocketed Hutton took a sudden turn for the better when he married the daughter of a well-to-do broker. In 1904, with the financial backing of his father-in-law, Hutton founded a small brokerage firm, E. F. Hutton & Company, Inc. Ever the opportunist, Hutton recognized the growth potential for his industry in California and opened a San Francisco office of his firm in 1905. E. F. Hutton & Co. was the first brokerage with operations on both coasts and the first to have a private telegraph wire connecting New York City and San Francisco. With this communications link, Hutton's firm could complete bi-coastal securities transactions in a matter of three minutes.

A devastating earthquake registering an estimated 8.3 on the Richter scale struck San Francisco shortly before dawn on April 18, 1906. One of the few direct communication linkages between San Francisco and New York that survived the earthquake was E. F. Hutton & Co.'s private telegraph wire. Because no other Wall Street brokerage firms were aware of the earthquake for several hours, Hutton's brokers were able to use their knowledge of that event to "sell short" securities of companies adversely affected by the disaster and to "go long" in the securities of companies that stood to benefit from the huge trembler. E. F. Hutton & Co.'s executives encouraged their subordinates to exercise such ingenuity and opportunism throughout the firm's existence. Those executives disdained bureaucratic policies, centralized decision making, and organizational charts, all of which they believed stifled employee creativity. Instead, Hutton's management urged subordinates to be innovative, particularly when it came to integrating new technologies and management strategies into the firm's operations—technologies and strategies that would provide the firm with a competitive advantage over other brokerages. Ironically, the aggressive management style of Hutton's top executives, a management style established by Edward F. Hutton himself, ultimately proved to be the firm's undoing.[1]

E. F. Hutton & Co. grew and prospered over the first three-quarters of the twentieth century. By the late 1970s, Hutton enjoyed the brokerage industry's highest return on stockholders' equity and ranked second only to Merrill Lynch in terms of annual revenues. But, disaster struck the firm suddenly and unexpectedly in the early 1980s. Several executives of banks scattered across the United States began complaining of huge cash overdrafts run up by Hutton branch offices that maintained accounts at their institutions. Those complaints triggered a lengthy investigation by federal law enforcement authorities—an investigation that resulted in the firm pleading guilty to 2,000 counts of mail and wire fraud in 1985.

The overdrafts that Hutton's retail offices rang up on an almost daily basis, which collectively approached $1 billion at times, stemmed from a complex "cash management" scheme used by the firm. The funds that Hutton's branch offices withdrew from their local bank accounts, withdrawals that created the overdrafts in those accounts, were immediately deposited in interest-bearing clearing accounts maintained with major metropolitan banks. Since Hutton's local banks did not charge the firm interest on the overdrafts, those overdrafts effectively provided the brokerage firm with interest-free loans. Hutton relied on these "loans" to inflate its revenues and profits. In 1981, interest profits accounted for almost three-fourths of the net income of the firm's retail brokerage division, an abnormally high percentage for the brokerage industry. Federal authorities alleged that if Hutton's scheme had been used on a wide scale by other financial services firms, the nation's entire banking system might have been threatened. Fallout from the huge scandal cost the Hutton firm credibility with the investing public.

---

1. See the following source for an in-depth discussion of the history of E. F. Hutton & Co.: M. C. Knapp, "E. F. Hutton & Company, Inc." *Contemporary Auditing, Real Issues*, 4th ed. (Cincinnati: South-Western College Publishing, 2001).

Within three years, the once prestigious brokerage firm was hovering on the brink of insolvency when it was purchased by a competitor.

If E. F. Hutton & Co. had survived until the early 1990s, the firm would likely have been one of the first brokerages to take advantage of Internet technology. The Internet revolution has been led by opportunistic executives who have recognized before their competitors the potential applications that the Internet and World Wide Web have for their businesses. Hutton's former competitors, including industry leader Merrill Lynch, were slow to embrace the Internet. Instead, several smaller brokerage firms took the lead in introducing U.S. investors to the joys and frustrations of online trading. By the end of the millennium, millions of investors routinely bought and sold securities while watching their favorite daytime television program or while "hard at work" at the office.

CHARLES SCHWAB: FIRST COMMANDER OF THE DISCOUNT BROKERAGE

Despite the aggressive and sometimes illicit strategies used by E. F. Hutton & Co., the brokerage industry was among the most highly regulated industries during most of the twentieth century. Much of that regulatory oversight was prompted by the involvement of brokerage firms in various stock manipulation schemes that contributed to the stock market collapse of 1929. To curtail such abuses and to restore the credibility of the nation's capital markets, Congress passed several federal securities statutes in the 1930s and 1940s. These securities laws imposed rigorous reporting requirements and other regulatory restrictions on publicly owned companies and on the investment firms and brokers involved in marketing those companies' securities. Most prominent among these statutes were the Securities Act of 1933, the Securities Exchange Act of 1934, and the Investment Advisors Act of 1940. In the early 1930s, Congress also created the Securities and Exchange Commission (SEC) to oversee and police the nation's securities markets. Joseph Kennedy, Sr., was appointed the SEC's first chairman.

The regulation of the securities industry even extended to brokerage commissions. Standard commission rates for brokerage transactions gave the large brokerage firms, such as Merrill Lynch and E. F. Hutton, a sizable competitive advantage over smaller brokerages. The large brokerages could offer much more extensive and varied services to investors than could their smaller rivals. Smaller brokerage firms faced the proverbial Catch 22: they were not large enough to offer high-quality customer services, nor could they use offers of lower commissions to lure potential customers who did not need or want such services.

During the early 1970s, Congress and federal regulatory agencies began rethinking the regulatory infrastructure that the securities markets and brokerage industry had operated under for the previous four decades. The biggest change that resulted from this reexamination was the deregulation of brokerage commissions on May 1, 1975. Initially, many of the "old-line" brokerage firms saw the deregulation of brokerage commissions as an opportunity to raise their commission rates. But, a handful of smaller firms did just the opposite. These firms, principal among them Charles Schwab & Co., dropped their commission rates and in doing so created a new breed of brokerage firm, the discount brokerage. Most discount brokerage firms offer only limited customer services. Those services typically include little, if any, investment counseling or "stock-picking" recommendations. Instead, the key thrust of these firms is offering brokerage services at a much lower cost than full-service brokerage firms.

Charles Schwab graduated with an MBA from Stanford University in the mid-1960s. He and two friends decided they wanted to be their own bosses, so they founded a small company that sold an investment newsletter to the public. That company enjoyed only limited success. In 1971, the restless and ambitious Schwab borrowed $100,000 from a relative and created his own brokerage firm, First Commander Corporation. Taking a page from the annals of Edward F. Hutton, Schwab later renamed his firm after himself.

In 1975, the 37-year-old Schwab realized that the deregulation of brokerage commissions provided an opportunity for his firm to pry customers away from full-service brokers. Schwab believed that many individuals, particularly those well-versed in the art of investing, would flock to a brokerage firm that offered them discounts of up to 70 percent off the commissions charged by full-service brokers. Schwab was right. Within a few months of converting his firm into a no-frills, reduced commission brokerage, Charles Schwab & Co. became recognized as the leading "discount broker" in the industry.

To attract more customers of full-service brokers and to beat back the competitive challenge posed by hordes of upstart discount brokerages, Charles Schwab continually implemented new and aggressive strategic measures. One of his first major initiatives was opening retail brokerage offices scattered across the nation. Before placing trades, cautious investors could first drop by and meet their Schwab & Co. broker face-to-face. Other measures implemented by Charles Schwab included offering customers the ability to place orders 24 hours a day, carrying out a nationwide advertising campaign to build a reputation as a credible and trustworthy brokerage firm, and investing heavily in new technology. Schwab's most daring move in the late 1970s was investing in an automated transaction and recordkeeping system, an investment approximately equal to the net worth of the firm at the time. That gamble paid off handsomely since the new system allowed Schwab & Co. to provide more timely service to its customers, while significantly reducing internal transaction costs.

The financial success of Charles Schwab & Co. during the late 1970s and early 1980s made the discount broker a prime takeover target. In 1983, Charles Schwab sold his firm to Bank of America for approximately $55 million, although he remained its principal executive. For the next few years, Schwab grew increasingly unhappy with how Bank of America was operating the firm. So, in 1987, Charles Schwab formed a syndicate of investors and bought back his company. A few months later, Charles Schwab took the firm public with an initial public offering (IPO).

One opportunity that Charles Schwab bypassed was becoming one of the first brokerage firms to establish a full-scope presence on the Internet. An executive with the online service provider Prodigy approached Schwab with the revolutionary concept of offering brokerage services over the Internet. Although Schwab & Co. had created a rudimentary online service for its customers, Charles Schwab believed that few investors were ready to go online with their investment decisions. Once again, he was right. The online brokers that began operating in the early 1990s struggled to sustain their operations.

In 1996, Charles Schwab decided that the time was right for his firm to begin a major push into online brokerage services. Just like it had two decades earlier when it entered the discount brokerage business, Schwab & Co. quickly established itself as the leading firm in the newest sector of the brokerage industry. In early 1998, Charles Schwab & Co. made another bold move. Because Charles Schwab and his top subordinates decided that the Internet would likely have a much more dramatic impact on brokerage services than they had expected just a year or so earlier, they developed a plan to totally restructure their firm and convert it into a primarily Internet-based operation. By cannibalizing Schwab & Co.'s core conventional brokerage business, Charles Schwab was taking another huge risk. Effectively, he was gambling his firm's future on the future popularity of the Internet.

CHUCK TAKES TO THE INTERNET

During the early and mid-1990s, large numbers of technically inclined entrepreneurs decided that the Internet was the "place to be." These brave souls established cyberspace businesses that marketed pet food and supplies, furniture, access to offshore gambling sites, scholarship application services, and literally thousands of other products and services. Within a few years, a large number of those early Internet-based businesses would fail. Why? One common reason was that many of these businesses were not well suited for the Internet. Charles Schwab's decision to convert his company into an Internet-based operation was inspired by the realization that brokerage services were among the business activities best suited for the Internet.

Market researchers documented during the mid-1990s that a disproportionate number of the individuals swarming to the Internet were adventurous, do-it-yourself spirits who were more affluent than the general public. Market researchers also found that Internet users tended to be much more sophisticated and informed regarding the capital markets and investing, in general, than the great unwashed masses. Charles Schwab and his top lieutenants believed that they could persuade large numbers of the risk-seeking, do-it-yourself, investment-savvy Internet users to become online investors. Schwab's management team reached that conclusion despite the failure of early online brokers to establish large customer bases. In fact, in early 1998, online brokerage trades by retail customers hovered at an anemic 7,000 per day.[2]

The two lynchpins of Schwab & Co.'s effort to convert to an Internet-based business model were large investments in technology and extensive advertising. Internet breakdowns due to hacker attacks, sudden spikes in online traffic, and other causes posed major headaches for e-commerce companies and their executives during the 1990s. Charles Schwab realized that a key to attracting and retaining customers was making his firm's website as breakdown-proof as possible. To accomplish that objective, Schwab insisted that his company's systems utilize state-of-the art technology that had been rigorously tested before being integrated into the *Schwab.com* website. To minimize disruptions in customer service,

---

2. C. Coolidge, "Buyer's Market," *Forbes.com*, 12 June 2000.

Schwab & Co. also built extensive redundancy or back-up features into its computer systems. A corporate mantra often repeated by Schwab & Co. executives reflects the firm's commitment to technology: "Schwab is a technology company that happens to be in the brokerage business."[3]

Schwab & Co.'s large marketing staff developed a massive and effective advertising campaign to entice potential customers to access *Schwab.com*. A key element of that campaign was a series of print and television commercials featuring the man known by company insiders as simply "Chuck." Thanks to those commercials, Chuck Schwab's face easily became one of the most recognized corporate images in the United States. To persuade existing customers to take advantage of the speed and efficiency of online trading, the firm's marketing staff used a barrage of brochures mailed to those customers and stuffed inside their monthly statements. Increasing the effectiveness of those appeals were the seemingly interminable waits that phone-dependent Schwab customers were forced to endure before having their calls answered by a broker. To make online investing even more appealing, Schwab & Co. continually added links to its website that provided customers with easy access to investment information and analysis that they previously had been forced to search for on their own.

The dramatic shift to the Internet by Schwab & Co. that began in 1996 and took full effect in 1998 was less than welcomed by many of the company's long-time, Internet-phobic customers. Wall Street also reacted negatively to the announcement that Schwab & Co. was converting to a principally Internet-based operation. That news sent the company's stock price lower on expectations of reduced revenues. But, the plan worked. By early 2000, Schwab & Co. boasted more than seven million online accounts. The company's stock price also recovered when investors realized that the company's new business model could potentially be much more profitable than its previous model. After dropping sharply in mid-1998, Schwab & Co.'s stock price nearly tripled by the end of the year.

In a brief four-year period beginning in 1996, Charles Schwab & Co. successfully "morphed into an e-business" in the words of one Internet analyst.[4] In 1995, Charles Schwab had established a "stretch" goal of having $1 trillion in assets under management by 2005. But, thanks to the company's Internet initiative, Schwab & Co. reached that goal five years early, in mid-2000. Schwab & Co.'s "thrive-on-change" culture and dedication to technology allowed the firm to become the dominant online broker and to challenge Merrill Lynch's long-entrenched position as the nation's largest and most prominent brokerage firm. In fact, by late 1999, the collective market value of Schwab & Co.'s common stock surpassed the market valuation of Merrill Lynch's stock.

JUST WHO IS #2?

Even as Schwab & Co. was assuming a leadership position in the rapidly evolving online sector of the brokerage industry in the late 1990s and setting its sights on overtaking Merrill Lynch as the premier brokerage firm in the nation, several

---

3. C. Wilder, "Leaders of the Net Era," *InformationWeek*, 27 November 2000.

4. *Ibid.*

online brokers were working on strategies to challenge Schwab & Co. In fact, more than 200 brokers would eventually establish websites to attract investors. The more noteworthy of these firms included E*Trade, TD Waterhouse, Datek, Ameritrade, and CSFBdirect, which is owned by the financial services conglomerate Credit Suisse First Boston.

By early 2000, nearly one-half of all retail securities trades were made online.[5] The growing interest of the public in online investing and online brokers prompted the leading business periodicals to begin publishing rankings of the major online brokers. Periodicals attempt to out duel each other in developing the most credible or, at least, the most widely referenced online brokers' "poll." *Smart Money*, *Barron's*, *Business Week*, among other publications, have come up with their own unique criteria for ranking online brokers. *Barron's*, for example, assigns a 1 (worst) to 5 (best) score for six features of online brokers' operations: trade execution, ease of use, range of offerings, research amenities, reports and customer access, and costs. In summarizing the results of its 2001 poll and in revealing the "winner" of that poll, *Smart Money* bluntly told readers who were trying to choose an online broker that, "You want a Charles Schwab account."[6]

Most publicly available "hard" metrics confirm that Schwab & Co. easily qualifies as the dominant online broker.[7] The percentage share of daily online trades is the measure most commonly used to determine the largest online broker. Schwab typically accounts for approximately 22 to 25 percent of all online trades compared to E*Trade's 14 to 16 percent, and 10 to 12 percent for the third largest firm based upon this metric, TD Waterhouse. In terms of the collective dollar value of online accounts, Schwab again claims the top spot among online brokers, while Fidelity and TD Waterhouse rank second and third, respectively, on this measure. The only hard metric for which Schwab does not occupy the top position among online brokers is the number of online accounts. Fidelity claims that distinction with Schwab & Co. a close second and TD Waterhouse a distant third.

Although second place among online brokers is "up for grabs" in most respects, one firm can easily lay claim to being the clear leader among Schwab & Co. wannabes. That firm is E*Trade. Christos Costakos took over as E*Trade's chief executive officer (CEO) in early 1996. Immediately, Costakos informed his subordinates that his objective was to overtake Schwab & Co. In fact, Costakos has set his sights even higher. Costakos's "ambition is to assemble a financial-services empire that not only surpasses that of online rival Charles Schwab & Co. but also matches the breadth of the brick-and-mortar giants such as Merrill Lynch & Co. and Citigroup."[8]

When E*Trade's board of directors hired Christos Costakos, he had no experience in the brokerage and financial services industries. In his previous position, he had served as co-CEO of A. C. Neilsen Corporation, the market research firm. E*Trade's board hired Costakos because it realized the firm needed an aggressive CEO to compete effectively in the dynamic and highly competitive online

---

5. T. W. Carey, "Better, Not Just Bigger," *Barron's*, 13 March 2000, 42.

6. T. Delaney and M. Heimer, "Trading Up," *Smart Money*, August 2001, 111.

7. The data in this paragraph and the following paragraph were taken from recent quarterly research reports prepared and distributed by the financial services firm U.S. Bancorp Piper Jaffray.

8. L. Lee, "Tricks of the E*Trade," *Business Week e.biz*, 7 February 2000, EB 21.

brokerage field. Financial analysts tracking online brokers quickly learned that aggression is one of Costakos's strong suits.

Costakos, the son of two Greek immigrants, grew up in a tough New Jersey neighborhood. After serving in Vietnam where he was awarded the Bronze Star for heroism and the Purple Heart, he returned home and earned a degree in communications from small Patterson State College in his home state. Following graduation, Costakos drifted to Los Angeles and took a job as a package handler for Federal Express, a job that paid all of $3 per hour. A self-professed workaholic, Costakos's work ethic, initiative, and insight on "how to do things better" impressed his superiors and allowed him to quickly work his way up the employment hierarchy of the rapidly growing air courier service. In 1988, at the age of 40, the company's CEO placed Costakos in charge of FedEx's European operations. A few years later, Costakos left FedEx to become co-CEO of A. C. Neilsen.

In describing his management style, the fiery Costakos often uses references to his tour of duty in Vietnam. "One of the things I learned from my experiences in Vietnam is that if you go in halfway, you can't win. You've got to have not only ground cover but air cover. You've got to bring in the heavy artillery. You've got to say, 'I'm here, I've arrived, and I'm not going to be messed with.'"[9] Within the ranks of his subordinates, Costakos constantly attempts to instill an attack-dog mentality. "At E*Trade, we're an attacker, we're predatory. We believe we have a God-given right to market share."[10] Individuals who know Costakos best insist that such statements are not simply locker-room rhetoric intended to inspire the troops. Costakos approaches the online brokerage business as a battleground, realizing that most of the 200-plus companies that have entered the business in recent years will fail, routed by their more aggressive competitors.

To build *esprit de corps* and make his troops battlefield ready, Costakos uses what some competitors have described as "bizarre" team-building exercises. Those exercises range from Costakos and his key subordinates taking gourmet cooking lessons so they can learn how to better work together by producing an elaborate ten-course meal, to competing against each other by racing Formula One cars at speeds topping 150 miles per hour. Costakos uses such exercises "to build a company that's jammed with people who are wildly creative, arch-competitive, yet so closely knit that they're almost family."[11]

When Christos Costakos arrived at E*Trade, the company was struggling to survive, having a meager 75,000 customer accounts. At the time, E*Trade offered online brokerage services through the websites of America Online and CompuServe. Shortly after his arrival, Costakos established E*Trade's own website where investors could place trades. A few months later, in August 1996, Costakos took his company public to raise funds that the company desperately needed to make a name for itself in the increasingly crowded online brokerage field. Costakos intended to accomplish that objective principally with an intensive marketing campaign. After spending heavily on advertising during his first two years with the firm, Costakos stunned E*Trade's board in 1998 by insisting that the company's advertising budget be quadrupled. Costakos's plan, which the board

---

9. D. Roth, "E*Trade's Plan for World Domination," *Fortune* (online), August 1999.

10. Lee, "Tricks of the E*Trade."

11. *Ibid.*, EB 20.

reluctantly approved, called for E*Trade to spend $150 million on advertising, a figure that equaled two-thirds of the company's previous year revenues.

E*Trade quickly became recognized for its memorable commercials. To steal customers from full-service brokers, E*Trade flooded the airwaves with the classic commercial that relied on the punch line, "If your broker is so smart, why is he still working?" E*Trade became a regular advertiser during the Super Bowl, featuring a chimpanzee that became known as the "E*Trade Monkey" in a series of commercials that received critical acclaim. During Super Bowl XXXV, in January 2001, E*Trade spent $5 million on two thirty-second commercials in which the E*Trade Monkey rode a horse through a dot-com ghost town—a commercial pointing to the fact that E*Trade had survived the bursting of the "Internet bubble" in the stock market.

Costakos's heavy emphasis on advertising made E*Trade one of the four most-recognized brand names on the Internet by early 2001. Although E*Trade easily outshone Schwab & Co. in terms of creative advertising efforts, Chuck Schwab's company easily outdistanced Costakos's firm on the technology front. E*Trade's disproportionately large advertising expenditures limited the funds that Costakos could commit to information technology projects. In 1999, E*Trade spent approximately $3 on advertising for every $1 spent on technology.[12] The relatively low priority that E*Trade has placed on technology apparently accounts for the firm's website being less dependable than those of its major competitors. In one of its annual surveys of online brokers, *Barron's* reported that during busy trading periods E*Trade's site often "slows to a crawl."[13]

E*Trade has also lagged behind Schwab & Co. in terms of the content available at its website. Schwab & Co. offers more extensive online research materials than E*Trade, including research reports on major companies prepared by leading financial analysts. E*Trade is one of the few online brokers whose customers can routinely purchase IPO shares, a fact that the company broadcasts in promotional materials to gain a competitive advantage over smaller online brokers such as Ameritrade and Datek, which have largely been shut out of the IPO market. But, here again, Schwab & Co. has a significant advantage over E*Trade. Alliances that Charles Schwab and his subordinates have cultivated with the major Wall Street investment houses that sponsor most IPOs allow Schwab & Co. to obtain much larger "chunks" of IPO shares than E*Trade.

Costakos has gained an upper hand on Schwab & Co. in two important respects. E*Trade's standard commission rate of $14.95 easily undercuts Schwab & Co.'s standard rate of $29.95.[14] E*Trade can also offer a wider range of financial services than Schwab & Co. In 1998, E*Trade acquired its own online banking firm. Three years later, E*Trade Bank ranked as the eighteenth largest federal savings bank in the nation, the only "pure" online bank within the top 20 largest federal banks. Costakos expects his firm's online brokerage and online bank to operate as "feeders" for each other, that is, to funnel customers to their sister unit. Access to online banking services, online brokerage services, and other ancillary

---

12. J. Frederick, "Why Online Brokers Can Win the Web War," *Money*, July 1999, 103.

13. Carey, "Better, Not Just Bigger."

14. Then again, Ameritrade's standard commission rate of $8 easily undercuts E*Trade's standard rate.

services offered by E*Trade, such as the ability to invest in mutual funds, have made E*Trade a one-stop shopping center for financial services.

In less than five years, Christos Costakos built E*Trade into a major financial services company. From the relatively paltry 75,000 customer accounts that E*Trade had when he joined the firm, Costakos could point to more than 3.6 million customer accounts by early 2001. Plus, his company boasted a bank having nearly $13 billion in assets. Despite those and many other impressive data points for E*Trade, Christos Costakos was not satisfied. He was still No. 2 to Schwab & Co. in the minds of most Internet analysts and was ranked even lower in online broker polls by other analysts. As a journalist for *Fortune* suggested, Costakos will apparently only be satisfied with "world domination," at least within the financial services industries.[15]

THE LIFE AND TIMES OF ONLINE INVESTORS

When the time comes for Charles Schwab, Christos Costakos, or the top executives of any other online broker to make an important strategic decision affecting the future of their business, you can rest assured that a critical factor in that decision will be how it affects online investors. Online brokers cater to, dwell on, and fret over the needs, interests, and idiosyncrasies of their customers and potential customers. The profitability, if not viability, of online brokerages depends largely upon their executives' ability to obtain a thorough understanding of the new generation of investors produced by the Internet, including the key issues and challenges facing those investors.

The Internet, aided by the deregulation of the brokerage industry, has empowered investors and has led to what one executive of a stock exchange referred to as a "rapid and sweeping democratization" of the stock market.[16] Online investors literally have at their fingertips access to a treasure trove of financial information regarding thousands of publicly owned companies. In the past, access to such information was limited to the privileged few, principal among them large "trust fund" investors and Wall Street brokers and analysts. Ready access to the data needed to make informed investment decisions and an ability to easily execute securities trades via online accounts have resulted in the United States becoming a nation of the "self-invested." Most stock market mavens predict that the trend toward online investing will continue in the future, fed by the "do-it-yourself impulse" that is a "deep cultural force" within American society.[17]

The explosion in online investing in recent years promises potential monetary and intrinsic rewards for millions of cyberspace investors, but these investors also face a long list of problems and challenges. Ironically, the major obstacle that online investors face is posed by the most appealing feature of the Internet, namely, the easy access to a wealth of free financial information. Online investors have available to them more information than they could possibly ever use. The Yahoo! Finance site alone, provides links to more than 1,000 sources of financial data. Motley Fool, Raging Bull, and dozens of other popular investment forums on the

15. Roth, "E*Trade's Plan for World Domination."

16. E. Jovin, "Fair Trades," *Financial Planning*, June 2000, 187.

17. Frederick, "Why Online Brokers Can Win the Web War."

World Wide Web serve as watering holes for information-thirsty investors. Unfortunately, these investors often leave those websites punch drunk from information overload. At one point, Raging Bull reported that its message boards were attracting nearly 400,000 messages weekly.[18]

More problematic than information overload is the risk that online investors will fall prey to the huge amount of misinformation and fraudulent information that parades on the Internet disguised as the unvarnished truth. The host of an investment website and author of a popular book on the stock market notes that "the ability to defraud convincingly has been democratized, and the effects of a fraud are instant."[19] The most common fraud that online investors face is the garden-variety pump and dump scheme. Federal law enforcement authorities have investigated hundreds of such scams. These frauds typically involve a small number of individuals who purchase shares in a relatively unknown company and then begin "hyping" that company's future prospects on the Internet, most often by way of message board postings. When the price of the given stock rises, the scammers "dump" their shares, leaving the gullible individuals who purchased those shares with large losses when the stock's price eventually settles to its original, "pre-pump" price.

Arthur Levitt, former SEC chairman, often shares the story of the 15-year-old New Jersey schoolboy who orchestrated a large pump and dump scheme. The young man used numerous online pseudonyms or "ghosts" to post illicit messages to various electronic message boards and to place buy and sell orders on the stocks he targeted. The young man's total haul? A profit approaching $300,000. The head of the SEC's Internet Enforcement Division has repeatedly urged investors to avoid making decisions based upon "information" they obtain from Internet message boards. "A person should never base their investment decision on what they read on a message board. Period."[20]

Another common problem that Internet-based investors face is becoming too wrapped up in their online investing. One online investor interviewed by a reporter for *The Wall Street Journal* confessed that for her "trading [online] is addictive."[21] The addictive feature of online trading stems largely from the real-time, real-life nature of the activity. With the help of an online portfolio tracking service, investors can assess minute by minute the wisdom or folly of their investment decisions. Many investors fear that they may miss a big move in the market or in the price of one of their stocks if they spend more than a few moments away from their online ticker tape.

A researcher who serves as the director of the Center for Online Addiction reports that online stock trading has replaced online pornography as the most serious workplace distraction.[22] Numerous corporations have been forced to resort to using surveillance to identify employees who are spending their days mes-

---

18. J. R. Emshwiller, "Reining in Stock Hype Strips Silicon Investor of Its Luster," *The Wall Street Journal* Interactive Edition, 30 November 2000.

19. J. K. Glassman, "Stock Hoax Should Affirm Faith in Markets," *The Wall Street Journal* Interactive Edition, 30 August 2000.

20. C. Lee, "Raging Bull Unveils Ratings for Stock Postings," *The Wall Street Journal* Interactive Edition, 3 August 2000.

21. R. Simon and E. S. Browning, "Some Online Investors Can't Seem to Say No to Playing the Market," *The Wall Street Journal*, 4 August 2000, A1.

22. D. Setton, "On the Job Trading," *Forbes*, 22 May 2000, 28.

merized by wild swings in tech stocks rather than focusing on their more mundane job responsibilities. Former SEC Chairman Levitt worries that workplace investors are using their ready access to the Internet to take inordinate risks in hopes of profiting on short-term market swings. Many of these individuals, Levitt fears, are gambling away their student loan funds, their retirement nest eggs, and cash raised from second mortgages taken out on their homes.[23]

The Internet has also created a new breed of "professional" day traders who attempt to earn a livelihood by trading on hour-to-hour or even minute-to-minute swings in stock prices. Some day traders are very successful. *Investor's Business Daily* reported that one lucky or skilled day trader earned more than $10 million in the turbulent stock market of 2000.[24] Despite such isolated reports, reputable studies repeatedly find that most day traders consistently lose money. A study by a brokerage industry trade group, for example, revealed that 77 percent of day traders lose money annually.[25]

The inability of most day traders to profit from their "job" has not put a damper on the volume of their online investing. *Fortune* reported in early 2001 that an estimated 50,000 individuals were professional day traders. "Those trigger-happy types now perform an average of 44 trades a day—about one every nine minutes—and represent a stunning 81 percent of total online retail trades."[26] Many experts question whether the staggering volume of online trades is good for the stock market. Day traders contribute significantly to the tremendous volatility that has characterized the stock market in recent years. This is particularly true of the NASDAQ that is heavily laced with high-tech stocks. One source reports that 50 percent of the trades executed by online brokers involve high-tech stocks, while the comparable percentage for "off-line" investors is only 10 percent.[27] The trading volume—and commissions—produced by day traders has caused several online brokers to cater to this relatively small but important group of investors. These brokers provide incentives to attract day traders, including free high-speed Internet access and wireless Internet devices.

A few years ago when online trading was in its infancy, two factors in particular deterred many investors from going online. Those factors were the reliability of online brokers' websites and the degree of security that online brokers provided for their customers' account information. As online trading has matured, those issues have generally dissipated. Disruptions of service due to hacker attacks, faulty software, or other problems still occur; however, most online brokers have taken aggressive measures to minimize the frequency and severity of those disruptions. According to *The Wall Street Journal*, "online brokerages have become one of the most successful e-commerce businesses partially because they have been able to convince customers that their information and accounts are se-

23. M. McNamee, "The SEC Has Words of Warning for Online Investors," *BusinessWeek Online*, 27 January 1999.

24. P. McKenna, "Some Traders Are Making Hay by Day," *Investor's Business Daily*, 29 June 2001, B4.

25. M. Maiello, "Day Trading Eldorado," *Forbes.com*, 30 May 2000.

26. N. D. Schwartz, "Can't Keep a Good Day Trader Down," *Fortune*, 19 February 2001, 147.

27. M. Krantz, "Volume May Turn Down for Online Trading Firms," *USA Today*, 4 August 1999, 3B.

cure."[28] Nevertheless, security breaches still arise for online brokers and can be very damaging to their reputations and pose significant risks for their customers. In August 2001, both Schwab & Co. and E*Trade publicly revealed that until a few months earlier their websites had shared a common flaw. That flaw had made it possible for skilled and determined hackers to gain access to the customer accounts of each broker.[29]

LOOKING TO THE FUTURE

The past century has witnessed dramatic changes in the brokerage industry. The stock market collapse in 1929 led to the end of the nearly-anything-goes attitude that plagued the industry in the early 1900s. Rigid regulatory oversight characterized the next four decades—regulation highlighted by the passage of the federal securities laws during the Great Depression. Then, the deregulation of commissions on May 1, 1975, gave birth to the era of discount brokerages. Finally, in the early 1990s, several forward-looking individuals introduced the industry to the Internet. Over the next few years, large numbers of schemers and scammers invaded the world of online investors, prompting many parties to question whether the industry had gone full cycle and returned to the wild and raucous days of the 1900s. No doubt, the changes resulting from the integration of the Internet into the brokerage industry are not over. The "disruptive technologies" of the Internet and World Wide Web will almost certainly continue to trigger pervasive and unexpected changes in the brokerage industry. Among the parties most affected by those changes will be online brokers—the firms that have benefited the most from the new era of cyberspace investing.

The biggest change facing online brokers in the next few years is the decision of full-service brokers to move en masse to the Internet. Throughout most of the 1990s, executives of full-service brokers, including Merrill Lynch's management, disparaged the concept of online investing. In mid-1999, Merrill Lynch established an online trading unit only ten months after referring to online investing as a "threat to Americans' finances."[30] A.G. Edwards, another full-service broker, went online a few weeks after Merrill Lynch. Edwards' CEO seemed much less than enthusiastic regarding that decision. "I don't think online trading is good for the client. . . . We're pressed by competition to provide it, but that doesn't mean we have to recommend it."[31] By late 1999, every major full-service broker had established a website where their customers could place orders.

The key factor that accounted for the reluctance of full-service brokers to move to the Internet was fear that doing so would "cannibalize" their existing offline

28. T. Bridis and S. Forster, "E*Trade Fixes Flaw That Made Customer Accounts Vulnerable," *The Wall Street Journal* Interactive Edition, 26 September 2000.

29. D. Howell, "Online Trading Companies Take on the Hackers," *Investor's Business Daily*, 29 August 2001, A13.

30. J. Frederick, "When an Online Broker Goes Offline," *Money*, May 1999, 151.

31. J. Frederick, "Full-Service Firms Are Finally Fighting Back, but Their Hearts Aren't in It," *Money*, July 1999, 153.

business. Charles Schwab and his subordinates had faced that dilemma more than a year earlier and decided that the future of the brokerage business was on-line not offline. The tardiness of full-service brokers to move online provided a window of opportunity for Schwab & Co. and a handful of other major online brokers. These latter firms took advantage of that brief period of time to establish an impenetrable beachhead in the online brokerage sector of the industry. Al-though Schwab & Co.'s position as the leading online broker seems secure, at least for the foreseeable future, the mass invasion of the online brokerage field by the full-service brokers poses a major risk to the large number of small online bro-kers. Within one year of the full-service brokers' en masse move to the Internet, those firms had captured 28 percent of the market value of online customer ac-counts and 11 percent of all active accounts.[32]

Another piece of bad news for the scores of smaller online brokers was the downturn in the stock market that began in early 2000. Leading stock indices for the NASDAQ, the stock exchange that is home to the high-tech stocks favored by day traders and other online investors, declined by more than 60 percent between the spring of 2000 and fall of 2001. That downturn slowed the growth in the num-ber of new online accounts and had an even larger impact on the trading activity of online investors. During the 18 month period between March 2000 and June 2001, many online brokers realized more than 50 percent declines in the total number of trades made by their customers each month. As NASDAQ stock prices continued their downward spiral during 2001, many of the smaller online brokers began laying off employees. Even the largest online brokers, among them Schwab & Co. and E*Trade, initiated cost-cutting measures. By the fall of 2001, Schwab & Co. had laid off nearly 20 percent of its workforce.

Industry analysts doubted that even a prolonged "bear" market would have a long-term, adverse impact on the financial condition of Schwab & Co. or E*Trade. But, those same analysts were less optimistic regarding the viability of most smaller online brokers under such circumstances. One British journalist noted that "many online brokers are keen to move away from a 'primitive' business model based on capturing clients with low-cost deals as they realize that it is not sustainable in the long term."[33] The problem smaller online brokers face in mov-ing away from a "primitive" business model to a model that involves providing more customer services is that the big, full-service brokers have now staked out that portion of the online market. Similarly, Schwab & Co., E*Trade, and other major online "discount" brokers have now incorporated a significant customer service component into their product lines.

A final challenge that online brokers must confront in coming years is the dy-namic regulatory environment in which they operate. As proven in 1975, sudden shifts in the federal government's regulatory philosophy for the brokerage in-dustry can have pervasive implications for individual brokerage firms. Many in-dustry observers believe that the extreme volatility that has characterized the stock market in the Internet era may force the federal government to once more impose more regulatory restraint on the market. Online brokers that fail to antic-ipate such changes in the regulatory environment may find themselves joining

---

32. E. Thornton, "Take That, Cyber Boy," *Business Week*, 10 July 2000, 58.

33. *Financial News* (online), "Online Brokers Fight for Market Share in Low-Margin Landscape," 15 January 2001.

the ranks of E. F. Hutton & Co. and other formerly high-flying but now permanently grounded brokerage firms.

QUESTIONS

1. This case mentions three federal statutes that Congress enacted to regulate the securities industry: the Securities Act of 1933, the Securities Exchange Act of 1934, and the Investment Advisors Act of 1940. Choose one of those statutes and research its key requirements. List those requirements in a bullet format.

2. In your opinion, does the federal government have a responsibility to protect irresponsible online investors from their own poor judgment? Defend your answer.

3. A relatively small number of online day traders have a disproportionately large impact on the stock market. Should the SEC, other federal authorities, or online brokers implement measures to curtail the impact that day traders have on the stock market? Why or why not?

4. Full-service brokers delayed establishing online trading operations because they feared that doing so would "cannibalize" their core or offline operations. Identify a prominent company in another industry that established a major online operating unit. Discuss how that decision apparently influenced the overall financial health of the company.

5. Choose either Schwab & Co. or E*Trade. For the company you chose, research recent developments affecting or involving that firm. Summarize these developments in a bullet format.

6. Access to relevant and reliable information regarding publicly owned companies is critical to investors. Identify three or more items of information that publicly owned companies *should not* be required to report to investors and other interested parties. Defend your choices.

Electronic Hatcheries

Imitation is the sincerest flattery.

Charles Caleb Colton

The Internet incubator ranks among the most revolutionary business models developed by cyberspace's commercial pioneers. Internet historians generally credit Bill Gross with originating the concept of the Internet incubator when he organized idealab! in 1996. Gross intended his new firm to serve as an electronic hatchery, of sorts, for online business ventures. Prospective entrepreneurs brought ideas for Internet-based businesses to idealab!. Gross and his colleagues then provided financial support, technological resources, administrative skills, and other services to help create sustainable businesses from those ideas. In return, idealab! received a sizable ownership interest in each company that it successfully incubated.

The initial success of Gross's new firm prompted a mad rush to develop businesses mimicking idealab!. In less than four years, an estimated 800 Internet incubators existed worldwide, more than one-half located in the United States. Since the inception of Internet commerce in the early 1990s, e-commerce pioneers have been forced to cope with opportunists who quickly replicate their business plans. "The current trend of incubators everywhere is a perfect illustration of the Net economy at work. In the fast changing Internet economy, it seems the only certainty is that if you have a smart idea, expect someone to duplicate it in less than a month."[1]

Founders of new incubator companies brazenly copied Bill Gross's business model but made every effort to develop unique and memorable names that outshone the catchy handle Gross had applied to his firm. Most favored were names that alluded directly or indirectly to the incubator concept. These names included eHatchery, unHatched, The Nest, and the more subtle—and clever—Oxygen. Other reasonable, if not pretentious, labels for new Internet incubators included ExperTelligence, Quantum Leap Ventures, and Brainspark. Chicago-based Divine InterVentures seemed appropriate since the firm's principal investors included

---

1. O. Malik, "Hatch Them Young," *Forbes.com*, 15 December 1999.

none other than the Windy City deity, Michael Jordan. Finally, among the more thought-provoking names chosen for Internet incubators were BeastoftheEast, Camp Ants, Ant Factory, and Jelly Works.

As the field of Internet incubators became increasingly crowded, many of these companies soon discovered that an eye-catching name could not overcome a weak business plan. In fact, even the largest Internet incubators, among them Bill Gross's idealab!, encountered trying times as e-commerce emerged from its infancy in the early days of the new millennium.

An Idea Factory

Bill Gross commenced his entrepreneurial career in 1970 as a 12-year-old junior high student. The young businessman purchased candy bars en masse from local merchants and then hawked them from his locker at prices that lowballed those charged by the school cafeteria. A few years later, while a high school student, Gross organized and incorporated Solar Devices, Inc., a company that manufactured solar power kits. Sales for that business, produced primarily by ads placed in *Popular Science* magazine, helped Gross finance his college education at the prestigious and pricey California Institute of Technology.

At CalTech, Gross created two companies. One of these businesses manufactured loudspeakers, while the other marketed accounting software linked to the then-popular *Lotus 1-2-3* spreadsheet program. A few years after graduating from CalTech with a B.S. in Engineering and Applied Science, Gross sold the accounting software company to Lotus for $10 million and immediately turned his attention to several other projects including Knowledge Adventure, a company that marketed educational software designed for adolescents. Knowledge Adventure quickly became the third largest seller of educational software in the United States. Gross eventually sold this company to CUC International, a large public firm, for $100 million.

Proceeds from the sale of Knowledge Adventure allowed Bill Gross to tackle his most ambitious business project in March 1996. Gross encountered little difficulty convincing prominent investors and celebrities to pony up large sums to purchase ownership interests in his new company, idealab!. Movie mogul Stephen Spielberg had become acquainted with Gross after purchasing Knowledge Adventure software for his children. Spielberg gave his stamp of approval to idealab! by noting bluntly, "If he [Gross] is involved, I want to invest in it."[2] Actor Michael Douglas, Jack Welch, the chief executive officer (CEO) of General Electric, and Compaq Computer's CEO Ben Rosen were just a few other high-profile investors who became part owners of idealab!. Within two years of founding idealab!, the energetic Gross had raised more than $250 million from private investors to finance his new company.

Thanks to idealab!, Gross would soon become recognized as one of the leading Internet visionaries by the business press. When asked by a journalist to describe his new firm, Gross responded nonchalantly, "I run an idea factory."[3]

---

2. L. Armstrong and R. Grover, "Bill Gross, Online Idea Factory," *BusinessWeek Online*, 29 June 1998.

3. *Ibid.*

HATCHING BUSINESSES

The concept of a business incubator did not originate with Bill Gross. Instead, he simply applied the concept to e-commerce. Business incubators began appearing in the United States in the early 1970s. Government agencies, universities, and private foundations sponsored most early incubators. Many of these incubators were intended to develop and nurture small businesses in financially blighted inner-city neighborhoods. By the mid-1990s, an estimated 500 business incubators existed, a disproportionate number located in large urban centers along the East Coast.

Before Internet incubators appeared on the scene, new e-commerce businesses typically relied on venture capital (VC) firms to provide "seed money" to finance their early operations. VC firms that became recognized as key underwriters of new e-commerce ventures included Sequoia Capital, Kleiner Perkins, and Benchmark Capital. In most cases, one or more partners of a VC firm that financed a new Internet company accepted a position on the company's board of directors. But, these venture capitalists seldom offered more than general advice and recommendations to the management teams of e-commerce ventures.

During the early 1990s, Bill Gross had repeatedly encountered individuals who had stumbled upon promising concepts for Internet-based businesses. Most of those individuals lacked the financial resources and the necessary technical or business-related "know-how" to construct a comprehensive and viable business plan. Since VC firms typically refused to consider business ventures that had not progressed beyond the embryonic or "idea" stage, Gross decided that he would create a company to make a wide range of resources available to potential Web entrepreneurs. idealab!'s original website noted that the company's mission was "to develop individual ideas into highly focused and successful Internet businesses." That website also provided a general description of the company's operations.

> In addition to capital, idealab! provides a full range of resources to infuse start-up companies with the development strategies and financial support needed to rapidly introduce innovative products and services. Resources include office space and the accompanying network infrastructure, consulting and services relating to development and technology, graphic design, marketing, competitive research, legal, accounting and business development support and services. In addition, idealab! provides advice on strategy, branding, and corporate structure.

From idealab!'s inception, speed was a key element of the firm's incubation strategy. Gross realized that the business opportunities offered by the Internet's rapid expansion into the fabric of the nation's everyday life would not go unnoticed for long. To build successful e-commerce companies, Internet entrepreneurs not only needed to identify a viable business concept, they also had to beat competitors to the market. Gross believed that by quickly establishing a significant market presence, individual e-commerce companies could erect a barrier to entry that would discourage other firms from duplicating their business model.

An even more important element of idealab!'s incubation strategy was allowing entrepreneurs to focus their efforts on the core operations of their businesses. One study suggests that owners of new businesses spend 90 percent of their time raising funds, hiring employees, and performing other administrative tasks.[4]

---

4. D. Vrana, "California Dealin', Financing the State's Emerging Companies," *Los Angeles Times*, 5 June 2000, C1.

Access to idealab!'s resources largely freed owners of new Web-based businesses from those responsibilities during the first several months of their firm's existence. Instead, those new entrepreneurs could concentrate their time and energy on developing strategic initiatives, improving their products and services and, most important, locating a critical mass of customers for those products and services.

Over the first three years of its existence, idealab! successfully incubated more than 30 companies. Those companies included eToys, which markets toys online; GoTo.com, a search engine; and Ticketmaster Online, an online seller of tickets for a wide range of events. Each of those companies eventually went public via an initial public offering (IPO). At one point, those three companies had a total market capitalization exceeding $10 billion. Since idealab! retained a significant ownership interest in most companies it incubated, Bill Gross and his fellow investors profited handsomely from former clients that went public. Financial analysts estimated that idealab!, a private company, had a market value measured in the billions by early 2000.

TAKING ON IDEALAB!

By the late 1990s, Internet incubators were operating or being organized in practically every major metropolitan area in the United States. Incubators were also popping up in London, Paris, and other major commercial centers around the world. Two U.S.-based incubators, CMGI and ICG, emerged as the leading challengers to idealab!'s reputation as the most prominent and successful creator or sponsor of new Internet firms.[5]

CMGI: AN AMERICAN KEIRETSU

David Wetherell, a mathematician turned programmer turned entrepreneur, built CMGI into one of the Internet's leading companies in the late 1990s. Wetherell graduated from Ohio Wesleyan University in 1976 with a mathematics degree. After bouncing from job to job for several years, Wetherell became enthused with computers and landed a position as a computer programmer. In the mid-1980s, Wetherell became his own boss when he established a software company. When that venture quickly floundered, he took over a small, financially troubled company, College Marketing Group, Inc. (CMGI), whose principal line of business was marketing textbooks to college professors. The headstrong, if not pushy, Wetherell convinced a bank to extend a large loan to CMGI that allowed the firm to avert almost certain bankruptcy. Over the next several years, Wetherell built CMGI into a substantial company, which he took public in 1994.

As the Internet began mushrooming in popularity in the early 1990s, Wetherell recognized that this new technology provided an entirely new method of mar-

---

5. Both CMGI and ICG are most commonly referred to as Internet incubators by the business press. However, many Internet analysts refer to the two companies as "quasi-incubators" since they differ in several important respects from idealab!. Here, we will simplify matters and refer to all three firms as Internet incubators.

keting books, particularly to tech-savvy book buyers such as college professors. Wetherell diverted much of the proceeds from CMGI's initial public offering (IPO) into a project to develop a Web browser, Booklink, that targeted online book buyers. Within a few months, both Microsoft and America Online (AOL) approached CMGI, offering to purchase Booklink. Wetherell agreed to sell Booklink to AOL. The AOL stock that CMGI received in the transaction soon had a market value of $75 million, an impressive figure since CMGI had spent less than $1 million developing Booklink.

Wetherell used the huge profit realized from the sale of Booklink to purchase ownership interests in several dozen Internet ventures. In some of these firms, CMGI purchased a majority ownership interest, but in most Wetherell acquired only a minority equity interest. In these latter cases, CMGI typically purchased a sufficiently large minority interest to gain effective control over the given company's operations. The Internet-related businesses in which CMGI invested included AltaVista and Lycos, the Web portals; Raging Bull, an online investor forum; Furniture.com, a furniture e-tailer; and MotherNature.com, an online marketer of vitamins and other health products.

Unlike Bill Gross, Wetherell concentrated on existing Web businesses rather than developing new Internet ventures; similar to Bill Gross, Wetherell saw his responsibility as nurturing the companies in which CMGI invested. Wetherell's approach to accomplishing that goal primarily involved creating a network of interrelated Internet companies.

> At the core of Wetherell's vision is a plan to create a network of interlocking Net companies that work together. He wants each of CMGI's sites to feed its users into the others in a virtuous, ever-growing circle. Wetherell's network draws individual customers through his AltaVista and Lycos portals, which generate the traffic that is crucial to the rest of the enterprise.[6]

Wetherell borrowed the underlying concept for his organization from a long-standing tradition in the Japanese economy. The companies in a Japanese keiretsu operate in a variety of different industries but form an economic cartel by pledging to transact business with each other, whenever possible, rather than using the services or purchasing the products of companies outside the keiretsu. During the post-World War II occupation of Japan by the United States, General Douglas MacArthur attempted to break down the keiretsu system in the Japanese economy. General MacArthur, who oversaw the U.S. occupation forces, believed that keiretsu would be disruptive to the free market economic system that U.S. leaders wanted to foster in Japan. He ordered that the Mitsubishi keiretsu, the most powerful in Japan at the time, be disbanded. Fifty years later, the Mitsubishi keiretsu has been re-established. The more than 40 companies that display the distinctive, three-diamond Mitsubishi logo make up one of the largest corporate empires in the world.

Another central element of Wetherell's initial business plan for CMGI was obtaining as much Internet "real estate" as quickly as possible. Wetherell believed a key factor that would contribute to the success of his online keiretsu was traffic—Internet traffic. If he could create a sizable network of Internet businesses that offered a range of products and services to meet the needs of most Internet users,

---

6. P. C. Judge, "Who Is David Wetherell? And Why Is Everyone Talking About Him and His Hot Company, CMGI?" *Business Week Online*, 25 October 1999.

he could keep those users circulating from one CMGI site to another. The lynch-pins of Wetherell's grand plan were his two Web portals, AltaVista and Lycos, which he hoped would eventually rival Yahoo!'s position as the Web's most popular entry point.

During the late 1990s, David Wetherell became a legend on Wall Street. Under Wetherell's leadership, CMGI invested in more than 60 Internet companies. Wall Street's preoccupation with Internet stocks caused the value of CMGI's investment portfolio to soar. Over a five-year period between 1994 and 1999, CMGI 's stock rose more on a percentage basis than any other common stock in the United States. That meteoric stock rise made Wetherell, who owned approximately one-sixth of CMGI's stock at the time, a billionaire several times over.

In commenting on his wealth, Wetherell once remarked, "If you can't make money in this business, then you might as well pick oranges."[7] The self-deprecating executive was more than happy to tarnish his own image as a Wall Street icon by pointing out that one of the Internet ventures that he passed on was eBay, a decision that cost him $4 billion by his own estimate.

ICG: AN ECONET

Walter Buckley and Kenneth Fox founded Internet Capital Group (ICG) in 1996 and took the company public three years later. Buckley graduated from the University of North Carolina in 1982 with a B.A. in Political Science, while Fox received a B.S. in Economics in 1993 from Penn State. Although the two men were ten years apart in age and very different in temperament, they became close friends while working with a Philadelphia investment firm in the early 1990s—an investment firm that concentrated on Internet-based businesses. In 1996, the odd couple decided to create their own firm.

Unlike many Internet enthusiasts, including Bill Gross, who expected that business-to-consumer (B2C) e-commerce would be the leading sector of the new Internet economy, Buckley and Fox believed that business-to-business (B2B) e-commerce would dominate the New Economy. That belief served as the motivating premise of ICG. "Our goal is to become the premier B2B e-commerce company by establishing an e-commerce presence in major segments of the economy. We believe that our sole focus on the B2B e-commerce industry allows us to capitalize rapidly on new opportunities and to attract and develop leading B2B companies."[8]

After studying business models for existing companies that sponsored Internet ventures, ICG's two co-founders settled on a model that blended the operating strategies adopted by Bill Gross and David Wetherell. Buckley and Fox intended to identify and invest in B2B ventures in an early stage of development or to purchase ownership interests in existing B2B companies. Upon obtaining an equity interest in these firms, ICG would provide them with a range of professional services including general management skills, marketing programs, and information technology services. ICG also intended to integrate these companies into a collaborative economic network or EcoNet. The firms in this EcoNet would cooper-

---

7. "Time Digital 50," *Time.com*, July 2000.

8. ICG website.

ate when possible by purchasing goods and services from each other and by sharing advances in technology, particularly Internet technology, that could benefit each of them.

> Our operating strategy integrates our Partner Companies into a collaborative network that leverages the collective knowledge and resources of ICG. Acting as a long-term partner, we actively develop the business strategies, operations and management teams of our Partner Companies.[9]

Buckley and Fox believed the factor that would largely determine the degree of financial success ICG ultimately achieved was the extent to which the firm could quickly gain control of a critical mass of Internet real estate, a concept borrowed from David Wetherell's business plan for CMGI. To establish ICG as a key player in B2B e-commerce, the ICG founders committed their company to gaining control of B2B Internet companies in 50 top sectors of the global economy. Within the first six months of going public, Buckley and Fox were well on their way to accomplishing that goal, having integrated more than 40 companies into ICG's EcoNet, including such Web-based ventures as eChemicals, PaperExchange.com, and VerticalNet.

Buckley and Fox were well-compensated for their intense efforts to build ICG into a dominant B2B company. The ICG stock each received when they took their company public in 1999 had a market value exceeding $500 million shortly after the IPO was completed.

INCUBATION INTOXICATION

By the late 1990s, Internet incubators patterned after idealab!, CMGI, or ICG were "spreading like a virus."[10] As one business journalist noted, investors seemed "intoxicated"[11] by the concept of Internet incubators as they eagerly snapped up stock in those companies although most of them lacked a proven track record. Among these investors were some of the most respected on Wall Street. Legendary financier George Soros and Wall Street's leading investment broker, Goldman, Sachs & Co., invested heavily in the upstart incubator eCompanies based in Los Angeles. The management teams of many incubators also seemed less than sober. Symbolic of that insobriety was the $7.5 million paid by eCompanies for the rights to the Internet domain name *business.com*.

A precipitous drop in the market prices of dot-com stocks in the spring of 2000 put a major dent in investors' fascination with Internet incubators. Since the principal assets of these firms were dot-com stocks, their stock prices plummeted as well. Over a period of several months in early 2000, the market values of most publicly owned incubators nosedived anywhere from 60 to 90 percent. Privately owned Internet incubators suffered large losses on their investment portfolios as well. The executives of several incubators that intended to go public during the first half of 2000 were forced to postpone those IPOs. Chicago-based Divine

---

9. *Ibid.*

10 C. Palmeri, "Is idealab! Running Dry?" *Business Week*, 5 June 2000, EB 50.

11. *The Economist* (online), "Hatching a New Plan," 12 August 2000.

InterVentures seven times announced that it would be going public and seven times postponed its IPO.

The tailspin in the stock prices of Internet incubators that began in early 2000 caused many investors, financial analysts, and business journalists for the first time to critically examine the upstart Internet incubation "industry." These in-depth examinations raised several serious concerns regarding not only the economic viability of individual incubators but also the integrity of the incubation process. Many critics maintained that the explosive growth in the number of Internet incubators had left too many of these firms chasing too few Internet business concepts that were viable. These same critics also pointed out that although hundreds of Internet businesses had been "successfully" incubated, that is, had become independent firms, very few of those companies were actually profitable. Despite that "minor" technicality, before the swoon in dot-com stock prices in early 2000 investors had ascribed huge valuations to firms such as eToys and GoTo.com that were products of the incubation process. Those valuations had translated into equally incredible valuations for the incubators that retained large ownership interests in their former clients.

The most common criticism of Internet incubators was that few actually created a nurturing environment that spawned sustainable businesses. The Internet incubation industry developed so rapidly that there was little agreement on the types of services that Internet incubators should provide, nor was there any consensus on how the incubation process should be structured and managed. Practically any company could label itself as an Internet incubator although it provided few, if any, of the professional services that idealab! and other early incubators offered to the firms they sponsored. Many Internet incubators supplied potential clients with little more than office space and basic business services, such as access to copiers and off-the-shelf accounting packages.

> At one point, Jackpot Enterprises, a Las Vegas gambling operator, announced that it would become "J Net," an Internet incubator, and saw its shares rise by 50% on the news. Why rent space to a few scruffy start-ups if you can call yourself an incubator instead? . . . Why lose deals to bigger and better venture-capital firms when you can convert a conference room or two into *incubator* space and claim a competitive advantage?[12]

The crush of excitement generated among investors by early Internet incubators sparked the get-rich-quick mentality that triggered the stampede to establish copycat firms. Many of these second-generation Internet incubators were under-financed, overhyped, and managed by individuals lacking the skills necessary to support and promote new Web-based ventures. As the year 2000 progressed, articles and exposés criticizing these latter firms began appearing with increasing frequency in the business press. The image of incubators became so tarnished that many of these firms began avoiding the "I" word when referring to themselves. "Even the word [incubator] itself seems cursed: companies that just a few months ago were proud to be on the incubation bandwagon today claim they are something else entirely: business accelerators, venture catalysts, e-campuses—anything but incubators."[13]

---

12. *Ibid.*

13. *Ibid.*

Wall Street analysts predicted a large shakeout among the hundreds of second-generation Internet incubators following the abrupt end to the mania surrounding those firms that accompanied the collapse of dot-com stock prices during 2000. Those same analysts predicted that the surviving firms would likely fall into two categories: those well-financed firms that offered a wide range of essential services to potential clients and those that offered highly specialized services intended exclusively for start-ups operating in one segment of the new Web-based economy.

BIG THREE ALSO FACE BIG CHALLENGES

The Big Three firms among Internet incubators did not escape the problems encountered by their lesser known competitors during 2000. Cynical investors pummeled the stock price of both CMGI and ICG. At one point during 2000, CMGI's stock price had slid by 80 percent from its yearly high, while ICG's stock price had plunged by nearly 90 percent. Although the stock prices of the two companies rallied occasionally during 2001, the overall trend in those prices continued to be downward. idealab!, again, a private company, saw the value of its investment portfolio of dot-com stocks plummet and found that its investors and lenders were hesitant to fork over additional funds to finance Bill Gross's latest "hot" projects. During 2000, Gross's plan to take idealab! public was delayed several times by the Securities and Exchange Commission (SEC), creating more financial headaches for him and his colleagues. The SEC maintained that since idealab! qualified as an "investment company," the firm faced more stringent requirements for going public than the typical firm. One year earlier, the SEC had made a similar argument when ICG applied for an IPO but later relented and allowed Walter Buckley and Kenneth Fox to take their company public.

As 2000 progressed, the business press focused increasing scrutiny and criticism on the Internet incubation industry, particularly on idealab! since that firm had effectively launched this new industry. For example, an article that appeared in *Business Week* in June 2000, openly criticized the exorbitant compensation package that idealab! had given its chief executive and founder.[14] That compensation package included options permitting Bill Gross to purchase 150 million shares of idealab! common stock for slightly more than $1 per share—assuming the company was eventually successful in going public. Many business journalists also began questioning Bill Gross's strategy of focusing almost exclusively on developing B2C dot-coms. By mid-2000, B2B e-commerce seemed to offer the most profitable long-term opportunities for Internet business ventures. Other critics charged that the B2C business plans developed by Gross, although innovative, were easily copied by other dot-coms.

> A close examination of idealab!'s IPO documents shows that there are good reasons to question the company's prospects—even beyond the fall in tech stocks. One major problem may be that Gross's incubator often finances cookie-cutter business plans that are easily replicated. Competitors can quickly set up similar sites, and many idealab! companies haven't been able to lead in their markets.[15]

---

14. Palmeri, "Is idealab! Running Dry?"

15. *Ibid.*

Reporters became increasingly strident in pointing out that most of the dot-coms "successfully" incubated by idealab! incurred huge and recurring operating losses after being jettisoned into the business world by Bill Gross's firm. Even more disturbing to these critics was that Gross often sold large blocks of the shares idealab! owned in its former clients before their stock prices crashed to earth. Take eToys, for example, the most prominent of idealab!'s graduates. Near the end of 1999, idealab! sold 4 million shares of its eToys' stock at a gain of approximately $200 million. A few months later, eToys' common stock had fallen by nearly 90 percent, to just a few dollars per share. In early 2001, eToys filed for bankruptcy. One disgruntled observer charged that Bill Gross and his colleagues had taken advantage of naïve investors swept up in the euphoria surrounding the Internet and dot-com stocks.

> After 30-plus start-ups, only incompetence can explain this pattern of failure. idealab! seems to be essentially operating on the "greater fool theory." Consider their pattern of development. Find a believable concept for a Web-based business. Next, quickly generate some revenue, increase the hype and then come to market with an IPO. Their last step is to pocket millions of dollars on the sale of stock options, management fees and other services, at premium prices.[16]

As the mystique and aura surrounding Internet incubators gradually morphed into suspicion, and even contempt, the business press also turned on idealab!'s two close cousins, CMGI and ICG. Many reporters began questioning the "speed at all costs" strategy adopted by David Wetherell, a strategy later emulated by Walter Buckley and Kenneth Fox. "The traditional advice to young companies [Internet start-ups] is speed at all costs. Not bad advice, but not quite accurate; what is more important is that key strategic call. Strategy has to go beyond hiring quickly, marketing heavily and running big deficits."[17] Legal analysts also questioned the legality of the keiretsu concept advocated by David Wetherell and the comparable EcoNet concept embraced by ICG's co-founders. These analysts suggested that the Federal Trade Commission and Department of Justice could reasonably argue that both of those organizational strategies qualified as restraints of trade.

The most common complaint lodged against CMGI and ICG was that the complex organizational structure of each firm made it extremely difficult for their executives to exercise effective control over their operations. For example, consider the daunting task that faced David Wetherell throughout 2000. At the time, Wetherell rode herd on a corporate domain that included approximately 60 firms representing a varied assortment of lines of business involving e-commerce. Even the mundane but important task of "keeping in touch" with the chief operating officer (COO) of each subsidiary proved to be an enormously difficult assignment for Wetherell. According to press reports, Wetherell hosted an 8 A.M. telephone conference call each Monday morning with those COOs. During that conference call, each COO provided Wetherell a briefing that summarized the key issues facing his or her firm. Wetherell and a handful of his lieutenants in the CMGI headquarters had to digest those reports and provide each subsidiary's management

---

16. *Los Angeles Times*, "idealab! A Good Example of a Bad 'New-Economy' Business," 3 July 2000, C3.

17. H. Anderson, "Internet Companies Are Finding There Is Strength in Numbers," *Canadian Business and Current Affairs*, 19 November 1999, 15.

team with policy and strategy recommendations to cope with the rapidly changing business environment of the Internet.

A related problem posed by the complex organizational structure of CMGI and ICG was the overlapping lines of business pursued by some of the companies they sponsored. In the case of CMGI, several of the company's majority-owned subsidiaries were involved in the same general line of business as a company in which CMGI had a minority ownership interest. CMGI's management had an incentive, in most circumstances, to provide preferential treatment to the majority-owned subsidiary to the detriment of the firm in which it was a minority stockholder.

Finally, the organizational structure of CMGI and ICG resulted in individual companies within their ownership groups being pressured, at least implicitly, to do business with "sister" firms even though a better deal was available from an external firm. As a former CMGI executive noted, the interdependencies central to the keiretsu concept resulted in an "inherent conflict of interest built into the structure"[18] of firms utilizing that concept and related strategies, such as the EcoNet organizational strategy of ICG.

By late 2001, the common stocks of both CMGI and ICG qualified as "penny stocks" since each traded for considerably less than five dollars per share. Investors' general hostility to Internet-related stocks by late 2001 contributed to the huge decline in the stock prices of the two firms. But, the factor most responsible for the collapse of their stock prices was the dismal operating results they consistently reported each quarter. During the third quarter of 2001 alone, CMGI reported a staggering loss of nearly $1 billion. In May 2001, ICG's stockholders filed a class-action lawsuit against Walter Buckley, Kenneth Fox, other top executives of the firm, and the firm's investment bankers. Among other allegations, the lawsuit charged that ICG's top brass had circulated "materially false and misleading statements" in connection with the company's IPO during the summer of 1999.[19] Those statements reportedly helped drive ICG's stock price to approximately $212 per share in December 1999; a little more than one year later, the stock was selling for $1.25 per share.

The Internet incubator concept conceived by Bill Gross and re-engineered by CMGI and ICG executives served as a launching pad for thousands of dot-com companies. No doubt, the early apparent success of The Big Three incubators created expectations that were far too lofty for this new business model. Most Internet analysts believe that the Internet incubation model will remain intact and eventually prove to be economically viable and the source of a large number of substantial and profitable Internet ventures. But, over the next few years, Internet incubators may need to scale back their expectations. One of the co-founders of eCompanies noted that his firm's objective "is not to create public companies, but companies that change the world."[20] That may be an appropriate long-range goal; however, over the short term, the investing public would likely accept a more modest goal, such as producing dot-coms that can string together a few quarters of solid profits.

---

18. P. C. Judge, "One Big Happy Family—But for How Long?" *Business Week Online*, 25 October 1999.

19. *PR Newswire* (online), "Class Action Lawsuit Commenced Against Internet Capital Group, Inc.," 23 May 2001.

20. Vrana, "California Dealin.'"

QUESTIONS

1. Choose either idealab!, CMGI, or ICG and research recent developments involving or affecting that firm. Write a brief summary of your findings that includes a status report for the firm you selected. Among other items, that status report should comment on the apparent financial condition of the given firm, important problems or challenges it apparently faces, and your assessment of its prospects for future success.

2. Locate the website of an Internet incubator other than the "Big Three" that were the focus of this case. Document the location of the website, the company's stated mission, the services that it provides to clients, and related information.

3. Identify an "Old Economy" industry in which an apparently strong business model developed by a new company was quickly replicated by several other firms. Identify the company that developed the new business model and several of its competitors.

4. List the key challenges that a "start-up" or developmental stage company faces. Do these challenges vary across industries? What unique issues or problems do new Internet-based companies face? Explain.

5. Do you believe that Bill Gross acted ethically when he sold most of his company's ownership interest in eToys? Why or why not?

6. Critics have complained of the allegedly exorbitant compensation package that idealab! provided to Bill Gross. List the key factors, in descending order of importance, that you believe should be used in determining the compensation of a company's chief executive officer (CEO). Defend your ranking.

7. Legal analysts have suggested that the keiretsu and EcoNet organizational strategies may qualify as "restraints of trade." What exactly is meant or implied by the phrase "restraint of trade"? Identify other business strategies or policies used by Internet-based companies that might qualify as restraints of trade.

Brainiacs, Inc.: The Brave New World of E-Consulting

Pride goeth before destruction, and a haughty spirit before a fall.

Proverbs 16:18

Top management of companies large and small make decisions each and every day to protect and promote their firms' economic interests. Decisions made in the best interests of individual companies often have unpleasant consequences for a wide range of parties closely associated with those firms, including their creditors, vendors, employees, and even stockholders. Laying off employees easily qualifies as one of the most unpleasant tasks faced by corporate executives. Loss of market share, cost-saving technologies that reduce a company's manpower needs, economy-wide downturns, and strategic blunders by management rank among the most common factors triggering workforce reductions by businesses. Among the most immediate and understandable aftermaths of employee layoffs are expressions of anger by those individuals who lose their jobs.

After arriving for work on a Monday morning in early February 2001, more than 400 employees of Razorfish Inc., received a rude shock when they learned that their positions had been eliminated due to an unexpected loss of clients by the high-profile, Internet consulting firm. By the end of that day, many of those employees had clogged online bulletin boards with bitter, and sometimes vicious, personal attacks directed at their former boss, Jeff Dachis, Razorfish's co-founder and chief executive officer (CEO), who had been widely praised by the press for being an e-business pioneer. "Die, die, die" and "So long, Rotten flounder" were some of the more civil of those angry missives.[1] Online hate campaigns targeting CEOs of once high-flying e-commerce firms were not uncommon following the bursting of the Internet Bubble in 2000. Two factors likely accounted for the especially malicious attacks launched on Dachis by his former subordinates.

Even more so than most e-commerce concerns, the Internet consulting firms developed tightly knit cultures. Dachis and the top executives of his competitors cultivated an all-for-one and one-for-all atmosphere within their firms. That attitude helped those executives maintain effective control over their organizations

---

1. H. Green, "A Web Hotshot Learns Humility," *Business Week e.biz*, 19 March 2001, EB 28.

and to persuade subordinates to accept the long hours, extensive travel, and often tedious and complex work assignments that characterized most e-commerce consulting projects. Dachis personally recruited many of Razorfish's employees and regularly organized employee retreats, including ski trips and other excursions, to build *esprit de corps* among his troops. Such personal attention made those individuals feel as if they were members of a team, if not a family, rather than simply being employees. No doubt, the stronger the bonds that exist within an organization, the more angst felt by individuals who are asked to leave the organization.

The other factor that likely accounted for the nasty personal assaults on Dachis by his former employees was his in-your-face approach to all aspects of doing business, including overseeing his subordinates. Despite attempting to create a tightly knit, family atmosphere within his firm, Dachis was not prone to coddling his subordinates. Instead, he apparently relied on a demanding, if not overbearing, management style to get the most out of them. In commenting on his leadership strategy, the always self-assured Dachis told a reporter, "There are sheep and shepherds, and I fancy myself to be the latter."[2]

CONSULTANTS ON STEROIDS

Large business consulting firms became prominent within the U.S. economy following World War II. As the corporations that dominated the nation's major industries grew in size and complexity, they wrestled with increasingly intricate marketing issues, multidimensional production constraints, and other problematic circumstances not encountered by earlier generations of "Mom and Pop" businesses. Because many corporations did not have the in-house expertise to address those challenges or because their executives did not want to be diverted from their routine, day-to-day responsibilities, these companies began turning to outside consultants for assistance.

In the decades following World War II, several consulting firms established themselves as the leaders in their new industry. Those firms included Booz Allen & Hamilton, Bain & Co., The Boston Consulting Group, and, most notably, McKinsey & Co. Each of these "consultancies" developed similar business practices and methods that focused on delivering a wide range of strategic business advice and problem-solving skills to large public companies across the complete spectrum of industries within the U.S. economy.

McKinsey & Co. became recognized and widely respected for its highly regimented, buttoned-down professionalism. McKinsey's management insisted that each consultant in each practice office conform to the smallest details of the firm's extensive policy and procedures manuals. That iron-fisted control allowed McKinsey to ensure that a high quality of service was provided to each client regardless of the specific individual or groups of individuals assigned to a given consulting project. Network sitcoms during the 1960s and 1970s often parodied the no-nonsense approach to doing business popularized by McKinsey's large workforce. Television directors portrayed business consultants as unemotional,

---

2. *Ibid.*

one-dimensional "efficiency experts" who marched through a client's office in starched shirts and dark suits, all the while barking out solutions to largely imaginary problems. Another business practice popularized by McKinsey was hiring highly qualified B-school graduates. Throughout the latter decades of the twentieth century, entry-level positions with the leading business consultancies ranked among the most coveted job opportunities of freshly minted MBAs and a few fortunate individuals possessing only undergraduate business degrees.

By the end of the twentieth century, several new members had joined the elite fraternity of prestigious business consultancies. These new members included the consulting divisions of the Big Five accounting firms—Arthur Andersen & Co., Deloitte & Touche, Ernst & Young, KPMG, and PricewaterhouseCoopers. Initially, these firms' consulting divisions focused on projects involving technology issues linked to the accounting and information systems of the Big Five's thousands of large audit clients. But, as time passed, the scope of the Big Five's consulting services evolved and began to overlap with the mainstream strategic consulting services provided by McKinsey, *et al.* By the turn of the century, all but one of the consulting divisions of the Big Five had become independent firms. In fact, the former consulting division of Arthur Andersen & Co., renamed Accenture after a less than amiable split with its former parent, reigned as the largest consulting firm worldwide by most benchmarks.

The large computer manufacturers also created consulting divisions to compete for the growing market for business-related consulting services. Foremost among these entities is IBM Global Services, a subsidiary of its giant parent company. Among independent consultancies that elbowed their way into the increasingly crowded ranks of the consulting industry was EDS (Electronic Data Services), the firm founded by frequent presidential candidate H. Ross Perot. Business journalists who track the consulting industry typically refer to the two dozen or so, large consulting firms with decades-long track records of profitability and credibility as the "Old Guard."

The explosion of e-commerce during the 1990s created an entirely new breed of consulting firm, e-commerce consulting firms or e-consultancies. These new consulting firms concentrated on recruiting two types of clients: new Internet-based companies, particularly the thousands of dot-coms retailing goods or services over the Internet, and "Old Economy" companies that wanted to renovate their operations to include some degree of online capability. As one information technology (IT) expert noted on *CNNfn*, these new consulting firms "are helping corporate America move from an offline to an online world."[3] The business press struggled to characterize the services provided by e-consulting firms since there seemed to be little consensus even among those firms regarding the nature and scope of their services. "E-consulting is a catch-all term for high-tech consulting, and it encompasses a variety of vague jargony terms like 'business solutions provider' and 'systems innovation.' Some [firms] in the category focus mostly on Internet strategy—designing and managing websites—while others do more in-depth hardware and software work."[4]

---

3. T. Guida and K. Pilgrim, "Market Coverage," *CNNfn*, 31 August 1999, Transcript #99083145FN0119.

4. J. Pope, "Glory Days Fading Fast for E-Consultancies as Bigger Players Muscle in," *Associated Press State & Local Wire*, 9 February 2001.

The demand for Internet-related consulting services grew steadily with each passing year during the 1990s. Thanks to an effective public relations campaign, e-consultancies claimed the bulk of the New Economy consulting projects. Spokespeople for these firms repeatedly insisted to the business press that the Old Guard did not have the requisite skills needed to complete consulting projects for pure-play Internet businesses. Nor did the traditional consultancies allegedly have the insight to help Old Economy companies renovate and transform their cultures to suit the demands of the radically new world of e-business. A Razorfish executive suggested that, compared to Old Guard consultants, his firm had a much "deeper understanding of information technology. . . . We think and breathe digital, our soul is digital. That is what sets us apart."[5] Such claims apparently resonated with corporate executives charged with overseeing their firms' Internet development efforts.

After retaining Razorfish and another e-consultancy to design Nokia's online strategy, that company's top IT executive remarked, "their specialization is one of the key reasons why we opted for these types of consulting companies, because they do understand the medium [Internet] better."[6] That prevailing attitude among corporate executives meant that the new e-commerce consulting firms had to invest only limited resources in conventional marketing programs. In fact, when asked to explain how his firm obtained new clients, a top official of an e-consulting firm smugly replied, "Inbound calls."[7]

Another facet of the e-consultancies that appealed to potential clients was speed, that is, their ability to complete consulting projects quickly. Viant, a Razorfish competitor, claimed that it could take a dot-com company from "concept" to "launch" in nine months or even less, which was reportedly one-third the time that a traditional consulting firm required to complete such an assignment.[8] Another major e-consulting firm, Sapient, incorporated speed of execution in its corporate mission statement: "To help companies, big and small, get wired—and fast—to the Web."

By early 2000, scores of e-consulting firms existed, ranging from one-person proprietorships to multinational firms employing several thousand consultants. Approximately three dozen of these firms had gone public and had their stock traded on a major stock exchange. Five of the e-consultancies had managed to separate themselves from their competitors and become recognized as the leading firms in their new industry. These firms, referred to as the Fast Five by some business journalists, included iXL Enterprises, MarchFirst, Razorfish, Scient, and Viant.

The growing market for e-commerce consulting services seemed to ensure that the Fast Five and their smaller competitors had a promising and profitable future. Internet research firms predicted that the market for such services would grow to $60 to $80 billion per year by 2003, up from $12 billion in 1999. The most pressing problem these firms had to address was a shortage of what *Business Week* referred

5. *Time International*, "Swimming with the Big Fish: A Group of E-Savvy Newcomers Is Making Waves in the Once Serene Management Consultancy Industry," 15 May 2000, 46.

6. *Ibid.*

7. L. B. Ward, "Internet Consulting Firms Face Shakeout as Dot-com Clients Wobble," *The Dallas Morning News* (online), 6 January 2001.

8. M. Stepanek, "Clash of the E-Consultants," *Business Week*, 19 June 2000, 123.

to as Internet "brainiacs,"[9] individuals who had the experience and expertise required to design and carry out major Internet-based consulting projects. To solve this problem, executives of e-consultancies regularly raided the ranks of "e-literate" employees working for Old Guard firms. Particularly targeted in these raids were employees of the Big Five firms' existing or former consulting divisions since many of those individuals had extensive IT backgrounds. One report estimated that by early 2000, at least 30 percent of all Big Five consultants had accepted positions with e-commerce consulting firms. These individuals were lured away from the Big Five firms by stock option grants and lucrative compensation packages. Among the e-consulting executives most successful in recruiting Old Guard consultants was the mercurial CEO of Razorfish, Jeff Dachis.

RAZORFISH AND THE BOUNCING BLUE DOT

Razorfish was the prototypical e-commerce consulting firm in many ways. Aggressive, young entrepreneurs created most of these firms—individuals who knew a great deal about the Internet and the World Wide Web but typically had limited or no prior experience in traditional business consulting. Most of these "Web geeks" began developing Web pages for friends and acquaintances as a hobby and then gradually migrated into earning cash from that hobby by designing websites for local businesses. Individuals who earned a reputation for doing high-quality work could convert themselves into "Web strategists" by simply moving into a small office in a low rent part of town and nailing a catchy company name on their front door. In 1994, Jeff Dachis and Craig Kanarick created a website design business that they named "Blue Dot." The name came from a bouncing blue dot appearing on the home page of the business's website. At the time, Web graphics were very primitive. The bouncing blue dot qualified as "high tech" and served to convey to potential clients the expert status of Dachis and Kanarick in website design.

Dachis and Kanarick had grown up together in a middle-class, Minneapolis neighborhood. Dachis was the more outgoing of the two. While Kanarick enjoyed tinkering with computers and reading science magazines, Dachis was more interested in applied economics, that is, earning extra cash from a variety of part-time jobs. Scalping tickets to University of Minnesota football games ranked among young Jeff's favorite pastimes. The two childhood friends split up when they went to college. Dachis attended the State University of New York at Purchase where he completed an undergraduate degree in dance and dramatic literature in 1988. He then moved to New York City where he earned a masters degree in performing arts administration at New York University. Throughout his college days, Dachis relied on his instinctive entrepreneurial skills to pay his bills. Among his most successful ventures was a small marketing company that promoted a wide range of products appealing to college students. Craig Kanarick earned dual undergraduate degrees in philosophy and computer science at the University of Pennsylvania and later a masters degree in visual technology at the Massachusetts Institute of Technology.

---

9. *Ibid.*

The two friends eventually reunited in New York City. While "hanging out" together, Craig Kanarick gave his good friend an introductory tour of the World Wide Web, which was still in its infancy at the time. Dachis was immediately captivated by the new sister technology of the Internet. Always the entrepreneur at heart, Dachis recognized that as the Web grew in popularity among Internet users, companies and other organizations would almost certainly begin using it for promotional and marketing purposes. With some coaching from Kanarick, Dachis taught himself the fundamental principles of website design in less than one month. After creating their Blue Dot website, the two young men began marketing website design and related services on the Web. They agreed that Dachis would serve as the new company's CEO since he would be overseeing the "business end" of the operation. Kanarick, on the other hand, chose the title "Chief Scientist," since he would be the two-person firm's technological guru.

A small office near the trendy SoHo district of Manhattan served as Blue Dot's headquarters. That neighborhood would soon become known as Silicon Alley because of the large number of Internet start-ups that congregated in the area. After deciding that "Blue Dot" was too bland a name for their business, Dachis and Kanarick searched a dictionary to find a more cutting-edge, high-tech sounding moniker to hang on their company. They eventually chose "razorfish," a term that refers to a genus of fish having a "vertically compressed, sharp-edged head." The term had nothing to do with the Internet. Dachis and Kanarick simply liked it.

After making a convincing presentation to several Time Warner officials, Razorfish's two executives signed a contract to develop a new website for one of the media company's internal divisions. The marketing leverage produced by that high-profile engagement allowed Dachis to sign up a long list of impressive clients over the following months. Razorfish's clients would eventually include American Express, AOL, Charles Schwab & Co., Encyclopaedia Britannica, Excite, Ford Motor Company, Ralph Lauren, Reuters, Sega, and the Smithsonian Institution. Along the way to acquiring those clients, Razorfish expanded the scope of its operations and the product line of services that it provided. At Razorfish's website, Dachis informed potential clients that, "I only want to do really cool projects." The company's website listed the following services that Dachis apparently considered "cool": Web strategy, brand extension and integration, content strategy, information architecture, interface and interaction design, platform integration, system re-architecture, usability analysis, and user intelligence.

During the late 1990s, Dachis adopted an aggressive growth strategy for Razorfish that included buying out smaller e-consulting firms and recruiting top talent from other firms in the industry. That strategy allowed Razorfish to post a double- or triple-digit increase in revenues each quarterly reporting period during the late 1990s. In April 1999, Dachis and Kanarick took their company public with a successful initial public offering (IPO). Dachis poured much of the $55 million raised by that IPO into his expansion plan. Eventually, the firm's more than 2,000 employees would be scattered around the globe in 9 countries and in 15 offices located in cities such as Helsinki, London, Los Angeles, Oslo, San Francisco, and Stockholm.

Razorfish's rapid growth caught the attention of Wall Street and the business press. From a struggling, two-person office in early 1995, Razorfish boasted a market capitalization of nearly six billion dollars by early 2000, thanks to investors driving the company's stock price far beyond its initial offering price in April 1999. Razorfish was the fourth-fastest growing technology firm in North

America between 1995 and 1999—a period over which the firm's annual revenues shot from $300,000 to more than $170 million. During that time frame, *Forbes* magazine named Razorfish one of the nation's "200 Best Small Companies." Jeff Dachis also received numerous awards and recognition for his leadership skills. Ernst & Young named Dachis New York City's Entrepreneur of the Year for 2000, while the *New York Post* tabbed him as one of "Silicon Alley's Top 20 Movers and Shakers."

Dachis's rapid rise to wealth and fame vaulted him into the inner circle of Manhattan's social elite. He became a regular at some of New York's most chic after-hours establishments, developed a taste for expensive vehicles and art, and began dabbling in film production. Dachis also became known for something else: his ego. He never tired of discussing his success as a chief executive. And the press gave him many opportunities to do just that in newspaper interviews and during numerous appearances on national television programs including CBS's *60 Minutes*.

An executive of an e-consulting firm confessed that he and many of his colleagues at competing firms were guilty of allowing their egos to get the better of them. "The arrogance was unbelievable. We took ourselves way too seriously and Jeff was one of the ones who took himself the most seriously."[10] That arrogance apparently extended to the manner in which Dachis dealt with clients. Former clients commented on the abrasive, "know-it-all" attitude that Dachis and his subordinates displayed toward them. "The way they spoke to us, the way meetings were conducted, it made me wonder who was working for who."[11]

Such criticism failed to ruffle Jeff Dachis or deter him from his self-appointed mission. He believed that Razorfish was leading a revolution that would transform business processes not only in the United States but internationally as well. Dachis frequently downplayed suggestions that the Old Guard consulting firms might eventually pose a significant challenge to Razorfish and other e-consultancies. He insisted that the Old Guard can't "deliver unique user experiences with an integrated skill the way we can."[12] In commenting on his role as Razorfish's CEO, he was just as adamant and self-assured. He pledged to "stay the course" to stockholders and other stakeholders in Razorfish. "I am the CEO and will remain the CEO until they throw me out. This is my company. This is my vision. I want to create the future, and I have an army of people who want to do the same thing. They believe in me and I believe in them. That's absolutely how this works."[13]

SNAKE OIL AND IMPLODING DOT-COMS

E-consultancies became a mainstay of the Internet Revolution during the mid- and late 1990s. But, as early as late 1999, critics began questioning the quality of

10. Green, "A Web Hotshot Learns Humility."

11. *Ibid.*

12. A. H. Germain, III, "The Art of Empire Building—Razorfish Ignites a Powerhouse," *VAR Business*, 16 August 1999, 11.

13. *Ibid.*

these firms' work and the credentials of their executives and founders. Since the inception of the business consulting industry, corporate executives have often voiced complaints that their expectations were not fulfilled by a major project that they paid a prestigious, top-shelf firm to perform. However, such complaints against the major e-consultancies began arising with alarming frequency as the end of the century approached. Many of those complaints resulted in lawsuits filed against the Fast Five firms by disgruntled clients.

In the spring of 1999, Isaac Tigrett, the co-founder of the Hard Rock Café restaurant chain, hired iXL Enterprises to write a business plan and create a website for a new venture that he was developing. The agreed-upon fee for that project approached $1,000,000. Eighteen months later, frustration stemming from constant turnover among consultants assigned to the project, missed deadlines, and the poor overall quality of work allegedly performed by the Fast Five consulting firm prompted Tigrett to abandon the project. He later reported that the project had been "a complete disaster."[14] Adding insult to injury, iXL eventually sued Tigrett for refusing to pay the more than $300,000 unpaid balance for the defunct project.

Also in 1999, the CEO of the online wine retailer Wineshopper.com contracted with Scient, another Fast Five firm, to build an elaborate database for his company. Scient's shoddy work on the project reportedly resulted in the key feature of the database working only 1 percent of the time.[15] The cost to complete the project? $3 million. Razorfish had its own litigation problems in the late 1990s. IAM.com, an online talent promotion company, filed a lawsuit against Razorfish that claimed the website designed for the company by Jeff Dachis's firm had been "flawed by grave technical and navigational problems."[16] IAM.com executives also maintained that Razorfish had missed nearly every delivery milestone or completion deadline specified by the consulting contract.

Critics charged that the large number of lawsuits and complaints filed against e-consulting firms by former clients were not isolated incidents but instead reflected the generally poor quality of work performed by those firms. According to one industry expert, the e-consulting firms used a haphazard, "code-and-fix" strategy to developing software for online ventures. That strategy caused 40 to 80 percent of the budgets on such projects to be spent correcting software defects resulting from errors made by the software engineers assigned to those projects.[17] An official of the respected market research firm Forrester Research leveled an even broader indictment against the e-consultancies when he accused those firms of misrepresenting "their capabilities in alarming ways. A lot of the stuff was snake oil, and the clients didn't know it. That makes their actions more vile."[18] The journalist who interviewed the Forrester official went on to suggest that although e-consultant firms had a wealth of expertise in technological issues, their lack of in-depth expertise in fundamental business issues doomed many of their projects. "One lesson of the Web consulting fiasco is that getting e-business right

---

14. M. Newman, "Dotcom Inferno: Money to Burn," *eCompany* (online), November 2000.

15. R. King, "Scient and the Bursting of the E-Consulting Bubble," *eCompany* (online), April 2001, 67.

16. Green, "A Web Hotshot Learns Humility."

17. Newman, "Dotcom Inferno: Money to Burn."

18. King, "Scient and the Bursting of the E-Consulting Bubble," 64.

is a lot harder than it looks. The technology is complex, alien to many clients. The consultants, for their part, may know the technology, but sometimes have no feel for the true business needs of their customers."[19]

In retrospect, many of the e-consulting firms' executives were their own worst enemy. Their "know-it-all" attitude caused them to rush headlong into new projects without first obtaining a clear understanding of their clients' needs. They also overstated the benefits those projects would yield, creating an environment in which their clients' expectations would almost certainly go unfulfilled. Another serious mistake apparently made by the executives of e-consulting firms was focusing too much attention on acquiring new clients, which took away from the time and energy they could devote to their existing clients. "They made the same mistake as their [dot-com] clients: pursuing growth for growth's sake rather than developing a more sustainable business."[20]

As criticism of the work performed by e-consulting firms mounted, those firms were suddenly blindsided by another huge problem: the collapse of hundreds of dot-coms—the primary market for their services. The nosedive in the stock prices of Internet-based companies that began in earnest in the spring of 2000 and continued well into the following year spelled the end of the dot-com craze in the stock market. Most upstart, online companies were not generating positive cash flows from their operations, which forced them to rely heavily on loans and investments from external sources. When these companies lost access to new debt and equity capital, they were destined to go out of business, meaning they would no longer be asking the e-consultancies to perform large consulting projects for them. Many of the e-consulting firms had taken ownership interests in their clients rather than accepting cash payments for their services. So, the collapse in dot-com stock prices served as a "double whammy" for these firms. Not only did they lose a large number of clients, they also saw much of the revenue they had previously earned evaporate in the stock market.

Making matters even worse for Razorfish and its competitors was that the large public companies, the so-called Fortune 1000 companies, began backing off on their e-business initiatives as they saw the competitive threat posed by dot-coms quickly fading away. The Fortune 1000 did not cancel those initiatives but instead recognized that they could take the time to make sure that their new e-business strategies and the hardware and software infrastructure required to implement those strategies were properly designed to meet their needs. In short, the e-consultancies saw a sudden and large drop-off in the flow of revenues from both major markets that they served.

The bad news for the e-consultancies did not end there. Following the dot-com implosion and the deferral of many online initiatives by Fortune 1000 companies, a huge and relatively untapped market still remained for e-commerce consulting projects. During the late 1990s, thousands of second-tier "Old Economy" companies, that is, companies smaller than the Fortune 1000, recognized that to compete effectively in the future they had to integrate the Internet into their basic business processes. The e-consulting firms had previously ignored these companies, choosing to target instead the "sexy" dot-com market and the lucrative

19. *Ibid.*

20. J. D. Glater, "A High-Tech Domino Effect: As Dot-coms Go, So Go the E-Commerce Consultants," *The New York Times* on the Web, 16 December 2000.

Fortune 1000 market. As the revenue potential for the latter markets dimmed, the e-consulting firms finally turned their attention to the second-tier market.

Razorfish and the other e-consultancies had to overcome two large barriers before they could hope to exploit the second-tier market for e-commerce consulting projects. First, as noted earlier, most of these firms had weak marketing departments, which made recruiting new clients a difficult assignment for them. Second, the bulk of the Internet consulting projects demanded by second-tier companies involved more than website design and the other fairly rudimentary types of services that the e-consulting firms specialized in providing. Instead, these prospective clients required more complex, long-term projects that often included the development of extensive hardware and software infrastructure for their key business functions.

One by one, the Fast Five e-consulting firms began issuing profit and revenue warnings in late 2000 and early 2001. Viant shocked its stockholders in early 2001 when it announced a large loss, a loss 100 percent larger than that forecast just a few months earlier by Wall Street analysts. MarchFirst reported a huge loss for the final quarter of 2000, which was a prelude to a bankruptcy filing in early 2001 intended to protect the firm's assets from nervous creditors. Razorfish added to the dismal earnings reports for Fast Five firms by reporting a loss of $163 million in the fourth quarter of 2000. The massive losses reported by the Fast Five firms prompted each of them to announce large employee layoffs. Scient had the most drastic workforce reduction, releasing more than 50 percent of its employees. By mid-April 2001, the total market value of the common stock of each Fast Five firm had dropped by at least 95 percent in a little more than one year. Razorfish's stock price plummeted 98 percent over that time frame.

The colossal financial and operating problems besieging the Fast Five firms was bad news for their creditors, employees, bankers, and stockholders. But, those problems presented a golden opportunity for the Old Guard consulting firms such as McKinsey & Co., Accenture, and EDS. These well-established consulting firms had been lurking in the background for the previous several years as their upstart competitors lured away their top employees, claimed hundreds of large and lucrative consulting projects, and received widespread praise from the business press that was clearly enamored with the likes of Jeff Dachis and other brash and brassy e-consulting executives. Not surprisingly, many consultants with Old Guard firms gloated in the miseries of the e-consultancies and shared the sentiment of one of their colleagues when he noted, "The Internet consultants will crawl back into the hole they came from."[21]

OLD GUARD LEARNS NEW TRICKS

During the late 1990s, the Old Guard consulting firms had been quietly retooling their professional practices to better serve the needs of rapidly evolving pure-play Internet companies and to meet the needs of old-line, offline companies that wanted to join the "wired" world. Particularly aggressive efforts to develop

---

21. B. Hammer, "The Return of Big Consulting," *The Industry Standard*, 30 April 2001, 47.

e-business capabilities were made by the Old Guard firms that had historically specialized in technology consulting projects, including the Big Five consultancies, IBM Global Services, and EDS. Most of these firms created new operating units to target potential e-business clients.

In 1999, the CEO of Deloitte Consulting warned his colleagues that Razorfish, Scient, Viant, and other e-consulting firms were rapidly gaining momentum and market share within the business consulting industry, particularly within the industry's high-tech segment long catered to by Deloitte. At that point, he posed a simple but important question to his colleagues: "How do we reinvent ourselves while continuing to serve our traditional clients?"[22] After considerable study and introspection, Deloitte's leadership developed a plan to focus the organization on the rapidly developing e-business economy. That strategy would address the consulting needs of both new Internet-based companies and the needs of the metropolitan banks, insurance companies, manufacturing firms, and other large corporations that made up the bulk of Deloitte's clientele—companies that wanted to use the Internet to become more competitive within the New Economy.

A major feature of Deloitte's plan to reinvent itself was requiring every professional within the firm to pass an online "e-certification" course. This unique and costly measure ensured that each member of the organization would understand the key issues, opportunities, and problems posed by the rapidly changing business environment. Deloitte also totally overhauled its organizational structure. An important goal of that restructuring was to make Deloitte Consulting more nimble—more capable of responding quickly to the dynamic changes in technology driving e-business initiatives. Management replaced Deloitte Consulting's heavily centralized, bureaucratic structure with a large number of autonomous units, each of which provided a set of related but highly specialized services demanded by specific types or categories of clients. For example, Deloitte developed eStudio to compete head-to-head with Razorfish and other e-consultancies whose primary revenue streams were produced by website design and development projects. Other new, e-focused units created by Deloitte included a B2B consulting group, a business "accelerator" designed to help new Internet start-ups get off to a "fast start," and a venture capital fund to provide financing for promising Internet-based ventures.

Even the major strategy consultancies, such as McKinsey & Co., made a significant resource commitment to developing e-business consulting capabilities. McKinsey organized a new e-business consulting unit "@McKinsey" manned by 500 highly trained Internet and Web specialists and also launched an Internet incubator. A key plank of McKinsey's new e-business development strategy was targeting the Far East—a region of the world where the e-business revolution was still in its early stages.

The e-business development activities of the Old Guard began paying dividends almost immediately. Granted, the problems gripping the e-consultancies accounted for much of that success. But, whatever the reason, the Old Guard firms eagerly embraced the windfall of new clients. Deloitte Consulting projected that one of its new e-units would produce $40 million of revenues during its first full year of operation; the unit easily surpassed that goal. Within one year of its

---

22. K. Cross, "Bang the Drum Quickly," *Business2.com*, 1 May 2001, 28.

e-makeover, McKinsey acquired more than 1,000 e-consulting projects.[23] Similar results were reported by most of the Old Guard firms.

Soon, McKinsey, Deloitte, and the other Old Guard business consultancies faced a new problem: finding sufficient IT specialists to staff the flood of new e-consulting projects. A shortage of IT professionals was a major problem not only for consulting firms but for private industry as well. In late 2000, the federal government estimated that nationwide 800,000 to one million IT jobs were going unfilled.[24] Eventually, the Old Guard firms zeroed in on the largest available source of IT professionals, namely, the existing and former employees of the e-consultancies. In early September 2000, Deloitte Consulting took the daring step of running a full-page employment ad in *The Wall Street Journal* appealing for employees of pure-play e-consulting firms to "Come work for Deloitte."[25] That ad contrasted the financial problems and turmoil facing the e-consulting firms with the long-term profitability and stability that Deloitte Consulting had enjoyed for nearly four decades. The ad worked. A spokesperson for Deloitte Consulting reported that "We got tons of resumes and hired a bunch of people."[26]

A large percentage of the e-consultants hired by Deloitte and other Old Guard firms were familiar with their new employers. Why? Because they were among the thousands of consultants Razorfish, *et al.* had "stolen" from the staffs of the Old Guard firms over the previous several years. In fact, Accenture sent letters to more than 1,000 former employees who had left the firm in the height of the blitzkrieg by e-consultancies. That letter invited those individuals to return and promised them special bonuses, referred to as "loyalty e-units," if they remained with Accenture for at least three years.

When e-consulting "re-treads" returned to their former employers they brought with them an assortment of new concepts and approaches they had learned during their brief stints with e-consulting firms. The Old Guard firms adopted many of these "revolutionary" ideas including relaxed dress codes, flexible work schedules, and new methods of billing for services. These new billing methods included accepting equity positions in clients that were new business ventures or, alternatively, negotiating revenue-sharing arrangements with such clients in lieu of cash payments.[27] Ironically, in past years, many of the traditional consulting firms had harshly criticized e-consultancies for using those non-conventional billing methods, insisting that those methods could potentially taint the professional judgment exercised by consultants.

CDs, T-Shirts, and Humble Pie

Business journalists who had praised Jeff Dachis and other founders of leading e-consulting firms throughout the 1990s, eventually became those New Age en-

23. Stepanek, "Clash of the E-Consultants," 124.

24. J. Dodge, "Old School Consultant Deloitte Gets Its Revenge on Web Firms," *The Wall Street Journal* Interactive Edition, 12 September 2000.

25. *Ibid.*

26. Cross, "Bang the Drum Quickly," 30.

27. Hammer, "The Return of Big Consulting," 48.

trepreneurs' harshest critics. Along with many financial analysts and economists, those business journalists suggested that the founders and executives of the e-consultancies bore much of the responsibility for the dot-com fiasco that cost investors billions of dollars. These critics alleged that the fraternity of e-consulting executives had convinced new Internet firms to sink enormous sums into online ventures that had little chance of success. Their motivation? Lining their pockets with cash earned from huge consulting projects carried out to help develop those ventures.

Criticism directed at the e-consulting firms prompted different responses from their founders and executives. "Facing this increased skepticism, some consultants have turned openly apologetic. But others are unrepentant."[28] Count Jeff Dachis among the former. The previously brash and egotistical Dachis told a *Business Week* reporter in early 2001 that the sudden and dramatic turn in Razorfish's fortunes had taught him a lesson he needed to learn, namely, how to be humble. According to Dachis, his new creed was "Be humble because in success, humility will win, and in failure, humility will win."[29] Despite Razorfish's financial problems, Dachis remained certain that his company would survive and ultimately return to a profitable position. But, as Razorfish continued to wallow in large losses, Dachis finally admitted defeat. In April 2001, Dachis reneged on his earlier pledge and resigned as the company's CEO, although he remained a member of its board of directors.

After his resignation, Dachis decided to once again collaborate with his old friend, Craig Kanarick, who also resigned his management position with Razorfish. The two buddies decided that they would jumpstart Razorfish Studios, a small subsidiary of the parent company. Dachis and Kanarick planned to produce and sell music CDs, computer games, t-shirts featuring Razorfish's logo, and assorted other products.

QUESTIONS

1. Certain critics questioned the professionalism of at least some of the e-consulting firms, their executives, and their employees. Identify the traits typically associated with a "professional." Are business consultants "professionals"? In your opinion, did some of the e-consultants behave unprofessionally?

2. Choose two of the "Old Guard" consultancies. Research these firms, including visiting their websites. Write a brief report comparing and contrasting the two firms you selected. In your report, indicate the nature of the e-business consulting services provided by each firm.

3. Many of the e-consulting firms, and ultimately some of the Old Guard firms, accepted equity interests in their clients or agreed to revenue-sharing arrangements in lieu of cash payments for their services. Describe the potential problems that this practice may pose for consulting firms and their clients.

28. A. Harmon, "What Have E-Consultants Wrought?" *The New York Times* on the Web, 13 May 2001.

29. Green, "A Web Hotshot Learns Humility."

4. The Old Guard consulting firms rehired many of their former employees who had left to join an e-consulting firm. Discuss the advantages and disadvantages posed by the rehiring of former employees.

5. Research online or hard copy databases and find an article that discusses a major Internet-based consulting project performed for a large public company. Obtain the following information for that project: the name of the consulting firm, the name of the client, the specific nature of the project, and the cost and duration of the project, if available.

Index